At the Precipice

THE LITTLEFIELD HISTORY OF THE CIVIL WAR ERA

Gary W. Gallagher and T. Michael Parrish, editors

Supported by the Littlefield Fund for Southern History, University of Texas Libraries

At the Precipice

AMERICANS
NORTH *and* SOUTH
during the
SECESSION CRISIS

Shearer Davis Bowman

THE UNIVERSITY OF
NORTH CAROLINA PRESS
CHAPEL HILL

© 2010 THE UNIVERSITY OF NORTH CAROLINA PRESS
All rights reserved. Set in Miller and Edwardian Script types by Tseng Information
Systems, Inc. Manufactured in the United States of America

The paper in this book meets the guidelines for permanence and durability of the
Committee on Production Guidelines for Book Longevity of the Council on Library
Resources. The University of North Carolina Press has been a member of the Green
Press Initiative since 2003.

Library of Congress Cataloging-in-Publication Data
Bowman, Shearer Davis.
At the precipice : Americans north and south during the secession crisis /
Shearer Davis Bowman.
p. cm. — (Littlefield history of the Civil War era)
Includes bibliographical references and index.
ISBN 978-0-8078-3392-6 (cloth : alk. paper)
1. United States—Politics and government—1849–1861. 2. United States—
History—Civil War, 1861–1865—Causes. 3. Secession—United States—History.
I. Title. II. Title: Americans north and south during the secession crisis.
E415.7.B64 2010
973.7′11—dc22

2010013478

14 13 12 11 10 5 4 3 2 1

Contents

Illustrations

At the Precipice

1 Introduction and Overview

When did the secession crisis that precipitated the Civil War begin? More broadly, when began the longer era of antebellum sectional conflict that culminated in the secession crisis and then Civil War? Some historians see the beginning of this antebellum era in the 1819–20 North-South political conflict over Missouri's admission to the Union as a slave state. The Show-Me State was the first situated entirely west of the Mississippi to apply for admission to the Union and was geographically situated so that the traditional borders between free and slave states, the Mason-Dixon Line and the Ohio River, could no longer apply. The Missouri Controversy anticipated much of the sectional tension over the western expansion of the "peculiar institution" that moved again to the front burner of American politics with the annexation of Texas in 1845 and the Mexican War of 1846–48. The flames receded temporarily after the Compromise of 1850 seemed to settle the issue of slavery expansion in the southwestern Mexican Cession of 1848. Yet sectional tensions roared back after the Kansas-Nebraska Act of 1854 rescinded the Missouri Compromise's 36°30′ latitudinal line separating free from slave territories in the vast national domain that had been acquired by the Louisiana Purchase of 1803. The mid-1850s, despite the temporary political florescence of anti-immigrant and anti–Roman Catholic Know-Nothings, saw the birth and rapid growth in the free states of a Republican Party committed to the geographical containment of slavery. To some extent during the Mexican War but especially after the Kansas-Nebraska Act, the notion of a political and judicial Slave Power and its apparent success in using the Democratic Party to promote the security and spread of the South's peculiar institution shaped the perceptions of increasing numbers of free state residents.

Sectional controversy over slavery in the territories of the trans-Mississippi West, strongly linked with different interpretations of state versus federal authority under the Constitution, did not directly cause the secession crisis and Civil War. Even so, during the 1840s and 1850s, the territorial question sectionalized American politics and made possible the 1860 victory of a northern sectional president.[1] During the 1850s, disputes over enforcement of the new Fugitive Slave Law, likewise connected with different views about the proper balance between state and federal authority, also contributed significantly to the sense of alienation between northerners and free southerners. When the new and explicitly antislavery Republican Party almost captured the White House in 1856, many residents of the slave states declared that the election of such a candidate would provide just cause for secession. Although the Democratic Party retained the executive branch by electing a Pennsylvanian—a "northern man with southern principles"—ongoing controversies and anxieties in the Congress, in territorial Kansas, in the federal courts, and in the press over the interrelated issues of slavery's expansion and security set the stage for the Republican victory of 1860. Abraham Lincoln's win created the crucial precondition, well before his inauguration in early March 1861, for action by aggressive southern disunionists in seven slave states.

Other historians see the effective start of antebellum America as the 1830s, when religiously inspired abolitionist immediatists, especially in Massachusetts, condemned slavery as a serious sin and sought to persuade Americans north and south that the process of emancipation should begin forthwith. Some proslavery ideologues, concentrated in South Carolina, not only denied that the Christian Bible ever condemned the institution of slavery but also portrayed the peculiar institution as a positive good for blacks and whites alike. Between 1837 and 1845, these debates spilled over into complicated splits within the Presbyterian, Methodist, and Baptist denominations. Some scholars have opined that these denominational divisions, especially those among the Methodists and Baptists, dramatically increased the potential for a rip in the fabric of the nation's political unity.[2]

North-South tensions and recriminations escalated dramatically after the Kansas-Nebraska Act, drawing fuel from the mini–civil war between proponents and opponents of slavery in territorial Bleeding Kansas, from southern congressman Preston Brooks's caning of Charles Sumner at his Senate desk, from the Supreme Court's 1857 proslavery ruling in the *Dred Scott* case, and from recurring disputes over enforcement of the Fugitive Slave Act in the free states. For many scholars, John Brown's aborted October 1859 abolitionist raid at Harpers Ferry, Virginia, marked the start of the secession crisis. Anger, fear, and resentment beset white southerners, especially when northerners hailed the executed Brown as a righteous martyr. Growing numbers of residents of the slave states thought that antislavery violence, whether coming from "ultras" in the free states or rebellious slaves themselves, would receive unacceptable encouragement from a Republican victory in the 1860 presidential election. In the minds of white southerners, northern Republicans appeared to be infected with the disease of radical abolitionism; these

U.S. troops under Colonel Robert E. Lee storm John Brown and his men in the firehouse at Harpers Ferry, fall 1859. (From Albert Shaw, Abraham Lincoln: His Path to the Presidency, *2 vols. [New York: Review of Reviews, 1929])*

antislavery ultras warranted the label "Black Republicans" by virtue of their alleged determination first to destroy simultaneously black chattel bondage and southern power within the Union and then to permit or promote the fearsome "degradation" of racial amalgamation and equality. Southern leaders expressed concerns that a Republican administration would inevitably use its powers of appointment and patronage to build an antislavery constituency in the slave states. Sectional partisans on each side had come to see their opponents in terms of antislavery or proslavery conspiracies intended to degrade the interests, rights, and honor of citizens in the other region. Northerners nurtured palpable anger and resentment at the Slave Power conspiracy emanating from Dixie, while southerners became convinced that Yankees nurtured a Black Republican conspiracy. Partisans on both sides viewed their sectional interests and their rival understandings of the rights and honor owed to the country's citizenry as grounded in the American nation's founding documents of 1776 and 1787. They thus also tended to see serious challenges to these assumptions and perceptions as the product of nefarious conspiracies with whose perpetrators no reliable or satisfactory compromise was feasible.

The likelihood of an antislavery Republican in the White House appeared to rise dramatically during the late spring of 1860, with the sectional fracturing of the Jacksonian Democratic Party. In the 1850s, the "Democracy," established a quarter century earlier under Andrew Jackson of Tennessee and New Yorker Martin Van Buren, became the only major party with a substantial following both in the North and in the South. The Democrats captured the presidency in 1852 and 1856 with one-term northerners who proved overtly sympathetic to the slave South. In the minds of more and more citizens of the free states, Presidents Franklin Pierce and James Buchanan seemed "doughfaced" toadies to the "slave interest," "slaveocracy," or "Slave Power." That is, they appeared to be "northern men with southern principles," determined to protect and enhance the security of black bondage in the South even at the expense of white nonslaveholders in both sections. However, in 1860, thanks in part to the machinations of "hotspur" secessionist fire-eaters intent on provoking disunion and southern independence, the Democratic National Convention split along sectional lines over the vexing issue of slavery's status in the federal territories. Two Democratic nominees, Stephen A. Douglas of Illinois and John Breckinridge of Kentucky, ran on different platforms, and their rivalry precluded the possibility of a united front against what supporters of both nominees deemed ultraradical Black Republicans. Even though the "Republican platform denounced disunion," in the words of historian Peter J. Parish, "the party itself was a symbol of the breakdown of national unity."[3] Even if all the votes cast against the Republican nominee in both sections had been united behind a single opponent, Lincoln's sweep of the free states (with the exception of New Jersey) would still have won the presidency in the Electoral College, just as the U.S. Constitution prescribed. In addition to the Republican and two Democratic nominees, a fourth candidate, former Whig and nativist John Bell of Tennessee, became the nominee of a newly formed Constitutional Union Party, whose platform consisted of a nonconfrontational and conservative commitment to maintaining the Union.

Although the Harpers Ferry raid and the Democratic Party split must be considered crucial signposts on the final stretches of the road to disunion, the secession crisis began in earnest in October 1860, when Republican organizations won several state elections across the lower tier of northern states—Indiana, Ohio, and Pennsylvania. (In antebellum America, as historian William Gienapp writes, "political power was concentrated in state and not federal government," and, therefore, "politics was state- and not national-oriented.")[4] The border free states along the Ohio River had appeared to constitute the crucial battleground between the northern Democrat, Douglas, and his Republican opponent, a fellow Illinoisan. These state elections convinced almost all observers that Lincoln would carry the presidential contest in November. Indeed, by winning all the northern electoral votes save New Jersey's three, Lincoln captured the constitutionally mandated majority in the Electoral College without a single electoral vote from a slave state.[5] The Republican ticket did not even appear on the ballot in two-thirds of the fifteen slave states.

Yet despite widespread rhetoric to the contrary in both the North and the South, the victor was not a radical abolitionist and color-blind immediatist. Instead, Lincoln qualified as a firm Unionist whose gradualist and colonizationist stance on the peculiar institution struck his supporters—that is, the less than 54 percent of the northern electorate who voted for him—as at the same time constitutionally conservative, racially sensible, and unabashedly antislavery. Lincoln insisted that he and his party's other leaders decried Brown's criminal violence at Harpers Ferry. Moreover, Lincoln declared that he harbored neither desire nor design to interfere with the peculiar institution in the existing slave states and would enforce the provisions of the 1850 Fugitive Slave Law. Yet he also stood firmly against southern radicals' insistence that both the Constitution and the Supreme Court permitted—even mandated—the spread of slavery into all territories, present and future, that would at some point enter the Union as sovereign states. During the secession winter, the Republican leadership upheld Lincoln's insistence that the more moderate southern demand for a restoration of the old Missouri Compromise line (embodied in the proposal named after Kentucky senator John J. Crittenden, who aspired to wear the late Henry Clay's mantle as the Great Compromiser) could and should not be accepted if the agreement allowed the slaveocracy to continue agitating for ongoing U.S. expansion south of the 36°30' line into Latin America.

In addition to weakening the Slave Power, containing the spread of slavery would have the long-run effect, over many decades, of persuading slaveholders to endorse proposals for the gradual and compensated emancipation of their human chattel as long as these proposals were coupled with a program to deport or "colonize" freed African Americans beyond U.S. borders. This process, Republicans believed, would ultimately promote the interests, rights, and honor of citizens in both sections and hence of the nation as a whole. Lincoln and Jefferson Davis, chosen president of the independent Southern Confederacy in February 1861, could agree that both the security of slavery and the integrity of the Union hung on the fundamental question of slavery's continued geographical expansion into present and prospective American territory. Both would have concurred with former president John Tyler's emotional declaration in February, when he was chosen president of the Washington Peace Conference, that what "our godlike fathers created, we have to preserve."[6] Yet what the Mississippian Davis and the Virginian Tyler saw in the Founding Fathers' legacy as requiring preservation was very different from what the Illinoisan Lincoln, like former Democratic president Van Buren, saw as needing to be preserved. Davis, a U.S. senator until late January 1861, seems to have spoken for most whites in the Lower or Cotton South by refusing in the end to vote for the Crittenden Compromise. Following the lead of the late John C. Calhoun as well as the Supreme Court's contested *Dred Scott* decision, most free men in the seven states of the Deep or Lower South—the ones that would secede and formally organize the Confederate States of America even before Lincoln's inauguration on 4 March—seem to have concluded that their sectional interests, rights, and honor required at least temporary separation from the United States while keeping open the option of acquiring more southern slave territory.[7]

After Lincoln's victory, the secession crisis continued through and well beyond the four months remaining in Buchanan's Democratic administration. The Pennsylvanian wanted desperately to maintain the Union and avoid a civil war and believed that the only way to do so was on terms sympathetic to southern slaveholders—that is, through the same sorts of sectional compromises that had made possible the composition and ratification of the Constitution and had preserved the Union in 1820, 1833, and 1850. During the secession winter, the most pressing questions became how Buchanan's administration should and would respond to the reality of separate-state secession after South Carolina announced its exodus on 20 December and how many slave states would still consider themselves members of the Union when the new chief executive was inaugurated. Well before that day, seven slave states extending from South Carolina to Texas—known variously as the Cotton, Gulf, Lower, or Deep South—had already seceded and sent delegates to centrally located Montgomery, Alabama. There they had organized a new republic, the Confederate States of America, and composed a constitution modeled in most ways on the 1787 document that southern representatives saw the populous and sectionalized free states as undermining and perverting.

From December 1860 to March 1861, Buchanan presided over a stalemate between the U.S. government and those first of the seceding states and then of the new Southern Confederacy. Several attempts to effect Union-saving compromises—first among members of special Senate and House committees and later among delegates to the Washington Peace Conference—proved unsuccessful. The stalemate continued under President Lincoln until mid-April

1861. Buchanan denied the constitutionality of secession but also claimed that the executive branch alone had no power under the Constitution to force or "coerce" a seceded state back into the United States of America. Although Lincoln also denied the legitimacy of both secession and the Confederacy, he did not rule out the propriety or necessity of presidential and military "coercion" in response to palpable aggression against U.S. government sovereignty. During the six weeks beginning in early March, the most pressing questions became how Lincoln's new Republican administration would respond to disunion and the new Confederacy's claims to independent nationhood and how durable were Unionist loyalties in the eight states of the Upper South. With an inflated estimation of lingering attachment to the Union among citizens of the Lower and Middle South slave states (i.e., the eleven that would eventually join the Confederacy), the new president hoped that avoiding armed confrontation would bring that latent southern Unionism to the forefront.

In April 1861, the new Confederate administration determined that the interests, rights, and honor of the seceded states and the new Confederate States of America confronted an unacceptable challenge emanating from a U.S. Army garrison that refused to surrender a federal fortification to South Carolina or the Confederacy. Fort Sumter, at the time still under construction and commanded by Major Robert Anderson, is situated "on a man-made granite island four miles from downtown Charleston at the entrance to the bay."[8] Confederate shore batteries pounded Fort Sumter into submission on 12–13 April. In response to this bombardment, Lincoln quickly ruled that a violent rebellion against U.S. authority had commenced, an unconstitutional insurrection "too powerful to be suppressed by the ordinary course of judicial proceedings, or by the power vested in Marshals" by law.[9] U.S. interests, rights, and honor required that this rebellion be suppressed and the old Union restored. A *rage militaire* swept across slave states and free states alike; in the words of one scholar, the war fever "cut across social classes, creating a heady sense of solidarity."[10]

On 15 April, President Lincoln declared that the rebels had twenty days to renounce their rebellion and return to the status of de jure peace that had existed before the bombardment of Sumter. At the same time, Lincoln called on loyal state governors to provide seventy-five thousand militiamen to the U.S. government for ninety-day tours of duty. The eight slave states still in the Union had to choose sides. Divided state conventions in Virginia, North Carolina, Tennessee, and Arkansas cast their lot with the Confederacy, which transferred its capital to Richmond. Faced with the choice of remaining in the Union or taking up arms against sister slave states, these four Upper South

The course of secession, 1860–61

states joined their fates and substantial resources to those of the earlier Confederate states, thereby prolonging the Civil War. Tennessee's governor captured the spirit of Middle South secessionism when he declared that his state "will furnish no troops for the wicked purpose of coercion, but fifty thousand if necessary for the defense of our rights and that of our Southern brothers."[11] The four border slave states—Delaware, Maryland, Kentucky, and Missouri—and later West Virginia (after its "secession" from the Old Dominion) ultimately remained loyal to the Union. However, all except Delaware experienced intrastate civil wars.

After Fort Sumter, from almost every corner of the North came what historian James M. McPherson has labeled an "eagle-scream of patriotic fury" against treasonous Confederates. Even northern Democratic newspapers joined in the patriotic indignation, thundering, "Let our enemies perish by the sword." To southern moderates who had opposed both secession and coercion, Lincoln's call for troops meant that the North had inaugurated what Bell decried as an "unnecessary, aggressive, cruel, unjust wanton war" against the South.[12] Just as most Confederates at that moment expected a brief and exciting war for southern independence from Black Republican tyranny, so most northerners anticipated a short and glorious war against treasonous southern rebels. The subsequent reality of a bloody, costly, internecine conflict extending over four years appears today as one of the two most notable historical ironies and unintended consequences from the Civil War era. The other, related to the first, is the immediate and uncompensated abolition of slavery, along with the end to any prospect of colonizing freedpeople abroad, when slaves fled their masters and mistresses for Union lines; Lincoln issued the Emancipation Proclamation, effective 1 January 1863; and the Thirteenth Amendment was enacted in 1865.

The story of the 1860–61 secession crisis has been told and amplified many times in great detail and with penetrating analysis by such authors as Allan Nevins in the 1950s, David M. Potter in the 1970s, and James M. McPherson in the 1980s. In this volume, I take what I have learned from generations of scholarship—especially works not available to Potter and McPherson and a number of well-edited and invaluable primary sources—and mold it into a coherent and accessible interpretation of Americans north and south during the secession crisis.

The number of both specialized monographs and ambitious syntheses has multiplied since I took my doctoral qualifying exams in the late 1970s. Scholars have authored a rich and diverse array of relevant volumes and journal articles, some focused on political parties, others on states or communities, and still others dealing with social groups defined by such criteria as class, ethnicity, gender, race, and religion. Numerous publications have made worthwhile contributions to the ongoing understanding of the background forces, fascinating characters, and contingent chain of events that led to our American Iliad, the Civil War.[13]

As historian Jean H. Baker has observed, "The present endlessly laps on the shores of the past."[14] All historians should recognize that their assumptions, experience, and agendas influence their views and interpretations of the past. I have purposely avoided using the words "bias" or "prejudice" on the optimistic and perhaps self-deluding grounds that today's academically trained, professional historians should strive first and foremost to survey and integrate fairly into their accounts of the past as much of the available evidence and testimony as possible. Then they should try to let the content and logic of that research steer them away from biased or prejudicial judgments that find no clear and firm grounding in the extant sources. The best historians are those who realize that self-understanding and self-mastery are prerequisites to balanced understanding and mastery of the past, even as they acknowledge that achieving both goals is a chimerical vision.[15]

In the absence of the "scientific" opinion polls that began to shape American politics in the mid–twentieth century, the records left by articulate persons become absolutely invaluable sources of popular perceptions and understandings. Some illiterate former slaves, including Sojourner Truth and Harriet Tubman, proved themselves powerfully articulate. The scholarly efforts of latter-day biographers, editors, and archivists have enabled me to attempt to blend broad historical analysis of supraindividual movements and tendencies with the fascinating stories of significant, intriguing, and unique persons. I have made extensive use of several unpublished manuscript collections when they provided testimony regarding important experiences and perspectives that seemed unavailable in published sources. For example, the diaries of Michael Luark in Iowa, Robert Granniss in Virginia, and E. N. Tailer in New York City and the letters Kentuckian Henry Waller wrote from Chicago offer rich insights that I have not found illuminated so well elsewhere. Like Granniss, Luark, Tailer, and Waller, most of the men discussed in this volume were white males, though no historian of the era can overlook former slave turned abolitionist Frederick Douglass. Many of the people I examine were high-profile politicians, including Douglas, Tyler, Davis, and Lincoln. Some women, too, merit sustained attention, especially white South Carolinian Keziah Goodwyn Hopkins Brevard and black New Yorker Sojourner Truth. These people illustrate a variety of cultural economic, geographic, intellectual, political, and social cross-currents in antebellum America's complex national and regional societies.

Long-term economic, social, cultural, and political processes increasingly differentiated the slave states from the free, in the process raising the level of sectional tensions and mutual recriminations among southerners and northerners. However, not until the winter of 1860–61 did a critical mass of citizens in the states of the Lower, Cotton South become willing to quit the Union and establish a new confederacy. At the same time, the preponderance of these disunionists, whether believers in constitutional secession, in the natural right of revolution, or perhaps in both, remained deeply "American." They could explain their decision to themselves and justify it to others only by framing disunion in terms of preserving what they perceived to be genuinely American institutions and values, including express commitments to both the republican ideology and the Protestant Christianity that then pervaded American culture.[16] It is well known that the members of the Confederate convention in Montgomery modeled their new constitution, their body of fundamental law, after that of the United States while giving explicit sanction to the principles of state sovereignty and black chattel slavery (as opposed to the U.S. Constitution's euphemism, "persons held to service or labor"). The new document, like U.S. law as of 1808, also prohibited the new federation's involvement in the international slave trade, in part to assure Upper South states still in the Union that joining the Confederacy would not jeopardize their long-standing outlet for surplus slaves, who were sent south to cotton and sugar plantations. The Confederate Constitution also stipulated its president's election to a single six-year term, thereby seeking to insulate the office of chief executive more effectively from partisan politics and their corrupting influence. Perhaps most important, to remedy the U.S. Constitution's failure to include any acknowledgment of God or Divine Providence, the preamble to the Confederate Constitution identified the new southern confederation as a Christian republic by "invoking the favor and guidance of Almighty God." Although a wartime campaign in the North to rewrite the preamble to the U.S. Constitution failed in its goal of declaring America a Christian country, Secretary of the Treasury Salmon P. Chase did place "In God We Trust" on Union coins during the conflict.[17]

The creators of the new Confederacy saw dire threats to the well-being and even survival of the slave states coming from perfidious Yankee betrayers of fundamental American principles. In turn, the preponderance of people in the states loyal to the Union became convinced, no later than the aftermath of Fort Sumter, that they were engaged in a necessary crusade to protect their own American version of republican freedom and constitutional liberty. "The themes of liberty and republicanism formed the ideological core of the cause for which Civil War soldiers fought, Confederate as well as Union," as McPherson has written. Lincoln, Jefferson Davis, and "Americans in both North and South believed themselves custodians of the legacy of 1776."[18] Southern Confederates and northern Unionists alike elevated themselves into devotees of liberty doing glorious battle against the denizens of despotism, though they defined the character and roots of that despotism in very different ways. In the process, they sought to appropriate for themselves the contested legacy of true Americanism—what we might call American nationality or nationalism, each side viewing it through sectional lenses.[19] Tragically, however, both the sectional and national lenses of free Americans on both sides were strongly tinted with Negrophobia. "Fundamentally," in the words of one recent scholar, "most white Americans harbored a deep core of what can only be called racism."[20] Historians have found ample testimony to strong racial prejudice among northern Unionists as well as southern Confederates, among those hostile to the peculiar institution as well as defenders of black bondage.

Despite their common antipathy to black Americans, northern and southern partisans of white sectionalism tended to see their respective sections as engaged in the high-minded defense of vested interests, outraged rights and liberties, and imperiled honor, all embedded in a society and way of life they deemed authentically American. Of course, the precise content of sacrosanct words such as "rights" and "liberty" assumed rather distinct configurations in the competing capital cities of Washington and Montgomery/Richmond. Republicans, with their many Unionist allies among northern Democrats, had the distinct advantage of administering the direct institutional legatee of 1787, the United States of America. Secessionist Confederates had to establish a new institutional base for their geographical and sectional version of American nationalism. This project did not seem as daunting to them as it does to us today. In the words of historian Maury Klein, "The federal government barely intruded on the lives of people." For "the vast majority of Americans" outside of Washington, D.C., which impressed visitors as more southern than northern, the "only real tangible [federal] presence was the post office, which was staffed by locals," among them young Abraham Lincoln.[21] "In a century of rampant nationalism throughout the Western world," observes Potter, "there were probably no people who carried national patriotism and self-congratulation to greater lengths than the Americans, and this included the South." But the nation was still young and fragmented, and what appear to us today as the beginnings of modern means of communication, the railroad and telegraph, had only begun their penetration of American society. Hence, at the beginning of 1860, as Potter recognizes, the North and the South each proclaimed devotion "to its own image of the Union, and each section was indistinctly aware that its image was not shared by the other."[22]

What did Americans on the eve of the Civil War believe about themselves and the world around them, and how did their thoughts inform their actions and decisions? These concerns have led me to focus on the complex and divergent perceptions of what contemporaries understood as the crucial and interrelated issues of interests, rights, and honor. Historian Elizabeth Varon has

The official seal of the
Confederate States of America
(Courtesy of the Museum
of the Confederacy)

recently shown how "provocative and potent" the rhetoric of disunion could be in the United States during the decades of the early republic and ante-bellum era, whether those words were employed as threat or counterthreat, prophecy or accusation, process or program. And she has rightly emphasized that disunion, despite its "wide range of meanings" in different historical contexts and for different agendas, should not be equated with secession, which "referred to a specific mechanism whereby states could leave the Union" and "reflected complex constitutional theories on the boundaries of state and federal power."[23] When the secession crisis brought tensions between staunch disunionists and devoted Unionists to a boiling point, the most important dichotomy among Americans' complex and divergent perceptions became the one separating disunionist southern secessionists from loyal northern Unionists. Secessionist Confederates and perpetual Unionists alike glorified the Declaration of Independence and the U.S. Constitution; most paid homage to what one author has recently termed "a political religion that worshipped the Founding Fathers and the Revolution."[24]

Yet they interpreted their sacred documents and glorious ancestors in markedly different ways and came to very different understandings of their Americanism—that is, what it meant in theory and practice to be a citizen or resident of the U.S. republic. It was hardly coincidental that those who designed and endorsed the official seal of the new Southern Confederacy sought to appropriate the metaphorical father of the United States, George Washington—the first U.S. president as well as commander of the Continental Army that had won independence from Great Britain—as the personal symbol of the Confederacy's claim to national independence in the name of both state's rights and individual liberty. Just as General Washington had become a heroic and chivalrous symbol of free Americans' fight for independence from despotic Britain, General Robert E. Lee became a symbol for white southerners fighting for independence from the tyrannical North.[25] Confederate southerners believed that Black Republicans had betrayed and corrupted America's constitutional essence.

Secessionist and Confederate understandings of "southern rights" in 1861 encompassed the fundamental liberties of citizens in the slave states, understood in gendered terms as autonomous or independent white adult males. Those liberties and rights could be construed as constitutional, revolutionary, or both. These citizens had the liberty and the right to vote in favor of rescinding their state's ratification of the U.S. Constitution; seceding from the Union to become a separate, independent, and sovereign republic; and joining with other disunionist states in creating a new Confederacy whose founding document, or constitution, was modeled in most respects after that of the U.S. republic these states had just left. This right of state secession and the liberty to form an independent Confederate States of America could be based on Confederates' interpretation of the old U.S. Constitution and the Union as created by sovereign states in 1787–88. The right to leave the Union could also be derived from the inherent liberty and freedom of any body of republican citizens to rebel against some political authority they viewed as threatening despotism, tyranny, and metaphorical enslavement and therefore by definition oblivious to the inalienable natural rights described in the Declaration of Independence. Or the arguments regarding the U.S. Constitution and humanity's natural rights could be blended and combined. From whatever principle the disunionist right of secession derived, seven slave states found it necessary to withdraw from the Union during the secession winter of 1860–61. As their state conventions explained in formal declarations, their rights as republican citizens living in sovereign slave states—in particular, their right to maintain the security of a society that denominated African Americans as chattel black slaves—seemed at serious risk in the aftermath of Lincoln's election to the presidency. Contrary to the Supreme Court's 1857 ruling, both the candidate and his party platform insisted that citizens of the slave states could and would be prevented from exercising their basic liberty and right to take slave chattel property into the existing western U.S. territories or into territories that might be acquired in the future. These territories had been or would be acquired by citizens from the slave as well as the free states. As many secessionists made abundantly and unabashedly clear, black chattel slavery constituted without doubt the most distinctive and important private interest of citizens in the region. They deemed this regional interest as essential to their way of life, which was based on slavery's crucial function as a system of both property rights and racial control. Antislavery and abolitionist Republicans denied free southerners the liberty and right, constitutional as well as inherent and natural, to enjoy free and protected disposition over their slave property in the nation's territorial domain, a stance that boded ill for the future security of human bondage in the existing slave states and therefore for the safety and prosperity of free southerners. They told themselves and others that the Republican stance posed an unacceptable challenge to their interests, rights, and honorable reputations as slaveholding citizens of the American republic; by presenting a challenge to the future of their peculiar institution in the federal territories that would eventually join the Union as states, the Lincoln administration also presented unacceptable threats to security in the existing slave states. Of course, from the perspective of almost every U.S. citizen in the early twenty-first century, despite white southerners' public paeans to liberty and independence, chattel bondage for African Americans in antebellum America appears to have been a fundamentally antidemocratic and inhumane institution. Slave owners and family proprietors composed a decided minority of free residents in the slave states—about one-third of the population of the eleven states that joined the Confederacy. Yet this regional elite firmly believed that the Founding Fathers of the United States had intended the Constitution to guarantee and protect the interests, rights, and honor of southern slave owners. Indeed, some members of this elite saw disunion as dangerous, because secession would jettison the protections of the slave interest that were woven into the U.S. Constitution. One scholar has suggested that "the elementary principle of southern nationalism" received apt expression in December 1859 from South Carolina congressman Milledge L. Bonham: "There is a treason, now known to the South greater than the treason of disunion, and that is treason to the South itself, and her constitutional rights."[26] That is, southern nationalists believed that an independent Southern Confederacy would be truer to the letter and spirit of the 1787 Constitution than the United States under a Republican president who decried black bondage as a "monstrous evil" destined for "ultimate extinction." Even as slavery apologists engaged in proslavery exegesis of the Christian Bible, they tended to uphold what one scholar has termed "a hierarchical, organic ideology that considered relations of dependence a necessary part of the natural ordering of things." Just as children should be subordinate to adults and women to men, savage people should be subordinate to the civilized and black people to white.[27]

By consistently labeling the enslavement of black people in the South a palpable evil or sin, free state Republicans appeared to citizens in the slave states to have insulted, demeaned, and degraded their manly dignity and honor. Republicans withheld from these men, their families, and their communities the essential esteem and respect that was owed to dignified and honorable fellow citizens and Christians. Hence, citizens from the free and slave states no longer held themselves in the mutual esteem and honor absolutely necessary to the survival of harmony and liberty in the U.S. republic. In April 1861, the executive branch of the self-styled Confederate Israel determined that the despotic U.S. government's refusal to surrender control of Fort Sumter represented an intolerable affront to its rights and dignity. By denying the new southern nation and its leaders the appropriate respect and honor, the Lincoln administration justified and warranted a preemptive assault on the military installation to force its surrender.

In response, the newly inaugurated Republican administration determined that the attack on Fort Sumter marked the decisive beginning of a treasonous and violent insurrection against duly constituted federal authority. Lincoln, as commander in chief, summoned troops from all the loyal states to subdue the unprovoked and unconstitutional rebellion against a federal union designed as perpetual by its framers. In reply to Lincoln's coercive and intolerable call for troops to be dispatched against fellow slave states that had joined the Confederacy, the conventions of four more slave states also revoked their ratifications of the U.S. Constitution, declared themselves independent and sovereign republics, and became constituent members of the Confederate States of America.

In the free states north of the Mason-Dixon Line and the Ohio River, most citizens, whether Republican or Democratic partisans in 1860, felt firmly that a slave state had neither substantial cause or constitutional warrant to sever its ties to the United States simply because a man of antislavery principles had won the presidency. Indeed, Lincoln won the White House precisely in accordance with the terms of the Constitution. Secessionists appeared to display the privileged arrogance and sense of preferential entitlement that Republicans had for years attributed to the slaveocrats and their political minions. When the election of 1860 showed the Democratic Party and the Slave Power incapable of maintaining their rule over the executive branch, disunionists and secessionists seemed determined to ruin the glorious republican and constitutional Union. And this decision came even before the Republican president had the opportunity to take any clear and concrete steps that would have threatened slavery and the slave states. Republicans could find in the U.S. Constitution no evidence of or testimony to secession as a constitutional right. If slaveholders were determined to invoke the natural human right of revolution against perceived tyranny, Republicans responded that their party had done absolutely nothing to attack or endanger the slave states' rights and interests. Disunionist rebellion and Confederate insurrection were unwarranted and should be suppressed, by force if necessary. To Republican minds, secessionists and Confederates in the Gulf or Lower South had betrayed and jettisoned the glorious Union simply because the political opponents of the old Democracy and the Slave Power had won the presidency fair and square, according to the constitutional rules of the game. This arrogant and unwarranted behavior effectively insulted and demeaned the dignity and honor of the free states and their citizens and did so for no better reason than because the North's electoral and popular votes had put a man in the White House who criticized and intended to rein in (but certainly not attack directly) the southern slave interest and its peculiar institution. All men loyal to the glorious legacy and vision of the Founding Fathers should join hands against arrogant and treasonous rebels who seemed hell-bent on crippling and dishonoring history's greatest example of republican self-government. Secessionist slaveocrats were willing to sacrifice the noble experiment in liberty embodied in the United States of America simply because they wished to perpetuate a distinct, distasteful, and anachronistic regional interest, black chattel slavery. The republic's Founding Fathers, like their successor, Lincoln, had viewed human bondage as a stain on the escutcheon of American liberty, fervently hoping that it would remain on the gradual, nonviolent, but steady path to ultimate extinction that they saw beginning in the Northeast during and after the American Revolution. When the illegitimate Confederate government launched a violent, unprovoked, and dishonorable military attack on U.S. property and personnel at Fort Sumter, the nation's dignity and honor demanded that all loyal sons rally to Columbia's defense.

My interpretation and perspective both complement and modify those presented in Anne Sarah Rubin's and Russell McClintock's recent monographs on the South and the North, respectively. In *A Shattered Nation: The Rise and Fall of the Confederacy, 1861–1868* (2005), Rubin admirably synthesizes an immense amount of historical analysis and research as she traces the evolution of Confederate identity and nationalism from the beginning of the Civil War to the postwar implementation of a more radical approach to

"Reconstruction"—that is, the process of reconstructing the Union as well as the South without chattel slavery. In the process, she addresses in clear and concise fashion a number of important issues relevant to my focus on the secession crisis. Rubin's book opens with a recognition that some Americans today continue to argue over the real "meaning of the Confederacy . . . the argument most often devolving into 'it was about slavery . . . it was about state rights,' back and forth, neither side listening to the other, each side convinced it is right." From my perspective, both sides are right. No reputable historian today would gainsay Rubin's statement that "the Confederacy was emphatically a slaveholders' republic," even though "the vast majority of white Southerners did not own slaves." There would have been no secession crisis and Civil War if white southerners had not been deeply concerned about the economic and social security and stability of their section's peculiar institution.[28] At the same time, their words and actions during the secession crisis reveal their deep commitment to what they saw as fundamental principles of state's rights embodied in the Constitution and the Tenth Amendment. However, not all Confederate disunionists were certain that the Constitution expressed the extremist version of state's rights—that is, thoroughgoing state sovereignty. Although this principle could undergird the argument for separate-state secession as a constitutional right, many Confederates invoked the natural right of revolution against tyranny and despotism that they saw articulated in the Declaration of Independence.

Most of their opponents in the Republican Party, like Lincoln, interpreted the Declaration as a manifesto for republican liberty against despotic slavery, which constituted a decidedly anti-American institution embodying tyranny. And they saw the Constitution, properly interpreted, as having created a substantial degree of state's rights but not state sovereignty within a prosperous, powerful, and perpetual Union. This judgment led them to view secession as a form of unreasonable and insufferable treason against the authority of the finest constitutional republic and most successful democratic experiment in the annals of history. As McClintock concludes in *Lincoln and the Decision for War: The Northern Response to Secession* (2008), spokesmen for both the slave-labor South and the free-labor North strove to identify themselves with "the revered Founding Fathers of the Revolutionary era" while "using the other as a negative reference." McClintock also argues that each side in the oratorical contest pursued this strategy "to mask its own internal worries." Free southerners reacted out of "defensiveness about slavery," northerners out of "anxiety toward modernization."[29] Many southerners also appear to have been concerned about the long-term impact of modernization, if that protean process is associated with the growth and spread of industrial production, wage labor, and egalitarian principles. At the same time, northerners felt defensive anger about what they perceived as the despotic political aggressions of the southern and Democratic Slave Power against northern interests, rights, and honor.

Rubin provides clear definitions for some important but potentially ambiguous terms and concepts. She defines the crucial word "nation," as opposed to the political construct and structure identified by the word "state," as "an emotional, ideological, and frequently sentimentalized construct, created by individuals who-self-consciously share the belief that they are all united by a common culture, history, and social personality." She recognizes that the construction or creation of Confederate nationalism was "not a difficult problem." In fact, it was and remains "startling" to see how quickly "white Southerners, many of them staunch Unionists through the election of 1860, shed their American identity and picked up a sense of themselves as Confederates." Yet by 1867, their "call for separate nationhood had largely subsided, replaced by a desire for equal treatment within the American Union." In response to the threat and "insult" coming from the Radical Republicans and their version of Reconstruction, southerners portrayed themselves as victims and reacted "not by threatening secession but by protesting the loss of their rights as Americans." Having taken oaths of loyalty to the United States and "become American citizens again, they wanted to be treated as equals by the North."[30]

Rubin's view of white southerners after the war, like McClintock's interpretation of northerners on the eve of the war, implies a fundamental truth about citizens in both sections during the secession crisis. Partisans on each side tended to see themselves as more genuinely American than their opponents and therefore as entitled to assume a stance of moral and political superiority to the other. Northern Unionists viewed the secessionists as frustrated denizens of the oppressive Slave Power; having lost their bid to extend the slave South's rule over the executive branch, the slaveocracy was now engaged in a treasonous scheme to ruin the glorious Union created by the Founding Fathers. Southern secessionists saw themselves as heirs to both the revolutionary and constitutional principles of these same Founding Fathers, who had asserted the inalienable liberty and right of rebellion against tyranny, and viewed a proper understanding of state's rights, including state sovereignty, as the surest defense against the possibility of federal despotism. Where unionists saw secessionists as aristocratic and proslavery ultras embracing an extremist version of state's rights (i.e., state sovereignty) that found no sanction in the U.S. Constitution, disunionists saw the Black Republican Party as embracing an antislavery fanaticism alien to the nation's founders, a fanaticism that appeared all the more menacing because it was linked to a consolidation-ist form of federal tyranny that sought to promote the interests of the more populous free states at the expense of the slave states through such policies as high import taxes (federal tariffs) and a homestead bill. Furthermore, some free states had refused to honor the Fugitive Slave Law, essentially nullify-ing it. Most Confederates, like Jefferson Davis, believed that their determi-nation to preserve the security of slave property, white privilege, and state's rights rendered them more committed to the true letter and spirit of both the Declaration of Independence and the U.S. Constitution than were radi-cal and power-hungry Republicans. In 1861, Davis and most Confederates, like Lincoln and most Republicans, saw their cause as loyal to the Founding Fathers' simultaneously libertarian yet conservative principles and heritage. Again, most Americans on both sides viewed such iconic terms as "liberty" and "honor" through the prism of a strong racial prejudice, Negrophobia. Hence, they could not envision blacks, whether free or slave, as entitled to the liberty and honor—in particular, the equality before the law, suffrage, and social respect—that accrued to republican citizenship in the United States. Military defeat in 1865 would leave the white South no choice but to recognize that blacks could no longer be owned as chattel property and that the Union would have to be treated as perpetual. However, white southerners were still Americans, just as they had been in 1861. After 1865, having suffered military defeat in an honorable cause, they deemed themselves entitled to dignity and respect, worthy of being viewed by victorious Yankees as equal and hence honorable citizens in the Union. And by the end of the nineteenth century at the latest, most Yankees seem to have accepted that their former enemies were correct about the wisdom, even necessity, of keeping the preponder-ance of "free" African Americans in a state of dependency and subjection. The freedmen were still not worthy of the same liberty and honor that accrued to full-fledged American citizens.

Not to be treated as an honorable equal in antebellum America suggested that one's detractors and opponents intended to wield degrading and despotic power over one and in the process reduce one to a metaphorical form of dis-honorable slavery, to the figurative status of a tyrant's bondsman inherently deficient in dignity and self-respect. In eighteenth-century Anglo-American politics, the terms "slavery" and "enslavement" had become potent and endur-ing tropes or metaphors for the result of corrupt tyranny's victory over hon-orable liberty. To be sure, the persistence and spread of black chattel bond-age south of the Mason-Dixon Line and Ohio River into the mid–nineteenth century meant that white southerners remained particularly touchy about their reputations as free men worthy of respect and honor within both their regional slave society and the American republic at large. Antislavery radicals in the free states refused to recognize what most citizens in the slave states wanted to see as the benevolent and patriarchal character of the South's peculiar institution, in the process demeaning the Christian and American character of slaveholding Americans. These Yankee ultras seemed intent on reducing or degrading them to the blatantly disreputable and dishonorable status of metaphorical slaves subject to corrupt, exploitative, and tyrannical majorities in the more populous and numerous free states.

To be sure, religiously inspired abolitionists on the eve of the Civil War also drew on the powerful American dichotomy of liberty versus tyranny, portraying slavery as at the same time despotic and sinful. During the Second Great Awakening earlier in the century, this antislavery interpretation of America's republican legacy and principles had begun moving toward a kind of cultural fusion with the North's relatively egalitarian and reformist version of evangelical Christianity. By the mid-1850s, the South's peculiar institution, along with those people who had invested in it economically, emotionally, and politically, appeared to many (perhaps most) citizens in the free states as corrupt and despotic obstacles to the ongoing progress of both true Christianity and genuine Americanism. Yet the vast majority of the North's citizenry rejected radical or extremist solutions to the problem of slavery, which threatened not only the Union's integrity but also traditional and desirable hierarchies based on gender and race.

A coherent if intricate fabric of American evangelical reform had been woven by what historians term at least two Great Awakenings between the 1730s and 1830s, but this fabric quickly frayed, as scholars such as James H. Moorhead and Robert H. Abzug have suggested.[31] When the American Colonization Society was founded in 1817, evangelical Christian leaders in both sections could believe that God was slowly but surely preparing the earth for the apocalyptic millennium by empowering the converted to help him, in his own good time, put such evils as demon rum and chattel slavery on a path to gradual and peaceful extinction. This process would take place without fundamental challenges to divinely ordained social hierarchies, especially those based on Negrophobia and patriarchal assumptions about proper gender relations. Mainstream and responsible Christian evangelicals would imprint divine principles on the turbulent hearts and minds of an increasingly democratic citizenry. Without such instruction, Americans would succumb to the Scylla of anarchy or the Charybdis of tyranny. However, during the 1830s, a small number of radical reformers, proponents of color-blind abolitionist immediatism in tandem with woman's rights, came to reject both antislavery gradualism and traditional hierarchies of race and gender. This tiny but vocal minority came to reject the assumption that blacks and women must and should be content with subordinate positions in American society, the former in chattel bondage and the latter in patriarchal households. To these radicals, gendered and racial hierarchies involved manifestly sinful evils. Those truly born again and converted would quickly gain the vision and discipline to repent of these sins and would then take dramatic steps to extirpate them. These "Come-Outers" lambasted American Protestants for their hypocrisy and inconsistency. This ultra stance found personification in former slave Sojourner Truth and former South Carolina lady Angelina Grimké. However, few antebellum northerners responded positively to radical calls for abolitionist immediatism and woman's rights. The great majority of Americans north and south alike preferred not to challenge directly conventional hierarchies of gender and race. Because these hierarchies seemed bolstered by so much precedent and tradition, secular and divine, Americans accepted the necessity for both white supremacy and male domination of the public sphere. Instead, they focused their anxieties and fears on the far more palpable and unifying threat to the legacies of 1776 and 1787 coming from the tyrannical and corrupt machinations of an aggressive, unscrupulous, and ultimately secessionist slaveocracy and Slave Power.

Few antebellum northerners were willing to follow either the antipolitical Garrisonians or the Liberty Party men. While the former denounced slavery and even the 1787 Union itself as sinful and un-Christian and favored northern separation from the South, adherents of the Liberty Party interpreted the Constitution as permitting the federal government to take aggressive steps against the South's peculiar and un-American system of human bondage. However, hostility to slavery and the Slave Power drew clear impetus from the annexation of Texas as a slave state and the Mexican War in the 1840s; the mills of antislavery drew more grist from the Fugitive Slave Act and then much more from congressional adoption and selective executive enforcement of the Kansas-Nebraska Act of 1854. Two years later, northern popular opinion became inflamed against slave state celebrations of South Carolina's Preston Brooks for brutally vindicating the honor of his family and state from the abolitionist insults of Massachusetts's Charles Sumner. The 1857 *Dred Scott* decision by a proslavery Supreme Court majority confirmed in the minds of more and more northern citizens that the southern Slave Power and its northern "doughface" allies in the Democratic Party had begun an aggressive proslavery campaign. This campaign sought not only to preserve slavery but also to expand its reach and power in the Union, obviously at the expense of dominant free state assumptions about American rights, interests, and honor. After antislavery Republicans won the presidency, the secession movement in the Lower South aroused northern anger and indignation at the Slave Power's apparent disrespect for constitutional government and majority will.

Historians have also recognized that the remnants and remembrance of slavery above the Mason-Dixon Line seem to have disappeared from public memory during the first half of the nineteenth century. Following the full-blown glorification of free wage labor during the 1840s and 1850s, chattel slavery increasingly appeared to northerners as a regional anomaly incompatible with republican and natural rights principles. The peculiar institution was also less amenable than free labor to the kind of economic and cultural dynamism coming to characterize society in the free states. The Founding Fathers had idealistically proclaimed America's devotion to the universal cause of human freedom while pragmatically accepting the reality of slavery's durability, though not its permanence, in the planting and slave states. If slavery could be contained geographically—a process that Lincoln saw the Founding Fathers as intending to jump-start with the Northwest Ordinance of 1787, the abolition of the foreign slave trade as of 1808, and the Missouri Compromise of 1820—then the slave states would eventually lose their political clout, and slaveholders themselves would become more and more willing and able to recognize in slavery an economic as well as social liability. White southerners eventually would endorse a gradual process of compensated emancipation, necessarily coupled with the colonization or deportation of freed blacks outside the country's borders.

At midcentury, as historian Anne C. Rose has suggested, most mainstream Protestants rejected radical nonconformism "from the safe haven of Victorian religion, with its comforting conviction that slow, systematic growth was God's preferred way."[32] Yet beginning with the annexation of Texas as a slave state and especially after the Kansas-Nebraska Act and the *Dred Scott* ruling, mainline Protestants in the North began to see the slaveocracy and Slave Power as having embarked on a course of aggressive machinations to promote both the security and spread of their peculiar institution at the expense of the rights, liberties, honor, and religious sensibilities of nonslaveholders in both the free and slave states. Perhaps the best-known exponent of Victorian Christianity in antebellum America was Henry Ward Beecher, pastor at the Congregationalist Plymouth Church in Brooklyn. When he first arrived at Plymouth Church, he expressed an optimistic and gradualist "belief in peaceful evolution, that with patience and time liberty would naturally drive out slavery." Yet after the Compromise of 1850, Beecher came to demonstrate the "combativeness" that biographer Debby Applegate posits as the "temper of the times." In the 1850s, he illustrated how formerly mainstream, moderate evangelicals could direct more and more of their combative spirit against slavery and the South. "What was disappearing," in the words of Moorhead, "was the integrating center that gave a sense of participation in one united evangelical crusade to bring in the millennium"—that is, a holy crusade to promote the creation of a society infused with justice and righteousness that would hasten the return of the resurrected Christ to assume divine dominion over God's creation. (This was a postmillennial rather than premillennial vision, since the latter tends to see the world as descending into a vortex of corruption and paganism from which only the Second Coming of a militant and angry Son of God can redeem the chosen and saved.)

Beecher's response to the Fugitive Slave Law of 1850, whose provisions allowed federal marshals to compel the cooperation of free state citizens in recovering alleged runaways, infuriated white southerners: "The North is to have the guilt and the South the profits of Slavery." In the conclusion to her powerful novel, *Uncle Tom's Cabin*, Beecher's sister, Harriet Beecher Stowe, pointed to a palsied national will before the nation's sin of slavery and prophesied that the "wrath of Almighty God" would soon descend on the United States if its people failed to take appropriate antislavery measures during the "day of grace" that a gracious but insistent God would soon bring to an end.[33] Her stance suggested some kind of premillennial punishment from God.

Some southern preachers—in particular, influential South Carolina Presbyterian James Henley Thornwell—expounded a form of pro-slavery millennialism whereby relationships between masters and slaves were becoming what one historian has termed "an intimate and continuous conduit of Christian spirituality into actual behavior and consequences." Such clergy "equated the moral regulation of slavery with the march of progress" and espied "a mysterious process by which slavery, in the hands of Christian masters, would purge itself of evil." In other words, far from being a sin or evil, chattel bondage in the South had been instituted by God with the divine expectation that it should and would evolve into a thoroughly Christian relationship. This position allowed Thornwell to acknowledge that slavery as then practiced in the South still had room for improvement but nevertheless represented part of "a vast providential scheme," whereby "God assigns to every man, by a wise and holy decree, the precise place he is to occupy in the great moral scheme of humanity," which involved "the education of the human race for liberty and virtue."[34]

During the 1850s, Harriet Beecher Stowe and Henry Ward Beecher became more and more identified nationally with northern antagonism toward slavery and the Slave Power even as they also espoused a Lincolnesque conservatism on the matter of racial equality and continued to endorse the increasingly impractical vision of gradual emancipation linked to colonization.[35] When war began, northern evangelicals such as the Beecher siblings came to see their region's struggle for the Union as part and parcel of God's plan to promote the divine cause of glorious freedom triumphant against corrupt and tottering despotism. Upholding the integrity of the Constitution and the Union became linked with upholding the Union's commitment to a higher standard of Christian morality for the nation's life, a standard derived ultimately from the Golden Rule. In contrast, Christian evangelicals in the South came to endorse a secessionist vision of their region's providential slave society as assuming the garb and role of latter-day Hebrews following a very different interpretation of godly precepts and divine guidance. Under Confederate rather than Mosaic leadership, they helped to effect and defend an exodus from metaphorical enslavement to corrupt and ungodly tyranny imposed by dangerous, heretical, and impractical northern Republicans rather than a pagan Egyptian pharaoh. As many partisans of disunion made clear, the God of Moses had endorsed Hebrew enslavement of savage and foreign gentiles, and neither Jesus nor Paul had made any statements that could be construed as antislavery.[36]

At least since the Declaration of Independence, most Americans have tended to see themselves as high-minded practitioners and purveyors of the greatest degrees of freedom and liberty in human history, an enviable condition deriving from a divine blessing and destiny reflecting God's Providence. Historian Lewis Saum maintains that during the nineteenth century, "no theme was more pervasive or philosophically more fundamental than the providential view. Simply put, the view held that, directly or indirectly, God controlled all things." Such an assertion may seem a bit hyperbolic, but Saum's position is accurate and important. More recently, historian Mark Noll has explored the mid-nineteenth-century perspective on Divine Providence, finding that the "belief that God controlled events has always been foundational wherever biblical religion prevailed, yet in nineteenth-century America confidence in the human ability to fathom God's providential actions rose to new heights." Even as the legacy of the eighteenth-century Enlightenment inclined Americans to think that common-sense observations could reveal more and more about the workings of the world in which they lived, they could still invoke God's Providence to explain the tragic power of ubiquitous and fatal diseases such as cholera and tuberculosis. Thus, Americans could be at the same time "children of Enlightenment as well as children of God."[37] Americans north and south could believe the ultimate blessings bestowed by Divine Providence and could invoke heavenly intervention or guidance when faced with political crisis as well as medical emergency.

Some Americans adhered to a simple theistic and supernatural assumption that God's often direct intervention in human affairs and the physical world should be as obvious to their fellow Americans as it was in the lives of Abraham and Moses as recorded in the biblical revelation of Genesis and Exodus. More citizens seemed to believe that God worked mysteriously and behind the scenes in the created world; to them, God was the supremely rational Creator of a physical universe operating according to certain divinely engineered natural laws, although he could also somehow work secretly, in ways inaccessible to human analysis, to direct or guide human history. Indeed, God's natural laws extended to the proper organization of human society in the form of the self-evident law of supply and demand in the economic sphere and the law of inalienable human rights in the political realm. Both of these ideas had been proclaimed in 1776, the former by Adam Smith in Scotland and the latter by Thomas Jefferson in America.

Even as they paid homage to Divine Providence, most free American men also held fast to the classical liberal principle or assumption that the individual must and should be responsible for his and his family's secular success or failure in the American land of liberty and opportunity. Historians term this perspective or ideology "classical liberalism" to distinguish it from the later, perhaps more modern, manifestation of political liberalism that endows federal and/or state government with the obligation and duty to provide all citizens with a minimum level of personal well-being and individual welfare. Twentieth-century political liberals also came to endow government in a democratic republic with the responsibility for protecting the corporate welfare of all citizens from the exploitation and duplicity orchestrated by often corrupt "special interests" entrenched in positions of wealth and power. However, facets of this more modern liberalism clearly extend back to the birth of American politics in the 1790s. During that seminal decade, some observers, often described as classical republicans, decried the federal government's support for a central Bank of the United States as promoting the interests of a despotic financial aristocracy. By the 1820s, the second Bank of the United States, chartered in 1816 with support from the same Madisonian

Republicans who had opposed the first national bank's charter in 1791, had become what its critics portrayed as a corrupt "Money Power" feeding on the vitals of genuinely republican governance. After the new Jacksonian Democratic political party destroyed the second bank in the 1830s while the slave plantations of the emerging Cotton Kingdom spread westward, the stage was set for northerners in the final two antebellum decades to espy and decry a southern-based slaveocracy working to promote the "slave interest" at the expense of the free states. At the same time, the manifestation of powerful antislavery and antislaveholder political sentiments in the North during the 1819–20 controversy over slavery's geographical expansion was followed during the 1830s by the emergence of a vocal and more radical abolitionist movement denouncing the South's peculiar institution as both un-Christian and anti-American and demanding emancipationist immediatism. Where citizens in the free states increasingly came to fear aggressive and dangerous machinations by the Slave Power, citizens in the slave states increasingly came to express fears of aggressive and dangerous machinations by an insidious conspiracy orchestrated by outspoken abolitionists, seemingly aided and abetted by those who proclaimed themselves conservative or moderate antislavery men.

During the antebellum era, northerners and southerners glorified the image and imagery of the self-made man, embodied in Tennessean Andrew Jackson and New Yorker Martin Van Buren. At the same time, Americans also maintained a conviction that their experiment in republican and constitutional liberty owed its success to the favorable circumstances and guidance offered by God's Providence. During the secession crisis, as northerners and southerners alike prayed for guidance and invoked Divine Providence, most people fervently hoped that God would somehow act or intervene to avert a permanent or violent rupture of the Union. Louisa Rodgers Meigs, wife of Unionist army engineer and captain Montgomery Meigs, wrote to her Unionist son, John, a cadet at West Point, on 20 November 1860, weeks after it had become clear that Lincoln would be the next U.S. president but weeks before South Carolina officially declared itself out of the Union: "The political state of the country fills every mind with anxiety. 'Secession' is the subject of every one's conversation. I think that the Union is in great danger, but I trust the Divine Wisdom will find some means that we do not know about to deliver us from the evils which threaten us."[38] South Carolina plantation mistress Keziah Goodwyn Hopkins Brevard had much the same outlook, although she privately acknowledged slavery's downside in a way that most slavery apologists never did in public. On 20 February 1861, as the Confederacy was being organized in Montgomery, the widow Brevard confided to her diary, "If I had had children I have always said that I would try to get them away from negro slavery—am I right or am I wrong—God's ways must be right—he has put them here for some wise purpose & I know I should leave all in his hands & not murmur as I do."[39] The Civil War's destruction of African American slavery demonstrated to both southerners such as Brevard and northerners such as Charles Hodge of Princeton Theological Seminary that God's purpose had willed an outcome unexpected by whites in both sections four years before. The Confederacy, by its desire to perpetuate "a system so fraught with evil," had only provoked "Divine Displeasure," concluded Hodge; "that it was the design of God to bring about this even cannot be doubted."[40] If one accepts the providential yet tragic view of history endorsed by Lincoln during the Civil War, perhaps the long and tortuous road from the election of 1860 to that of 2008 reveals evidence of some transcendent direction or goal that most human beings can comprehend only in retrospect.

A number of scholars have recognized the significance of the widespread American belief in the power of Divine Providence. As Harry S. Stout suggested in 2006, "The United States was first and foremost an idea built on a foundation of ideology and theology." That is, ideological adulation of the United States as a glorious example of constitutional and republican government generally accompanied a theological conviction that God had blessed the United States as a nation of liberty and prosperity. To be sure, once the old Union and new Confederacy came to blows, this "foundation of ideology and theology" could be and was tilted to support either cause. In the words of Edward L. Ayers, "Both sides, certain that God favored their cause, easily invoked His mercy and blessings."[41] Religious spokesmen in the slave states found it both necessary and correct to link the proslavery and disunionist crusades with traditions and values they believed rooted in both the U.S. Constitution and the Christian Bible, Old and New Testaments. At the same time, Republicans and their allies sought to ground their antislavery Unionism in scriptural as well as constitutional exegesis.

In short, leaders on both sides could lay claim to and invoke apologetically different facets of the complex American legacies of 1776 and 1787. Different sectional interpretations of these legacies could be and often were supplemented by different interpretations of Christian Scriptures and their message. Although neither Davis nor Lincoln displayed or appealed to overtly evangelical sensibilities, each wanted the public to see him as what one historian has called "the conservative defender of the nation's founding principles."[42] For Lincoln and Davis, both the Declaration of Independence and the Constitution were crucial founding documents, although they were viewed and interpreted through different sectional lenses. Lincoln interpreted Jefferson's Declaration as an antislavery manifesto, albeit hardly radically abolitionist, and the Constitution as establishing a perpetual union founded on liberty and majority rule. The United States was probably a providentially sacred nation but doubtless a progressive republic, within which slavery should be recognized as a regrettable and anomalous institution. Though black bondage was deeply rooted, Americans properly dedicated to liberty and ongoing human progress should and would acknowledge its shortcomings and someday agree to eradicate it, albeit gradually and safely. And in fact, as historian Phillip Shaw Paludan has concluded, the Union that Lincoln determined to save in 1861 "was not a union where slavery was safe."[43] For Davis, the Declaration was a revolutionary but implicitly racist document that endowed America's white citizenry with the God-given right of rebellion against any government becoming a tyrannical purveyor of political servitude and degrading dishonor. He viewed the Constitution, especially as supplemented by the Tenth Amendment (1791), as a republican compact or federation among sovereign states rather than a consolidated government, the latter claiming a dangerous legitimacy derived from the unenlightened populace at large. For Davis and his like-minded allies, the libertarian, Lockean, and Trinitarian concept of humanity's natural rights to life, liberty, and property still underlay and permeated the 1776 Jeffersonian version of "life, liberty, and the pursuit of happiness." Any government that could threaten individual property rights, guaranteed by the Fifth Amendment and including state-recognized property in human beings, could pose a despotic threat to individual liberty among the white citizenry, to state sovereignty as a bulwark of those liberties, and to a southern way of life inseparable from black chattel slavery as a system of benevolent racial control and respectable private property. White southerners generally viewed enslaved blacks as members of an inferior and brutish race and thus fervently defended the right to own and control these chattel.

Davis identified the oppressive northern free states in 1860–61 with corrupt and tyrannical England of 1775–76. The seceding slave states played the role of the American colonies rebelling against an imperial government seeking to siphon off wealth and crush the free colonists' rights, interests, and honor. Lincoln saw the northern free states as upholding a blessed republican and democratic union against despotic and secessionist traitors. Secessionists refused to accept the clearly constitutional decision of American voters, expressed through the Electoral College. It had elected as president a conservative and responsible Republican, not some radical, ultra, fanatical abolitionist. The elitist Slave Power may have begun to lose its traditional ability to control the federal government in the service of the South's peculiar regional interests, but that development gave slave states no justifiable warrant to abandon and undermine the world's greatest providential example of genuinely republican and democratic government. To the minds of Lincoln's fellow Republican Unionists, the Slave Power had betrayed the antislavery convictions of those who founded the American nation, refusing to accept one of their fundamental principles—that is, that human bondage in the United States be placed on the road to long-term, peaceful extinction. To Davis's fellow Confederates, a tyrannical northern antislavery majority refused any longer to make the substantial and equitable sort of sectional compromises made by the Founding Fathers in the interests of establishing and preserving the Union. Lincoln's election demonstrated that this Union no longer constituted an amicable and respectful confederation among free and slave states. Most citizens in the slave states understood that to accept Lincoln's election and administration, however much Republicans insisted on its constitutional legitimacy, meant that they had "to accept the ultimate death of slavery." In Paludan's words, "To demand that they stay in the Union forecast a future in which their world was lost."[44] Each side had a particular understanding of its interests, rights, and honor.

Many people at the time and a good many observers since have lamented that ambitious, shortsighted, and irresponsible politicians failed to engineer and endorse the substantive compromises that would have avoided what a Vermont newspaper in mid-December 1860 termed "the foulest minister of God's wrath, *civil war*!" The stability and health of representative, democratic government depends on effective political compromise. "It is their willingness to compromise that makes politicians so indispensable and so untrustworthy," historian James Oakes explains. "They build the coalitions that bring democracy to life by trimming their principles down to popular size. The best politicians know how to compromise to arouse a constituency without forsaking basic ideals."[45] Devout Unionist politician Henry Clay of Kentucky made much the same point during the Senate debates prior to adoption of the pieces of legislation known collectively as the Compromise of 1850. His conviction that slavery "is an evil, a social and political evil" would accompany him "to the grave," which in fact claimed his body two years later. Yet he would craft laws "doing equal and impartial justice to the South and to the North." Why? "All legislation, all government, all society is formed upon the principle of mutual concession, politeness, comity, courtesy." The foremost "recommendation" to "honorable" compromise, Clay declared, is to be found in the fact "that if you concede anything, you have something conceded to you in return."[46] However, this sort of political concession is usually anathema to the moral absolutist, for whom life appears not in shades of gray compromise but in diametrically opposed black evil and white good.[47]

The apparent inability to craft a sectional compromise during the secession winter did not mean that American leaders of the time were inferior to the men who had proposed and supported the Compromise of 1850. After all, the two politicians who probably did the most to guide the compromise measures piecemeal through the Congress—Democrat Stephen A. Douglas of Illinois in the Senate and Democrat Howell Cobb of Georgia in the House—were still alive and active on the national stage in 1860–61. Yet after Fort Sumter, Douglas offered unequivocal support to Lincoln and the Union, while even before Lincoln's inauguration, Cobb became the enthusiastic chair of the convention in Montgomery that organized the new Confederacy. The inability to engineer an acceptable compromise during the secession crisis reflected the reality that neither northern nor southern stalwarts could endorse concessions that did not seem to undermine what they perceived to be their fundamental interests, rights, and honor as citizens of the American republic. Avery Craven has powerfully concluded, "Neither the North nor the South could yield its position because *slavery had come to symbolize values in each of their socio-economic structures for which men fight and die but which they do not give up or compromise.*"[48] Partisans in both sections saw the causes and values for which they fought and died—their interests, rights, and honor—as unquestionably American in character because they were firmly rooted in the legacies of 1776 and 1787. These interests, rights, and honor were also buttressed by understandings of genuine Christianity.

Roy Nichols has argued that Americans north and south "set to killing one another in 1861" because "emotion in the United States" had become "supercharged." People tend to abandon compromise and resort to violence when they experience stressful, fearful "hyperemotionalism." This contention may be true, but such emotions also are fed by growing fears of those who appear to pose substantive challenges to common assumptions, principles, prosperity, and security. As Nichols recognizes, "in the spirit of 1776," secessionist southerners "would organize a second American Revolution" against a perceived new tyranny rooted in popular northern hostility to slave society. "They would create a reformed confederacy free from corruption and centralization in which their social and economic institutions would be safe." Almost all Confederate leaders in Montgomery and Charleston agreed, in the words of historians J. G. Randall and David Herbert Donald, that Lincoln's plan to re-lieve Sumter seemed "a threat, a challenge, a breach of faith"[49] and felt they had no choice but to fire the first offensive shot in angry resentment of Yankee self-righteousness. The bellicose response of the Lincoln administration in Washington quickly won northern backing from "an angered constituency that included most northern Democrats." The U.S. government, as Nichols writes, "determined to fight rather than permit the seceding states to break up a profitable partnership, a source of wealth and power, and an experiment in liberty and equality which Lincoln felt was the hope of the world." Far more recently, Ayers has poignantly made much the same point: "People invoked the Constitution and Declaration of Independence against enemies invoking the same icons. People enlisted God in their cause and anxiously waited signs of His approval for the blood they shed."[50]

Political psychologists offer helpful insights into the ways that many kinds of Americans have historically experienced or perceived a "normative threat" or challenge—that is, a "threat to the normative order" of their values and well-being." Karen Stenner posits the need to recognize that "there are politi-cal dispositions other than reasoned ideologies, and things that citizens want to express in politics other than ideas." She concludes, "The experience or perception of normative threat may certainly, even often, be a product of elite manipulation. But the predisposition to be hyper-responsive to those condi-tions is endogenous—a product of the masses."[51] The masses, like elites, can insist on respect and security instead of condescension and threats.

Historian Michael F. Holt has offered a perspective on the secession crisis that appears both to accord with and to diverge from Stenner's argument. Holt recognizes that the "Civil War was not exclusively a politicians' war. Far too many young Americans fought and died during it for that claim ever to be made." Nonetheless, the records of politicians from the era of the so-called second party system,[52] which pitted Whigs against Jacksonian Democrats, reveal clearly how "slavery extension became a political weapon rival parties use to exploit for political reasons." This phenomenon occurred even though the resulting "sectional polarization . . . could only help their intra-party rivals and endanger the very preservation of the Union."[53] Recalling Stenner's argu-ment, Holt seems to see political elites as playing an important role in pro-moting popular perceptions of a serious outside "normative threat" to each section's interests, rights, and honor. If so, these antebellum politicians seem to provide another tragic example of what Barbara Tuchman has identified as the frequently misguided and ultimately self-defeating behavior coming from those in political power: "the pursuit of folly," with "folly" defined as the perverse pursuit of policies contrary to a society's actual and/or long-term self-interest.[54]

A suggestion that southern politicians had engaged in the pursuit of folly came in mid-November 1860 from Alexander Stephens of Georgia, future Confederate vice president. Speaking in the Georgia state capital, Milledgeville, Stephens opined "that but for the policy the Southern people [themselves] pursued," those people would not then confront the "fearful result" of Lincoln's election—that is, "the result of a sectional election of a President of the United States, one whose opinions and avowed principles are in antagonism to our interests and rights, and, we believe, if carried out would subvert the Constitution under which we now live." By instigating and sustaining a sectional split in the Democratic Party earlier that year, southern politicians had jeopardized "this Government of our fathers." Despite "all its defects," the U.S. polity "comes nearer the objects of all good government than any other on the face of the earth." Stephens declared himself at that time "unwilling to support secession and disunion." What "if the policy of Mr. Lincoln and his Republican associates shall be carried out, or attempted to be carried out," if the new administration did in fact seek "to exclude us, by an act of Congress, from the Territories, with our slave property"? Then, declared Stephens, "no man in Georgia will be more willing or ready than myself to defend our rights, interest, and honor at every hazard and to the last extremity."[55]

I have changed the order of Stephens's triumvirate from "rights, interest, and honor" to "interests, rights and honor." Certainly, as Stephens made clear, the spread and security of black chattel bondage had become the most important "interest" in the sectional dispute, together with what Allan Nevins termed "its complementary problem of race adjustment."[56] Other "interests" were at stake for some southerners, but slavery was paramount. However, as Stephens's original order suggests, southerners—and northerners—generally preferred to discuss the questions of slavery and later secession in terms of threats to their constitutional and natural rights and to their honor as citizens of a state and a section within the Union. Although historians can see the economic and racial foundations of southern and northern complaints against each other, the sectional combatants, like the great majority of human beings, much preferred to address and defend those "interests" in terms of powerful abstractions such as "rights" and "honor." Such abstractions rendered sectional interests in language and concepts that seemed transcendent and universal and hence eminently admirable and defensible. As with Stephens, most free southerners and northerners in 1861 determined to defend and protect their self-evident interests, rights, and honor.

Perceptions and understandings of external reality often have far more important consequences than the elusive reality itself. History suggests that if Americans (like other peoples) can be persuaded of the necessity to use military force to forestall the imminent threat of direct enemy attack or even a serious challenge to our national security, then we are willing to endorse a war of assumed or alleged self-defense. However, as Mark Kurlansky has recently observed, "There is always a way to argue that a war is a case of self-defense."[57] In 1860–61, both American secessionists and Confederates on one side and American Unionists and Republicans on the other claimed they were engaged in defensive conflict against verbal insults and dangerous aggression, a conflict also necessary to preserve their sense of security and well-being.

When the specter of military conflict and war has loomed on the horizon, most Americans have seen their society's uniquely high quantum of providential freedom and liberty as challenged and threatened by an enemy that can best be described as tyrannical and despotic—versus constitutional and republican or democratic—and therefore as corrupt and depraved. Americans have been summoned to arms (whether borne by short-term volunteers, conscripted troops, or professional soldiers) by some mixture of three dominant impulses and objectives: first, the basic, fundamental, God-given human right of self-preservation against grave danger and imminent threat to the security of one's family and community; second, the heightened sense of duty and nobility involved in defending and preserving the rights, interests, and honor of an exemplarily and providentially free American society or community against contemptible and terrifying foes; and third, the still higher calling of serving as an example so that other, supposedly less blessed and advanced peoples can enjoy some measure of the extraordinary liberty and freedom that Divine Providence has seen fit to bestow on the United States. Regardless of the accuracy of these perceptions or the skill with which manipulative leaders have at times appealed to such self-congratulatory impulses and motives, they unquestionably have the power to shape not only Americans' idealistic, positive perceptions of themselves but also the negative and at times demonic images they have attached to their foes. During the secession crisis, most free Americans in both the North and the South came to understand and apply these assumptions, values, and impulses with regional blinders. And most of them assumed or prayed that Divine Providence ultimately would bless their side.

Four years of warfare inadvertently enabled Republicans to accomplish something about which radicals such as Frederick Douglass and William Lloyd Garrison had only dreamed in early 1860: the end of slavery in their lifetimes. Angelina Grimké, South Carolina lady become abolitionist, wrote prophetically on 12 December 1860, "The South are dissolving the Union in order to prevent the abolition of Slavery and yet they are too blind to see that this dissolution will only hasten instead of prevent its overthrow."[58] Some large slaveholders, especially in the Upper South, demonstrated similar foresight. Prominent among them was a former Whig governor of Tennessee, William B. Campbell, a resident of Middle Tennessee and nephew of a recently deceased former governor of Virginia, David Campbell of Abingdon. In mid-March 1861, William Campbell wrote, "The great upheaving of the Southern States has been avowedly for the protection of negro slavery, while I regard the whole [secessionist] movement as the most unfortunate and injurious to that institution. As a pro-slavery man I repudiate the Southern move as unwise and impolitic, and tending to the ruin and overthrow of negro slavery. The rights of the slaveholder cannot be maintained out of the Union so well as in it, and I fear cannot be maintained at all outside of it."[59]

A significant number of affluent slaveholders between Lincoln's election and Fort Sumter seemed to have agreed with Campbell that their interests, rights, and honor seemed safer under the U.S. Constitution than under the Confederate Constitution. Such men were correct. As Roger Ransom has noted, the United States as a whole "probably offered the most secure haven for a slave society in the world of the nineteenth century."[60]

To be sure, Lincoln insisted in 1861 and for most of 1862 that federal military coercion had nothing to do with slavery per se and everything to do with enforcing federal laws and preserving the Union. Maintaining the loyalty of border slave states, especially Kentucky, provided powerful and practical incentives for his administration to emphasize the perpetuity of the Union while restraining hostility to slavery. In early 1861, Secretary of State William Henry Seward overtly and Lincoln covertly supported a proposed Thirteenth Amendment to the Constitution that would have prohibited any future amendment—like the actual Thirteenth Amendment ratified in late 1865—allowing federal interference with property rights in human chattel held within the existing slave states. Such an amendment might have encouraged conditional Unionists and reluctant Confederates to remain in or perhaps even return to the Union. During the half century prior to the Civil War, explains Michael Vorenberg, "Americans had come to regard the constitutional text as sacred." Despite their sometimes vehement disagreements over what it said and meant, Americans "accepted the document's vagaries as the price of Union." Yet in late February 1861, the proposed Thirteenth Amendment received enough Republican votes to win a majority in the House of

Representatives, and three days later, Douglas led the Senate to approve it. Signed by President Buchanan, it was sent to the state legislatures, two of which voted for ratification before the process was derailed by the outbreak of the Civil War.[61] As late as September 1862, a month before issuing the preliminary Emancipation Proclamation, which took effect on 1 January 1863, the president insisted in a public letter to editor Horace Greeley that "my paramount object in this struggle *is* to save the Union, and is *not* either to save or destroy slavery."

This conundrum constitutes perhaps the fundamental irony among the many that abound in the background, course of, and outcomes after the Civil War. Various slave states and the president of the Confederacy made it clear that genuine concerns over the stability and future of slavery had prompted a secessionist response based on state's rights and state sovereignty.[62] Until October 1862, Lincoln denied any desire or intention to strike directly at slavery. However, he concluded at that time that the paramount goal of saving the Union through military victory required both the destruction of slavery in areas still outside U.S. authority and the enlistment of black troops in the Union Army. He followed the Emancipation Proclamation with a campaign for what became the Thirteenth Amendment, which abolished chattel slavery not just in Confederate territory but throughout the United States, including his obstinate native state of Kentucky. According to the ironic historical law of (or at least powerful tendency to) unintended consequences, the 1860–61 secessionist movement intended to secure slavery had the opposite effect. It brought an end to African American slavery far more quickly than Lincoln and most of his fellow Republicans had ever imagined or wished during the secession winter. The Confederacy's defeat and surrender in 1865 also marked the de facto demise of secessionist state sovereignty, its de jure death coming with the ratification of the Fourteenth Amendment in 1868 and the Supreme Court's 1869 ruling in *Texas v. White*.

Secessionism was the extreme version of a state's rights way of thinking, or "persuasion," that enjoyed widespread support in various parts of the United States from the 1790s to the 1850s. However, when secession led to civil war in 1861, the new Confederate government faced the reality of having to mobilize people and resources in eleven theoretically sovereign states against an invasion that both denied and threatened the infant nation's existence. In the process of the remarkable if ultimately unsuccessful mobilization by Davis's government in Richmond, the Confederacy provoked protests that it was engaged in despotic behavior contradicting the principles of state's rights and Lockean liberty that the 1861 Confederate Constitution had been written to protect. Most Americans who went to war in the spring of 1861, whether Unionist or Confederate, expected the fighting to be a glorious, uplifting, and brief adventure. They had little inkling of the carnage and destruction that four years of internecine conflict would bring. Yet the 620,000 U.S. casualties between 1861 and 1865 exceed those suffered by the United States in all its other wars and "conflicts" combined.

To paraphrase Potter, the Civil War had three major casualties: secession, slavery, and more than 600,000 American dead. Were those American lives worth the constitutional de jure emancipation of almost 4,000,000 slaves and the near-universal victory of Lincoln's conviction that the Union was in fact permanent? To paraphrase Kenneth Stampp, how should we decide whether the life of one person should be sacrificed to give legal liberty to six others and whether death and destruction were necessary sacrifices to the perpetuity of the Union? Answering these questions seems to require the kind of moral judgment that no individual can make for another.[63]

s of 1860, the future Confederate president, Jefferson Davis, owned well over a hundred African American slaves in Warren County, Mississippi. One historian has described Mississippi as "the most southern of southern states—a prototype where is mixed all the peculiar forces and tensions that have made the American South unique in the nation."[1] During the 1850s, the state's cotton production surpassed that of Alabama, transforming the Magnolia State into the statistical heartland of the Cotton Kingdom. By 1840, after the presidential administration of Andrew Jackson had effected the final dispossession and "removal" to western Indian Territory of the Chickasaw and Choctaw tribes, Mississippi had joined South Carolina as one of two states where African American slaves constituted a majority of the population. Although Mississippi followed South Carolina's December 1860 lead and became the second slave state to quit the Union, Mississippi's state convention did not achieve the secessionist unanimity of South Carolina's. The Magnolia State convention endorsed separate-state secession by a 88–15 vote that testified to the persistence of antisecessionist sentiment in some nonplantation areas outside the fertile Delta-Loess soil region abutting the Mississippi River. The Delta-Loess region had come to constitute what James Cobb calls "the most Southern place on earth." It included the Yazoo Delta above Vicksburg, which had not been heavily settled until the development of a nascent levee system during the 1840s, and the Natchez District below Vicksburg, which had been home to settlers of British and African ancestry since the last third of the eighteenth century.[2]

While Davis's slaves in Warren County lived and worked on his cotton plantation, Brierfield, downriver from Vicksburg, in 1860 their owner represented the Magnolia State in Washington as a Democratic U.S. senator. Immediately after Lincoln's election, Davis appeared to be a halting cooperationist, as opposed to an ultra or fire-eater demanding immediate separate-state secession. Such cooperationists hoped that slave states considering disunion would first consult among themselves, present the Republican Party and northern Democrats with an ultimatum in the form of new constitutional guarantees for the security of the peculiar institution, and only then leave the Union en masse if these guarantees were denied.[3] At that point, Davis may have been less inclined toward immediate disunion than were the majority of voters in his state. Young Greenville attorney William L. Nugent, for example, reported to his wife from Vicksburg on 26 November 1860, "I find there is a decided tendency to Secession everywhere. Almost everyone I meet has come to the determination to vindicate the rights of our outraged section if need be at point of bayonet."[4] In mid-December, Davis joined Mississippi's other congressional representatives in signing a statement "To Our Constituents" that told voters that secession had become necessary to maintain their "honor, safety, and independence." A few days later, he reluctantly agreed to serve on the Senate Committee of Thirteen intended to ponder sectional compromise. The committee members accepted his proposal that the committee should make no recommendation to the Senate that had not been endorsed by a majority of both Republicans and Democrats. Like his political opponent but personal friend William Henry Seward, a New York Republican, Davis gave enthusiastic support to a proposed Thirteenth Amendment that would have precluded any direct federal interference with the peculiar institution in the existing slave states. Also like Seward, but for different reasons, Davis ultimately refused to endorse Kentucky senator John J. Crittenden's proposed restoration of the Missouri Compromise line in all federal territories, current or future.

The slave states could certainly choose to withdraw from the United States and could justify such a decision in one or both of two ways. Davis preferred to portray secession as a constitutional legacy of 1787–88 that each state retained by virtue of its ratification of the U.S. Constitution. Yet he also understood that separation from the Union could be construed as an inherent legacy from the 1776 natural right of revolution against political authority perceived as degrading and tyrannical. He preferred the constitutional argument, in part because opponents of secession liked to portray it as anarchic and treasonous rebellion. Hence, Davis insisted that calling secession a revolution constituted "an abuse of language," since slave states withdrew from the Union "to save ourselves from a revolution" that would render "property in slaves so insecure as to be comparatively worthless." Like John C. Calhoun, Davis believed he had devoted many years to preventing sectional separation, albeit only on terms that he deemed showing "due regard to the rights, the safety and the honor of the South." Just as equality of right among adult white males formed the foundation stone of politics in southern and northern states alike, so too was equality of right between slave and free states in territorial questions foundational to the preservation of both southern honor and national harmony.[5] Davis told the Senate in early January, before Missis-sippi's secession, "In the committee of thirteen, where the resolutions of the Senator from Kentucky were considered, various attempts were made, but no prospect of any agreement on which it was possible for us to stand, in security for the future, could be matured." From his perspective, "the only response which has come from the other side has been a stolid indifference, as though it mattered not, 'let the temple fall, we do not care.'" Should the U.S. govern-ment fail, "it will not be the defect of the system, though its mechanism was wonderful, surpassing that which the solar system furnishes for our contem-plation." Davis insisted that the disunionist movement begun by South Caro-lina found its cause in "the perversion of the Constitution," in the antislavery movement's "substitution of theories of morals for principles of government" and its "crude opinions about things not understood upon the domestic insti-tutions of other men."[6]

On 31 December, the Committee of Thirteen had reported to the Senate its failure to agree on compromise measures. In Davis's view, "Black republicans exultant over their recent success are not disposed to concede any thing." As he wrote to a good friend, Senator Clement Claiborne Clay of Alabama, "We have piped but they would not dance." The Mississippian had concluded that for the "planting states" to continue under the authority of the U.S. govern-ment, they would have to tolerate the dishonorable and unacceptable "alter-native of submission or compulsion." On 5 January, Davis met in caucus with all the senators from seven Lower South states. This group adopted reso-lutions in favor of immediate separate-state secession and the calling of an interstate convention to meet in Montgomery no later than 15 February to organize an independent confederacy. Three days later, the Magnolia State's convention gathered in Jackson, endorsing secession on 9 January. The state convention issued a Declaration of the Immediate Causes of Secession that announced forthrightly, "Our position is thoroughly identified with the insti-tution of slavery—the greatest material interest in the world. . . . There was no choice left to us but submission to the mandates of abolition, or a dissolution of the Union, whose principles have been subverted to our ruin."[7]

After the convention overwhelmingly adopted an ordinance of secession, Davis resigned his seat in the U.S. Senate and returned home to Brierfield. In early February, a messenger from the Vicksburg telegraph office brought word that convention delegates from the seceded states meeting in Montgomery had named him president of the new Confederate States of America. Davis accepted the post out of what seemed a rigid sense of public duty, for he may well have preferred a generalship. Then the "deplorable state of the rail system in the South . . . forced him to travel nearly seven hundred miles—north, east, and then south—to reach Montgomery," which lay merely a hundred miles east of Jackson.[8] Although Davis probably harbored as much inner hunger for public honor as did Abraham Lincoln, overt longing for political preference and acclaim was generally viewed as undignified and déclassé in midcentury and Victorian America. For many upper-class citizens, especially conservatives who remained privately skeptical of democratic passions and the popular will and who saw themselves as repositories of benevolent and responsible leadership serving the common good, the only public office worthy of an honorable gentleman was one proffered by expressions of popular respect for the candidate's principled integrity and dutiful disinterestedness.[9]

Davis's Mississippi, after its commitment to secession and the organization of the independent Confederacy, sent Fulton Anderson, a lawyer and Whiggish Unionist, as its official commissioner to make the case for secession before the newly inaugurated state convention of Virginia, still loyal to the Union. Anderson cited newly elected U.S. president Abraham Lincoln's well-known "House Divided" speech as evidence of northern and Republican hostility to the South. In June 1858, at the beginning of his campaign against incumbent Illinois Democratic senator Stephen Douglas, Lincoln had invoked the words of Jesus as reported in the New Testament Gospel of Matthew, chapter 12: "'A house divided against itself cannot stand.' I believe this government cannot endure, permanently half slave and half free. I do not expect the Union to be dissolved—I do not expect the house to fall—but I do expect it will cease to be divided. It will become all one thing, or all the other." In other words, Lincoln no longer agreed with the nation's Founding Fathers that free and slave states could coexist harmoniously within a federal republic. Since the Illinoisan had made plain his hostility to slavery as a substantial blot on the escutcheon of republican liberty in the United States, Anderson suggested, Lincoln obviously intended to effect what he had called the "ultimate extinction" of the South's peculiar institution and its regional way of life. Four months after Lincoln's 1858 speech, an analogous argument had come in Rochester, New York, from one of that state's U.S. senators, William Henry Seward, then the preeminent national leader of the Republican Party. Seward posited "an irrepressible conflict between opposing and enduring forces" that "means that the United States must and will sooner or later become either entirely a slave-holding nation or entirely a free-labor nation."[10] Earlier in the decade, during the conflict over Bleeding Kansas, he had exclaimed, "We will engage in competition for the virgin soil of Kansas, and God give victory to the side which is stronger in numbers as it is in right." Such speeches, Anderson argued in 1861, demonstrated that northern Republicans "are engaged in a holy crusade against slavery, [which] lies at the very foundation of our social and political fabric." Slavery, he insisted, constituted "the surest foundation of Christian moral order."[11]

Yet at that moment, Anderson's audience in Richmond proved more attached to the old Union than to Lower South secessionism. Of the 152 delegates elected to the Virginia Constitutional Convention on 4 February, at most 50, perhaps fewer than 40, endorsed immediate secession. Since more than 75 percent of the convention's members were slaveholders (in a state where only a quarter of white families owned slaves), even most of the slaveholding delegates still refused to endorse the Old Dominion's separation from the United States, which an earlier generation of state leaders (prominent among them George Washington and James Madison) had done so much to establish and frame in the 1780s. A provisional conservative coalition of staunch and conditional Unionists kept the secessionist radicals at bay until mid-April, when the Confederacy's bombardment of Fort Sumter elicited President Lincoln's call for troops from all the loyal states to suppress the violent and unconstitutional rebellion begun in South Carolina. Former conditional Unionists quickly became reluctant but determined Confederates, and on 17 April, the Virginia State Convention adopted an ordinance of secession by an 89–55 vote.

Among the swing-vote delegates to Virginia's convention was attorney Timothy Rives, representing the Tidewater counties of Prince George and Surry, situated southeast of Richmond along the James River. Rives served as the federal government's collector of revenue for the port of Petersburg, which bordered Prince George County. He had won election to the state convention in early February by receiving 400-plus ballots more than secessionist candidate Edmund Ruffin Jr., who lived with his famous fire-eating father at Prince George's Beechwood plantation. One of the voters in that contest was thirty-seven-year-old grain planter and physician Richard Eppes, owner of three inherited plantations and more than one hundred slaves. The doctor recorded in his diary, "I could not vote conscientiously for either candidate, and I cast my vote simply to have the acts of the Convention referred back to the people." (Secessionists opposed this call for a popular referendum because they wanted to effect disunion as quickly as possible, but the referendum was approved by a popular vote of 100,536 to 45,161.) To Eppes's mind, the young Ruffin appeared "a true type of South Carolina in politics." However, the doctor also disliked Rives's devotion to the United States "under all circumstances[,] besides being, almost entirely devoted, if he is to be judged by his resolutions and speeches, to the non slaveholding interest of Virginia and willing to sacrifice that of the slaveholder to perpetuate the Union." Eppes described himself as "a moderate man in my views, preferring the Old [Union] to a new if the South can have her rights guaranteed but if not feeling that our hope must be in another Union as a last resort."[12]

When the Virginia State Convention cast a pre-Sumter vote against secession on 4 April, Rives sided with the Unionist majority. During the post-Sumter balloting thirteen days later, however, he declared, "The Government being already overthrown by revolution, I vote 'aye,'" in favor of disunion. A less Unionist delegate, Thomas Branch, a merchant and banker who represented the city of Petersburg and with whom Eppes did business, had voted in favor of secession in the earlier vote after receiving secessionist petitions signed by his citizen constituents. Rives received such popular instructions just before he endorsed disunion on 17 April. Eppes reported in his diary on 15 April that neighbor James Proctor had called at Eppes's home, Appomattox Manor in City Point (nine miles from Petersburg), requesting the doctor's signature on a letter instructing Rives to support a secession ordinance. Eppes signed the letter, recording that he had "lost all hopes for our Union with the Northern States since President Lincoln has adopted the policy of coercion of the seceded states." He expressed pleasant surprise that "almost all the male inhabitants of the Point" had signed the letter, since "most of the inhabitants are nonslaveholders." He was struck by "the unanimity of opinion on this most important move." This state of mind seems to have prevailed among nonslaveholding citizens during the secession crisis.

Eppes blamed fanatical extremists on both sides of the Mason-Dixon Line for fomenting sectional conflict over slavery. In early December, after Lincoln's election, Eppes had observed, "The extremes both North & South have gone too far to recede and separation is almost inevitable." He viewed the Republican victory as evidence that the free states were more susceptible to disruptive, revolutionary fanaticism than were the slave states. Therefore, he saw the North as more likely than the South to succumb under President Lincoln to the sort of Napoleonic military despotism that had afflicted France after revolutionary turmoil in both the 1790s and 1848. As he explained to Proctor on 11 November, "A Republic could not long endure without a slave basis." In support of this assertion, the doctor cited the "Athenian and Roman Republics as examples," although he overlooked these republican polities' failure to endure even with slavery. He reiterated this rationale for slavery on 8 Decem-

ber during a conversation with his cousin, Peronneau Brown: "A strong monarchical government is the only one adapted to the free states where every
office is ruled by universal suffrage or rather mob Law Legalized."

Property qualifications for voting and officeholding had been almost elimi-
nated from American politics during the antebellum decades, and universal
white manhood suffrage had come to Virginia under the state constitution of
1851. A good many upper-class Virginians agreed with Ruffin, at least in private, that universal suffrage had corrupted and demeaned the reputedly high
tone of Virginia politics of the late eighteenth and early nineteenth century.
Eppes, conversely, subscribed to the proslavery counterargument that black
bondage protected the slave states from the worst consequences of democracy—that is, the extension of suffrage to what Ruffin termed "the lower &
meaner class," whose members were enslaved chattel rather than free citizens.
The South's peculiar institution thus rendered the slave states the world's last,
best hope for a successful long-term experiment in republican government,
preserving it from degenerating into irresponsible mobocracy and "agrarianism" (what is now called socialism). As Eppes informed Brown, "I believe, that
with a slave basis such as we have in the South, the slaves occupying the place
of Northern free Laborers, we can still retain our republican institutions and
be a permanent Government."

Eppes had doubtless been schooled in this line of thought at the College of
William and Mary, where he had studied law before shifting to medicine at
the University of Pennsylvania. During the 1843–44 academic year, when he
was nineteen, he was among the forty students enrolled in the "Senior Political Course, embracing Political Economy, Government, and the Philosophy of
the Human Mind," taught by Thomas Roderick Dew, the school's president.
As historian Michael O'Brien has pointed out, Dew qualified as "the most influential social philosopher, certainly of Virginia, possibly of the South," during the antebellum era. His seminal proslavery treatise, *Review of the Debate
in the Virginia Legislature of 1831-'32* (1832), one of four required texts in
the "Senior Political Course," maintained that black slavery enhanced white
equality. Young Eppes more than likely heard Dew make arguments similar to
those contained in an 1836 address he had delivered before the Virginia Historical and Philosophical Society in Richmond: "One of the most fatal evils
with which the republican system of government is liable to be assailed, is
the diffusion of a spirit of agrarianism among the indigent classes of society,"
a spirit that excites "that most blighting and deadly hostility of all, the hostility of the poor against the rich." However, Dew expressed confidence that
the slave South had little to fear. "Domestic slavery, such as ours, is the only

institution which I know of, that can secure the spirit of equality among freemen, so necessary to the true and genuine feeling of republicanism, without propelling the body politic at the same time into the dangerous devices of agrarianism and legislative intermeddling between the laborer and the capitalist." Dew thus offered an early formulation of the highly influential proslavery argument that posited the enslavement of blacks as the best available foundation for genuine republican government among whites. This idea certainly informed the thinking of Eppes and other educated Virginians as they contemplated the future of slavery and the South in the aftermath of Lincoln's election. Free southerners who did not really understand the North's free-labor society could take comfort in such dire and dramatic predictions of northern society's imminent internal collapse as appeared in the *Richmond Enquirer* on 10 May 1861. The newspaper saw "in the present condition of affairs at the North, the elements of a terrible revolution." "Beneath the thin crust of Black Republican hostility to the South, there rage the awful fires of civil anarchy and social chaos. The disruption of the Union, and the consequent withdrawal from Northern society of Southern wealth and labor, which have sustained it, have brought millions of the laboring classes of the North face to face with utter want and starvation. Northern capital trembles for its safety; Northern conservatism shakes with terror in the presence of the unchained demons of anarchy and starvation."[13] During the 1830s, the argument for a positive connection between black slavery and white republicanism also emerged in South Carolina; a notable formulation came from Senator John C. Calhoun in his 6 February 1837 speech against congressional reception of abolition petitions.[14] On the eve of the Civil War, Eppes's personal library included a number of Calhoun's published speeches. The apologia made by Calhoun and Eppes may well have become what one historian has called the "dominant public ideology" in the slave South. Some historians, following the lead of George M. Fredrickson, have labeled this the racist argument for a *"Herrenvolk* democracy," a political democracy for the master race.[15]

Eppes termed his decision to sign Proctor's secessionist letter of instruction "perhaps the most important of my Life" and recognized that he and his family must be prepared "to endure trials & afflictions" to preserve their liberty. Especially trying would be "our separation from our numerous friends & relatives in Philadelphia." Not only had Eppes, like many prominent southern physicians, studied medicine in Philadelphia,[16] but he was also married to the daughter of one his former professors at the University of Pennsylvania, Dr. William E. Horner. Nonetheless, both his "feelings and interest" called him to side with the new Confederacy.

The inauguration of Confederate president Jefferson Davis, Montgomery, 1861
(Courtesy of the Library of Congress)

When Confederate president Jefferson Davis delivered his inaugural address in Montgomery on 18 February, he did not directly discuss the subjects of slaves or property rights. Davis asked for God's favor and invoked the U.S. Constitution. If the new Confederacy "be assailed, it will but remain for us, with firm resolve, to appeal to arms and invoke the blessings of Providence on a just cause." Why was the cause just? "The Constitution formed by our fathers is that of these Confederate States," organized by leaders who understood the "well-known intent" and "true meaning" of those who wrote, ratified, and amended the earlier document.[17]

Davis later reportedly expressed dismay at the forthright fashion in which his vice president, Georgian Alexander Stephens, addressed the subjects of bondage and race in his "Cornerstone Speech," delivered in Savannah the following month. This speech seems all the more remarkable because Stephens, a former Whig, had supported northern Democratic Unionist Stephen A. Douglas in the 1860 election and then fought hard to inhibit the spread of secessionist fever. After Davis had been chosen the Confederacy's president, Robert Toombs proposed his fellow Georgian as vice president. Stephens's candidacy carried largely because it would appeal to hesitant Upper South states, who admired his attempts to hold back the tide of secessionist immediatism. On 21 March 1861, Stephens identified "our peculiar institution, African slavery" as "the immediate cause of the late rupture and present revolution" that had culminated in the Confederacy's foundation in Montgomery. None other than Thomas Jefferson in 1820 had "anticipated this as the 'rock upon which the old Union would split,'" although Stephens expressed doubt whether the Sage of Monticello had "fully comprehended the great truth upon which that rock *stood* and *stands*." Jefferson, like "most of the leading statesmen at the time of the formation of the old constitution," viewed "the enslavement of the African" as "in violation of the laws of nature." To their minds, human bondage "was wrong, in principle, socially, morally, and politically." In marked contrast, the new republican and slaveholding Confederacy "is founded upon exactly the opposite idea; its foundations are laid, its cornerstone rests upon the great truth, the negro is not equal to the white man; that slavery—subordination to the superior race—is his natural and normal condition"—precisely what the U.S. Supreme Court had said in 1857.

Vice President Stephens's attempt to discredit the more radical and reckless Jefferson of the 1770s and 1780s found many parallels among Republican opponents in the North. As James Gordon Bennett of the *New York Herald* had argued in late February 1860, when he, like Stephens, supported Douglas for the Democratic presidential nomination, "It is true that Jefferson for a time became tainted with the French revolutionary leveling notions about negro slavery, and other things; but he afterward changed these opinions."[18] In fact, in retirement, Jefferson had become an avid opponent of any federal intervention to prevent the spread of slavery into the trans-Mississippi West and particularly into Missouri.[19]

Davis's discomfort at Stephens's comments and irritation with the attention they received reflected the Confederate president's concern that the new country's public stance should emphasize "state versus national sovereignty" rather than slavery as the crucial issue.[20] Such a public position was far more likely to win sympathy and perhaps recognition from foreign powers, especially Britain and France, leading importers of southern cotton. Both of those countries had abolished chattel slavery in their colonial possessions years earlier, and popular sentiment in both nations was decidedly antislavery. Confederate leaders, Davis believed, should direct their appeals for sympathy and recognition to those republican legacies of the American Revolution and the Founding Fathers that involved the defense of individual and local rights and liberties against the threat of external tyranny and despotism. This time, what Davis viewed as "wanton aggression" came not from the British monarchy but from hostile free states and Black Republican voters north of the Mason-Dixon Line and the Ohio River. Although some European observers responded positively to the disunionist and Confederate invocation of the "principle of self-determination," its firm connection in this instance with the defense of human bondage alienated the cause of southern independence from those in Europe who promoted "liberal nationalism"—that is, national self-determination and/or unification in league with constitutional and representative polities based on the principle of individual liberty. Those most opposed to the promotion of republican governments and universal manhood suffrage in Europe, including noble members of Prussia's Junker landed elite, would express the most sympathy for an independent Confederacy. In England, the pro-Confederate *London Times* spoke for both antidemocratic British conservatives and those worried that a successful Union blockade of Confederate ports would drive the huge British textile industry to economic ruin by cutting off cotton imports from North America. Ironically, by November 1861, the *Times* espied an "exact analogy between the government in Washington and the Government of George III, and the South and the Thirteen Revolted Provinces" of 1776. However, in 1861–62, Confederate leadership, perhaps overly confident that the power of King Cotton would bring European recognition and intervention, "undervalued the importance of diplomacy," concludes the authoritative historical synthesis on U.S. foreign relations, and the men who held the post of Confederate secretary of state proved less competent than their U.S. counterpart, Seward. Despite the "questionable legality" of the Union blockade, even European leaders sympathetic to the Confederacy "were not disposed to intrude" in the American Civil War, in part as a consequence of forceful warnings from the Lincoln administration. As English prime minister Lord Palmerston observed, "They who in quarrels interpose, will often get a bloody nose."[21]

Jefferson Davis summoned the Provisional Confederate Congress to a special session at Montgomery on 29 April 1861. His presidential message to the gathering openly addressed the slavery issue. Davis sketched the history of North-South political conflict, culminating in the capture of the American presidency by a political party whose "avowed object" was "the total exclusion of the slave States from all participation in the benefits of the public domain acquired by all the States in common." In other words, Lincoln had won the presidency on a sectional, northern party platform that called for the total exclusion of slaveholders and their human property from all federal territories even before they could apply for statehood. To Davis's way of thinking, this stance most certainly did not derive from sincere concern on the part of Republicans for the well-being of the enslaved, who had "been elevated from brutal savages into docile, intelligent, and civilized agricultural laborers . . . under the supervision of a superior race." The free republican citizens in the seceding slave states, he argued, had simply acted out of the ancient and necessary right of "self-preservation." They had responded to the victorious agenda of an antisouthern sectional party whose goals involved "rendering the property in slaves so insecure as to be comparatively worthless, and thereby annihilating in effect property worth thousands of millions of dollars." To Davis, this concern for valuable property complemented and upheld the citizens' judgment "that our cause is just and holy; we protest solemnly in the face of mankind that we desire peace at any sacrifice save that of honor and independence."[22]

After the war, Davis, like many former Confederates, denied slavery as the cause of secession. His two-volume tome published in 1881, *The Rise and Fall of the Confederate Government*, presents a perspective rather at odds with his message to the Confederate Congress twenty years earlier: "The truth remains incontrovertible, that the existence of African servitude was in no wise the cause of the conflict, but only an incident." This argument became central to the late-nineteenth-century glorification of the Confederacy as a tragic "Lost Cause" in defense of local self-determination against federal despotism as well as a struggle between rural gentility and coarse industrialism. In 1881,

Davis had no doubt that that he had acted during the secession crisis and Civil War as a "constitutional patriot" rather than a treasonous rebel. The North and the Republican Party should have accepted the constitutionality of southern secession rather than "prosecuting a destructive, uncivilized war" and then, during Reconstruction, "imposing an oppressive peace on honorable men who had laid down their arms." As historian David Blight has emphasized, Davis and the other "major spokespersons of the Lost Cause could not develop their story of a heroic, victimized South without faithful slaves and benevolent masters." For Davis in 1881, much as before the war, the slaves' "servile instincts rendered them contented with their lot, and their patient toil blessed the land of their abode with unmeasured riches," even as they became "enlightened by the rays of Christianity."[23]

If Davis's *Rise and Fall of the Confederate Government* does not demonstrate that sectional disputes over constitutional interpretation rather than slavery really caused the Civil War, then Mississippi's Declaration and Davis's address to fellow Confederates in 1861 do not demonstrate that the institution of slavery apart from ideas about state's rights caused the secession crisis and the Civil War. No proper understanding of what happened in 1860–61 is possible without emphasizing the close dialectical linkages between slave society and ideas about state's rights and state sovereignty in the South at that time. (Americans could and can believe in various degrees of state's rights relevant to a variety of political issues yet not take the concept to the point of invoking state sovereignty as a rationale for disunion and secession.)[24] Just as most white southerners saw the stability of slavery as fundamental to the health and security of their regional society, so too did they see state's rights principles as fundamental to their political system and values. An emphasis on state over federal prerogatives, bolstered by the Constitution's Tenth Amendment, appeared an integral part of their professed commitment to limited federal power and strict construction of the Constitution. To be sure, as many Confederates made explicit, slave states left the Union first and foremost because their peculiar institution and the regional way of life it supported seemed in dire peril after Lincoln's presidential victory. Yet they could also believe sincerely in the principle of state sovereignty (the extreme version of state's rights thinking) as the political justification of immediate separate-state secession from what they claimed was a potentially despotic federal government, headed for the first time by an unabashedly antislavery chief executive. At the same time, most northerners saw their free-labor society as well as their more dynamic and productive economy as more true to America's libertarian and constitutional ideals than was the South's slave society. Residents of the free states firmly believed that the authority and prosperity of the Union under the glorious U.S. Constitution trumped the extremist and dangerous version of state's rights trumpeted by secessionists.

The doctrine of state's rights, like that of federal supremacy, can promote or protect any number of agendas or interests. During the Federalist and Jeffersonian eras of the early republic, state's rights principles could be invoked against Alexander Hamilton's national bank of 1791, against John Adams's Alien and Sedition Acts of 1798, against the Madison administration's prosecution of the War of 1812, and against some rulings by John Marshall's Supreme Court between 1801 and 1835. Given subsequent southern justifications of secession and northern insistence on the need for federal coercion against disunionist treason, it is one of American history's wonderful ironies that during the last two antebellum decades, many free states appealed to the doctrine of state's rights to justify their antislavery stances against de facto proslavery legislation adopted by the federal government. Free southerners and their conservative northern allies found themselves in the position of asserting federal power against resistance in the free states to congressional implementation of the Constitution's Fugitive Slave Clause.[25] A prime example of a reluctant free state supporter of the 1850 Fugitive Slave Law was Moses Stuart of Andover Seminary in Massachusetts, "widely recognized as the nation's most learned biblical scholar." Although he believed that committed Christians should view slavery as "a self-evident moral evil" that should be put on a path to "gradual, peaceful, and voluntary elimination," he accepted both the "self-evident" (versus scriptural) inferiority of black Americans and the constitutional obligation that runaway slaves should be returned to their legal Christian owners.[26]

The sectional dispute over fugitive slaves warrants attention not only as an important historical irony but also because it continued to reverberate just prior to the Civil War. Article IV, Section 2 of the Constitution states that persons "held to Service or Labour" in one state who escape into another state are not to be "discharged from Service." Instead, stipulated the Founding Fathers, such persons are to be "delivered up on Claim of the Party to whom such Service or Labour shall be due." The euphemistic phrase "held to Service or Labour" reflected not just the Founding Fathers' reluctance to use the word "slavery" or "bondage" in a document whose preamble proclaimed its intention to "secure the Blessings of Liberty to ourselves and our posterity." The phrasing also reflected the fact that indentured servitude and formal apprenticeship for whites remained legal in many states. Later, when New York and other northern states began the process of gradual emancipation, slaves born after a certain date would still be required to serve a lengthy term as indentured servants before attaining personal freedom. Moreover, in the words of two constitutional scholars, "the precise meaning" of the Fugitive Slave Clause "was vague in that it did not make clear what agency, state or federal, was charged with its execution." Since Article IV dealt with various issues related to "interstate comity"—that is, the principle by which the court system of one state might accede to or give effect to the laws of another state—it could be and was at first deemed, particularly in Congress's Fugitive Slave Act of 1793, that responsibility for the return of runaway slaves lay with the individual states rather than with federal authorities.[27]

In 1842, the Supreme Court attempted to clarify the meaning and intent of Article IV, Section 2, in *Prigg v. Pennsylvania*. Justice Joseph Story composed the official opinion and thereby helped set the legal stage for the Fugitive Slave Law of 1850. According to legal historian Don E. Fehrenbacher, Story was the country's "foremost legal scholar" as well as "a devoted supporter of federal authority in the tradition of John Marshall," a Federalist enemy of Jefferson. The Fugitive Slave Clause, wrote Story in 1842, was a "fundamental article, without the adoption of which the Union could never have been formed." Slaves were a "species of property," and the slaveholder's right to recover a fugitive constituted "a right of property."[28] At the same time, Story's logic undercut the argument that states were responsible for the return of fugitives and thus constituted an unacceptable "reading of law" to many partisans of the peculiar institution. Story stipulated that the obligation to enforce the Fugitive Slave Law of 1793 belonged to federal agencies and that state law enforcement officers did not have to participate.

A total of nine free state legislatures subsequently adopted "personal liberty laws" that either expressly forbade state officers from involvement in the pursuit of fugitive slaves on pain of criminal penalties for kidnapping or prohibited the use of state and local jails to hold arrested fugitives. Since slave catchers and sympathetic judges might identify free blacks as runaway slaves, a state's personal liberty laws might give alleged fugitives the right of habeas corpus, the right to trial by jury, and the right to testify. The personal liberty laws could be justified as state interpositions, or actions to protect the liberties of a state's citizenry from a particular imposition of federal tyranny. Indeed, defenders of these laws could invoke much of the state's rights logic that Jefferson and Madison had incorporated into the Kentucky and Virginia Resolutions of 1798, which had protested Federalist limitations on personal liberties and served as campaign documents for the election of 1800. Northern personal liberty laws became an important reason for southern insistence on a new and stronger federal Fugitive Slave Act as part of the Compromise of 1850. During the compromise debates, Senators James M. Mason of Virginia and Andrew Butler of South Carolina plainly opted for the creation of "an elaborate bureaucracy," a veritable "army of 'commissioners' . . . to facilitate the recovery of fugitive slaves." The law as finally passed in 1850, concludes Fehrenbacher, "would surely have failed if it had been considered as an independent measure at any other time" other than the years of fearsome sectional tension following the Mexican War of 1846–48.[29] On 7 March 1850, New England Whig senator Daniel Webster supported the Butler-Mason Bill as part of a general settlement. On this issue, he declared, "the South in my judgment is right, the North is wrong," thereby infuriating most northern Whigs. This nationalist, who had contributed so much two decades earlier to the formulation and dissemination of the argument for a "perpetual" Union, received "howling criticism, especially from Massachusetts." Webster became "truly nettled" when Free-Soil congressman Horace Mann, the former executive secretary of the Massachusetts Board of Education who now occupied the late John Quincy Adams's seat in the U.S. House, described the senator as a "fallen star." Instead of turning to "the Ten Commandments" to solve "a great question of political duty," Webster had combated slavery by citing the Constitution and pointing to "the mild influences of Christianity" and climate.[30]

The 1850 Fugitive Slave Law assigned federal marshals responsibility for pursuing fugitive slaves in the free states but also gave these marshals the authority to coerce or compel assistance and cooperation from local residents. Newly appointed federal commissioners were authorized to issue warrants for the arrest of runaway slaves, and commissioners could summarily issue rulings without jury trials when accused persons claimed to be free blacks. This summary decision was not subject to appeal, and state courts could not issue writs of habeas corpus.[31] What if a slaveholder or his agent swore that a particular black person was an escaped slave when in fact the accused was not a runaway but a free black resident of a free state? The person falsely identified seemed at a serious disadvantage to the accuser: the accused could not testify on her or his own behalf and had no legal claim to a jury trial. The federal commissioner also received only five dollars if he ruled against the slaveholder but ten dollars for ruling in the slaveholder's favor, presumably because of the greater paperwork involved in implementing the latter decision.

The 1850 legislation helped inspire Harriet Beecher Stowe's 1851–52 composition of the heartrending antislavery novel *Uncle Tom's Cabin; or, Life among the Lowly*, whose "astonishing success" among northern readers in turn elicited vehement denunciations in the southern press. The story and characters were designed to portray the peculiar institution as cruel and sinful by virtue of its inability to protect slaves and their families from forced sales and brutality. The novel's popular appeal in the North and the denunciations that it elicited in the South testify to the sentimental sanctification of the nuclear family and affective family relationships that had emerged in transatlantic Victorian culture as well as to the popularity of Stowe's concerns about the pervasiveness of economic greed in American society. Young Eliza Harris flees Kentucky with her four-year-old son across ice floes in the Ohio River, escaping vicious dogs and the boy's rumored sale. The saintly Christian character, Uncle Tom, is sold away to a sadistic plantation overseer, Yankee-born Simon Legree. Legree beats Tom to death for refusing to reveal the hiding place of two runaways.[32]

Northerners could and often did view the Fugitive Slave Law of 1850 as one more example of tyranny coming from a federal government too much under the sway of the South's aristocratic and crafty slave interest, or slaveocracy, which in turn controlled the national Slave Power. This label, which became perhaps the era's most powerful political slogan in the free states, had appeared in the 1830s, but it first became popular because of sectional disputes over the annexation of Texas and the outbreak of the Mexican War during the mid-1840s. The term reflected a rising northern perception that the federal government was controlled by a political coalition of southern slaveholders and northern allies in the Democratic Party. This Slave Power sought to secure the expansion and long-term security of slavery in the United States, even at the expense of nonslaveholding whites in both sections. "Usually conspiracy arguments have limited appeal, inspiring a handful of true believers but not a wide audience," historian Leonard L. Richards has argued. "The Slave Power thesis, in contrast, attained the status of conventional wisdom in Republican circles" after the party's founding in 1854–55 "and had wide appeal across the North."[33]

The case of an antislavery businessmen and politician in Rhode Island, Rowland Gibson Hazard, is illustrative. His father, also named Rowland Gibson Hazard, had played an important role in the establishment and expansion of New England's textile manufactures during the early nineteenth century. The son had spent much time in New Orleans during the 1830s and into the 1840s for both personal and business reasons, and his experiences there accentuated the hostility to slavery he had inherited from his Quaker forebears. Although his factories continued to manufacture "negro cloth" for the southern market throughout the 1850s, the younger Hazard became involved in political antislavery as a Free-Soiler in the aftermath of the Mexican War, later becoming a founder of the Republican Party in Rhode Island and a delegate to the new party's Philadelphia convention in 1856 and its Chicago convention four years later. In late February 1850, he spoke out in the Rhode Island House of Representatives against the Fugitive Slave Law proposed a month earlier by U.S. senator Henry Clay as part of an omnibus bill to reconcile sectional differences. "It seems hardly fair," argued Hazard, that slaveholding southerners "should ask us not only to leave them alone, but to insist that we shall become what they themselves most heartily despise, *slave-hunters*."[34] Clay had been known to implore antislavery northerners simply to leave the South's peculiar institution alone. For example, in October 1842, he delivered a speech in Richmond, Indiana, when he was presented with a petition asking that he set an example by freeing the slaves at his Ashland estate just outside Lexington. Like most of his fellow slaveholders in the Bluegrass State as well as in the Border South as a whole, Clay refused to defend slavery in the abstract, following the example set by the Founding Fathers. He called American slavery "a great evil" but insisted that "greater evils" would "inevitably flow from a sudden, general, and indiscriminant emancipation." The greatest evil would be the "revolting admixture" of blacks and whites, "alike offensive to God and man." Without the colonization of free blacks abroad, Kentuckians would face a racial "civil war" that would result in "the ultimate extermination or expulsion of the blacks." Clay, like Jefferson in 1776, sought to exclude his society from moral condemnation by insisting that slavery was "introduced and forced upon the colonies by the paramount law of England."[35] Nonetheless, Clay insisted that Kentucky law clearly and unambiguously recognized "the right of property in slaves" and condemned "the unfortunate agitation of the subject" by monomaniacal abolitionists. He reported owning about fifty slaves, worth some fifteen thousand dollars, and asked if the abolitionists were willing to pay him that sum for the freedom of his slaves. Near the close of his speech, he thundered, "Go home and mind your own business, and leave other people to take of theirs."[36]

In 1850, Hazard insisted that New Englanders would never cooperate in executing the proposed Fugitive Slave Law because doing so would "degrade" them. To work as "a slave-catcher" was to become "despicable . . . vile and execrable." Such degradation was clearly incompatible with the honor of free men. Though acknowledging that many slaveholders had "humane motives" and that Americans north and south should have "charity" for the "defects" of the other section, Hazard described slavery as "the worst existing form of society for all concerned." Southern politicians certainly could not endure such slurs against their honor with equanimity.

Six years later, Hazard delivered the Narragansett Speech a number of times while campaigning in Rhode Island on behalf of Republican presidential nominee John C. Frémont. Hazard insisted that the "incompatibility of sectional domestic slavery with free national political institutions is continually manifesting itself in practical results." The Fugitive Slave Act, for example, awarded "an extra five dollars per head" to slave catchers in the North. More recent "practical results" included a "civil war" in territorial Kansas between proslavery and antislavery forces and the highly publicized caning of outspokenly antislavery senator Charles Sumner by South Carolina congressman Preston Brooks. Hazard referred to Sumner as "a Senator stricken down and mangled for exercising the right of a free man to defend freedom."[37] The Democratic Party's presidential nominee, James Buchanan of Pennsylvania, was "the selected champion of slavery." Hazard lambasted Buchanan for something he had done while serving as America's minister to Great Britain. In 1854, he had signed the Ostend Manifesto in favor of aggressive action to take slaveholding Cuba from Spain. Hazard claimed that the South's peculiar institution lay at the heart of the Democratic Party's 1856 Cincinnati Platform. He identified Buchanan's political ally, Caleb Cushing of Massachusetts, as instrumental in constructing this platform, which Hazard saw as implying that slavery should be legal throughout the country. The Democrats seemed to be aiding the Slave Power in its efforts to break down "the defenses of rational liberty." As president, Buchanan's nominees to the Supreme Court would work by "judicial fiat" to "extend slavery over this whole country." At issue in the 1856 election, declared Hazard, was "the great issue of the cause of liberty against despotism, of freedom against slavery."

The Rhode Islander clearly belonged to the anti-Catholic, nativist, and temperance wing of the Republican Party, with its fears that too many Roman Catholic immigrants from Ireland and the German states were undermining the interests of native-born workers and could become tools of "Papal domination." Hence, Hazard wanted to make sure that his listeners understood his opposition not only to Buchanan but also to former Whig president Millard Fillmore, the 1856 nominee of the nativist American Party, popularly known as the Know-Nothings. Fillmore had been elected vice president in 1848, "when the slave-power held undisputed sway over both parties." Hence, when he assumed the presidency after Zachary Taylor's death in 1850, Fillmore "had felt compelled to recognize [the Slave Power's] supremacy and submit to its authority."

Hazard asked whether the slave states and the Slave Power would submit to the election of an antislavery Republican in 1856. He reported having "numerous friends" in the South. When he looked at the citizens of the slave states, he saw "too much manliness of character" among them first "to permit them to take the chance of winning" in the presidential election and "then meanly refuse to abide the results when they lose." In addition, despite Frémont's strong opposition to slavery in California, he was not a radical abolitionist like Gerritt Smith of Ohio, the nominee of the Liberty Party. Though southerners feared a Frémont victory, acknowledged Hazard, the candidate had never done or said anything "to indicate ultra sentiments or extreme measures on the subject of slavery." Republicans in 1860 would make the same case for Lincoln, and the Rhode Islander would be a member of the committee that composed the party platform on which Lincoln campaigned.[38]

In the earliest states of the Old Northwest (Ohio, Indiana, and Illinois), the notion of a Slave Power conspiracy seems to have resonated not only with New Englanders and their descendants, who dominated settlement near the Great Lakes, but also with many persons who migrated across the Ohio River from the interior Upland South (especially western Virginia and Kentucky). According to historian Nicole Etcheson, significant numbers of "Upland Southern Midwesterners" drew on "personal experience of a planter class that they felt attempted to oppress white nonslaveholders"—for example, by buying up and consolidating the most productive agricultural lands. Even as they condemned abolitionist fanatics and expressed racialist concerns that allowing the immigration of free blacks into their states would degrade and disadvantage free white labor, these migrants disliked the provisions of the 1850 Fugitive Slave Act that allowed what one called "converting the Freemen of the North into a gang of Slave catchers for the South." In other words, the Slave Power threatened to subject free whites to a form of degrading despotism and powerlessness that had disconcerting analogies to the subservience of enslaved blacks. Upland South settlers usually held equal disdain for proslavery and abolitionist ultras. Lincoln followed this way of thinking, though in the 1850s he proved highly unusual in his willingness to speak out in support of basic natural rights for African Americans. Only a decided minority of southern-born midwesterners supported the Republican Party during that decade, in part because Democrats became viciously racist and in part because the Democratic principle of popular sovereignty seemed to provide a political alternative to radical ultras both north and south.[39]

During the 1850s, nine northern states adopted new personal liberty laws to protect the rights of their citizens from enforcers of the 1850 law. Between 1854 and 1859, the Wisconsin Supreme Court issued three different rulings that upheld the state's personal liberty legislation and declared the Fugitive

Slave Law unconstitutional. In 1855, the state court ordered the release of a prisoner "duly tried, convicted, and sentenced" in a federal circuit court for violating the measure. In March 1859, the U.S. Supreme Court ruled unanimously against Wisconsin in the case of *Ableman v. Booth*; the opinion came from Chief Justice Roger Brooke Taney, who two years earlier had written the dramatically proslavery majority opinion in *Dred Scott v. Sandford*. A solid Republican phalanx in the Wisconsin legislature, supported by Governor Alexander W. Randall, passed resolutions condemning the Supreme Court's "arbitrary act of power" and declaring it void and of no force. According to David M. Potter, "In the history of resistance by the states to federal authority, few acts of defiance have exceeded this one, which involved nullification in a form that even John C. Calhoun had not advocated." Less than two years later, as Mississippi became the second slave state to endorse secession, Governor Randall delivered his annual message to the state legislature. "On this occasion," according to historian Richard N. Current, "the governor repeated none of his old states-rights challenges to federal authority." Indeed, "he concluded with a resoundingly nationalistic peroration: 'Secession is revolution, revolution is war; war against the government of the United States is treason.'"[40] In retrospect, the Fugitive Slave Law of 1850 proved a pyrrhic proslavery victory, costing far more in northern goodwill toward the South than it yielded in the value or number (perhaps 350) of alleged runaways remanded to their masters.

White southerners often accused what one called "Ultra Abolitionists and free negroes up north" of acting to render the 1850 legislation unenforceable, fomenting slave flights to freedom, and organizing an Underground Railroad to facilitate escapes. In 1860, this point of view became amusing hyperbole in a pamphlet from the pen of Georgia native Augustus Baldwin Longstreet, already famous for the intentional humor evident in his 1835 literary classic, *Georgia Scenes*. After practicing law, winning election to the state legislature, gaining appointment as a judge, and becoming ordained as a Methodist minister, he assumed the presidency of Emory College in 1839. The peripatetic Longstreet subsequently became president of Centenary, the University of Mississippi, and the University of South Carolina, from which he retired in 1861. As the Palmetto State approached secession, Longstreet composed for the *Southern Guardian* a portrait of "the domestic bliss" that awaited the slave states out of the Union, where slave discipline would present no problems: "Get us away from Republican influences, and [master and slave] shall dwell together in peace on earth, and mingle hymns in heaven."[41]

A more prosaic warning had come in 1856 from a newspaper in western

Virginia, the *Shepherdstown Register*, which advised locals that "agents hereabouts" had conducted a "secret operation, by which so many of our citizens are robbed of our property."[42] Residents of the slave states exhibited great reluctance to concede publicly that probably "the most prevalent reason for running away" was the prospect of being sold or having a family member sold.[43] Nor did slaveholders like to admit that the irrepressible human passions of masters and mistresses could at times drive bondsmen and bondswomen to temporary or permanent flight, perhaps simply for a brief escape from emotional or physical abuse. Nor did slaveholders and their allies want to believe or acknowledge that enslaved people, living amid a civic culture that glorified republican independence and liberty, might consider fleeing northward just to pursue visions of freedom from bondage. To be sure, the substantial skills of dissimulation demonstrated by slaves and free blacks alike usually enabled African Americans to disguise their true feelings and thoughts from whites. As Solomon Northup explained in his 1853 slave narrative, ninety-nine out of one hundred slaves "cherish in their bosoms the love of freedom," though they dared not utter such thoughts "in the hearing of the white man."[44]

During a stopover in the Virginia port city of Norfolk in mid-April 1861, the often perceptive English correspondent William Howard Russell found white men on "all the street corners . . . discussing the news" of Fort Sumter's surrender to General P. G. T. Beauregard "with every symptom of joy and gratification." He also saw "Negroes" everywhere, "male and female, gaudily dressed or in rags. Not a word were they talking about Sumter." When Russell asked "a respectable looking Negro," "Any news today?," the man reputedly replied, "Well, sare, I tink nothin' much occur." Russell then wondered, "Was it a very stupid *poco-curante* [doltish person], or a very cunning, subtle Sambo?"[45] A similar uncertainty afflicted many white southerners, including Mary Boykin Miller Chesnut, wife of South Carolina U.S. senator James Chesnut Jr. and a noted diarist. In Charleston as Confederate artillery pounded Fort Sumter, Mary Chesnut penned musings much like those of Russell: the slaves must have heard "the awful row that is now going on in the bay . . . dinning into their ears night and day." Nonetheless, "Not by one word or look can we detect any change in the demeanor of these negro servants. Laurence sits at our door, as sleepy and as respectful and as profoundly indifferent. So are they all." Chesnut could not read their inner thoughts. Although "people talk before them as if they were chairs and tables," still "they make no sign. Are they stolidly stupid or wiser than we are, silent and strong, biding their time?"[46]

Many elite masters and proslavery intellectuals wanted to believe that ownership of valuable human property produced powerful but enlightened motives of self-interest when guided and refined by the influence of Christian and chivalric calls for care and protection of the weak and dependent. These influences allegedly worked to further humane and even benign treatment of black slaves and thereby to promote the enslaved's acceptance of what antebellum apologists for the South's peculiar institution often termed a patriarchal system of familial or domestic servitude.[47] Some important and influential scholars during the last third of the twentieth century sought to recast the family metaphor into the analytical and value-free concept of paternalism, a term unknown and unused in America before or during the Civil War.[48] Eugene D. Genovese posits antebellum paternalism as the defining characteristic of the South's precapitalist system of labor and class relations. This paternalism involved different sets of "reciprocal demands and expectations" on the part of masters and slaves that produced a complex variety of subtly negotiated give-and-take interactions among groups and individuals.[49] Other scholars have expressed serious reservations about the accuracy and clarity of the precapitalist/paternalist construct. Ira Berlin has suggested that an international and transatlantic perspective on American slavery "illuminates how the struggle between master and slave moved onto new ground, articulated in the language of domesticity." This broader perspective "places the vexed matter" of paternalism (which Berlin seems to equate with seigneurialism) "in the context of not only the historic affinity of traditional elites for familial metaphors, but also in the context of the middle years of the nineteenth century," with their often romantic apotheosis of affective but efficient patriarchal families as models for healthy social and economic relations.[50] From this perspective, it makes sense to distinguish between paternalism as ideology, or "a prevailing ideal" among slaveholders, explains Steven Deyle, and as an accurate depiction of "historical reality."[51]

Many northerners testified to the power of such familial metaphors, including Frederick Law Olmsted, an antislavery Republican who achieved his greatest fame as a landscape architect who helped design and construct New York City's Central Park. Olmsted was a native of Hartford, Connecticut, which his ancestors had helped found in the seventeenth century. At age twenty-five, Olmsted became a "country squire and scientific farmer" in Staten Island, New York, on land purchased by his father, where the young man proved "fair but exacting with his hired laborers." In 1852, he accepted a job touring the South as a special correspondent for the *New York Times*. His reports became important contributions to the Republican Party's free-labor and free-soil ideology. As historian Lawrence N. Powell explains, Olmsted "believed a 'civilized' community" should, like New England, "be settled in compact villages and small towns populated by artisans, tradesmen, and modest-sized manufactures, linked by ties of trade to small commercial farmers on tidy homesteads in the surrounding countryside."[52] Yet in 1853, he reported being very much charmed after spending several days on a rice plantation in the Georgia low country. He described the owner as "a religious, generous, and humane-minded man" and "found Slavery under its most favorable circumstances, and the agriculture with which it was conducted under the most economical and profitable management." The editors of Olmsted's papers explain that the traveling correspondent saw this plantation as "a model of what he believed slavery should be in America—a benevolent, patriarchal, and civilizing institution."

According to Olmsted, the near-utopia of White Hall plantation (situated on the Ogeechee River in Bryan County) reflected in large measure the New England background of its proprietor, who had "brought to the management of the estate all the keen talent for organization and administration, and the exact business habits of a man trained in the rugged fields of New-Hampshire, among the looms of Lowell, and in the counting rooms of Boston." The plantation's proprietor, whom Olmsted did not identify by name, was Richard James Arnold, the younger son of a wealthy mercantile Quaker who had graduated Phi Beta Kappa from Brown University in 1814 before studying law and becoming a merchant in Providence, Rhode Island. Arnold had acquired the estate at his 1823 marriage to heiress Louisa Caroline Gindrat and by the time of Olmsted's visit had added to his holdings four additional nearby plantations (totaling some eleven thousand acres and more than two hundred slaves). Arnold's biographers point out the importance of the "language of domesticity" and "family metaphors" to the New Englander and his peers by stressing how his personal papers and business records "reveal the easy accommodation of most upper-class white northerners to the institutions of slavery as part business and property and part paternalistic society." He and his bride spent winters in Georgia and summers in Rhode Island at a townhouse in Providence or at the seaside resort of Newport, which had drawn wealthy vacationers from the South since the eighteenth century. "Paternalism was the key to the social acceptability of Arnold as slave owner by his northern friends and family" explain Charles Hoffman and Tess Hoffmann, "and religious doctrines and property rights were the moral and economic justification. The portrait that emerges from the documents is that of a kind and good master, an image he himself fostered." He opposed Georgia's secession in January 1861 but in late February pledged seventy-five dollars in his name and that of his disunionist son, Thomas, "to uniform the Bryan County Troops." Fearing expropriation of his

Georgia properties because of his Unionist stance, Arnold transferred all his Bryan County property to Thomas and spent the war years in Rhode Island with his dutiful wife, who had strong Confederate sympathies. He devoted summers to traveling and looking after his other business interests, including investments in northern and western railroads, "commercial blocks and a dock company in Chicago," and "mining companies in Michigan and Canada." The yields from these investments seem to have bought in more than enough income to compensate for his family's ultimate wartime losses in plantation land and slaves.[53]

Both before and during the Civil War, some slaves—including the mulatto engineer and head driver, Amos Morel, at Arnold's White Hall plantation, where Morel had been born to "a favorite house-servant"—behaved in ways that seemed to confirm their masters' familial and patriarchal aspirations.[54] However, the overwhelming majority did not do so, often engaging in either passive or active resistance to their bondage.[55] Those slaves who protested by running away played an absolutely essential role in fomenting both northern discontent and southern dissatisfaction with enforcement of the 1850 Fugitive Slave Law. Historians thus have come to see a "vital connection" between slaves who resisted bondage by running away "and the volatile politics of the 1850s."[56] Upper South slaves, especially those, such as Frederick Douglass, who had some education and skills and might be hired out by their owners to other employers, proved especially prone to pondering the possibilities of flight toward freedom. "The most successful resistance to exploitation helps end the system," explains William Freehling. "While slavery ended in a war between whites, fugitive slaves helped provoke that combat" and from 1861 to 1863 helped transform a war to preserve the Union into a war against slavery as well.[57] Although historians have no access to reliable statistics about how many late antebellum slaves became runaways,[58] exact numbers were and are less important than the impact of their actions on fears and perceptions in both the South and the North. Northerners came to see unsavory slave catchers as agents of the Slave Power, working to compromise civil liberties and threatening a form of federal tyranny in the free states. Southerners saw antislavery fanatics in the North as interfering recklessly and unconstitutionally with the stability and security of their distinctive domestic institution. In mid-November 1860, the *New Orleans Daily Crescent*, published in the Old South's largest city, pointed to personal liberty laws in the free states as proof that "the Constitution affords no remedy for Southern grievances." Echoing the common southern misperception of president-elect Lincoln as a radical abolitionist, the editor claimed that the Illinoisan's victory provided evidence of the North's "fanatical desire to subjugate" the South. Later that month, the *New Orleans Bee* described the Fugitive Slave Act "as a solemn enactment of Congress, adopted in virtue of an imperative mandate of the Constitution." It compared free state nullification of the 1850 law to South Carolina's nullification of protective tariffs passed by Congress in 1828 and 1832.[59] Few southerners appear to have known or cared that only a single free state had passed personal liberty legislation prior to the Kansas-Nebraska Act of 1854. Galvanizing moderate antislavery sentiment anew by overturning the Missouri Compromise line of 1820, the opening of territorial Kansas and Nebraska to the possibility of slavery gave birth to the Republican Party in the North. After the 1854 act, eight more free states adopted personal liberty legislation.[60] White southerners' anger and resentment toward these personal liberty laws only intensified after abolitionist John Brown's fall 1859 attack on Harpers Ferry, and these feelings in turn fed into anxieties about the prospects of further Republican electoral victories in 1860.[61] In December 1859, proslavery Virginia ironmaster Joseph R. Anderson wrote to a Philadelphia agent for Pennsylvania pig iron producers that he and his business partners believed they had "some good and true friends of a fair and constitutional lean in the North." However, "in view of recent events, and so long as the Legislatures of those States are inimical to us, and laws remain on their statute books unfriendly to us and denying our just rights, we believe it is becoming a pretty general resolution in our State not to buy anything that we can do without from the Northern states."[62]

Anderson, like many other white southerners, lumped all hostility to slavery under the heading of abolitionism. As early as 1849, well before the emergence of the Republican Party, Anderson had complained of "the Whig party in the North being infected with abolitionism, or free soilism, which is the same thing, or but another name for abolitionism."[63] Nonetheless, a crucial distinction existed between the two major wings of antebellum northern antagonism to slavery. The small number of abolitionist immediatists, including William Lloyd Garrison, wanted the process of abolishing the sinful injustice of human bondage to begin almost immediately and believed that freed blacks could and should remain in the United States and enjoy equal civil and political rights. Such radicals probably never composed more than 1–2 percent of the North's population, though many of them sided reluctantly with more moderate Republicans. The far greater number of moderate antislavery opponents, including Lincoln, focused on containing slavery geographically and saw emancipation as a gradual, long-term process. Given the pronounced racial prejudices pervasive among white Americans, this process would necessarily involve the deportation and colonization of freed blacks beyond the borders of the United States. More conservative moderates also spoke and wrote in support of what they understood to be their constitutional obligations to enforce the Fugitive Slave Clause. What historian Robert Cook has written about the preponderance of Iowans on the eve of the Civil War also held true for white northerners in general: they "had little affection for slavery, but even less for black people themselves." The electorate was both "antagonistic toward blacks" and "fearful of racial amalgamation and disunion." In a comparative study of Virginia's Augusta County and Pennsylvania's Franklin County, Edward L. Ayers observes that "despite the high-flying rhetoric about justice," neither the Democratic nor the Republican Party "displayed any sympathy toward their black neighbors."[64] The North's strong popular desire to curtail southern arrogance and power and then to preserve the Union against slave state perfidy proved far more powerful than concerns about the plight of enslaved African Americans.

Although the doctrine of state's rights is not necessarily linked with either the protection of slavery or postbellum defenses of racial disfranchisement and segregation, slave state conventions explaining secession expressed a political logic based on extrapolation from state's rights principles. That is, the U.S. Constitution had been ratified by conventions in thirteen different states, each elected by voters in the former dependent colonies, which had already become independent state republics during the American Revolution against Britain. Therefore, a later state convention could determine that the liberties and rights of the state's citizens were threatened by some Madisonian tyranny of the majority. Southerners saw powerful potential for such tyranny in the far more populous North's hostility to slavery and the South's way of life. State's rights and state sovereignty could be invoked to protect the right to secure ownership of slave property and thereby the security of slavery as a means of racial control. All these factors seemed central to the interests, rights, and honor of the slave states that seceded from the Union. The obvious popularity in the North of Republican hostility to southern domestic institutions required that slave states rescind their ratifications of the Constitution and resume their independent status as distinct republics or commonwealths.

Not all citizens in the eleven states that joined the Confederate States of America believed that the U.S. Constitution included the unambiguous right of state secession. America's founding document and fundamental law frequently appear ambiguous if not ambivalent about the precise dividing lines between federal and state authority (or sovereignty). An illuminating exchange emerges from the correspondence of two South Carolinians in late October 1860. According to historian William Kauffman Scarborough, Columbia newspaperman A. G. Baskin chided former governor John L. Manning, "a relative moderate amid the ultra-secessionists of his state" and a resident of Millford plantation in the Sumter District, for failing to go "far enough" along the road to disunionism. In Baskin's words, "A Southern Confederacy is the object of us all," and "the only difference between [us] is as to the *modus operandi* of bringing it about." Manning still hesitated to endorse immediate separate-state secession and viewed secession not as a right derived from the Constitution but as the inherent right of revolution against tyrannical oppression. Baskin disagreed. Defining "revolution" as "insubordination or resistance to authority," he argued that each state in the Union constituted a sovereign entity; a state's secession from the Union, therefore, could not be "revolution in a political sense." But immediate separate-state secession was not necessarily wise or expedient. Like many southerners, Baskin and Manning agreed that a South Carolina committed to leaving the Union should first seek the cooperation of other slave states in determining the procedure and timing of secession. However, should efforts at cooperative disunion fail, secession by a single state could become necessary. "Rather than submit to Northern aggression," declared Baskin, "I would raise the banner of resistance, and if we fail, 'let us die with our feet to the foe and our face towards heaven.'"[65]

In short, advocates of a southern confederacy could always resort to the fundamental right of self-protection that preceded any constitutional body of fundamental law. The imperative of self-preservation entitled any free people to rebel or foment a revolution against what they deemed a tyrannical power posing substantial threats to their natural or inherent interests, their rights, and their honor. "To say the least of it, the right of Secession is an extremely doubtful one," opined an article in a 17 November 1860 Natchez newspaper, yet there remains "the unquestioned right of revolution."[66] During the secession winter, North Carolina politician Jonathan Worth told the citizens of Randolph and Alamance Counties that the convention that had taken the Palmetto State out of the Union "is a modern invention of South Carolina, to bring about a sort of legalized revolution." In another public address the following spring, Worth stated, "I have always believed and still believe that the doctrine of secession, as a peaceful and constitutional mode of withdrawing a state from the Union, [is] an absurdity." At the same time, in response to Lincoln's call for troops to subdue rebellion against federal authority, Worth "deemed it highly inexpedient for the Government to attempt coercion by military force" and believed that the new U.S. president "showed want of common sense in adopting the course he did." In mid-March, Worth had begun to "fear" that the revolutionary "current" of secession "can't be stayed." In the aftermath of Lincoln's coercion and North Carolina's subsequent secession, Worth argued in mid-May that a "peaceable separation" offered the country's "best hope for ultimate re-union." However, "I am left no other alternative but to fight for or against my section. I can not hesitate. Lincoln has made us a unit to resist until we repel our invaders or die."[67]

Such was the legacy and spirit of 1776 as immortalized in the Declaration of Independence and America's heroic struggle for independence from despotic England. The same revolutionary rhetoric against tyranny could be invoked by both black and white abolitionists. Frederick Douglass asked in 1851 what slaves should do if the American creed, as articulated in the Declaration of Independence and the Constitution, did not provide a "warrant for the abolition of slavery in every state in the union." For example, what if the U.S. government continued to enforce a proslavery rather than abolitionist interpretation of the Fifth Amendment, with its declaration that no person could "be deprived of life, liberty, or property without due process of law?" Douglass, like most black leaders, refused to accept the despairing alternative of black emigration to Africa and believed that the only acceptable option was the kind of violent revolution that free Americans had launched against Great Britain in 1775–76.[68] From a very different perspective, Republican antislavery editor Horace Greeley expressed some sympathy with white southern appeals to America's revolutionary heritage. Although Greeley's *New York Daily Tribune* condemned South Carolina's secessionism as a "dictatorial, reckless course" of action, "we could not stand up for [military] coercion or subjugation, for we do not think it would be just." Why not? Because "our devotion to Human Liberty [and to] the Rights of Man" impel us to accept the probable "secession of Five Millions of Southerners from the Federal Union in 1861" as analogous to "the secession from the British Empire of Three Millions of colonists in 1776." This conciliatory stance and the associated admonition to let the erring sisters go in peace seems to have been a minority position in the ranks of the Republican Party in mid-December, when Greeley wrote. By the end of February, when the new Confederate government was up and running in Montgomery, even Greeley's *Tribune* had begun the shift from conciliation to coercion. "We must either treat the fact of Southern Secession as a revolution, and recognize the independence of the seceding states, or we must confront it as treason, and put it down by the military forces of the loyal states. Either course will be frank, honorable and comprehensible."[69] The latter course — military coercion of the treasonous and arrogant South — was endorsed by almost all Republicans as well as most northern Democrats after the Confederate assault on Fort Sumter.

Whether or not pro-Confederate southerners believed in and cited the constitutional right of secession, the natural right of revolution against despotism, or both, they could agree on the legitimate right and absolute liberty of their state conventions, embodying the will of their citizens, to quit the Union and establish independent state republics analogous to those created in 1776. These state republics could then cooperate in creating a new and independent confederation whose constitution emulated that of the United States. As President Davis emphasized during his inaugural address in February, southern citizens had "merely asserted a right which the Declaration of Independence had defined to be inalienable," one that could never be taken away from or totally surrendered by any people.[70] The statement approved by Virginia's state convention in April subtly appealed to secession as concurrently a constitutional and a revolutionary right: "The people of Virginia" had ratified the U.S. Constitution with the understanding that "the powers granted under the said constitution . . . might be resumed whensoever the same should be perverted to their injury and oppression." After Lincoln had summoned soldiers, most members of the Old Dominion's convention believed that "the Federal Government" had in fact "perverted said powers not only to the injury of the people of Virginia, but to the oppression of the Southern slaveholding states."[71]

The case of Texas, the last of the seven Lower South states to quit the Union before Lincoln's inauguration, is especially noteworthy for two reasons. Texas governor Sam Houston proved himself unique among state chief executives in the Lower South by his staunch unconditional Unionism. Famous as a protégé of Andrew Jackson and the architect of Texas independence in 1836, Houston won the governorship in 1859 before John Brown's raid at Harpers Ferry. Houston opposed secession in 1861 and refused to take an oath of loyalty to the Confederacy. Second, Texas was the only seceding state to hold what most observers deemed a legitimate popular referendum on the question of withdrawal from the United States. On 23 February, Texans endorsed secession by a vote of 46,188 to 15,149; nonslaveholders, who constituted more than three-quarters of the state's electorate, voted for disunion by a two to one ratio. The first six states to exit the Union after Lincoln's election had declined to submit the decisions of their secession conventions to popular votes. This fact encouraged many critics, then and later, to conclude that shrewd, well-organized, and conspiratorial fire-eating extremists understood that most white southerners had not yet become committed disunionists and therefore engineered the falling dominoes of separate-state secession by promoting and exploiting a public atmosphere of fear and political panic. It can be tempting to see the secession crisis as an example of the influential conspiracies that many Americans have seen in their nation's history. However, the fact remains that elections for conventions in all the states that seceded, Upper as well as Lower South, proved just as democratic and fair as most electoral contests of that era, and the candidates had made their positions rather clear to the electorate. As James M. McPherson has pointed out, the U.S. Constitution had been ratified by state conventions without popular referenda, and proponents of ratification in 1787–88, like advocates of rescinding ratification in 1860–61, were determined to move the process along as quickly as possible. "Unfortunately," as one recent study has concluded, "historians will never know as much as they would like about the motivations of Texas voters at the time of the referendum." Even so, regression analysis of voting returns demonstrates that disunionism, there as elsewhere, generally proved strongest in the more affluent plantation districts. Why did "the wealthy East Texas planters who launched the secession juggernaut" succeed in mobilizing overwhelming support for disunion? Dale Baum argues persuasively that after years of sectional agitation dating back to the national political contest over Texas annexation in 1844–45, southern rights Democrats persuaded voters that Free-Soilers and Republicans, the so-called "revolutionary party of the North," threatened the slave states "with the contagion of abolition — an evil that would render property in slaves worthless and cause the slaves themselves to 'descend to the vilest barbarism.'" Secession, these Democrats convinced the overwhelming majority of their fellow citizens, nonslaveholders and slaveholders alike, offered "the best way to ensure social stability and maintain economic prosperity," even if it risked the real possibility of war.[72]

Nonetheless, white Texans seem to have greatly exaggerated the short-term threat posed by the contagion of abolition, and their hyperbolic fears clearly shaped the decision to quit the Union and join the Confederacy. Although Unionists such as Houston had virtually swept the state's August 1859 elections, in the summer of 1860, panic about an alleged slave revolt fomented by outsiders pushed the citizenry toward panic about the aftermath of a Republican presidential victory. Suspicions focused on "the great fire of July 8, 1860," in Dallas as part of an abolitionist conspiracy, although scholarly observers today see a far more likely explanation in the tendency that hot Texas summer for "the spontaneous combustion of [new and unstable] phosphorous matches, which were just at this time being extensively stocked by stores." According to the most thorough recent student of the "Texas terrors,"

Donald E. Reynolds, the argument for "a conspiracy theory, built by southern rights editors and politicians, and subsequently supported by many historians," simply does not hold water.[73]

Far to the east, South Carolina had played the crucial, decisive role in jump-starting the process of separate-state secession after Lincoln's election. That the Palmetto State took the first step surprised almost no one familiar with the nation's political history over the prior three decades, ever since that state alone had nullified the federal tariffs of 1828 and 1832 during Andrew Jackson's presidency. As William Freehling has written, South Carolina contained only "scant mountains (really only foothills) and constricted pine barrens (seldom barren of plantations)" and therefore "fostered few clusters of white belts without slaves, the southern condition that elsewhere most encouraged defiance of black belt extremists." The strength of Unionism in the Upper South, whether conditional or unconditional, reflected the far greater number and power of "white belts," fostered by far mountainous terrain and a more temperate climate. South Carolina was "so saturated" with slavery in 1860 that only one of its thirty counties contained fewer than 30 percent slaves, and a still hefty 23 percent of that county's population was African American. Such demographics seem to have nurtured a highly elitist and haughty kind of slaveholding republicanism and to have enabled the Palmetto State, alone in the Old South, to function without a two-party system. South Carolina became the first in a line of falling dominoes, a metaphor suggested by former president John Tyler's son and namesake, writing under the pen name Python in the New Orleans periodical *DeBow's Review*.[74] In understanding both how and why South Carolinians embraced this role, the devil is in the details and in the always elusive balance between the broad and deterministic sweep of impersonal forces on the one hand and on the other the unpredictable impact of historical contingencies involving personalities, accidents, and the unfolding of unintended consequences. The Palmetto State provides an important and illustrative example of an influential group of political insiders who shaped the chain of decisions and events that brought about their state's crucial initial assertion of state sovereignty.

After Lincoln's election, many cotton state leaders still believed that separate-state secession entailed more risks than would, in the words of Jefferson Davis, "seeking to bring these states into cooperation before asking for a popular decision" by voters. According to biographer William Cooper, Davis "had long believed that secession would result in war, though he considered conflict might be avoided if all the slave states left the Union."[75] In September 1860, however, a group of wealthy and sophisticated planters from Charleston and the South Carolina low country had organized a propaganda organ for secessionist immediatism known as the 1860 Association. Its avowed purpose was to arouse the South "in the event of the accession of Mr. Lincoln and the Republican party to power," even before the new administration committed some "overt act" of aggression against slavery. The association orchestrated attempts at what Freehling calls "interstate conspiratorial planning" to promote state-by-state secession, lest continued membership in the Union or even the delaying movement for a cooperationist southern convention prove ultimately disastrous to proslavery disunionism.

John Townsend, owner of a cotton plantation on South Carolina's Edisto Island, became the 1860 Association's most prolific and effective pamphleteer, authoring such titles as *The South Alone Should Govern the South*. After having opposed first Calhounite nullification in 1832 and then the impetuous notion that South Carolina should secede in 1850–51, Townsend had concluded during the summer of 1860 that paralyzed submission to the Republicans could only "postpone for a few brief years" the "ruin and degradation" of white southerners, lowering them "to an equality with our slaves." The association's premier organizer was Robert N. Gourdin, chair of the executive committee and principal proprietor of Gourdin, Mathiesen, and Company, whose offices in Charleston and Savannah marketed Sea Island cotton. The group's "fifteen or so" genteel grandees usually met on Thursday evenings at Gourdin's "grand mansion" on South Battery Street.

That such a group of anxious gentlemen as the 1860 Association emerged in the South Carolina low country no doubt reflected in large part the density of the area's slave population. The association's creation also resulted from anxieties produced by the relative lack of prosperity that the area's slaveholding rice producers experienced during the decade prior to the Civil War—that is, relative to cotton producers across the Lower South and tobacco planters in the Upper South. As Robert Fogel has pointed out, prior to the American Revolution, the slave South's three principal cash crops were rice, tobacco, and indigo. Indigo suffered most in the aftermath of U.S. independence. "Cut out of the British system of imperial tariff preferences and bereft of her bounties," American growers "could not withstand the competition of the West Indies and other British colonies." Rice, whose production occupied a fifth of the slave force before 1776, "fared only slightly better." Although producers of high-grade, long-staple cotton on the Sea Islands of South Carolina and Georgia prospered during the antebellum decades, after 1790, South Carolina's "rice industry stagnated for most of the next 60 years, relieved only by a moderate expansion between the 1820s and the 1840s."[76]

On 7 November 1860, as wire reports confirming the Republican victory reached Charleston, Gourdin was serving as foreman of a grand jury in the U.S. District Court headed by judge Andrew Gordon McGrath. When McGrath opened the day's proceedings by asking if the jury had any formal statements to make, Gourdin declared that Lincoln's election had "swept away the last hope for the permanence, for the stability, of these Sovereign States." Consequently, the federal grand jury "respectfully decline[d] to proceed with their presentments." McGrath then announced that he was submitting his resignation. "As far as I am concerned, the Temple of Justice, raised under the Constitution of the United States, is now closed."[77] Gourdin was a good friend of Major Robert Anderson, who in that same month became commander of the U.S. Army garrison at Fort Moultrie; in December, his command evacuated Moultrie for the more defensible Sumter.

Soon thereafter, Gourdin, as chair of the 1860 Association's executive committee, encouraged editor James D. B. DeBow to pen an essay, headed "Nashville, Dec. 5 1860." First included in a pamphlet, *The Interest in Slavery of the Southern Nonslaveholder*, the essay later appeared in *DeBow's Review* under the title, "The Non-Slaveholders of the South: Their Interests in the Present Sectional Controversy Identical with That of the Slaveholders." DeBow maintained that "a class conscientiously objecting to the ownership of slave property does not exist in the South." The essay can be seen as part of an ongoing effort to refute arguments, quite popular among Republicans but "arousing violent antagonism in the South," that had been presented in the 1857 "digest of a book," *The Impending Crisis of the South: How to Meet It*. The book led critics to brand its author, Hinton Rowan Helper, who had been born in western North Carolina, the "spawn of 'poor white trash'" who turned traitor against his neighbors. Although Helper had no sympathy whatsoever for slaves and insisted that blacks should be deported outside the United States, he portrayed the peculiar institution as a wasteful and inefficient economic curse on the free South, especially its decided majority of nonslaveholders. Helper "appealed to class divisions between the slaveholding and the nonslaveholding whites," Potter has explained. "No dogma of the southern creed was held more sacrosanct than the tenet that race transcended class and, indeed, extinguished it—that all whites were on the same footing, simply by virtue of their status as whites." Evidence indicates that Helper's book found a few sympathetic readers in the slave states, most notably the Reverend Daniel Worth, brother of hesitant Confederate Jonathan Worth. Formerly a Quaker in Guilford County, North Carolina, Daniel Worth became a Wesleyan Methodist minister. The Wesleyan Methodists had seceded from the

Methodist Episcopal Church in the 1840s over the issue of slavery. "Poorer whites composed most of the Wesleyan membership throughout the South," explains historian Charles C. Bolton, "and many of the denomination's clergy were northern missionaries who preached abolition." In the aftermath of John Brown's raid, anxious authorities arrested Rev. Worth and sent him packing for distributing abolitionist literature, including Helper's *Impending Crisis.* Helper's name even appeared in North Carolina discussions of tax policy. During March 1860, some Whigs (then known as the Opposition) had proposed ad valorem taxation (i.e., proportional taxing of assets or goods at full value) not only for slave chattel but for all articles of personal, moveable property. Democrats responded by appealing to nonslaveholding yeoman farmers with the "so-called 'tin cup' argument," saying that the proposed policy would tax "farming implements, household furnishings, livestock, even one's tin cups." Edward Jones Erwin, a banker, slaveholder, and Democrat in western Burke County, explained privately to his son why slaveholders should oppose the tax: if enacted, "this will carry out the very plan suggested by Hinton Rowan Helper, to usher every negro out of the state or render him worthless."[78]

The flames of Helper's notoriety had been fanned in the winter of 1859 by a protracted, two-month conflict in Washington over who would become speaker of the House of Representatives. The leading Republican candidate, John Sherman of Ohio, finally had to withdraw his name because he had allowed it to be linked with Helper's book. Although Sherman claimed he had never seen the volume, he had joined some sixty Republican congressmen in signing a letter endorsing a plan to publish and distribute an abridged version. Potter describes the third-term Ohio congressman as "not a militant on the slavery question" but rather "a thoughtful, moderate man, primarily interested in finance."[79] Yet many southern leaders suspected that Sherman would be part and parcel of a Republican effort to exploit the reality of internal divisions within the slave states, among both social classes and intrastate geographical subregions, to encourage the cancer of indigenous Republican interests in the South, largely through the use of presidential appointments and patronage after Lincoln captured the White House.[80]

South Carolina secessionists perceived no individuals as more dangerous and treasonous than Brown and Helper. The members of the 1860 Association not only sought to enlist fear of the two men in support of secession but also looked anxiously across the Savannah River. Far more internally diverse and divided than the Palmetto State, Georgia was also home to a more potent streak of Unionism. Without a disunionist decision by Georgians, if and when the more reliably secessionist states of Alabama and Mississippi left the Union, "a gaping geographic hole" would separate South Carolina from the Old Southwest as well as Florida. The crucial town in Georgia was Savannah, where the role of contingency loomed large, as Roy Franklin Nichols has pointed out. Quite coincidentally and "quite fortuitously" for the Carolinians in the 1860 Association, some three hundred black laborers had finished work on the first railroad connection between Charleston and Savannah exactly one week before Lincoln's election. The Charleston and Savannah Railroad had been chartered in 1854, at a time when the economy of the latter city boomed and that of the former limped along. While Savannah merchants hoped that some of Charleston's trade could be redirected to their thriving harbor, Charleston merchants, including Gourdin, hoped that some of Savannah's prosperous coastal trade with Atlantic port cities in the North could be redirected their way.[81] Some of Charleston's ambitious and proud partisans had long dreamed that their town should and could become the commercial emporium of the Southeast, much like the position reached by New York City in the Northeast.

On the morning of 2 November 1860, "eighty prominent Charlestonians" boarded a train for a celebratory six-hour ride over one hundred miles of often swampy terrain to the Savannah River. The train was met by Savannah's young but blue-blooded mayor, Charles Colcock Jones Jr. Although educated at Harvard, Jones described Yankees as "a poisonous brood" whose "hissing tongues and noxious breath" uttered "heresies and false conceptions of a higher law" allegedly superior to the proslavery provisions of the U.S. Constitution. At a banquet held that evening at Savannah's Pulaski Hotel, the principal Georgia orator was another youthful blue blood, Francis Bartow, who the following summer would become an early southern casualty as captain of the Oglethorpe Light Cavalry at the first Battle of Bull Run (Manassas). After schooling at the University of Georgia and Yale, Bartow had returned home, been named partner in a prestigious Savannah firm, and become master of eighty-nine slaves. In his speech, Bartow admitted that the time for secession and disunion had not yet arrived for most Georgians. But should the Carolinians "choose" to quit the Union "without consulting us" cooperatively, "you have the power of precipitating us into any kind of revolution you choose." Receiving "tremendous applause," he pledged that Georgia's sons "will defend South Carolina, rash though we think her, precipitate though we deem her, with all the energy and courage of a brother." Otherwise, white residents of both states would become a "degraded people" and therefore without honor.

The visitors from Charleston then prevailed on their Savannah hosts to make a return visit a week hence. When this train reached the Ashley River station on the afternoon of 9 November, everyone knew that a Black Republican would be inaugurated president of the United States in less than four months. That evening, 77 Georgians joined 124 Carolinians for a sumptuous feast at Charleston's plushest hotel, the Mills House. After supper, Gourdin and some associates escorted Bartow and another "handpicked" speaker from Georgia over to Institute Hall, where a "monster public rally" had been planned for days. Before a crowd of at least a thousand, Bartow first portrayed himself as a devoted American nationalist: "I am a Union man, in every fibre of my heart." However, he had become "tired of this endless controversy" and "wearied with seeing this threatening cloud." He finally felt ready for South Carolina to take the first step toward a new southern confederation. "Put it off not till tomorrow," he advised, for "we shall not be stronger by waiting."

The second speaker from Georgia was another former Unionist who had helped his cousin and political ally, Howell Cobb, derail secessionist sentiment in their state during the furor over the Compromise of 1850. Henry Rootes Jackson had also attended Yale, graduating with the highest ranking in his undergraduate class, but nevertheless excoriated all things Yankee as "impure, inhuman, uncharitable, unchristian and uncivilized." Northerners themselves were "demons of hell in the guise of men," spewing forth such "hellishisms" as "equalityism and negrophilism." Jackson's speech offered additional assurance that Georgians would rally behind a secessionist South Carolina.

Before midnight, members of South Carolina's state legislature, then meeting in Columbia, received telegraph messages that "the greatest meeting ever held" in Charleston had heard "Mr. Jackson, Mr. Bartow, and others from Georgia" pledge their state to support a disunionist Palmetto State. Aroused Charlestonians wanted a state secession convention called "at an early date" and "cannot be restrained." The next day, a special train carried a delegation from the port city to the inland capital. According to Mary Boykin Chesnut, also a passenger on that train, the members of the delegation constituted "a deputation from Charleston against tyrants" that urged the state legislators "to hurry up, dissolve the Union" before extralegal mobs forced the state government's hand by attempting to seize federal forts. The telegraph news and the deputation had the intended effect later that day.

On 9 November, the state senate had voted 44–1 to hold elections on 8 January for delegates who would convene a week later. The next afternoon, the House voted 117–0 in favor of moving the elections up to 6 December, with the delegates gathering on 17 December. That same evening, the Senate concurred, 42–0. On 11 November, the presiding officer of the South Carolina Senate, William Porter, a prominent member of the 1860 Association, wrote to one of South Carolina's senators, James Henry Hammond, a hesitant disunionist who had indicated support for interstate cooperation through a southern convention, that the secessionist "ball is in motion." Since Hammond was "known to have inclined against immediate action," he now could and should "help us with Georgia and with Georgia we can do everything." Two days later, Hammond followed the example of James Chesnut Jr. and resigned from the U.S. Senate, though his state had not yet renounced its formal membership in the Union. South Carolina gave the secessionist ball a furious push and almost irresistible momentum on 20 December when its convention voted in favor of separate-state secession with nary a dissenter.

Georgia voters elected their state convention on 2 January. The members of the electorate split their votes between hesitant delayers preferring interstate cooperation and fervent immediatists insisting on single-state secession. As Anthony Gene Carey has pointed out, the cooperationists could appeal to "powerful sentiments," among them hearts still beating with "love for the Union" and fears of provoking a swift military response from Washington. Republicans might opt for war against a few rebellious states in the Lower South rather than waiting for Upper South states to join in a united front of resistance. If united, argued cooperationists, the slave states could make a stronger case for substantive concessions and guarantees from Black Republicans. At a minimum, unity would result in a more organized South better prepared for intersectional war. However, in the final analysis, southerners' "antipathy to outright Unionism exceeded their opposition to immediate secession." Those counseling cooperation and deliberation "conceded that unmitigated Republican rule was intolerable and that disunion was the appropriate final remedy."[82] The case for delay suffered further when, five days before the Georgia convention gathered on 16 January, Alabama became the fourth state to endorse secession, doing so by a vote of 61–39. Mississippi and Florida had already followed South Carolina's lead.

On the Georgia convention's second day, the delegates heard a speech from South Carolina commissioner James L. Orr, former speaker of the U.S. House of Representatives. He had stood firm against the unwise ultra proposal to reopen the foreign slave trade and had converted to secessionism only when his Democratic Party had divided in 1860. Orr followed the tried-and-true script of presenting himself as an essentially "conservative and Union-loving man." However, Republicans had most of the North in the grip of "a blind and relentless fanaticism," and southerners had already endured too many "indigni-

White Savannah celebrates Georgia's secession from the Union, 1861.
(Courtesy of the Library of Congress)

ties." After Lincoln's inauguration, the new administration would surely seek to accomplish the South's "degradation and dishonor."[83] On 19 January, Georgia's convention delegates voted 208–89 to secede.

The following month, delegates from the six states whose conventions had already approved separate-state secession, including Louisiana, organized the Confederate States of America. They chose as president and vice president not secessionist fire-eaters but individuals whom Freehling has indentified as "the two most prominent late stallers on disunion," Jefferson Davis and Alexander Stephens. Historian Emory Thomas has explained that incessant drum majors for secessionist immediatism, such as the senior Robert Barnwell Rhett of South Carolina and William Lowndes Yancey of Alabama, "were root-and-branch radicals whose talents and tempers well suited the destruction of the old Union but ill became the construction of a new Confederacy." Freehling has applied analogous logic to the late antebellum North: "The more moderate Abraham Lincolns had to replace the more extreme William Lloyd Garrisons for antislavery men to sweep Northern elections."[84]

3 Honor and Degradation

Section, Race, and Gender

*I*n 1860, Charles Colcock Jones Jr., age twenty-eight, became the youngest man ever elected mayor of Savannah, Georgia, a victory his father termed "a high honor." Charles Sr. used the word "honor" according to its fundamental connotation: something worthy of esteem and respect. Although it is difficult to reduce the term to a concise definition, the "essence" of honor, in the words of a noted medievalist, "combines the self-esteem of an individual with the respect accorded by others." Human beings seem inclined not to separate and divorce their self-esteem from "the respect accorded by others." The basic question for historians is always how and why others in a particular place and time deem someone worthy of honorable respect.[1]

Charlie Jones had thoroughly absorbed from his parents, Charles and Mary, the principle that he and his two siblings should develop and employ "mind and heart and manners" for the purpose of "usefulness in society." Charles Sr., owner of several slave plantations in low country Georgia, was an ordained Presbyterian minister and a professor at Columbia Theological Seminary. He had achieved a measure of fame as, in the words of historian Erskine Clark, "a leading advocate for the reform of slavery in an attempt to make the system of slavery more humane"—and thereby more readily and forcefully defensible. In 1860, a young South Carolinian, William States Lee, "the son of a venerable and highly esteemed minister" at the Presbyterian church on Edisto Island, volunteered to assist Jones in preparing a manuscript history of the Christian church for possible publication by Charles Scribner's New York publishing house. Lee spent several months in 1860 living in the Joneses' plantation home. Early the following summer, Jones learned that Peggy, "an attractive young slave" in training as a chambermaid, had just given birth to a mulatto girl and had named Lee as the baby's father. Jones wrote to the young man, who had since established a school for young ladies in Columbus, "There is a resemblance to you beyond mistake." Jones was indignant not only that a free white man, especially "a gentleman, a married man, and a Christian," had abused his power over an unfree black girl by engaging in "illicit intercourse"

77

but also that Lee had violated basic standards of hospitality while a guest. Having "debauched a young Negro girl," Jones wrote, Lee had become "the only man who had ever dared to offer to me personally and to my family and to my neighbors so vile and so infamous an insult." Lee's inexcusable behavior had simultaneously besmirched his honor and compromised that of Jones; the master seemed far less concerned about any damage to Peggy's honor. Jones did not follow the protocol that might lead to the elegant violence of a formal duel, a recourse often denounced by evangelical Christian clergy, although he sought, without success, to have Lee's criminality punished by the leadership of the Presbyterian congregation in Columbus.

Charlie Jones had attended South Carolina College and Princeton before graduating from Harvard's law school in 1855. Within the year, he began practicing law in Savannah with a family friend, John Elliott Ward, the city's mayor at that time. In mid-October 1860, the new mayor recognized that Republican Party victories in Pennsylvania, Ohio, and Indiana state elections rendered Abraham Lincoln's November presidential victory "almost a fixed fact." That prospect meant that "the action of a single state, such as South Carolina or Alabama, may precipitate us into all the horrors of intestine war." Like so many Americans north and south, Jones expressed sincere hope and trust "that a kind Providence, that has so long and so specially watched over the increasing glories of our common country, may so influence the minds of fanatical men and dispose of coming events so as to avert so direful as calamity." Like his son, Charles Sr. prayed that God would work to prevent a dissolution of the Union and preserve sectional peace: a "separation" of the slave and free states might have such "consequences in the future" as would "be disastrous to both sections. Union if possible—but with it we must have *life, liberty, and equality*." Without them, father and son understood, a republican citizen could have no honor. Instead, he would experience what contemporaries often termed "degradation," which brought unacceptable shame.[2]

Honor in its "most basic form," as James Bowman has explained, is the "foundational social reflex" in a human being "to let others know one is not to be trifled with." In other words, "honor is the good opinion of the people who matter to us, and who matter because we regard them as a society of equals who have the power to judge our behavior." These people constitute our "honor group," peers whose judgments we value highly.[3] Yet we can simultaneously belong to a number of peer or honor groups, some more central to our identities than others. Loyalties to one honor group can compete with loyalties to another peer or honor group in our local, regional, or national community, and people may find that the principles endorsed by one group conflict with those advocated by another. On the eve of the Civil War, white male southerners such as the Joneses belonged to at least three significant honor groups: the community's, state's, or region's predominantly slaveholding elite of respected gentlemen and ladies and aspirants to recognized membership in that group; all white males in the southern slave states; and all free and white U.S. citizens. All three honor groups would have agreed in public that Lee's sexual intercourse with a slave girl while a guest in the Jones home constituted a form of dishonorable behavior. However, Charles and Charlie Jones, like most members of the first two honor groups, concluded that most northern members of their third and largest honor group considered it a challenge and insult to U.S. well-being and honor. That is, southern gentlemen and citizens determined, however reluctantly, that they had no choice but to secede from the Union to preserve the interests, rights, and honor of peers in their states and section.

Just before the 1860 presidential election, Mayor Jones welcomed a delegation from Charleston with a speech scorching "poisonous" Yankees for invoking some "higher law" than the U.S. Constitution when insulting slaveholders. After Lincoln's victory and South Carolina's secession, Jones continued to call for "the defense of southern rights and southern honor." Father and son seemed in accord that the slave states would forfeit their interests, rights, and honor if they were not treated as entitled to equality and respect within the federal union by the politically dominant free states. Georgia's state convention cast a 208–89 vote in favor of secession on 19 January, meaning that 89 politically prominent Georgians still did not view disunion as necessary to their dignity and honor. Just over a week later, Charlie Jones wrote to his father that during the debates leading to the Missouri Compromise of 1820, southern leaders should have "manfully resisted" the incipient "anti-slavery North." At the same time, white southerners should have "called upon the good and true men of the North" to assist them in stifling the antislavery "serpent in its den." Had this been done, the South would "not now have been suffering from the poisonous brood which with hissing tongue and noxious breath are crawling everywhere and polluting the otherwise wholesome air of this once pure and happy country." In other words, southern willingness to negotiate and compromise during the antebellum decades had only whetted antislavery northerners' hostility and aggression. The younger Jones claimed to "have long believed that in this country have arisen two [sectional] races which, although claiming a common parentage, have been so entirely separated by climate, by morals, by religion, and by estimates so totally opposite of all that constitutes honor, truth, and manliness, that we cannot longer coexist under the same government."[4] Such sentiments of what might be termed southern nationalism have provided fine grist for the mills of scholars who have seen in southern honor something unique within the United States, a phenomenon generally foreign to or at least fast fading in the North's less traditional, more dynamic, and modern culture.

More than the Joneses, Texas senator Louis Trezevant Wigfall, a native of South Carolina, epitomized the fire-eating, hotspur persona in the South. He combined aggressive calls for reopening the African slave trade and disunion with a devout adherence to the code duello, whereby a gentleman could demand personal satisfaction on the field of honor in response to what he perceived to be an insult to his character and reputation. In the early 1840s, on an island in the Savannah River, Wigfall and Preston Brooks had engaged in a duel. Wigfall took a bullet in his thigh but shot Brooks through the hip. Brooks used a cane for the rest of his life, pressing the walking stick into service in 1856 as a weapon with which to beat Charles Sumner on the floor of the Senate. Even after the Texas State Convention endorsed secession by a vote of 166–8 on 1 February 1861 and the state legislature named Wigfall a delegate to the Provisional Confederate Congress in Montgomery, he did not leave Washington. He liked keeping an eye on—and taunting—the Yankee leaders and helped the new Confederate War Department establish a Baltimore office that funneled both volunteers and weapons to South Carolina.[5]

On both 13 and 18 December 1860, Wigfall had addressed the Senate during discussion of a motion made in response to President James Buchanan's State of the Union address earlier in the month.[6] Senator Lazarus Powell of Kentucky had proposed that "a special committee of thirteen people" be appointed to investigate "the present agitated and distracted condition of the country and the grievances between the slaveholding and the non-slaveholding States." The United States "do not compose one single political community, but are divided into thirty-three separate communities called States," each of them "sovereign." Wigfall made it clear that he adhered to the southern rights or radical version of state's rights doctrine—what can be called the principle of state sovereignty, according to which individual states rather than the American people as a whole comprise the constituent, sovereign members of the U.S. constitutional compact. Declared the Texan, "It is known to every Senator upon this floor that one of the States of the Union will, before this day next week, cease to be one of the United States." That state, South Carolina, "in convention assembled, will have revoked the ratification of the treaty which makes her one of these United States." In response to Republican declarations that a state had no constitutionally recognized right to negate unilaterally its link to the Constitution and to withdraw or secede from the Union, Wigfall exclaimed, "A more monstrous outrage will not have been committed in any country, than will be committed if [the U.S.] government attempts coercion in any manner." For the federal government to employ coercive force against a sovereign state would represent an "attempt to reduce one of the parties to the compact to the condition of a conquered province," an assault on "constitutional liberty," and a step toward "military despotism." Those Americans who would sacrifice liberty and submit to despotism would be dishonored. Wigfall's logic clearly implied that slaves, who submitted to the indignity of coerced bondage at the hands of freemen, had no respectability or honor, no capacity for a reputation worthy of esteem and respect in a republican polity.

Wigfall acknowledged that U.S. military power might "conquer" small South Carolina and "trail that palmetto banner in the dust; but you will never reduce that people to slavery. No, sir; South Carolina may be made a graveyard of freemen, but, before God, it will never be the habitation of slaves." Wigfall's words brought forth "manifestations of applause in the galleries" of the Senate chamber. Of course, his boast contained grand irony: South Carolina, like Mississippi, was already home to more black slaves than free whites.

Lincoln's Black Republican followers often referred to the "barbarism of slavery" in the South, Wigfall noted. However, the southern states were home to "men who, even in this utilitarian age, are not dead to all sentiment; who defend with the hazard of their lives and with their blood their personal honor and will be as ready to defend the honor of their States as they are their individual respectability." The honor of a state as well as an individual depended on recognition of the bearer's entitlement to respect as a worthy equal. According to Wigfall, because antislavery Republicans "regard a sense of honor as one of the relics of barbarism and the incident of the institution of slavery," they "do not understand, or comprehend, or appreciate the feelings which influence the people of the slaveholding States." Those feelings would preclude the free citizens of South Carolina and other slave states from "submission" to "indignity" and coercion. Wigfall's persona and behavior, from his duel with Brooks to his ardent disunionism, lend credence to historian Bertram Wyatt-Brown's argument that the "threat to slavery's legitimacy in the Union prompted the secession crisis, but it was Southern honor that pulled the trigger."[7] And for many northerners, the disunionist challenge to their honor and that of the nation stoked a patriotic response in defense of the Union. On 10 March 1861, at the U.S. Naval Academy, a midshipman from Iowa and Oregon composed a letter in which he asked, "How did you like the Inaugural?" Roswell H. Lamson, an antislavery Republican, wrote, "I think it is just the thing: let us know if we have a government or not." If not, "allow it to be trampled upon, and the honor of its flag covered with insult by traitors." Lamson reported that some "southern fellows have resigned recently, but there are a good many here yet, who denounce the government as everything that is despotic and bad." Lamson had told these ingrates "that they yet should remember their oath and that as long as they wear its uniform their own honor is connected with it." Indeed, "for of all things that would dishonor an *American*" such as he, "it would be to serve a government such as they represent ours to be."[8]

On 17 December 1860, one of the foremost Republican senators had taken the floor and begun an extended reply to recent speeches by disaffected southern senators, including Wigfall.[9] Benjamin Franklin Wade, son of a Massachusetts farmer, had moved to Ohio and become a lawyer and antislavery Whig in the 1830s. In 1851, he had been elected to the first of three terms in the U.S. Senate with combined support from Whigs and Free-Soilers, a group that included many former northern Democrats who broke with their party when the Mexican Cession of 1848, following hard on the heels of the annexation of Texas, appeared to demonstrate conclusively that the national Democracy had become captive to the political Slave Power and its determination to enlarge the geographic range and public clout of despotic slaveholders. After the Kansas-Nebraska Act of 1854 opened two new territories in the trans-Mississippi West to the possibility of black slavery under the Democratic Party principle of popular sovereignty, Wade helped found the Republican Party in the Buckeye State. Reputed to be "a fearless radical," he did not share Massachusetts Republican Charles Sumner's condescending disdain for dueling. When Wade was threatened with a challenge to his personal honor, according to biographer Hans Trefousse, "he let it be known that as a senator he would refuse to fight, but as Ben Wade he would not hesitate to do so." Along with fellow senators Sumner and Salmon P. Chase of Ohio, Wade belonged in 1860 to the ranks of what one historian has termed "abolitionists in all but name"; their condemnations of the slave South seemed not too far behind those of the small band of color-blind abolitionist immediatists that included Wendell Phillips and William Lloyd Garrison.[10] As Wade's 17 December address demonstrates, Republican leaders clearly employed the language of honor. Yet their use of the term revealed their membership in a different set of honor groups than those of fire-eaters such as Wigfall. They therefore understood their honor as demanding different principles and behavior.

Wade told the Senate that southern members seemed less focused on "specific acts that northern people had done injurious to your property" and more on what they "took to be a dishonor and degradation." Rather disingenuously, the Ohioan insisted, "I am the last man that would be the advocate of any law or any act that would humiliate or dishonor any section of this country, or any individual in it." Indeed, "I would rather sustain an injury than an insult or dishonor; and I would be as unwilling to inflict it upon others as I would be to submit to it myself." Wade professed as much concern about personal dishonor as had Wigfall. For Wade and his peer group in the Republican Party and the free states, however, honor seemed to require taking a clear and firm political stand against slavery and slaveholders.

Wade declared that far from threatening to "commit any overt act against the Constitution," Lincoln and the Republicans in fact "hold no doctrine that can possibly work you an inconvenience." Again, he was disingenuous. Wade refused to acknowledge that southerners had expressed genuine concerns or had reason to be concerned about the Republican Party's position that the normal condition of the federal territories was free soil and that the U.S. government could constitutionally prohibit the expansion of chattel slavery into any new territories. Instead, he attempted to turn the tables on slave state politicians for having cooperated with toadying northern allies in the Democratic Party to pass the Kansas-Nebraska Act, which repealed the "sacred" Missouri Compromise, despite his warning that this repeal would foment "sectional bitterness." Secessionists now proclaimed that they were not going to wait for an overt act from the newly elected Republican administration: "The election of Mr. Lincoln showed hostility to you and your institution." Southerners wanted some sort of effective "compromise to be brought about by act of Congress," assuring them of the safety and security of "this peculiar institution of yours." Wade then returned to the issue of honor stressed by Wigfall: "Sir, it would be humiliating and dishonorable to [Republicans] if we were to listen to a compromise by which [Lincoln] who has the verdict of the people in his pocket should make his way to the presidential chair." That is, the Republican Party had won the election fair and square, according to the terms of the Constitution, and it would be humiliating and dishonorable for the victors to submit to threats from the losers—threats that only a compromise settlement with disgruntled southerners would allow Lincoln to enjoy the privilege of a March inauguration as president of the same United States that had elected him. Moreover, those making such threats should understand that Republicans did not see the doctrine of secession as a constitutional remedy for grievances. Like almost every American after 1776, Wade did "acknowledge, to the fullest extent, the right of revolution" against perceived tyranny and injury to one's interests and rights. Indeed, "I believe nobody at this day denies the right; but they that undertake it, undertake it with this hazard: if they are successful, then all is right, and they are heroes; if they are defeated, they are rebels . . . and the Government from which they have rebelled treats them as traitors" and their rebellious war as "treason." Wade concluded, "I am for maintaining the Union of these States. I will sacrifice everything but honor to maintain it," to keep "that glorious old flag of ours" waving "over the integrity of the Union as it is." Wade seems to have employed the language of honor for different political ends but in much the same tactical manner as Wigfall.

It was hardly unusual for a mid-nineteenth-century American orator north or south to declare his adamant refusal to sacrifice honor. In early December 1859, South Carolinian Wade Hampton III delivered an address before the state senate in opposition to the fire-eating "Ultra party" of "agitators" urging "the Slave Trade foolery" in the legislature. Pleading for regional unity in the face of antislavery threats from the North, Hampton condemned the divisiveness within the South caused by proponents of reopening the foreign slave trade. He believed that reopening the United States to slaves from abroad would "involve cruel and inhuman practice" while demoralizing "the slaves now owned in the United States." He continued, "The South has pressing need for all her sons. Cannot some platform be found broad enough to sustain us all? Show me such a one, and I will sacrifice everything but principle and honor to place myself upon it by the side of the true patriots of the South." Hampton, a future Confederate general, "did not question the morality of slavery itself or express doubts about the institution's future," and he had a reputation among his South Carolina peers as "a firm opponent of dueling," having "acted more than once among his acquaintances to prevent arguments from leading to pistol shots." Perhaps he had learned from his father that those who violated the family's reputation and honor should be brought low "by dogged opposition at every turn, over a period of years," with the long-term goal of effecting the trangressor's "social ostracism and political destruction." In 1843, Wade Hampton II had accused his brother-in-law, James Henry Hammond, a prominent planter-politician and at that time the state's governor, of attempting to seduce four of Hampton's daughters.[11]

A sectional understanding of honor far more complementary to Wade's than to Hampton's came from a second-term Democratic congressman from Illinois in mid-January 1861. Isaac Newton Morris was a member of the House Committee of Thirty-three appointed to find some peaceful way out of the sectional impasse. A Democrat and a lawyer, Morris was the son of Ohio's first U.S. senator.[12] Morris had supported fellow Illinois Democrat Stephen A. Douglas in the 1860 election and continued to argue that the popular sovereignty plank in the platform of Douglas's northern Democracy represented the best solution to the vexing North-South conflict over slavery in new U.S. territories. Resident "in the heart of the valley of the Upper Mississippi," Morris lived "where the Democratic masses love the Union, and are conservative, and where the rights of all are respected." He warned "the inhabitants of the Lower Mississippi" that ten million northerners would not and could not sit back and watch slave states downriver secede and create or join another government: "We never can, and we never will, consent to allow any foreign Power—and they will be foreign when they leave us—to retain possession and control of the mouth of that great highway of commerce. We do not mean to boast; we do not intend to threaten; but we *do mean to protect ourselves.*" The ultimate and undeniable right of every free citizen was self-preservation, and Morris saw the self-preservation of his midwestern region as dictating a firmly Unionist stance. The interests and rights of the Old Northwest simply would not permit the states of the Lower Mississippi Valley to leave the United States; their secession would create an "enemy" who "will find an army opposing him far more numerous than any which ever besieged imperial Rome, and blood will flow like water. This will be one of the results of disunion."[13]

Some outspoken opponents of secession in the Upper South also clearly understood that midwestern free states could and would not tolerate disunion. "Will not the North West submit to self-immolation if they recognize secession?," asked Whiggish Unionist Jonathan Worth of North Carolina in early May 1861. After the post-Sumter wave of secession in the Middle South, the Reverend Robert Jefferson Breckinridge in Kentucky argued that the Lower Mississippi was "controlled" by the three slave states of Louisiana, Mississippi, and Arkansas, "unitedly inhabited by hardly as many white people as inhabit the city of New York." Moving up both the Mississippi and Ohio Rivers but for some reason skipping Tennessee and commencing with Missouri and Kentucky, Breckinridge counted "nine of ten powerful States" whose populations rivaled that of "all the revolted states." He then asked, "Does any one suppose that these powerful States—this great and energetic population—will ever make a peace that shall put the lower course of this single and mighty natural outlet to the sea, in the hands of a foreign government far weaker than themselves?"[14]

In his speech, Morris also noted the continuing standoff between South Carolina and the U.S. government over Fort Sumter. Pointing to "the heroic band of sixty-five" stationed there under the command of Major Robert Anderson, "a true national patriot," the Illinois congressman exclaimed, "Let but a drop of blood be spilt at Sumter, or one of our noble troops be injured, and a million swords will leap from their scabbards to avenge his wrong and vindicate the national honor."[15] Morris's words suggested that the values of manliness and honor would drive him and his constituents to defend U.S. national honor against any aggressive injury or wrong committed against the troops in Charleston Harbor because honorable manliness "called for an open, aggressive, and appropriately manly response before their peers."

In late December 1860, when northerners had learned of Anderson's surreptitious transfer of his garrison from Fort Moultrie, exposed on the mainland, to the more defensible island redoubt of Fort Sumter, citizens in many cities fired thirty-three-gun salutes (one gun for each state, minus treasonous South Carolina) to honor Anderson's defense of federal authority. On 28 December, the *Boston Courier* quoted a local businessman who said, "These are times to develop one's manhood."[16] Anderson was a native Kentuckian and a former slaveholder, and his wife, Eba Clinch Anderson, came from a slaveholding Georgia family. A career army officer and artillery expert, he was firmly devoted to the Union but at the same time fervently wished to avoid bloodshed in Charleston Harbor and any provocation that might trigger civil war. In January, Anderson received notes from President Buchanan's new secretary of war, Joseph Holt, an attorney from Kentucky. Holt described the transfer of the garrison as "brilliant" and expressed "the great satisfaction of the Government at the forbearance, discretion, and firmness with which you have acted" in the midst of "perplexing and difficult circumstances." For his part, Anderson wrote about the prospect of war, "I shall do all that I can with honor, to prevent the occurence of so sad an event." According to historian David Detzer, Anderson's letters from around that time reflected occasional "anxiety, but most echoed his trust in the Lord's wisdom." In one missive to secessionist South Carolina governor Francis Pickens, Anderson penned, "I hope in God that the time may come when a change in circumstances, and the pleasure of an acquaintance will justify my subscribing myself—Your friend." For many Americans in both the North and the South, "Major Anderson at Fort Sumter" became the most important symbol of the Union.[17]

Morris also inextricably linked the rights and interests of the Old Northwest to the Union's authority and national honor: "I cannot, I will not believe it—that the fires of patriotism have died out all over the country; that we are only the degenerate sons of a brave ancestry, and fit only to be mourners in the funeral *cortège* of Liberty, or to desert its standard in the hour of peril." Morris here expressed the understanding, common across both regions of the country, that to be "degenerate," "degraded," or "submissive" was to forfeit one's claim to both liberty and respect. After declaring "PRESERVE THE REPUBLIC," Morris concluded with the almost obligatory reference to Divine Providence: "The Great Ruler is moving mysteriously in this storm; and as He 'does all things well,' let us look to Him for wisdom, guidance, and support in our *great extremity.*"

The speeches of Wigfall, Wade, Hampton, and Morris illustrate how both northern and southern leaders could and did invoke the powerful language of honor and manliness. Nevertheless, many recent scholars have seen in the phenomenon of southern honor something both quite different and far more significant than anything in the less traditional North's cultural lexicon. For example, Nicole Etcheson, building on the influential work of Bertram Wyatt-Brown, Edward L. Ayers, Elliott J. Gorn, and others, has concluded that southern honor placed "heavy emphasis on manliness" and that at its center "was the maintenance of one's reputation before the public." Free male southerners lived in a cultural world "where the importance of honor made it vital to sustain that honor by public combat." Not to resist an insult or slight would be to reveal one's lack of manliness and honor—to say, in effect, that one was unworthy of the honor and respect that should be accorded by one's peers. "The form that violence took depended on class: Upper-class Southerners dueled and lower-class Southerners brawled."[18]

Etcheson's research focuses on upland southerners who migrated north and settled in Ohio, Indiana, and Illinois. In contrast to middle-class northern professionals, who "demonstrated manliness by their ability to provide for their families in an increasingly market-oriented economy, keeping their women and children in a state of economic non-productivity," yeoman southerners who settled in the Old Midwest brought with them an inclination to prove their honorable manliness "in the more elemental fashion of brute courage." Wyatt-Brown anticipated much of Etcheson's perspective on North-South differences, arguing that historians should recognize a distinction between the antebellum North's devotion "to conscience and to secular economic concerns" and the Old South's devotion "to honor and persistent community sanctions." Wyatt-Brown suggests that northern culture was shaped not only by men demonstrating honorable manliness through economic success but also by individuals whose standards of honest and moral behavior were dictated by internal conscience rather than the opinions of others.[19]

More recently, the sectional distinctions posited by Wyatt-Brown and

Etcheson have been adapted by Orville Vernon Burton to the person of Abraham Lincoln, himself the son of a migrant from Kentucky to first Indiana and then Illinois, where he became a politically ambitious attorney. According to Burton, Lincoln's "life's decision and his handling of the [sectional] crisis" were driven by "his understanding of and respect for southern honor." Burton invokes the 1842 story of the Whig Lincoln's refusal to back down from a challenge issued by Democrat James Shields. Although the duel itself was foiled when "seconds stepped in at the last moment to remove the fearsome weapons and proclaim honor and manhood affirmed on both sides," the incident illustrates Lincoln's belief that "winning honor entailed more than earning the esteem of his fellows." Indeed, during his legal and political career, he "strove to attain enduring honor through the effort to make his choices matter."[20] No doubt manliness and honor held great importance for Lincoln, but this importance need not be attributed solely or primarily to his southern roots.

Like so many mid-nineteenth-century affairs of honor on both sides of the Atlantic Ocean,[21] the 1842 altercation between Lincoln and Shields sprang from an episode of political and party rivalry. It also arose at a time when the young Lincoln's original engagement to Mary Todd had been broken up as a consequence of the actions of one of Todd's relations. After the failure of the state bank, Shields, an Irish-born politician who fancied himself quite the lady's man, took the appropriate step of ordering state offices to refuse to accept the bank's notes as legal tender. Lincoln, writing under the pseudonym Rebecca, poked fun at Shields and his fellow Democrats in a letter to the editor of the *Sangamon Journal*. Mary Todd and her closest friend, Julia Jayne, apparently "carried away by the excitement," wrote a "a rather clumsy" follow-up letter from "Rebecca."[22] These articles enraged Shields, who felt insulted at missives "calculated to degrade me." When he demanded the author's real identity from the editor, Lincoln, apparently to shield the ladies from the Democratic auditor's wrath, identified himself as Rebecca, eliciting a letter from Shields demanding either a retraction or (implicitly) a duel. Lincoln, declaring himself "wholly opposed to dueling" but egged on by "a hot-blooded young Springfield physician, Dr. Elias H. Merryman," declined to offer an apologetic retraction. Facing a formal challenge and unwilling to do anything that might "degrade him in the estimation of himself and friends," Lincoln told Merryman that he preferred a duel to "such *degradation*." The future president's actions demonstrate the ubiquity of the widespread assumption that an adult male would appear shamefully degraded if he forfeited his manly honor.

Lincoln and Shields agreed to a location across the Mississippi River in Missouri, thereby avoiding prosecution under Illinois's antidueling statute. Since Shields had issued the challenge, Lincoln chose the weapons: cavalry broadswords, which gave an advantage to his greater height (by at least half a foot) and strength. As often happened, last-minute negotiations by friends on the dueling grounds avoided actual combat. Lincoln conceded that the letters had been intended as political satire rather than as personal attacks on his opponent's character, and Shields withdrew his formal challenge. The two principals shook hands and returned home.[23]

Traditional understandings of male honor seem to involve some form of violent confrontation, either to vindicate the dignity of an individual (as in the duelist's affair of honor) or perhaps to maintain the cohesive standards of a community (as in a lynching). The most famous duel in American history took place near the beginning of the nineteenth century between New Yorkers Alexander Hamilton and Aaron Burr, who had no family connections south of the Mason and Dixon Line. Although support for the duelist's honor waned more quickly in the North than in the South, the code duello does not appear to have become distinctively or exclusively southern before midcentury. Historian Amy Greenberg has concluded that "it is tempting to see honor as a sectional phenomenon" but that the "southern code of honor" does not appear to have differed substantively from the code for northern men.[24] Indeed, in March 1861, Stephen A. Douglas became irritated with Maine Republican senator William Fessenden and cursed him with epithets "better adapted to a pothouse than the Senate Chamber." "There were pointed references to settling the question 'elsewhere' in accordance with the 'code of honor,' but both parties wisely backed away at the last moment."[25]

The case of John Adolphus Dahlgren, born and bred in Philadelphia, exemplifies how an antebellum northerner could pay allegiance to the traditional notion of manly and martial honor. By the eve of the Civil War, Dahlgren, age fifty-two, had risen from the rank of midshipman to that of commander in the U.S. Navy. He had already achieved fame for perfecting the smoothbore naval cannon that bears his name, and he would go on to fight for the Union against the Confederate cause adopted by his younger brother, Charles. John Dahlgren "tried to maintain the views of a Union moderate who was willing to make concessions and compromises in order to preserve the Union," writing on 18 December 1860, "In the North there is no personal servitude, but there is the Slavery of the classes, so well understood that when a man rises from it, so much is made of it, as when copper approaches the White level. But however this may be, what right has the Northern man to infringe on the [slave's] admitted duty to the White man in order to discharge a factitious and gratuitous duty to the Negro? Let him see the starving laborers in Kansas and elsewhere at hand." Dahlgren thus expressed the sort of hostility to radical abolitionism that seems to have characterized the overwhelming majority of people in the free states. As a young naval officer, he had been involved in more than one affair of honor. In the early 1830s, Lieutenant Dahlgren felt he had been slighted when he failed to receive an invitation to a supper on board the *Cumberland*. Confronting the responsible officer to express his grievance, Dahlgren expected "a mortal quarrel"; instead, the officer apologized and offered a satisfactory explanation for the oversight. Dahlgren explained the affair to his family by employing the sorts of feelings and logic that had motivated self-consciously honorable men for centuries: "I know you would not have me tamely to submit to an insult, wherever I might be compelled to appeal for redress. What indeed can be so degraded as a man without courage, unless it be a woman without virtue."[26] Dahlgren's outlook resembled that of a medieval Irish "prophecy of doom" that "foretold social collapse into a world of 'women without modesty, men without valour.'"[27] Antebellum American culture, like that of Europe during the Middle Ages, denied personal honor to both cowardly men and promiscuous women.

During the secession crisis, Republicans did not want to appear cowardly and felt that their party would be degraded and dishonored by backing down on the issue of slavery in the territories before the challenge of disunionist threats. As president-elect, Lincoln expressed concern about issuing statements to "quiet alarm" in the South that might communicate "an appearance of weakness." He very much wanted to avoid any intimation that he possessed "the character of timidity and cowardice," for he understood that such a reputation pointed to degradation. A few months later, when the Confederacy's bombardment of Fort Sumter spurred the new president's call for volunteer soldiers, Lincoln described this summons to arms as an "effort to maintain the honor, the integrity, and the existence of our National Union," recalling the sentiments expressed by Morris.[28] Indeed, at the end of the century, a prominent Massachusetts Republican, Senator Henry Cabot Lodge, invoked much the same understanding of honor when advocating U.S. annexation of the Philippines after the Spanish-American War. He told anti-imperialist Democrats, "I do not shrink from intrusting . . . the fate and fortune" of the Filipinos "to the government which the American public create and sustain": "To the Americans and their government I am ready to entrust my life, my liberty, my honor, and, what is far dearer to me than anything personal to myself, the life and liberty of my children and children's grandchildren."[29]

Well before Fort Sumter, many northerners had lauded resistance to southern demands and insults, urging retaliation against aggression and violence perpetrated by the Slave Power as a form of honorable manliness. In response to Brooks's 1856 caning of Sumner and to horrific stories of proslavery violence coming out of Bleeding Kansas, mainstream Christians increasingly "began to see the honor and necessity of fighting back in the face of unrepentant lawlessness."[30] In late 1860, elitist New Yorker George Templeton Strong, despite his conservative dislike of radical agitators in both regions and his commitment to the Union, determined that he would not vote for the oil-on-the-waters Constitutional Unionist John Bell and would instead cast his ballot for Lincoln. At the end of October, Strong wrote in his diary, "Republicans refuse to believe secession possible (in which I think they are wrong). Bisection is disaster and degradation, but if the only alternative is everlasting submission to the South, it must come soon, and why should it not come now?" A few days later, Strong wrote, "Think I will vote the Republican ticket next Tuesday. One vote is insignificant, but I want to be able to remember that I voted right at this grave crisis. The North must assert its rights, now, and take the consequences," even if they included secession and civil war. Like the majority of northerners, Strong had come to believe that "submission to the South" involved a kind of degradation and dishonor. Citizens in the free states could not maintain their personal, regional, and national honor if, in the words of a Democratic newspaper in Iowa, they appeared to be among "the pimps and hirelings" of "the Slave Propagandists," like President Buchanan and his associates.[31]

Degradation, whether personal, political, or both, could come from many sources in antebellum America. For example, for devout Christian evangelicals, it could accompany the oppressive weight of unrepentant sinfulness, which they might associate with envy, intoxication, lust, or slaveholding. (The fact that slaveholding often involved white male lust exploiting enslaved black females made the peculiar institution all the more objectionable.) The correction and removal of sin could reverse the process and restore honor, as explained in a sermon on a passage from the New Testament Epistle of Hebrews (9:28: "Christ was offered to bear the sins of many") preached in New Jersey and Virginia during the 1820s. Presbyterian pastor William Jessup Armstrong of Richmond explained that sin involved transgression against God's law: "When a law is transgressed, its honor is stained, its authority is destroyed." However, punishment for sin "averts the consequences, . . . magnifies the law, and makes it honorable." If "the offering of Christ" constituted "a real and efficacious atonement for sin," concludes one historian of religion, then the crucifixion of Jesus becomes "the supreme exhibition of honor in human history."[32] Historians have no way of knowing how many Americans in either the 1820s or the 1850s understood the Christian Gospel in these terms, but scholars do know that Lincoln was not among them. During the mid-1850s, he opposed what he termed the "degeneracy" of the Know-Nothings and their anti-Catholic nativism because it involved the degradation of white people. "How can any one who abhors the oppression of negroes," queried Lincoln, "be in favor of degrading classes of white people?" In 1860, however, Lincoln welcomed former Know-Nothings into the Republican Party; the danger of political nativism had waned as the aggressions of the Slave Power had waxed, and northern Know-Nothings tended strongly to oppose slavery's geographic expansion. In the aftermath of the Kansas-Nebraska Act, Lincoln became more and more concerned about the kind of degradation that white families from the free states would experience from competition with slave labor in the territories. In New Haven, Connecticut, in March 1860, Lincoln declared that the Republican Party's commitment to free-soil territories would assure white northerners moving west that "you may not be degraded, not have your family corrupted by forced rivalry with negro slaves." Lincoln believed that by corrupting and degrading those who did hard labor, territorial competition for land and prosperity between nonslaveholding northerners and slaveholding southerners would disadvantage free white settlers. Had Indiana and Illinois been open to slavery during the Lincoln's youth, he implied, his rise to an honorable position would have been more problematic.

In response to the Supreme Court's 1857 *Dred Scott* ruling, Lincoln suggested that the next step on the Slave Power's agenda was to make slavery a national institution, perhaps by arranging for the federal judiciary to rule that no state had a constitutional right to deny legal protection to a slaveholder's human property. During the Lincoln-Douglas debates, the Republican candidate declared that both his senatorial opponent and President Buchanan were parties to some kind of proslavery conspiracy to nationalize the South's peculiar institution. Speaking in Carlinville, Illinois, on 31 August 1858, Lincoln declared that if they succeeded, "negro equality will be abundant, as every white laborer will have occasion to regret when he is elbowed from his plow or his anvil by slave niggers."[33] He clearly knew that his audience would see this prospect as degrading and dishonorable, much as they viewed northern submission to Slave Power demands and machinations.

To be personally degraded, Lincoln believed, was to lack both the prospect of advancement and an honorable reputation. Many poorer residents in the free states embraced this perspective on the connection between opportunities for upward social mobility and the accessibility of honor. During Lincoln's early 1860 speaking tour of the Northeast, which included his address in New Haven and contributed mightily to his capturing the Republican nomination in May, he paid a visit to a charity mission at Manhattan's Five Points House of Industry, which offered a home and education to more than 100 "abandoned and abused" boys in return for their "honest toil." Some three years later, after issuing the Emancipation Proclamation, President Lincoln received a letter signed by 118 boys at the mission who remembered that he had told them that "the way was open to every boy present, if honest, industrious, and [persevering], to the attainment of a high and honorable position."[34]

Free northerners and southerners alike often associated degradation with submission and the condition of slaves in general and black slaves in particular.[35] Of course, the importance and ubiquity of African American slavery in most of the South accentuated and intensified white southerners' anxiety and fear of becoming metaphorical slaves and thereby dishonored. As historians James Oakes and Ariela Gross have argued, "The concern for honor appears to be most pronounced in those societies where the gulf separating the upper from the lower class is widest." The Old South, with its glorification of individual freedom among members of a white ruling race lording over an underclass of black slaves, had a distinctly dishonored class.[36] Southern freemen thus responded with great fear and even rage to dire warnings about the consequences of the election of a Black Republican president. In addition to lowering whites to a condition of political and social equality with degraded black slaves, the Black Republicans were often perceived as intending to elevate ignorant African American males to the status of freedmen, where they could serve as tools of northern political ambition.

Many southerners sought to portray slaves as infantile inferiors requiring patriarchal guidance and discipline while doing their duty. Yet slaveholders also recognized that some slaves had the capacity for forceful resistance to the degradation of chattel bondage and understood that the slaves' potential for violent self-assertion required constant vigilance on the part of manly free males. On 12 November 1860, Thomas R. R. Cobb declared before a convention of Georgians meeting in the state capital, Milledgeville, "Our slaves are the most happy and contented, best fed and best clothed and best paid laboring population in the world, and I would add, also, the *most faithful* and least feared. But a discontented few here and there, will become the incendiary or the poisoner, when instigated by the unscrupulous emissaries of Northern Abolitionists, and you and I cannot say but that your home or your family may be the first to greet your returning footsteps in ashes or in death.—What has given impulse to these fears, and aid and comfort to those outbreaks now, but the success of the Black Republicans—the election of Abraham Lincoln."[37] Given this logic, white southerners mistakenly believed that the bloodiest slave rebellion in the antebellum United States, Nat Turner's 1831 rebellion in Southside Virginia, would never have erupted without outside meddling from irresponsible abolitionist editor William Lloyd Garrison and his Boston newspaper, *The Liberator*.[38] Yet southern whites also correctly understood that some male slaves "had chosen violent methods to defend their honor and rights as husbands or members of families," but this recognition only elevated their anxieties. One legal historian has concluded, "A Roman epigram— 'As many slaves, so many enemies'—illuminates the central feature of what Orlando Patterson has called the political psychology of slavery."[39]

For white southerners, slavery was inseparable from "regional identity, and it helped define southern masculinity and perpetuate honor."[40] Honorable masculinity was clearly incompatible with submission to tyranny and exploitation, the fate of degraded slaves, whether the kind of enslavement feared be literal chattel bondage or figurative political enslavement. Hence, the prospect of a president unabashedly hostile to the peculiar institution appeared both dangerous and dishonorable. One recent scholar has insisted that the "fundamental of southern identity" and therefore "the official cause of secession" was "not fears of white slavery, or fears of political slavery in a nebulous republican cosmology," but simply slavery as an antidemocratic system of property rights and racial control.[41] Yet editors and politicians often framed the issue in terms that appealed to white male perceptions of themselves as independent and honorable freemen and citizens in a society where the day-to-day reality of slavery provided constant reminders of what it meant to be degraded and dishonored. In the words of a Georgia newspaper that had supported Douglas in the 1860 election, "The South will never submit to such humiliation and degradation as the inauguration of Abraham Lincoln."

Frederick Douglass, the former Maryland slave become prominent black abolitionist, author, and lecturer, believed well before the Civil War that black men must acquire "an attitude of manly independence" to achieve freedom, respect, and honor. Honorable achievement and status required literacy and knowledge as well as the sort of physical self-assertion the young Douglass demonstrated in his fight with slave breaker Edward Covey. After the war began, Douglass insisted that recruiting black soldiers for service in the U.S. Army would not only bolster the Union war effort but also allow black males to demonstrate their capacity for manliness, honor, and citizenship. "The colored man only waits for honorable admission into the service of the country—They know that [those] who would be free, themselves must strike the first blow." In February 1863, after the Emancipation Proclamation had cleared the path to black military service, Douglass proclaimed that African American soldiers would "rise in one bound from social degradation to the place of common equality with the other varieties of men."[42] That November, Lincoln seems to have acknowledged, albeit indirectly, the validity of Douglass's argument. Recovering from a bout with smallpox about a week before delivering the Gettysburg Address, Lincoln sent a message to be read aloud in New York City: "Honor to the Soldier, and Sailor everywhere, who bravely bears his country's cause. Honor also to the citizen who cares for his brother in the field, and serves as best he can, the same cause—honor to him, only less than to him, who braves for the common good, the storms of heaven and the storms of battle."[43]

By 1865, black men came to constitute some 10 percent of the Union Army and about 20 percent of U.S. Navy personnel. Nevertheless, for many decades following the conclusion of Reconstruction in the 1870s, most white northerners and southerners discarded and repressed the nation's historical memory of the contributions made by African American sailors and soldiers. Doing so while insisting that occasional antebellum slave rebellions could be attributed simply to the inflammatory encouragement provided by radical and irresponsible abolitionists enabled the denial of any substantive African American claim to the kind of honor and privilege claimed by Americans of European ancestry.[44]

Douglass's speeches and essays clearly reflected the "male values of the Victorian Age."[45] In other words, an honorable gentleman combined independent and courageous manliness with a virtuous moral character. Hence Douglass described one slaveholder, William Freeland, "though not rich," as "what may be called a well-bred southern gentleman." Although he "shared many of the vices of his class," Freeland "seemed alive to the sentiment of honor," for he possessed "some sense of justice, and some feelings of humanity." Freeland stood far superior to another master, Thomas Auld, who showed himself "destitute of every element of character commanding respect."[46]

Douglass's praise of Freeland illustrates the cultural power in mid-nineteenth-century America and Britain of the Victorian ideal of the honorable, ethical, and usually Christian gentleman. The impact of this more bourgeois ideal on the evolving understanding of honor in antebellum America is evident in Lincoln's ultimate decision to wed Todd in 1842, just as the aborted duel with Shields demonstrated his retention of the traditional conviction that his personal honor required a public reputation for courageous manliness. As of 1840, Springfield society believed that Lincoln and Todd were a couple, concludes biographer Catherine Clinton, but they broke up "sometime shortly before or after New Year's Day, 1841." It is possible that Lincoln "became smitten" with the alluring Matilda Edwards (the niece of Mary's brother-in-law, Ninian Edwards), as did the future president's best friend, Joshua Speed. Neither Lincoln nor Speed won Matilda Edwards's affections, Speed called Lincoln a coward for trying to break off his engagement to Todd, and a melancholic Lincoln became temporarily estranged from both Todd and Speed. For two years, Lincoln could not escape the feeling that personal honor dictated that he stand by his earlier promise to wed. In November 1842, he and Todd suddenly pronounced their marriage vows in the parlor of Ninian Edwards's home. To regain and retain what he termed "the only, or at least the chief, gem of my character," Lincoln told Speed, "I must regain my confidence in my own ability to keep my resolves when they are made."[47]

Just as much as Jefferson Davis, Lincoln believed that the maintenance of personal honor required a public reputation for both courageous manliness and ethical excellence—what Douglass termed "character commanding respect." These dual standards and the tension between them extend far back in time, at least back to the thinking of classical Greco-Roman Stoics. A good premodern example of this tension within the understanding of what constitutes honorable conduct and character is evident in the evolution of chivalry in medieval France. Until the late twelfth century, "the Old French term *chevalerie* was used specifically to describe the warrior attributes of armed men on horseback, with no moral or social overtones." However, Stoic literature, with its emphasis on the virtues of "ethics, self-discipline, and refined social interactions," remained an important part of the classical education of medieval bishops, first at imperial and royal courts in the tenth century, where "these virtues received a religious imprint before spreading to bishops and priests everywhere" in Latin or Western Christendom. During the twelfth and thirteenth centuries, educated clerics, in tandem with authors of fictional romances, did much to spread ideals of Christianized Stoicism among young knights in training at French and German courts. Many of these ideals became incorporated into something known as courtliness. Because the model of chivalric and courtly honor prescribed a blend of warlike, Christian, and decorous behaviors, "the most chivalrous hero" could find himself "trapped between conflicting ideals." In short, honor among men "could take conflicting forms."[48]

Across the English Channel, the chivalric ethos reached full bloom during the fourteenth and fifteenth centuries. The inevitable tension within the notion of chivalric honor between the requirements of ethical and martial prowess was highlighted in the charges brought in Parliament against the Duke of Somerset in 1465: he had shown himself deficient in the "very gentleness and the noble honour that ought to be grounded in every gentleman." During the previous century, King Edward III had been portrayed as "the epitome of chivalry and prowess" by the notable French chronicler Jean Froissart, part of the entourage around Edward's French queen, Philippa of Hainault. In 1348, Edward officially established "the most exclusive club of chivalry and loyalty to the Crown—the Order of the Garter," which became England's most prestigious honor group. As English medievalist Miri Rubin points out, "The fellowship of the Garter was further reinforced by the Arthurian imagery of the round table revived and explored by Edward and his court."[49] The cultural power of legends and imagery surrounding King Arthur and his Knights of the Round Table was reinforced in the nineteenth-century Anglophone world by a number of romantic writers, first and foremost Sir Walter Scott in his historical novels.

For men, the primitive or primal call for chivalric knights to exact violent revenge retained much of its power for many centuries. However, vengeful violence, in Bowman's words, has "never quite sat easily with Christianity," because the religion includes prominent admonitions in favor of "humility and turning the other cheek." Although traditional notions of male honor included viewing females as the property of men, Christianity has also seen females as divinely created human beings, though carrying the biological curse of original sin and therefore generally consigned by God and nature to subordinate gender roles. Largely because medieval Western society experienced so much brutal violence and warfare, traditional notions of male and female honor became incorporated into the Christian ideal of chivalry. Insofar as this notion of chivalry required that upper-class men pay an exaggerated respect to upper-class womanhood, chivalry appears to be a distinctively Western notion. Christianized culture in the West has also produced "a long history of skepticism" about more "primitive" and traditional forms of honor, a skepticism that seems "unique in honor's realm."

The nineteenth-century transatlantic and Anglo-American world seems to have experienced a transformation analogous to though different from that which yielded the medieval notion of chivalry. This later cultural transformation created the model of the Victorian, Christian, honorable gentleman. English and American culture witnessed a widespread and powerful cultural impetus to redefine male honor further away from the old-fashioned martial values of European aristocracies and toward a more modern idea of virtue that Bowman labels both bourgeois and feminized: bourgeois in the sense of complementing commerce, finance, and industry, feminized in the sense of affirming a blend of sensitivity, modesty, and religiosity. Victorian England paid homage to the ideal notion that honor "included a sincere but not ostentatious Christian piety and was meant as a useful and living code of manners and conduct for the rising middle classes"—at least for those seeking admission to the genteel elite of ladies and gentlemen.[50]

In the United States, this Victorian ideal became superimposed on and blended with what the Declaration of Independence's authors and signers had identified as their "sacred honor." Such gendered, male honor retained its importance in antebellum public life in the basic sense that it offered a positive and prestigious reputation for that amalgam of courage, loyalty to one's peer group, and civic commitment that the Founding Fathers suggested was essential to durable republican government. As Samuel Haber argues, honor remained linked to the authority and power of traditional gentlemen (fundamentally those who did not have to do hard manual labor for a living) even as evangelical Great Awakenings imbued it with "a peculiar stoical and Calvinistic Christianity." In a republic, where independent citizens must do without the stabilizing though corrupting leadership of monarchy and nobility, the honorable ideal of civic virtue affirmed a citizen's disciplined, dutiful willingness, when required, to put the common good, the interests and well-being of the republican commonwealth, ahead of his personal and familial interests. (Significantly, the word "virtue" derives from a Latin noun, *virtus*, meaning "both physical strength and moral uprightness.")[51] The reward for such honorable devotion to good government would be the laurels of fame—that is, remembrance by subsequent generations for one's selfless and perhaps self-sacrificial commitment to the community. Of course, the laurels of fame could not be claimed by someone lacking an honorable reputation. Joanne Freeman, a careful student of politics in the early U.S. republic, has concluded that "a man of honor was defined by the respect that he received in public. Imagine, then, the impact of public disrespect. It struck at a man's honor and reduced him as a man." Such a man lost his metaphorical face. Wyatt-Brown makes much the same point when he emphasizes honor's "essentially defensive posture," its "pervasive fear of public humiliation" or shame.[52]

As antebellum America became increasingly democratic among and for white males, the process of political democratization was accompanied by an analogous cultural process that can be called (after the logic of Max Weber) the social democratization of gentility and honor. The descriptive phrase "honorable gentleman" in polite discourse could thus become synonymous with any free man. At the same time, manliness remained the preeminent trait of the honorable gentleman and chastity that of the honorable lady in the United States. As had been true centuries earlier for aristocratic nobles in medieval Europe, honor dictated "courage and martial prowess for lay men [as opposed to ordained priests], sexual modesty and careful household management for women." Yet the truly and thoroughly honorable gentleman in antebellum America needed also to maintain certain ethical standards. In Greenberg's vocabulary, genuine gentlemen should know when and how some situations required them to behave as "martial men" while other circumstances dictated behavior as "restrained men."[53]

The injunction to act as restrained men particularly referred to the honorable gentleman's relations with women, as shown in a February 1860 sermon by Henry Ward Beecher, the pastor of Brooklyn's Congregational Plymouth Church and perhaps the most visible paragon of Victorian, genteel, and Protestant Christianity in the free states. In "The Seducer," Beecher highlighted the sort of ethical behavior toward women expected from truly honorable men, addressing the issue of a publicly prominent man who took sexual advantage of an innocent and trusting female, "bewitched her noblest affections to become the suicides of her virtue," and thereby betrayed her honor. The preacher then illustrated how the concept of masculine honor was being reconfigured to encompass both a celebrated reputation and upright Victorian morality. In public, the selfish seducer "is fondled, courted, passed from honor to honor." Yet he had betrayed his trusting victim "without one pretense of honor—by lies; by a devilish jugglery of fraud; by blinding the eye, confusing the conscience, misleading the judgment." However, Beecher noted, the traditional double standard of sexual activity for men and women still retained much of its power. While "the infernal destroyer" of the female victim held on to his public reputation, hers became "crushed and mangled under the infuriated tramp of public indignation."[54]

As it bloomed in the Old South, the ideal of the honorable Christian gentleman entailed attempts to render relations between masters and slaves more Christian, familial, and humane even as it emphasized that exaggerated respect be paid to white women in a Negrophobic slave society. The ideal of Christian gentility and honor also elicited substantial criticism. As Ayers has concluded, "The most powerful critique" of the duelist's code of honor "came from within the South itself," largely as a consequence of the powerful influence of evangelical Protestantism.[55] Jefferson Davis's faith does not appear to have been evangelical, yet when the future president of the Confederacy emerged onto the public stage in the 1840s as a Mississippi planter-politician, he hardly expressed strong endorsement of dueling as the proper way to settle disputes among genuine gentlemen. In 1844, a year when Davis made numerous speeches in favor of annexing Texas to the Union and on behalf of the presidential candidacy of a Tennessee slaveholding Democrat, James Knox Polk, Davis also addressed the Mississippi Anti-Dueling Society in Vicksburg in the aftermath of the deaths by dueling of three Vicksburg newspaper editors. Only a minority at the meeting argued that the code duello still served to protect "gentlemen from gross abuse." The majority resolved to "sustain any person who refused a challenge, asserting that to give or accept a challenge was not a proof of courage." Davis presented more nuanced substitute resolutions, one of which read, "Resolved, That dueling, however irrational and immoral, can only be suppressed by the progress of intelligence, morality, and good breeding; Therefore, as the nearest approximation to the end we all desire, that the effort be made to prevent, unnecessarily, a resort to deadly weapons, and to regulate such a resort when it cannot be prevented by principles of fairness and as far as may be equality between the combatants."[56] Although Davis became involved in several affairs of honor, none led to a duel. And just as he was hardly a resolute advocate of dueling, so he would later be far from a fire-eating secessionist.

Both Jefferson Davis in Mississippi and Charlie Jones in Georgia clearly propounded southern versions of the Victorian ideal gentleman. This ideal, more clearly than that of medieval chivalry, envisioned an honorable gentleman who combined the antiviolent tendencies of Christianity with the physical courage of independent manliness. The Victorian ideal also enabled the protean notion of honor to evolve in harmony with emerging democratic practices and sensibilities, although they retained pronounced racial as well as gendered limitations. This form of honor could also meld with one's honorable success at a respectable vocation and among businessmen "became inseparable from the prescriptions of Christian virtue except for a special emphasis on trustworthiness in commercial dealings." The Victorians' amended version of traditional aristocratic and gentlemanly honor, argues James Bowman, helped to preserve much of the "traditional honor culture" into World War I. After 1918, the lessons of the war could include the discrediting of traditional martial honor and the sorts of masculinity (and femininity as well) that had prized it. During the twentieth century, many Americans and Europeans arrived "almost at the other extreme, where there is only morality and law for us to rely on and the key honor culture is despised as an offense to individual autonomy and moral progressivism." As the twentieth century progressed, the sort of honor that had valued modesty and chastity in women could come to value "sexual authenticity, undaunted by social convention."[57] New models of masculine and feminine behavior emerged and evolved. Honorable women could vote and have vocational ambitions, and honorable men could prove their mettle in ways that did not require physical courage and prowess, though such attributes have remained objects of respectful admiration. The traditional virtue of manly and martial honor survives today in a modified, nonlethal form in competitive sports, and it becomes more visible and powerful at times when people perceive their survival as at risk from some sort of unreasonable hostility or frightful savagery.

Middle-class and elite women in the South and North alike lived in an American version of Victorian culture imbued with a "cult of domesticity" that posited highly gendered understandings of honor. The cult of domesticity affirmed that women's natures impelled them to seek fulfillment, at the same time genuine and respectable, in a married household nurturing children and providing a domestic haven for their male providers, who became stressed and compromised by their necessary labors in the competitive work and political worlds. Indeed, one historian of antebellum politics has observed that the "public performance" inherent in partisan politics not only reflected but also "reinforced gendered virtues of manliness, honor, and character at a time when women lacked the vote."[58] Of course, educated women in both regions might accept woman's public subordination to men but rail privately at the restrictions on their activities. In April 1852 in East Texas, nineteen-year-old Lizzie Scott, from a well-to-do slaveholding family and about to become the bride of a man who had read law with her father, confided to her diary that "honors" "has been the ruling passion of my life, in all things save love. . . . Heaven in her wisdom has placed insurmountable barriers between me and my individual ambition. I can never gain worldly honors. Fame can never be mine. I am a *woman*! a woman. I can hardly teach my heart to be content with my lot."[59] Society presumed that genteel ladies would have slaves or servants to perform menial household work and gentlemen to provide protection and support. Because women's "female natures" gave them higher moral and aesthetic standards than men possessed, women were called to instill in their children and foster in men the ethical principles they needed to become productive and responsible adults. As the moral guardians and sheet anchors of a republican and increasingly democratic society, ladies could and did exert powerful political influence—though not as voters, since suffrage was a male prerogative. Women could and should, however, use their power over men to influence the voters' thoughts and actions with the goal of encouraging greater courage, decorum, piety, and social responsibility.[60] Elizabeth Barrett Browning effectively played this role in a powerful pro-Union letter that appeared in the *New York Independent* on 10 March 1861. She described her "serious fear" during the sectional crisis as that "of reconciliation and peace at the expense of a deadly compromise of principle. Nothing will destroy the republic but what corrupts its conscience and disturbs its frame—for the stain upon the honor must come off upon the flag." According to historian Allan Nevins, Browning's expression of "the tremendous sentimental and moral values attached to the Union" echoed that of the newly inaugurated president.[61]

Antebellum America was overwhelmingly patriarchal in that almost all of its free population assumed that men should dominate public life. Of course, traditional gendered notions of the honorable male's manliness and the honorable female's chastity presupposed a patriarchal culture and society. So, too, did the nineteenth-century cult of domesticity. Yet more people in the free states than in the slave states were willing to voice open challenges to both black bondage and women's subordination to men. Relatively few southern women and men voiced the sort of antiestablishment sentiments expressed by South Carolina's Sarah and Angelina Grimké or Basil Armstrong Thomasson of North Carolina. The Grimké sisters left their prominent Charleston slaveholding family and the Episcopalian Church to move north as Quakers and become both abolitionists and advocates of woman's rights. Sarah's *An Epistle to the Clergy of the Southern States* (1836) declared that "the slaveholding spirit . . . grants to man the privilege of sinning with impunity," in direct contradiction to "the gospel of Jesus Christ, which proclaims LIBERTY TO THE CAPTIVE." In March 1838, after Angelina had made an antislavery address that "occupied about 2 hours and a half in delivery," a newspaper opined that "she exhibited considerable talent for a female, as an orator; appeared not at all abashed in exhibiting herself in a position so unsuitable to her sex, totally disregarding the doctrine of St. Paul, who says 'Is it not a shame for a woman to speak in public?'"[62]

Thomasson was a devout Methodist nonslaveholding farmer. On 27 February 1854, after cutting "coal wood in the forenoon" and "haul[ing] in the afternoon," he engaged in "a regular chat to night, about women's work, etc." The discussion caused him to muse, "There are more slaves in the U.S. than most of us are aware of. Freedom is a great thing, but women can't be allowed to enjoy it; they are slaves to men & to fashion, but the time is coming when they will be free; may that time come quickly. Amen." Two years later, contemplating the Fourth of July, he wrote, "Great day throughout the U.S. in general—the people celebrating the Declaration of Independence—and a joyful time on our farm as to day we finished plowing our crop. May the people of the U.S. long remain free and independent—if, indeed, they are free—, and may our crop flourish and bring forth abundant harvest. Amen."[63]

Yeoman farmers such as Thomasson, freethinkers on the subjects of both human bondage and gender relations, seem hard to find in the Old South. Focusing on low country South Carolina, Stephanie McCurry argues that a free man without slaves or servants to work his land still qualified as the master of a small world by maintaining his "natural" authority over the dependent members of his household, especially his wife. It may be hyperbolic to posit that "the analogy of marriage and slavery lay at the very center of political discourse in the Atlantic world in the nineteenth century," yet most free southerners, along with many northerners, would have agreed with the argument presented in "Negro-Mania," written by South Carolinian Louisa McCord and published by *DeBow's Review* in 1852. The essay argued that the "Enfranchisement of Woman" was "but a piece with negro emancipation": both challenged "the beautiful order of God's developed thought in creation." In fact, "God has implanted in the white races, for their own preservation and for the perfecting of their high destiny, the strong antagonistic feeling of race which holds them aloof in their purity." McCord was "someone known to be a good wife and mother," according to one scholar, "and an excellent plantation mistress." Two other authors have evaluated her as "the most intellectually influential female author in the Old South, and the only woman in antebellum America to write extensively about political economy and social theory."[64]

McCord spoke for the overwhelming majority of southerners as well as many northerners who regretted that free-labor societies produced so many fanatics and ultras, especially abolitionists and what the twentieth century would come to call feminists. Northern society thus could appear to foment frightful and interrelated challenges to "natural" relations of authority and hierarchy in the slave South. Such northern apostasy was clearly evidenced in the 1848 meeting of woman's rights agitators at Seneca Falls, New York, where black and white abolitionists of both genders, including white suffragist Elizabeth Cady Stanton, a married Quaker, and Frederick Douglass, were welcomed. Two years later, the town of Cazenovia, New York, hosted a more obscure gathering of abolitionists hostile to the new Fugitive Slave Law at which Douglass was photographed next to a white woman. Such scenes could irritate and even infuriate white southerners.[65]

According to McCurry, during the secession crisis, nonslaveholding yeomen acted as "freemen in a world of dependents," sharing in the political symbolism of the moment, "in a definition of manhood rooted in the inviolability of the household, the command of dependents, and the public prerogatives manhood conferred."[66] Such assumptions about the value of male authority and independence could easily join hands with a powerful sense of duty to family and community, feeding powerful resentments against self-righteous outsiders interfering in local affairs. In turn, these ideas and feelings inflamed white southerners against the degrading and despotic military "coercion" they faced.

Slavery exacerbated the southern conviction that adult white men should dominate their households—both their immediate families and what slaveholders considered the dependent "servants" of their extended or household families. The slaveholding farmers of the Old South, explain Elizabeth Fox-Genovese and Eugene D. Genovese, "rooted the defense of their privilege in a vision of independent rural property ownership—of rural households. . . . To be happy meant to live independently, surrounded by family, on land that you (or your servants) cultivated and from which you drew the core of your sustenance."[67] Such visions also animated many northerners, yet in the South, labor on the farm and in the household was provided by human chattel who represented to their owner/employers both substantial capital investments and a suspect race. Northern visions of landed independence infrequently included black and enslaved laborers, although many free state natives moved to the slave states in search of fortune and perhaps fame.

One constant in the complex and evolving story of honor is the feeling or assumption that maintaining the appearance of significant power, control, and dignity was necessary. Honorable independence and dignity convey high status, while their absence conveys low status and degeneracy or shame. The Old South was a slave society in which slaves were always black, while the white population lived according to strongly gendered norms that prescribed very different roles for men and women. As in the free states, only white males could vote and hold political office. Indeed, unpropertied white males in the various slave states had received the right to vote only recently: universal white male suffrage did not come to Mississippi until the early 1830s and did not reach Virginia for two decades longer. Since slaves constituted valuable property and only a quarter of southern whites belonged to slaveholding families in 1860, the Old South blended high levels of social stratification based on both racial and socioeconomic hierarchies while the democratic political culture glorified egalitarian white manliness. As a result, "worship of the two-headed god Liberty-Honor permeated the white social order."[68]

Thus, whites in the Old South had a powerful preoccupation with both personal and regional honor at the same time that they bore strong racial prejudices and lived in a racially bifurcated society that encompassed 95 percent of the U.S. black population. Social and economic stratification among whites involved a predominantly slaveholding as well as masculine elite. Its members and aspirants to membership often demonstrated a touchy determination to maintain in the public eye their manly authority, respect, and honor as members of the elite and therefore as gentlemen. "The very debasement of the slave added much to the master's honor," explains Wyatt-Brown, "since the latter's claim to self-sufficiency rested upon the prestige, power, and wealth that accrued from the benefits of others."[69] The Old South's enduring reputation for violence, including the persistence of the "genteel" duel, seems to have reflected two fundamental historical realities: first, the fact that the region's peculiar institution and the white social order that overlay it became the target of increasingly harsh and moralistic attacks from northern opponents of slavery; second, the reality that physical violence, or the threat of it, was central to the peculiar institution as a system of both labor discipline and racial control.

Almost all whites in the Old South—rich and poor, male and female—fervently believed that the maintenance of their superior power and authority over blacks was essential to their gendered and racial understandings of honor and dignity. Since the reputation and character of an honorable man and his family should and could not be attacked with impunity, antislavery criticism of black bondage and of slavery's negative impact on the behavior and virtue of slaveholders obviously constituted an insult to which men of honor must respond. The prince of the Palmetto State, John C. Calhoun, exemplified this sensitivity in 1837, when he responded indignantly before the U.S. Senate to abolitionist petitions in which slavery "is pronounced to be sinful and odious, in the sight of God and man." In reply, Calhoun took the "higher ground," proclaiming that "the relation now existing in the slaveholding states" between the black and white races was "a good—a positive good. I feel myself called upon to speak freely upon the subject where the honor and interests of those I represent are involved." In a self-conscious and prideful republican polity such as that of the antebellum United States, reputable southerners had to counter insulting criticism of the South with demands for respect, dignity, and honor from citizens in the free states.[70] Some northern observers during the secession crisis empathized with white southerners' perception that their regional as well as personal honor within the American republic stood in the balance. In late February 1861, the politically independent *Philadelphia Inquirer* recognized and understood the southern insistence on "the point of honor, or abstract right, or equal right or chance."[71]

Implicit and sometimes explicit in white southerners' repeated use of the term "degradation" were fiery racial prejudices and fears. These fears were stoked by the palpable economic fact that slaves provided much of the propertied foundation for their owners' honorable independence, dignity, and gentility. At the same time, these chattel slaves were clearly identified in white minds and imaginations with members of a dark-skinned, troublesome, degraded, and dishonorable race. In Wyatt-Brown's words, "The most psychologically powerful expression of Southern honor was the sexual dread of black blood in a white womb. In the patriarchal imagination, no humiliation was greater."[72] Many northerners sympathized with such concerns. In the fall of 1860, prominent New York attorney Samuel Tilden, a Democrat, came out of retirement to help orchestrate electoral fusion among the three anti-Republican groups: hard-shell Democrats supporting John C. Breckinridge, soft-shell Democrats backing Stephen A. Douglas, and Constitutional Unionist supporters of John Bell. Although these fusion efforts proved futile, Tilden issued repeated spoken and printed warnings about free southerners' genuine fears of the prospect of northern voters endorsing the Republicans' platform of "moral coercion." The white South would view Lincoln's election as "a shock" to slavery's security and thereby associate it "with a pervading sense of danger to the life of every human being and the honor of every woman."[73]

Antebellum residents of the Old South repeatedly expressed patriarchal public fears about sexual violence by male slaves against white women, although few such incidents were recorded. These anxieties were much more pervasive in the slave states than in the free states as a consequence both of the South's far larger African American population and of the coercive power that white males exerted over male and female black slaves. Southern white women could feel dishonored and shamed if male relations, especially husbands or sons, engaged in sexual relations with African American women, resulting in the perceived degeneracy of "amalgamation." (The term "miscegenation" did not surface until the Civil War years.)[74]

Tryphena Blanche Holder Fox, a well-educated native of Massachusetts who moved south, married, and became a slave mistress from 1856 to 1861, offers a particularly powerful illustration not only of a woman's acceptance of patriarchy but also of her distaste for amalgamation. Schooled at Maplewood Young Ladies' Institute, where she knew half a dozen black servants, Holder probably took up teaching in 1851 at Gaylord's Bridge, Connecticut, as about one-fifth of all Massachusetts white women did at some point between the ages of fifteen and sixty. Soon thereafter, she became a plantation tutor, primarily to help support her widowed mother. From 1852 to 1856, Holder tutored the adopted daughter of George Messenger at his plantation, Bacon-ham, in Warren County, Mississippi, not quite twenty-five miles from Vicks-burg. In June 1856, hoping to find "protection from 'the hardships and trials of the world and its selfishness,'" she married David Raymond Fox, the son of a neighboring planter who was also a transplanted Yankee. The thirty-four-year-old Fox, a medical doctor, settled his bride where he had been practicing, in the village of Jesuit Bend, Louisiana, amid the sugar and rice plantations of Plaquemines Parish, about thirty-five miles up the Mississippi River from New Orleans. On 28 June 1857, Tryphena described David "as indeed a hus-band, in every sense of the word and if all who bear the name, were like him there would be far less misery, especially among our own sex, who are natu-rally dependent in disposition & sensitive in mind." She also reported her judgment that "Negroes are so peculiar—so utterly void of white folk's habits of cleanliness and energy!" and her dislike of "those ranting abolitionists" who "will think that *Triphen Holder* has turned out to be a Southern monster." In late March 1861, she expressed total exasperation with a household slave, Maria, who had been repeatedly punished for laziness and for "her fondness for *running out nights*." After Maria had left "all the dirty dishes standing untouched" in the kitchen, Tryphena informed her mother, "I disliked to say anything to her master he whips her so severely, so I punished her again my-self—not very severely & she promised to do better for she had troubled me all the week." Then Maria "took a notion to run away," apparently escaping through an unlocked window with the help of "some men," for "we found their tracks under the window in the mud." Tryphena subsequently "had a good many different reports about [Maria], but all attempts to find her" failed: "So much for her—if there had not been *fifteen*-hundred dollars expended for her, I should not care a picayune, if we never saw her again." Tryphena attributed Maria's flaws to her background: "It is not pleasant to have such a character around one, though most of these mulatresses are such & it is impossible to make anything different out of them."[75]

Especially since the post–World War II movement for African American civil and political equality, the public evidence for ubiquitous sexual relations between blacks and whites has become overwhelming. Yet members of the "ruling race" much preferred that this reality not be acknowledged and ad-dressed in public. Joshua Rothman points to a "growing intolerance" during the 1850s "even for the small amount of malleability" on the subject of black-white sexual relations evident "just a generation earlier." From the time of Jefferson to the late antebellum years, Virginia's citizens responded to "the discovery of sex across the color line with disapprobation but also with equanimity." They usually "recognized that exploitative, familial, commercial, and adulterous sexual liaisons were unavoidable in a multiracial world" that included many shades and mixtures of black and white. Rothman's evidence suggests that "anxieties about interracial sex and the maintenance of racial boundaries" probably became "more pronounced in urban than rural parts of Virginia," a finding that makes sense given the greater opportunities that cities such as Richmond provided for interaction among whites, slaves (including those hired out), and free blacks. The heightened concerns of the 1850s testified to growing white anxieties about rising North-South political tensions, which in turn help explain the sometimes hysterical responses to John Brown's raid. "'Blood' may have been the dominant metaphor of race since the colonial era, but only in the 1850s did some white Virginians begin to make the case that it was the only one." After the Civil War and the end of chattel slavery, laws and behavior evolved to support "the larger goal of white men to maintain their racial superiority in the absence of their literal ownership of black bodies."[76]

The subject of black-white sexuality and responses to it raises questions about human psychology that many historians are ill-equipped or poorly suited to address. White males may have harbored insecurities about the supposed sexual superiority of animalistic black males and may have dealt with these feelings of inferiority by constructing and projecting images of lascivious black females alongside black male beasts lusting after white women. Such images, in turn, may have expressed whites' discomfort over the disjuncture between the Victorian cultural apotheosis of the family unit as the seat of virtue and morality and true happiness and white men's frequent sexual exploitation of slave women. Some educated men in the Old South, familiar with the Greco-Roman classics, doubtless understood, as the ancient Greeks did, that "the body and its appetites" can yield "volatile, chaotic forces." While appreciating "the beauty and pleasure of sexual desire," classical Greeks also saw in sexual passion "a potentially destructive force of nature, a power that, if indulged to excess, could destroy not just the individual soul but the political and social institutions of civilization itself."[76] At least some antebellum Americans recognized that the awesome and terrible power of Eros needed to be controlled and contained, yet unlike the Greeks, Americans tended to view human sexuality through lenses that blended Victorian notions of propriety with admonitions from St. Paul that bodily lusts posed sinful distractions from devotion to God as revealed in Jesus Christ. These antebellum lenses could foster both guilt and shame over illicit sexuality, particularly across the lines of color and bondage.

Thomas Jefferson, a philosophe under the sway of the European Enlightenment, seems to have been too fond of the ancient classics and too skeptical of evangelical Christianity to feel much guilt or shame regarding genteel flirtations and discrete sexual liaisons with alluring women, even those who already had husbands. Since proslavery and/or secessionist ideologues and politicians on the eve of the Civil War often sought to invoke Jefferson's authoritative mantle by selectively citing from his historical record, Jefferson's life becomes an important subject for scholars striving to understand the interplay between public rhetoric and personal behavior among the southern elite. On 24 April 1788, the widowed Jefferson wrote to the flirtatious and married Maria Cosway with his observations regarding a provocative painting he had seen in Düsseldorf, Germany. The painting, by Adriaen van der Werff, offers an imaginative take on the Genesis account of a barren Sarah presenting the Egyptian bondswoman Hagar (alluringly though modestly bare-breasted) to Abraham as the future mother of his son, Ishmael. Jefferson described the painting as "delicious. I would have agreed to have been Abraham though the consequence would have been that I should have been dead five or six thousand years. . . . I am but a son of nature, loving what I see and feel, without being able to give a reason, nor caring much whether there be one."[77]

Most historians of the early U.S. republic now accept that Jefferson engaged in a long-term sexual relationship with Sally Hemings, a quadroon slave at Monticello. A few years before the beginning of their affair in the late 1780s, Jefferson set a highly prejudicial and powerful precedent whose impact reverberated in the United States well beyond the Civil War. Like many Americans of the revolutionary generation, Jefferson had accused the tyrannical British of seeking to reduce the free colonists to a metaphorical condition of degrading political slavery. How, then, could free Americans justify keeping blacks as enslaved chattel? In *Notes on the State of Virginia*, first published in the mid-1780s, Jefferson tortuously attempted to reconcile the contradiction between his 1776 apotheosis of God-given natural rights, "among them life, liberty, and the pursuit of happiness," and his deeply prejudiced "suspicion" that blacks could never be the intellectual and cultural equals of whites. Jefferson's resolution of the contradiction had to take into account the self-evident truth that his version of the good life at Monticello depended on the labors of many enslaved blacks. He insisted that the process of gradual emancipation in Virginia should and would certainly begin at some future date but that it needed to involve the colonization or deportation of the former slaves. "We must await with patience the workings of an overruling providence," he wrote at age forty-three, "and hope that that is preparing deliverance for these our suffering brethren."[78] The Sage of Monticello could never entertain the notion that free blacks and whites might be able to live together on harmonious or even peaceful terms under conditions of civil equality. As George Fredrickson suggests, Jefferson thus made a significant contribution to "the tragic limitation of the white racial imagination" in nineteenth-century America—that is, "its characteristic inability to visualize an egalitarian biracial society."[79] *Notes on Virginia*, which appeared in print well before the Haitian slave rebellion and civil war of the 1790s, testifies to its author's fear that blacks, in rebellious protest against bondage or vengeful retaliation when finally free, would seek violent retribution against whites, thereby provoking a race war. The Haitian experiences seemed to confirm this fear for Jefferson as well as for subsequent generations of antebellum white southerners.

Perhaps even more frightening were obvious if seldom publicized instances of consensual sexual relations across the color line, which would lead to the alleged degeneration of the white race biologically and culturally. The candid and detailed journal kept by Georgia plantation mistress Ella Gertrude Clanton Thomas from 1888 to 1899 illuminates the tortured blend of gendered, racial, and sexual dynamics involved in slaveholding. A devout Methodist, Thomas lived just across the Savannah River from the Palmetto State in Georgia's Richmond County, part of the hinterlands of Augusta. Thomas, like the more famous Mary Chesnut, privately believed that white southern women were "all at heart abolitionists" because of sexual relations between white men and black women. Because black women had the supposed innate advantage of a "tropical, passionate nature," Thomas feared competition between black and white women for white males, who seemed to have a particular weakness for mulatto women. "Like her peers, Thomas placed enormous importance on appearances, particularly on the appearance of self-mastery." Honorable mastery of herself involved viewing her husband as "master," seeing patriarchal hierarchy as natural and right, and agreeing that women should not speak in public or at church. She accepted the prevailing sexual double standard—that is, that women who failed to remain chaste before marriage should be judged more harshly than men. In marriage, she abjured contraception, bearing ten children by the time she turned forty-one.[80]

In 1861, in her late twenties, Thomas became a flag-waving southern nationalist. She hoped that the war would rejuvenate elite southern manhood, grown soft from luxury before the war and thereby further "degraded." In general, the moral fiber of men appeared rather weak. In the spring of 1855, she discovered that her husband, Jefferson, had been engaged in an intimate relationship with a light-skinned woman of African descent who had borne his son, Thomas Turner, in 1853. "The serpent" of a mulatto concubine had entered Thomas's home, and she had a "cross" to bear.[81]

Thomas's "long-standing conviction that slavery had a deleterious effect on the morals of white men" (whether antebellum planters or Union generals) anticipated a recent observation by historian Edward Baptist: "By the nineteenth century, the belief that black women were inherently sexually aggressive, in contrast to allegedly chaste white females, increased their attractiveness to white men, even as white men publicly proclaimed their disgust with African American women and their love for the pure and chaste belle."[82] At the same time, Thomas's assumptions about God's Providence and biblical authority meant that slavery had divine sanction. Not surprisingly, after the Civil War brought both Confederate defeat and the end of slavery, Thomas, like many other white southerners, faced a serious crisis of faith.[83]

4 The Second Party System and Its Legacy

The Careers of John Bell, John C. Breckinridge,

Howell Cobb, Stephen A. Douglas, John Tyler, and

Martin Van Buren

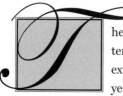he era of the second American party system, which extended from the mid-1820s into the mid-1850s, warrants extended discussion in any analysis of the late antebellum years and the secession crisis. The leaders of the Republican Party, the four principal candidates for national office in 1860, and the organizers of the Confederacy had entered the political arena during the years of Democratic-Whig rivalry. These two national party organizations contained North-South divisions during the 1830s and for most of the 1840s; their subsequent disintegration both reflected and presaged the sharpening sectional tensions that finally disrupted the Union. The legacy of the second party system on the eve of the Civil War included what one scholar has termed "the frenzied, all-consuming, society-defining political culture" of antebellum America.[1]

The contours and legacy of the second party system can be explored through the lives and careers of six important politicians, four southerners and two northerners, all of them involved at some point in presidential politics but each with a career that reflected the political dynamics of a different state. All took public stands during the secession crisis. Two—Martin Van Buren and John Tyler—were former presidents. Three—John Bell, John Breckinridge, and Stephen A. Douglas—ran unsuccessfully against Abraham Lincoln for the White House in 1860. And Georgia's Howell Cobb presided over the convention that organized the Confederate States of America in early 1861 and chose Jefferson Davis as its president. Despite the prominence of and influence wielded by these six men, the 1860 election placed in the White House a candidate whom they all opposed.

Like the victorious Lincoln, all of the three losing presidential candidates in 1860 rose to prominence in newer, post-Constitution states west of the Appalachian Mountains. Tennessee had entered the Union in 1796, and its favorite son in 1860 was Bell, a refugee from Upper South Whiggery and nativism who joined the new Constitutional Union Party's attempt to pour calming oil on the stormy waters of sectional conflict. The fractured Democratic Party nominated the sitting vice president, Breckinridge, a native of Kentucky, which had entered the Union in 1792, and Douglas, from Illinois, which had achieved statehood in 1818. Yet the Bluegrass State followed the Unionist tradition of Henry Clay and voted for Bell, a particular disappointment to Breckinridge, who stood for the firm assertion of southern rights. Illinois, home to two of the 1860 nominees, endorsed Lincoln over his longtime instate political rival, Douglas, who propounded the popular sovereignty stance on slavery in the territories that found great favor among free state Democrats. Both Bell and Lincoln had entered politics as Whigs, while Breckinridge and Douglas were lifelong Democrats, as was Cobb, who supported Breckinridge in 1860. The two ex-presidents had risen to political prominence in their native states, both of which were among the original thirteen: the New Yorker Van Buren endorsed his fellow northern Democrat Douglas, and the Virginian Tyler supported southern Democrat Breckinridge. Despite their Democratic votes in 1860, both Tyler and Van Buren had detoured off the Democratic path earlier in their careers. Tyler had been a state's rights Whig in the 1830s and 1840s, while Van Buren, the first president born after the American Revolution, had become a Free-Soiler in an attempt to return to the White House in 1848.

Van Buren and Douglas, like their states, became firmly Unionist in 1861. Georgia was one of the seven Cotton or Deep South states that seceded before Lincoln's inauguration. Virginia and Tennessee illuminate the power of conditional Unionism in the Upper South; they joined the Confederacy after the bombardment of Fort Sumter and Lincoln's call for troops. Tyler and Bell followed their states and supported the Confederate cause. Kentucky, internally divided between Union and Confederate partisans, attempted for a few months to remain neutral between the United States and the Confederacy. However, it never officially left the Union and ultimately provided more Civil War manpower to the United States than to the Confederate States. Breckinridge, newly elected to one of the Bluegrass State's seats in the U.S. Senate after Hannibal Hamlin's inauguration as vice president in early March, supported Kentucky's failed attempt at neutrality and eventually cast his lot with the eleven seceded states.

Before its sectional split in the summer of 1860, the national Democracy had won the presidential contests of 1852 and 1856 by nominating Franklin Pierce of New Hampshire and James Buchanan of Pennsylvania, northerners whom critics came to disparage as doughfaces because they usually sided

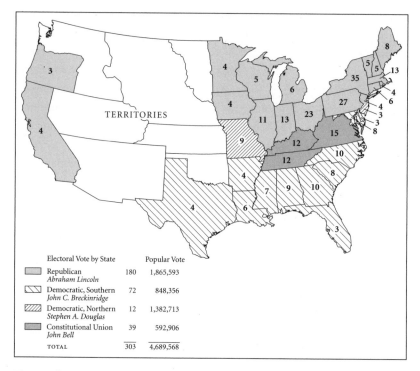

Electoral Vote by State		Popular Vote
Republican *Abraham Lincoln*	180	1,865,593
Democratic, Southern *John C. Breckinridge*	72	848,356
Democratic, Northern *Stephen A. Douglas*	12	1,382,713
Constitutional Union *John Bell*	39	592,906
TOTAL	303	4,689,568

The presidential election of 1860

with the increasingly powerful southern wing of the party. Buchanan had the advantage of being a diplomat abroad when the divisive Kansas-Nebraska Act received endorsements from both Pierce and Douglas in 1854, but in the same year, Buchanan had revealed his southern sympathies by endorsing the Ostend Manifesto, which called for intensification of U.S. efforts to acquire the slaveholding island of Cuba. In 1860, the national Democracy held its convention in perhaps the most sectionalized of all American cities, Charleston, South Carolina, where secessionist fire-eaters precipitated the party's split into northern and southern wings. Subsequent separate conventions in Baltimore nominated Douglas and Breckinridge. Ironically, the sectional divisions that resulted in this split nomination had been exacerbated by hard feelings between the two most prominent free state Democrats, Buchanan and Douglas. The Illinois senator had broken with the president over the latter's machinations in favor of Kansas joining the Union as a slave state under the Lecompton Constitution; the Nebraska territory to the North would certainly become another free state. Both Breckinridge and Douglas

Cartoonists depict the 1860 presidential election as a footrace and a baseball game. (top, Courtesy of Library of Congress; both from Albert Shaw, Abraham Lincoln: His Path to the Presidency, *2 vols. [New York: Review of Reviews, 1929])*

professed loyalty to state's rights as well as to the Union, rejecting the Black Republican call for a federal ban on slavery in all future national territories. They differed, however, on how state's rights doctrine affected the interests, rights, and honor of slaveholders in the territories and about whether state's rights principles, properly interpreted, extended to the legitimacy of secession. Bell portrayed himself as the most conservative and least divisive of the four candidates for the White House, avoiding a concrete stand on the burning question of slavery in the territories.

Stephen A. Douglas was the son of Stephen Arnold Douglass, a college-educated Vermont physician who died when his son was an infant. Not until 1846, when the younger man first won election to the U.S. Senate, did he drop the second "s" from his father's name. This change in spelling helped him avoid being confused or even associated with Frederick Douglass, the most famous—or infamous—black man in the United States, whose views on slavery, state's rights, and federal authority differed greatly from those of the senator. Frederick Douglass advocated racial equality and assimilation, interpreted the Constitution as permitting aggressive federal action against bondage, and came to see the War of the Rebellion as "a millennial struggle between liberty and tyranny." Although Douglass did not endorse Lincoln's relatively moderate opposition to slavery in 1860, the Emancipation Proclamations of 1862–63 won the former slave's enthusiastic support.[2] In contrast, Stephen Douglas made it perfectly clear in 1860–61 that preserving the United States as a unified country devoted to white supremacy was his first priority. Although some white southerners appreciated his platform of popular sovereignty and his commitment to the white "ruling race," his expression of willingness to endorse possible federal coercion against active disunionists cost him many slave state votes in the 1860 election.

Stephen Douglas certainly had less personal experience with slavery and slaveholders than did Frederick Douglass, but the Illinois Democrat had far more direct contact with the slave South as an adult than did his political rival, Lincoln. In 1847, shortly after winning the first of his three consecutive terms in the U.S. Senate, Douglas wed Martha Martin, the daughter of a wealthy North Carolina planter who died in 1848 and bequeathed to her a twenty-five-hundred-acre plantation on the Pearl River in Mississippi. She also inherited more than a hundred slaves. Douglas became responsible for supervising management of the operation in return for one-fifth of its income. Less than five years later, Martha Douglas died. She and her husband had two sons, who inherited the Mississippi estate. Douglas sold it on their behalf in 1857 but became joint owner of another Magnolia State plantation.

By this time, Douglas had a very attractive new bride in her early twenties, Adele Cutts Douglas, grandniece of Dolley Madison.[3]

Stephen Douglas, perhaps even more than Abraham Lincoln, appears to have embodied the fabled tale of a dramatic rise from modest beginnings achieved in tandem with western geographical mobility. After his father's death, the infant Stephen and his mother, Sarah Fisk Douglass, moved to a farm operated by her bachelor brother. Young Stephen worked as an apprentice to a cabinetmaker in Middlebury before moving with his family in 1830 to Upstate New York, a region being transformed by the Erie Canal, completed five years earlier. After attending a classical academy for a few years, he began to read law while working in the office of a local attorney. "A young man in a hurry," in the words of biographer Robert Johannsen, Douglas soon left the Empire State to seek his fortune to the west, where he could quickly establish himself. Toward the close of 1833, he settled in Jacksonville, Illinois, and the following year a judge admitted him to the bar after "a cursory examination" and an admonition "to learn more of the law."[4] He had become an enthusiastic devotee of Andrew Jackson, his party, and his principles, all of which were captured for Douglas in the capitalized word "Democracy."

Americans today tend to view Jacksonian Democrats as deeply flawed by virtue of their vehement denial of equal civil and political rights to women and people of color. However, the party's founders in the 1830s appeared to their supporters as both devoted to the glorious Union and hostile to aristocratic claimants to elitist privileges, whether acquired through family inheritance or financial machination. First and foremost among these founders were Jackson, a Tennessee lawyer-planter-general, and Van Buren, a New York attorney of modest beginnings. After the Missouri Controversy of 1819–21 over the expansion of slavery into the Louisiana Purchase west of the Mississippi River, most members of the old Jeffersonian Republican coalition had become determined, like Jackson and Van Buren, to push aside sectional differences to combat what they saw as the corrupt and despotic "Money Power" as embodied in the Second Bank of the United States, the clearest legacy from Hamiltonian Federalists of the 1790s.

Congress had awarded the Second Bank of the United States its charter in 1816 under Thomas Jefferson's presidential successor, James Madison, much to the dismay of diehard Old Republicans. These stalwarts, concentrated in Madison's Old Dominion and including the retired Sage of Monticello, insisted on continuing Jefferson's principled opposition to overreaching and despotic federal power coming from a "consolidationist" Federalist Party. Alexander Hamilton had secured approval from President George Washington and Congress of both the first bank and a loose or flexible interpretation of the federal government's implied powers under the Constitution. Jefferson's other nemesis, Supreme Court chief justice John Marshall, orchestrated an 1819 Supreme Court decision, *McCulloch v. Maryland*, upholding the federal government's power to charter a national bank and denying states the power to tax branches of the Bank of the United States to reduce its power vis-à-vis smaller state-chartered banks. The depression that followed the financial panic of 1819, apparently exacerbated by Bank of the United States policies, spurred a chorus of political voices, including those of Jackson and Van Buren, against what future Jacksonian Democrats such as Missouri's Thomas Hart Benton termed the exploitative and ruthless "monster bank." After the Second Bank's demise in the 1830s at the hands of President Jackson, the threat of another recharter receded during the 1840s, only to be replaced during the 1850s in the minds of most white southerners by the even more monstrous Black Republican conspiracy, which was determined to destroy and humiliate the slave states. The new monster, like the old, seemed to feed off a flexible interpretation of the powers granted to the federal government under the Constitution.

Douglas had great respect for Van Buren's skills and success at building a state party organization in New York and at working to contain sectional tensions on the national level. As a young man, Van Buren had followed his father's lead into the ranks of New York's Jeffersonian Republicans. Abraham Van Buren farmed, owned several slaves, and operated a tavern in the Hudson River Valley. Young Martin did not attend college but studied law in both his hometown of Kinderhook and in New York City before gaining admission to the bar in 1803. In Gotham, Van Buren learned much about the clannish and factional intricacies of Empire State politics, including the fierce rivalry between supporters of Aaron Burr and backers of DeWitt Clinton.[5] By the time Jeffersonian Republican voters in New York's Middle District (the counties south and southwest of Albany) narrowly elected him to the state senate in 1812 over a Federalist opponent, Van Buren seemed firmly committed to the party's traditionalist creed of political decentralization and state's rights. This creed carried the conviction that its defenders must do constant political battle against the Federalist financial and business elites who allegedly sought to enrich and empower themselves by supporting expanded federal authority. During the 1810s and 1820s, Van Buren battled the Clintonian faction of New York's Jeffersonian Republican coalition, which he saw as all too willing to form political coalitions with Federalist factions, and in the process he became leader of the state political machine known as the Albany Regency.[6]

In 1807, Van Buren married Hannah Hoes, a neighbor and distant cousin, who bore him five sons before her death from tuberculosis twelve years later.[7] Martin Van Buren never remarried, relying on the help of friends and relatives to raise his children. He always enjoyed a "vigorous and nonpartisan social life." Even after the failure of his 1840 bid for reelection to the presidency, he remained "gracious . . . fat and jolly," though he did not receive an invitation to the Whig victor's inauguration. Historian James Henretta has concluded that "a defining characteristic of Van Buren's life" was his "quest for respectability—nay, gentility." Henretta might have pointed to Van Buren's avoidance of overt and evangelical religiosity, following the example of the Founding Fathers. He worshipped regularly in Washington, D.C., at St. John's Episcopal Church, in part because the nation's capital lacked a congregation in the Dutch Reformed faith of his childhood. More obvious evidence for Henretta's evaluation was the president's purchase in the late 1830s of a landed estate near Kinderhook, a thirty-room mansion on two hundred acres that would enable him to enjoy the life of a country squire in retirement. He renamed the property Lindenwald. With a household staff of six and a farm manager, Van Buren had access to what Joel Silbey has described as "all the trappings of a contented gentleman enjoying his later years."[8]

Van Buren arrived in Washington as a U.S. senator in 1821, when the old Federalist Party no longer possessed a viable national organization. In the Senate, he became a leader of the radicals within the diverse ranks of the Republican Party; the appellation indicated that they held fast to the traditional republican and Jeffersonian dogma that both individual and local liberty required firm limits on and constant vigilance against the expansion of federal government power. In 1824, the radicals endorsed the presidential candidacy of Georgian William H. Crawford, who was, in the words of historian Robert Remini, the only candidate "committed to limited government and strict construction of the Constitution." Henry Clay and John Quincy Adams joined ranks to engineer the latter's presidential election by the House of Representatives, although Andrew Jackson had won a plurality of electoral as well as popular votes. After Clay received the coveted position of secretary of state, the radicals charged that his alliance with Adams represented a "monstrous union" cemented through a "corrupt bargain." In his first annual message, President Adams proposed an ambitious program of federal activism—in particular, a broad array of public works and internal improvements (roads, turnpikes, bridges, canals, harbor and river upgrades)—in line with "the spirit of improvement . . . abroad upon the earth." This favorable attitude toward U.S. government promotion and sponsorship of internal improvements would be embraced by leaders of both the Whig Party in the 1830s and the Republican Party in the 1850s. In making his case to Congress in 1825, Adams made a pair of statements that seemed directly to challenge the radicals' creed. First, said Adams, "Liberty is power"; moreover, the United States, as a "nation blessed with the largest portion of liberty," should "in proportion to its numbers be the most powerful upon the earth." Second, "Were we to slumber in indolence or fold up our arms and proclaim to the world that we are palsied by the will of our constituents, would it not be to cast away the bounties of Providence and doom ourselves to perpetual inferiority?" This speech and its endorsement of expanded federal activism even in the absence of support from voters did much to persuade Senator Van Buren that he and his fellow radicals should join political hands with General Jackson, whom the Tennessee legislature had already renominated for the White House. Clay, for his part, dismissed Jackson as simply a "military chieftain" lacking the experience or temperament of a statesman.[9]

Furthermore, from the moment he took his Senate seat at least until he moved out of the White House in 1841, Van Buren wanted to become a leader within some national party organization that would defuse and contain sectional tensions and conflicts. The ambitious New Yorker joined the Senate just after the Missouri Compromise. The Missouri Controversy had clearly demonstrated the potential of sectional antagonisms to undermine the intersectional health of the Jeffersonian Republican Party. During the 1820s, in the words of historian Jonathan Earle, Van Buren "cast about for southern allies to revive the old Jeffersonian coalition" between New York and Virginia, in the process "relegating sectional issues to the sideline."[10] Jackson emerged as the presidential vehicle for such an alliance. In January 1827, Van Buren wrote to Virginia editor Thomas Ritchie proposing "an alliance of 'the planters of the South and the plain Republicans of the North' that would provide 'a complete antidote for sectional prejudices.'" (To partisans of the nascent Jacksonian Democracy, the label "plain Republicans" encompassed "the working classes—a term they generally used in the plural and defined to include farmers and planters," as opposed to mercantile and financial nonproducers.)[11] During his rise to the summit of New York state's complex factional politics, Van Buren had earned a well-founded reputation as an ambitious and manipulative operator, symbolized by his nicknames: the Little Magician and the Sly Red Fox of Kinderhook. At the same time, he had also become convinced that disciplined party organizations were crucial to the health of American politics. Van Buren's national strategy seemed successful when Jackson became the Democratic Republican victor over the incumbent National Republican Adams in 1828. Although Van Buren was elected governor of New York in 1828, he resigned the following March to become President Jackson's first secretary of state.

At this point, Margaret "Peggy" Eaton became the crux of what historian John F. Marszalek has termed "the most famous debate over the meaning of womanhood in American history." A previously widowed innkeeper's daughter, Peggy Eaton was married to John Henry Eaton, Jackson's fellow Tennessean and Freemason as well as the president's confidant, political protégé, and first secretary of war. Her "brash, demanding, and voluptuous" persona encouraged much of Washington society to believe the hyperbolic accusation that her husband had "married his mistress, and the mistress of eleven doz. others." President Jackson came to Peggy Eaton's defense for the same reason that he had supported his wife, Rachel, against charges of adultery years earlier: he needed to defend his honor as a patriarch over his cabinet and family alike. Disputes over Eaton's character contributed significantly to Jackson's growing estrangement from Vice President John C. Calhoun between 1829 and 1833. According to Marszalek, Jackson "spent more time on this matter in his first two years in office than he did on any other question. His cabinet dissolved over it, and it became the underpinning for the worst split between president and vice president in American history," setting the stage for Van Buren's subsequent emergence as Jackson's heir apparent. In the words of William Freehling, Van Buren, a "crafty old bachelor," "paid court to Mrs. Eaton," while "hapless husband" Calhoun "watched his wife snub Peggy." Jackson biographer James Parton, writing on the eve of the Civil War, concluded that "the political history of the United States, for the past thirty years, dates from the moment when the soft hand of Van Buren touched Mrs. Eaton's knocker." The incident brought into play differing and gendered understandings of honor in antebellum America. As historian Daniel Walker Howe points out, American ladies proved unwilling and unable to recognize "the need to set aside morality in the interest of politics." American ladies understood themselves as defending the honor of respectable women, who would not stoop to "accord a man sexual favors without the assurance of support that went with marriage."[12]

Jackson, Van Buren, and their supporters challenged the national bank during the 1820s and 1830s and often took issue with the growing support for increasingly protectionist tariffs. Some New England merchants, most famously the Boston Associates, had shifted to manufacturing during the War of 1812. Like the national bank, growing taxes on imported goods, explain Nicholas Onuf and Peter Onuf, constituted crucial expressions of "a broader, neo-Hamiltonian program of nation building" that also included federal funding for internal improvements. The protectionists at first included Calhoun and other southerners, and the original critics of free trade included Daniel Webster and other New Englanders. Indeed, Kentucky's Clay took a phrase from Hamilton, announcing in 1820 the goal of creating an "American System."[13] Clay and his allies could speak for hemp and sugar producers in the slave states as well as manufacturing interests in the Northeast and devoted Unionists everywhere. The American System, including federal promotion of internal improvements, bespoke a desire to promote national self-reliance and economic independence against the constant threat of war against more developed foreign powers that, like England during the War of 1812, could exploit U.S. weakness when the country was cut off from foreign suppliers and trading partners. During the 1820s, the American System became the platform of the National Republican wing of the Jeffersonian coalition, which in turn organized the Whig opposition against "King" Andrew Jackson as he determined to destroy the Second Bank of the United States. Opponents of the American System included those who thought that free trade would promote peace through international economic interdependence and those commodity producers (especially cotton planters and overseas shippers, the latter concentrated in New York City) for whom the primary market was transatlantic rather than national. These interests, with their southern orientation, opposed federal government policies that taxed one sector of the economy or one region to benefit economic development in another sector or region. In 1837, Calhoun, at the time a senator, made an antitariff, anti-internal-improvement, and anti-Yankee argument that would be repeated many times during the 1840s and 1850s by southerners seeking to explain why economic development and diversification in the slave states lagged that of the free states: "In one thing only we are inferior—the arts of gain; we acknowledge that we are less wealthy than the Northern section of this Union, but I trace this mainly to the fiscal action of this Government, which has extracted much from, and spent little among us."[14]

Jacksonian Democrats often objected to the political corruption that resulted when government policies became linked to special interests benefiting from a congressionally legislated American System. Protectionists and free-traders alike raised questions about the selfishness and patriotism of their opponents. By the 1830s, the debaters had begun a process of polarization along sectional lines, a process symbolized by the transformation of Calhoun into a southern free-trader and sectionalist and of Webster into a northern protectionist and nationalist. During the Nullification Controversy of the early 1830s, Webster and his National Republican allies, soon to become Whigs, denounced Calhounites for daring to invoke state sovereignty (the extreme interpretation of state's rights) against the perpetual Union to justify South Carolina's constitutional prerogative to "nullify"—that is, declare null and void—protective tariffs adopted in 1828 and 1832. Calhoun became temporarily a state's rights Whig, part of the variegated opposition to Jackson during the mid-1830s. Such southern Whigs did not support the American System promoted by nationalist Whigs Clay and Adams but expressed indignation at Jackson's hard-line Unionist and militarist response to South Carolina's nullification campaign. The disparate anti-Jacksonian coalition began to adopt the label "Whig" in 1834, intending to invoke American memories of the glorious revolutionary struggle against an earlier kingly tyrant, George III.

The Whig Party attracted many evangelical Protestants born again during the Second Great Awakening. Some evangelicals in the free states manifested the growing perfectionist and postmillennial impulse among predestinarian Calvinists as well as free-will Arminians in the Protestant denominations.[15] This perfectionism might lead them to abjure politics as hopelessly dependent on inherently corrupt compromises with the sinful world; conversely, their interest in promoting a stable republican society through temperance, public education, and perhaps antislavery could incline them toward governmental activism. Support for activist government also came from economically nationalist Whigs who felt hurt by the impact of Jacksonian antibank, hard-currency financial policies. Most Democrats were hostile to both evangelical do-gooders and the sort of central state or federal banks that the Whigs supported as sources of stable growth. Democrats tended to see bankers as parasites feeding on producing citizens. Bankers did not create a real product, and their financial institutions often appeared "a vat of swindling machines" garnering speculative profits while hardworking citizens suffered. "The perennial Jacksonian question," one scholar explains, "queried rhetorically: 'Shall the banks govern the people or shall the people govern the banks?'"[16]

In Illinois, Douglas became a principal architect of the state's Jacksonian Democracy, helping create a well-organized and disciplined party organization on the model of Van Buren's Albany Regency. At age twenty-one, Douglas won election as a district state attorney, and in 1836 he captured a seat in the lower house of the Illinois legislature, where he served with anti-Jackson

Whig Abraham Lincoln. Only five feet, four inches tall, Douglas's brash aggressiveness and nervous energy resembled that of a bantam rooster, and his personal force and powerful oratory won him the nickname Little Giant. In 1838, Douglas ran unsuccessfully for a seat in the U.S. House of Representatives. Three years later, at age twenty-seven, he became the youngest man ever appointed to the Illinois Supreme Court.

Van Buren, who served as vice president from 1833 to 1837 and then occupied the White House for the next four years, agreed with his mentor, Jackson, that, in the words of historian Sean Wilentz, "legislating the people's will and preserving the Constitution had come to mean advancing the battle against concentrated monied power while quieting the growing tumult over slavery."[17] As presidents, Jackson and Van Buren declined to promote the annexation of Texas for fear that it would exacerbate sectional conflict over slavery. (However, Jackson did extend formal U.S. recognition to the newly independent Republic of Texas just before leaving office in 1837 and in 1843 expressed support for President Tyler's campaign to annex Texas as a slaveholding state.) Neither Jackson nor Van Buren had moral objections to black bondage. Both much preferred stable Unionism to either abolitionist or state's rights extremism. Of course, New York's Little Magician lacked the dramatic military and political credentials garnered by Tennessee's Old Hickory, first against American Indians and the British in the 1810s and then during the ensuing two decades against allegedly elitist National Republicans, an aristocratic Bank of the United States, and disloyal Calhounite nullifiers. For strong Unionists both north and south in 1860–61, Jackson's firm stance against the threat of disunion served as the gold standard of firm and decisive nationalism against which to measure the words and actions of Presidents Buchanan and Lincoln.

To placate the Democratic Party's powerful southern wing and maintain Jacksonian Democracy as an intersectional force for national unity during the mid-1830s, Jackson and Van Buren supported allowing postmasters in the slave states to impound antislavery literature. These free pamphlets and newspapers, sponsored by the American Antislavery Society (including William Lloyd Garrison, Theodore Dwight Weld, and society president Arthur Tappan) emerged as part of an abolitionist moral suasion campaign that, in the words of historian David Brion Davis, "fused religious zeal with a sense of irrevocable human equality."[18] The founding of the American Antislavery Society early in the decade had been inspired by the success of English predecessors in lobbying for the emancipation of slaves in Britain's West Indian colonies, particularly Jamaica. The society's organizers invited British abolitionists Charles Stuart and George Thompson to lecture in America. To proslavery Americans, the English could appear to be assuming the garb of philanthropy to strike at the foundations of both southern society and the nation's power and unity as a democratic republic. American advocates of moral suasion hoped to convince the American people, including slaveholders, of chattel slavery's sinfulness and corruption, thereby leading to their repentance and voluntary cooperation in beginning the process of emancipation and perhaps racial reconciliation. Some of the society's tracts labeled slavery "the foul stain of legalized plunder" and branded masters lascivious brutes or "villainous enslavers of souls." Offended southerners, feeling both their honorable reputations slandered and their sectional interests and rights threatened, responded with cries that such accusations were not only unjust and insulting but "inflammatory" and "incendiary," thereby anticipating the charges that most white southerners would level against Lincoln's Republican Party in 1860–61. At the same time, the abolitionists launched a massive petition campaign, supported by free blacks and reform-minded women in the North, calling on members of Congress to assert their constitutional and moral authority to terminate the sinful injustice of slavery in the federally governed District of Columbia.

President Jackson informed Congress in December 1835 that such antislavery agitation was "unconstitutional and wicked" and that northern mobs therefore were justified in launching physical attacks on abolitionist meetings and property. The abolitionists were hurling "inflammatory appeals" at "the passions of the slaves," attempting "to stimulate them to insurrection and to produce all the horrors of servile war," a phrase that recalled not only Nat Turner's short-lived 1831 rebellion in Southside Virginia but even more terrifying images of the Haitian Revolution from 1791 to 1804, in which Haitian slaves in revolt against their masters had been transformed into what David Brion Davis has described as "savage, tigerlike men or ferocious beasts gorged with blood."[19]

Virginia's Tyler, like many antebellum southerners, also harbored deep fears that the awful Haitian experience could be repeated in parts of the slave South. During the summer of 1835, Tyler, a second-term U.S. senator, voiced his horrified exasperation at abolitionist pamphlets and petitions in a speech delivered to neighbors and constituents gathered at the Gloucester County Courthouse, near the north bank of the James River in the Virginia Tidewater. "I have seen the Union twice in danger," he declared, citing as the second, more serious threat that posed by contemporary abolitionist agitators in the North, encouraged by their British compatriots. These abolitionists even enlisted women as "one of the instruments to accomplish their mischievous purposes," as shown in a petition to the Senate signed by fifteen hundred women and calling for abolition in the District of Columbia. Abolitionists libeled the South by portraying slaveholders as "demons in the shape of men," thereby "sharpening the dagger for midnight assassins, and exciting cruelty and bloodshed." More than two decades later, John Brown's raid at Harpers Ferry badly shook Tyler's faith in the durability of the Union. He praised Virginia's Democratic governor, Henry Wise, for his decisive role in bringing Brown to trial and execution but condemned President Buchanan's failure to act against northern individuals thought to be associated with Brown's conspiracy. In March 1860, Tyler added a revealing codicil to his will that testified to his awareness that harsh measures against slaves were sometimes necessary even on plantations as benign as he believed his own to be. After his death, his widow, Julia, would have explicit "authority to sell and dispose of any slave or slaves who may prove refranctory [*sic*], either reinvesting in other [slaves] or after such manner as she may deem most conclusive to the interest of my estate."[20]

Tyler's second and more serious threat to the Union had come from abolitionists in the mid-1830s; the earlier danger had come from northern politicians during the Missouri Controversy, when he had held a seat in the U.S. House of Representatives. He had condemned the 36°30' compromise line between free and slave territory in the Louisiana Purchase as unconstitutional on the grounds that Congress had no power to restrict the spread of slavery. But slave state representatives had voted 39–37 in favor of the compromise, although Virginia's unanimous delegation provided a quarter of the negative votes. Tyler and the Old Dominion's Old Republicans were more concerned about the security of slavery than were most southern politicians at that time.[21]

Like Jefferson, Tyler's livelihood depended on slave labor, but he also demonstrated a "lifelong ambivalence" about slavery. He endorsed Jefferson's notion of "diffusion" as an argument for the geographical expansion of the South's peculiar institution. This argument rested on both a deeply prejudiced view of blacks and a "climate-driven perspective on slavery." If slavery were allowed to expand west and south, then slave labor would inexorably be drawn out of the more temperate regions of the Upper South and into more tropical climes, whose crops made it more profitable. Temperate states, especially Jefferson's and Tyler's beloved Virginia, could export most of their slaves and then undertake a process of gradual and compensated emancipation. Since emancipation had to be accompanied by the mandatory deportation or colonization of freed blacks, the combination of slave exports and emancipations would bring the inestimable benefit of ridding former slave states of their dangerous and degraded black populations. The enslaved population might then be replaced with free, fair-skinned, and far move congenial European immigrants. Tyler, like Jefferson, defended slavery not in the abstract as a positive good but rather as a necessary if regrettable evil. It must be removed slowly, carefully, and with due regard for the interests, rights, and honor of slaveholders.

Despite his fierce antagonism to antebellum abolitionists, Tyler proved more open to one antislavery proposal than did Calhoun and Jefferson Davis. The Virginian was willing to entertain the idea of prohibiting slave trading in the District of Columbia, since the presence of auction blocks near the Capitol and the White House cast a discomfiting shadow on the nation's republican principles.[22] At the same time, he saw the far more radical 1840 platform of the new Liberty Party as both dangerous and unconstitutional. The new party attracted political abolitionists who interpreted the Constitution as a decidedly antislavery document, whereas Garrisonians saw it as hopelessly tainted and corrupted by concessions to slavery.

In the Senate, abolitionist petitions spurred Calhoun to sponsor a gag rule declaring that Congress could not touch slavery anywhere in the Union and should therefore refuse to accept any petition that portrayed the peculiar institution as some kind of evil or sin. However, such a formal gag rule could be easily painted as an extremist proslavery ploy that narrowed the First Amendment "right of the people to petition the government for a redress of grievances." From 1836 to 1850, the Senate generally abjured a formal gag in favor of what historian Daniel Walker Howe calls "an informal practice" based on the parliamentary rule that a motion to table rather than receive a petition is not debatable. Van Buren, then vice president and presiding officer of the Senate, shared the outlook of most northern Democrats, who wanted to avoid a formal gag rule in the House, to which most petitions were directed. The New Yorker helped orchestrate South Carolina representative Henry L. Pinckney's introduction of a more moderate bill that stipulated that antislavery petitions would be formally accepted but automatically referred to a new committee before any public discussion. The petitions were thus buried in committee rather than dismissed as unacceptable.[23]

The House approved Pinckney's motion in May 1836 by a vote of 117–68. Most northern Whigs voted in the negative, while the majority of southern Whigs, along with most Democrats in both sections, voted in the affirmative. When temporarily accepted by the Senate, the legislation pleased moderate southerners and placated northern Democrats anxious about having to defend an even more blatant gag rule before their constituents. Although Pinckney's formulation angered his more aggressively proslavery colleagues in Congress (especially fellow South Carolinians James Henry Hammond in the House and Calhoun in the Senate), it constituted the strongest anti-abolitionist response "consistent with the right of petition," in the words of Pennsylvania's Democratic senator and future president James Buchanan. Nevertheless, Massachusetts Whig Daniel Webster observed in 1838, "The anti-slavery feeling is growing stronger and stronger every day," because ever more northerners perceived that proslavery interests presented an arrogant and palpable threat to civil liberties. Abolitionist petitions and the negative reactions they generated in Congress helped lay the foundation for the idea of a Slave Power willing to limit the interests, rights, and honor of free northerners.[24]

Calhoun hoped to create a regional band of political brothers apart from both the Whig and Democratic Parties.[25] Such a southern phalanx might even carry the prince of the Palmetto State to the presidency. Calhoun claimed to disdain national parties in part because they encouraged the sort of partisan loyalties and corruption that the Founding Fathers, with their focus on republican virtue over factional rivalries, had intended to avoid. In particular, Calhoun singled out "the New York system of corruption and trickery," over which Whig and later Republican editor Thurlow Weed would come to preside. By the 1830s, Calhoun was convinced that citizens of the slave states must unite politically against the growing hostility to slavery and plantation agriculture in the free states. "Most of the time," explains historian Joel Silbey, "the Calhounites would gladly see the Whigs and Democrats shattered and driven from the scene in favor of a southern-rights coalition drawing on members of both parties" to "defend their section against the hostile intentions of its predatory enemies."[26]

However, Van Buren's satisfactory stance on the "abolition question" during the 1830s helped bring the South Carolinian and his allies back to the Democracy in time for the New Yorker's 1840 reelection bid. Van Buren received renomination by a national convention that officially changed his party's moniker from "Democratic Republican" to "Democratic" or simply "the Democracy." By this time, the panics of 1837 and 1839 had led the country into a serious depression that did not begin to abate until 1843. What Jules Witcover labels "Jacksonianism without Jackson" was crushed by an invigorated and well-organized Whig Party in the 1840 election.[27] The Whig victor, William Henry Harrison, was a Virginia native who had moved to Ohio and who had emerged as the Whig Party's answer to Jackson: Harrison had achieved a national reputation as a military hero against both American Indians and the British just before and during the War of 1812. He presented himself and was effectively packaged by his Whig handlers as a common man conducting a "Log Cabin and Cider" campaign, a sharp contrast to the "lily-fingered aristocrat," Van Buren. Yet Harrison, like his running mate, Tyler, hardly qualified as a common man; both were scions of plantation families on the north bank of Old Virginia's James River. Harrison and Tyler represented different wings of the disparate anti-Jacksonian coalition.

The Whigs proclaimed that their nominee did not pander after the presidency as did the Democracy's incumbent "political trickster." Harrison, supporters claimed, had been "brought forward by the Spontaneous Will of the People" rather than by the machinations of party insiders. Harrison crushed Van Buren in the election but held the presidency for only a month before becoming the first chief executive to die in office. In what Don E. Fehrenbacher has described as "an extraordinary historical accident," Harrison's death raised to the presidency "arguably the most resolute defender of slavery ever to occupy" the office.[28] Tyler and Calhoun became forceful allies in pressing for the annexation of Texas as a slave state. Under Tyler and his slaveholding successor from Tennessee, "Young Hickory" James K. Polk, the influence of what can be termed proslavery nationalism on U.S. foreign policy reached its apogee with the admission of Texas to the Union and the subsequent war with Mexico. Almost two decades later, after Lincoln's presidential victory, many southerners recoiled from the apparent threat of an antislavery nationalism become dominant in both the free states and in Washington.

John Tyler was a landed gentleman at birth as well as death. His father, also named John Tyler, served as Virginia's governor from 1809 to 1811 and passed on to his son strong state's rights principles, as evidenced by the senior Tyler's support for the Jeffersonian Republican Party and its dominant ideology of limited and localist government. Young John Tyler graduated from William and Mary College in 1807, then studied law and won admission to the bar in 1809, before he turned twenty. In 1813, he wed Letitia Christian, the daughter of another prosperous Tidewater planter. She bore him four daughters and three sons who lived to maturity. She died in 1842 after suffering two severe strokes in three years. Two years later, President Tyler, age fifty-four, married a woman thirty years his junior, Julia Gardner, daughter of a prominent New York landowner and former state senator. Julia bore him another seven children, the last born in 1860. As might be expected from most antebellum Virginia gentlemen, Tyler's Episcopalian religion embraced a decidedly deistic theology that honored God for creating a world organized around rational and generally beneficent natural laws. Such faith could issue forth ceremonial if also heartfelt invocations of God's providential favor but did not see much evidence of God's direct, physical, supernatural intervention in worldly affairs. Tyler projected a stereotypically southern charm and grace in the company of others from the upper crust but seemed rather aloof and ill at ease around those clearly less affluent and well-bred than he.[29]

Tyler, like Van Buren, decried sectional threats to the Union's integrity and often blamed foreign instigators for such threats to the American nation. Even more than Van Buren, Tyler expressed and exploited "a powerful Anglophobic strain in American political culture." Americans had battled Britain's "despotic imperial authority" first during the revolutionary era and again during the War of 1812, which most Americans saw as a patriotic second war for independence against English tyranny and arrogance.[30] Both Van Buren and Tyler saw themselves as ideological and political heirs to the original anti-English outlook of the first Republican Party as crafted in the 1790s by Founding Fathers Jefferson and Madison. The party then in power, the Federalists, found England far more congenial to its principles and interests than was republican or imperial France during the French Revolution and the Napoleonic Wars (1793–1815), into which the United States would be dragged during the War of 1812. Van Buren and Tyler absorbed some measure of the retired Jefferson's constant fear that the Federalist Party of Alexander Hamilton, though fatally crippled during the "Virginia dynasty" (1801–25), was always looking for an opportunity to reassert itself against the Jeffersonians. Van Buren and at first Tyler saw in proto-Whiggish National Republicans a sinister form of reinvented Federalism. Tyler, unlike Van Buren, turned against Jackson for his excessively militant and nationalist response to the Nullification Controversy.

Tyler had more than just partisan and patriotic reasons for viewing antislavery politics as part and parcel of an ongoing conspiracy by aristocratic and monarchical Great Britain to cripple and undermine the U.S. republic. Starting with thirteen slaves he inherited in 1813 and others acquired via his first marriage, Tyler ultimately owned a total of some two hundred slaves. During his retirement years at his plantation, Sherwood Forest, he seems to have owned an average of seventy at any one time. Some ten to thirteen worked as house servants, including three who lived in the big house. All the other slaves lived in about twenty cabins.[31]

Tyler and Polk, his slaveholding successor in the White House and a Jackson protégé, promoted and orchestrated the admission of slaveholding Texas to the Union in 1845. For both men, personal interest in and concern for the security of the South's peculiar institution encouraged energetic support for annexing the cotton-growing Lone Star Republic lest British interests and antislavery predilections gain dangerous influence there.[32] Tyler and Polk also saw U.S. acquisition of additional territory, including Texas, as promoting the health of the American republic as a whole. Their outlook echoed much of what Jefferson and Madison had thought about expansion of the republic externally as a way of strengthening it internally. To them, a large and diverse republic seemed less susceptible than a smaller one to the establishment of a tyrannical federal government dominated by one or more allied factions.

Nationalist Whigs in Congress, especially Clay and Webster, came to see Tyler as a traitor. While the president opposed such Whiggish domestic legislation as a new Bank of the United States and doggedly pursued the annexation of Texas, nationalist Whigs wanted to promote the economic and social development of the country's existing states and territories and feared that further territorial acquisitions might exacerbate sectional tensions over slavery expansion. While northern Whigs such as Webster came to endorse "the idea of the incompatibility of slavery with economic development," as historian Larry Menna has written, southern Whigs such as Clay sought "to move the Southern economy beyond plantation agriculture as a way to preserve and strengthen it."[33] Tyler so alienated his nominal party that he forfeited any serious chance of renomination for the presidency in 1844 despite his dream that he might ride the horse of geographical expansionism and Texas annexation back to the White House, perhaps even as the Democratic nominee. Tyler the Virginia aristocrat, much like the self-made New York Yankee before him, saw Whiggish economic support for a more powerful and activist federal government as persistent and insidious Hamiltonian Federalism seeking a disguised resurrection. Tyler, like Calhoun, also suspected that a more potent central government could eventually threaten the stability and security of slavery. If the number of slave states as well as their population fell behind those of the free states, the white South could face the fearful prospect of federal interference in the interstate slave trade as well as further restrictions on the spread of slavery.

With support from two successive slaveholding secretaries of state, Calhoun and subsequently Abel P. Upshur of Virginia, Tyler worked hard to accomplish Texas annexation. Reinforced by the Polk presidential victory on a nationalist platform of geographical expansion in the Northwest as well as the Southwest, Tyler secured Texas's admission to the Union before leaving office in March 1845. Texas and Florida, which joined the United States the same year, became the last two slave states to enter the Union. Three more free states entered the Union before 1860, causing proslavery southerners increasing concerns about their weakness relative to the free states in the Senate as well as the House. The Electoral College that chose Lincoln in 1860 represented fifteen slave and eighteen free states, containing total populations of twelve and seventeen million, respectively. Winning 55 percent of the northern popular vote gave the Republican well over the number of electoral votes he needed to become president despite the additional electoral votes awarded to the slave states according to the Constitution's three-fifths compromise.

Hesitation about annexing Texas cost Van Buren the Democracy's 1844 presidential nomination. In late April, both he and the eventual Whig nominee, Clay, published letters urging caution and deliberation. Their opponents portrayed these letters as testifying to the untrustworthiness of both politicians, to their "ambitious and artful" natures. Southern Democrats used the two-thirds rule inaugurated at their 1836 convention to block Van Buren's nomination, and his name was withdrawn after eight ballots. Polk emerged as the party's dark horse nominee. The disappointed Van Buren remained loyal to the Jacksonian Democracy and supported Polk, whose narrow victory over Clay constitutes one of the most important elections in American history. Just 5,107 of the more than 485,000 votes cast in New York would have given Clay both the state and the White House. Had upstate voters for the antislavery Liberty Party's nominee instead cast most of their ballots for Clay, he would have become president. If Clay rather than Polk had been inaugurated, 1845 would probably not have brought the annexation of Texas, and 1846 would not have brought war with Mexico. And as Gary J. Kornblith has argued, "The Mexican War was a necessary, if not sufficient, cause of the Civil War."[34]

Howell Cobb's support for Van Buren waned as the New Yorker hedged his bets on the Texas question. Both of Cobb's parents were natives of Virginia, and his father owned more than one hundred slaves in Georgia. Howell Cobb attended Franklin College (later the University of Georgia) before being admitted to the bar in 1836. He married Mary Ann Lamar, the daughter of a wealthy Bibb County planter and the sister of Cobb's college friend, John Lamar. Cobb served as a state representative from Clarke County beginning in 1836 and held a seat in the U.S. House of Representatives after 1842, positions in which he became a leading Unionist Democrat and an opponent of those party sectionalists prone to worshiping Calhoun. During the 1840 election, the national issues that most clearly distinguished the victorious Whigs from the losing Democrats in Georgia were the former's desire for the re-creation of a national bank and for some limitations on executive power.

Georgia had no protectionist party since the state had no substantive pro-tariff constituency; therefore, Democrats and Whigs alike claimed that they wanted revenue rather than protective tariffs. Cobb actively supported Van Buren's reelection in 1840, but Harrison took Georgia's eleven electoral votes. In the spring of 1844, however, the Georgian caught Texas fever and refused to endorse Van Buren. Like many southerners, Cobb saw Texas's annexation as a test of northern support for southern rights and institutions and there-fore as a test of the North's honorable respect for the South's claim to equality and dignity within the Union.

Considerable debate took place within Georgia about the impact of Texas's annexation on the health and security of slavery. Would it promote a slave exodus from Georgia and reduce the value of the state's human chattel, as Whig John Berrien believed? Or would Texas slaveholders' demand for more slaves drive up their market value? If Texas remained independent and fell under sway of the British abolition spirit, as Calhoun warned, would it be-come a haven for runaway slaves? A free-soil Texas would block the expan-sion and economic health of plantation society, encourage runaways from nearby slave states, and limit the South's opportunities to expand its political clout in the Union. Howell Cobb and his brother, Thomas R. R. Cobb, wanted Van Buren to be unequivocally pro-annexation, as was Polk, but the New Yorker was, in the words of historian Anthony Gene Carey, "seldom unequivo-cal about anything."[35]

American territorial expansion between 1845 and 1848, from the annexa-tion of Texas to the Mexican Cession, appeared to more and more free state Democrats as well as Whigs to have been orchestrated by an aggressive and manipulative Slave Power. Polk, the Democratic president-elect, cooperated willingly with another slaveholding politician, the lame-duck Tyler, nominally a Whig, in fast-tracking Texas's admission. And Texas entered the Union not by treaty with a foreign entity, the Lone Star Republic, which would have re-quired ratification by two-thirds of the Senate under the terms of the Consti-tution. Instead, Texas became one of the United States by the dubious mecha-nism of a joint resolution of Congress, which required only a majority vote in both the House and the Senate but helped inspire the potent phrase "Mani-fest Destiny" later that year.

After leaving the White House in 1845, Tyler returned to the ranks of the Democracy, and during the 1850s, he considered himself a Democrat loyal to the Union. In the 1860 election, he supported Breckinridge. After Lincoln's election and the secession of seven states in the Lower or Cotton South, Tyler made one final, dramatic effort to save the old Union on terms that he deemed compatible with maintaining slavery as a system of both property rights and racial control. He became presiding officer of the presumptive but ultimately futile peace conference that convened at Washington's Willard Hotel in early February at the same time that delegates from the seceded states gathered in Montgomery to organize the Confederate States of America. The Virginia General Assembly had summoned this conference "in an earnest effort to adjust 'unhappy controversies' and to afford the people of 'slaveholding States adequate guarantees for the security of their rights.'" The 132 delegates to this "Old Gentlemen's Convention" represented twenty-one states; eight slave states and five free states declined to send delegates. However, the Washington Peace Conference could not find a peaceful solution to the secession crisis. After the Old Dominion seceded in April, Tyler became the only living ex-president to embrace the Confederacy and the only president in U.S. history ever officially denominated a traitor. To Tyler's way of thinking, the leaders of the Republican Party should have made concessions to the slave states that respected the South's constitutional equality in the Union, particularly in the western territories, where the long-term future of the two sections would be decided. In the absence of such concessions, secession and disunion appeared both justified and absolutely essential to protect what he saw as the genuinely American interests, rights, and honor of the southern citizenry.[36]

After the close of Tyler's presidency and as war with Mexico over the disputed Texas boundary loomed in 1846, the Polk administration and the British government negotiated a partition of the Oregon Country. The United States gained far less of the Pacific Northwest than Polk had promised during his campaign. Since it was generally understood that this region was unsuitable for slavery, Free-Soilers opposed to the geographical spread of slavery felt betrayed and cheated by the negotiated settlement. Then the United States went to war with Mexico. President Polk identified his overarching goal as implementing the nation's "manifest destiny" by extending its boundaries to the shores of the Pacific Ocean. Yet antislavery men, including Whig congressmen John Quincy Adams and Abraham Lincoln, believed that Polk had provoked the war by sending U.S. troops into the disputed border region between Mexico and Texas. At war's end in 1848, Mexico ceded to the United States what became the American Southwest, including California. A good many northerners perceived that Polk was far more willing to fight for slave territory than for free soil and that the war had been part and parcel of an expansionist conspiracy orchestrated by the slave interest.

These concerns fueled the emergence of a short-lived antislavery third party in the late 1840s that anticipated the more durable Republican Party created during the mid-1850s. Ironically, Van Buren, Jackson's executive assistant in organizing the national Democracy as a bulwark against sectional strains, became the new Free-Soil Party's nominee for president in 1848. Despite his public support for the 1844 Democratic nominee, he felt anger against southern Democrats and their northern allies for choosing Polk. More important, Texas's quick annexation and the Mexican War seem to have convinced the Little Magician that the national Democracy had abandoned fundamental Jacksonian and Unionist principles in favor of subservience to the Slave Power's expansionist and proslavery agenda. As Jonathan Earle has argued, the free-soil movement that emerged among Jacksonian Democrats and temporarily attracted some future Republicans had sources that differed markedly from those of the far more Whiggish movements for "immediate abolitionism and evangelical reform." These movements had emerged in the 1830s and become associated with the Burned-over District of Upstate New York and Ohio's Western Reserve along with Puritan Boston and Quaker Philadelphia.[37]

Van Buren's acceptance of the Free-Soil Party's 1848 presidential nomination only reinforced the perception of his political enemies, especially in the South, that he was an unprincipled politician willing to shift position to advance his career. Not only was the Sly Red Fox of Kinderhook the party's standard-bearer, but one of his sons, John, became the new party's most effective campaign speaker. Free-Soilers were distinguished by their explicit support for the Wilmot Proviso of 1846, which the House but not the Senate had endorsed as a way to exclude slavery from any new western territories acquired from Mexico after an American military victory. This amendment to the war-funding bill was proposed by Negrophobic Pennsylvania Democrat David Wilmot, who called the proposal "Jefferson's Proviso," anticipating Lincoln's invocation of Jefferson on behalf of containment a decade later. Wilmot became the Keystone State's most prominent member of the Free-Soil Party and later joined the Republicans. Only two southern congressmen, both of them Whigs from the border state of Kentucky, originally voted in favor of the proviso. However, the population of the free states already so far exceeded that of the slave states that the House approved the Wilmot Proviso by a vote of 77 to 58.

The Free-Soil Party, organized at a Buffalo convention and taking as its slogan "Free Soil, Free Labor, Free Speech, and Free Men," clearly anticipated much of the platform of the Republican Party that first appeared in Michigan in 1854. However, after Whig Zachary Taylor, a military hero from the South, won the presidency in 1848, the Free-Soilers split along generational lines.

Some older party members, including the sixty-five-year-old Van Buren, could not shake the pull of the old partisan magnet and returned to the national Democracy. "Prince John" Van Buren reluctantly followed his father, declaring in 1849, "We expect to make the democratic party of [New York] the great anti-slavery party of this state, and through it to make the democratic party of the United States the great anti-slavery party of the United States." Younger Free-Soilers, among them Ohio lawyer Salmon P. Chase—for reasons that clearly included some blend of antislavery conviction, personal ambition, and the desire to exploit opportunities for interparty cooperation—preferred to retain a separate partisan identity. Doris Kearns Goodwin's astute evaluation of Chase applies to many other politicians present as well as past: "Advancement of self and advancement of the cause were intertwined in Chase's mind."[38]

Chase's hesitancy to divorce himself completely from the Democratic Party also seems to have reflected his ongoing loyalty to a set of democratic, egalitarian, and even anticapitalist Jacksonian principles that became associated with Loco-Focoism. The term itself seems to have originated in the cauldron of New York state politics in 1835, when a radical wing of the Democratic Party composed largely of workers' delegates broke from the regular wing dominated by Tammany Hall. After the Tammany group left the meeting hall and turned off the lights, the remaining radicals lit candles with "the new self-igniting friction matches called locofocos." Before adjourning, the radicals endorsed a Locofoco or Equal Rights Party with a separate electoral ticket and platform. Jacksonian Loco-Focoism, much of it incorporated into the Free-Soil Party's 1848 platform, included a strong preference for a hard-money, specie-based currency and a concomitant hostility to federal or state charters for a central bank. Such a bank, by virtue of both its right to issue paper money and its political ties to federal or state government officials, would inevitably become the seat of the aristocratic and corrupt Money Power.[39]

In 1848, Free-Soil/Democratic coalitions won an Ohio seat in the U.S. Senate for Chase and a Massachusetts seat for Charles Sumner. Both opposed the Compromise of 1850 as too favorable to the Slave Power. The Kansas-Nebraska Act finally led Chase and Sumner to cut their ties with the Jacksonian Democracy and join the new Republican organization. Other Free-Soilers followed Van Buren back into the national Democracy and its efforts to uphold the 1850 North-South armistice. The Little Magician seemingly reverted to his old Jacksonian Unionism and, like most American citizens, saw the compromise measures as flawed but essential to the paramount goal of sectional peace and preserving the Union. He remained committed to both the Democratic Party and Unionism until his death in 1862, voting for Douglas in 1860. Van Buren joined his fellow ex-presidents Millard Fillmore, Franklin Pierce, and James Buchanan in supporting Lincoln's refusal to recognize the Confederacy and determination to put down the southern rebellion. As Fillmore told a large crowd gathered at Buffalo's Metropolitan Theatre on 16 April 1861, "Our Constitution is in danger and we must defend it."[40]

Despite his dramatic sectional disagreements with Van Buren during the 1840s, Cobb later demonstrated his version of proslavery nationalism by promoting the Compromise of 1850 during his tenure as speaker of the House and in tandem with Douglas in the Senate. Despite his staunch Unionism at the time, he followed the lead of state's rights Democrats in affirming "the South's right to resist 'degradation' and 'inequality.'"[41] In 1857, Cobb became President Buchanan's secretary of the treasury. After Douglas broke with the Buchanan administration over Kansas's admission to the Union with a clearly bogus proslavery state constitution, the Georgian "masterminded" the administration's "drive to destroy the Little Giant." In the words of one historian, "Ostracizing Douglas would also, not coincidentally, further Cobb's long-shot bid for the 1860 presidential nomination."[42] By 1860, Cobb was prepared to insist that Congress would have to protect slave property in the territories if the federal courts failed to do so. Lincoln's election confirmed the Georgian's feeling that the process of educating northerners "to hate the institution of slavery" had advanced too far to be reversed, and he returned to his home state a disunionist. In a widely read pamphlet published toward the end of 1860, he told "the people of Georgia" that the Republican National Convention and Lincoln endorsed "the doctrine of negro equality." Indeed, the Republican Party had "succeeded in bringing into its organization all the Abolitionists of the North except that small band of honest [Garrisonian] fanatics who say, and say truly, that if slavery is the moral curse which the Black Republicans pronounce it to be, they feel bound to dissolve their connection with it, and are therefore for a dissolution of the Union." "The great object of" the Republican organization was slavery's "ultimate extinction." Consequently, insisted Cobb, "equality and safety in the Union are at an end; and it only remains to be seen whether our manhood is equal to the task of asserting and maintaining our independence out of it." He was both angered and grieved to realize that "the Union formed by our fathers was one of equality, justice and fraternity. On the fourth of March it will be supplanted by a Union of sectionalism and hatred." In February 1861, Cobb was chosen as the Montgomery convention's presiding chair, and he administered Jefferson Davis's oath of office when he assumed the provisional presidency.[43]

No individual had more to do with orchestrating congressional approval of the Compromise of 1850 than did Douglas, working in tandem with Cobb. First in the House of Representatives and later in the Senate, Douglas had become chair of the Committee on Territories. As an expansionist Young American and New Democrat, he supported both the annexation of Texas and the Mexican War as steps toward making the United States what he called "an ocean-bound republic" and "the first maritime nation in the world." Yet he opposed ratification of the treaty ending the war in 1848 because its terms might preclude the possibility of further American expansion south into Central America. He battled the free-soil Wilmot Proviso but also rejected the pro-slavery, Calhounite interpretation of the Constitution as mandating that all federal lands be open to slave property. In 1850, Douglas played a crucial role in the Senate's approval of popular sovereignty as the answer to the question of whether slavery should be permitted in the extensive new territories of New Mexico and Utah. Four years later, Douglas took the lead in securing congressional extension of the popular sovereignty, congressional-nonintervention principle into the northern portion of the Louisiana Purchase. Under the Kansas-Nebraska Act, signed into law by President Pierce in February 1854, applying the new policy would facilitate formal federal organization of new territorial governments on the northern Great Plains, thereby opening more western lands to settlers from both the United States and Europe and facilitating the northerly construction of a government-subsidized transcontinental railroad to California. The process of organizing these territories and building a transcontinental railroad had heretofore been delayed by strong North-South differences, including disagreements over whether the first railroad to the Pacific would follow a northern or southern route. These sectional disagreements could be sidestepped by extending to the new territories of Kansas and Nebraska what some critics called squatter sovereignty, which allowed new states upon admission to determine their status as slave or free.

Douglas and his supporters saw the doctrine of popular sovereignty as having at least two significant political advantages. First, its premise that the residents of territory should decide on such internal matters as domestic slavery paralleled the emphasis in the parties of Jefferson and Jackson on true liberty and freedom as rooted in local and state government rather than the national sphere. As historian Forrest McDonald concedes, "Douglas had his faults, and he was an opportunistic politician, but he was unvarying in his support of the principle underlying the doctrine of states' rights—local autonomy." Lincoln observed in early 1860 that "Senator Douglas and his peculiar adherents plant themselves upon the tenth amendment, providing that 'the powers not delegated to the United States by the Constitution, are reserved to the States respectively, or to the people.'"[44] Second, popular sovereignty promised to take the vexing and divisive issue of slavery expansion out of the hands of the federal government and localize it in individual territorial governments. This transfer would help free both the nation and Douglas's cherished Democratic Party from factional and sectional quarrels dangerous to their success and unity.

Douglas also hoped that applying popular sovereignty to the northern Great Plains, even if southern support required explicit repeal of the Missouri Compromise, might well achieve two additional goals. It would allow the first transcontinental railroad to funnel western traffic through Douglas's home state and its emerging metropolis, Chicago. Furthermore, the idea might win the Illinoisan enough support in both the free and slave states to make him presidential timber. The idea of popular sovereignty appealed to Douglasite Democrats because it offered some common ground on which voters North and South might stand. It promoted the expansionist nationalism so powerful in the Old Northwest, whose population was a blend of migrants from the Northeast and the South. Nonetheless, many antislavery Democrats in the North came to side with the Republicans in the aftermath of the Kansas-Nebraska legislation. Members of both groups could oppose the aristocratic slaveocracy's use of its control over the Democratic Party organization to expand slavery's range and power at the expense of closing off nonslaveholding whites from advancement opportunities in the western territories.

Douglas supporters responded that by insisting that all the territories be closed to slaves and their masters, northern Free-Soilers and Republicans in fact supported strengthening the power of the federal government relative to the interests, rights, and honor of all citizens in a particular territory. In a democratic republic, a territory's white male citizens should have the right to make local decisions about slavery, free from outside compulsion. Moreover, some Douglasites feared that behind the sectional principle of free soil lurked ghosts from the Federalist and Whiggish past, schemers who were always on the lookout for some political opportunity to implement their goal of increased national authority on behalf of business and financial elites. Last but not least, Douglas seems to have been convinced that fierce debates over slavery in the trans-Mississippi West were really sound and fury signifying nothing. Although the climates of the cold Great Plains and the arid Southwest made those regions uncongenial to slave plantation agriculture, this political noise could destroy the glorious American Union. If critics and defenders of slavery among the Founding Fathers could work out constructive compromises on slavery-related issues, why should not the current generation of Americans do the same? In 1854, neither Senator Douglas nor President Pierce sufficiently appreciated the depth of the North's opposition to the perceived tyrannical transgressions of the Slave Power. Neither man seems to have held strong moral or religious views about black bondage, and Douglas did not hesitate to employ racist and demagogic rhetoric against his political opponents.

The 1854 legislation quickly provoked a storm of protest in the free states. Kansas and Nebraska belonged not to the Mexican Cession but to the Louisiana Purchase. The new pair of territories lay north of the 36°30′ line of latitude established by the Compromise of 1820. Northerners not only viewed the Missouri Compromise line as an almost sacred compact between the sections but also perceived that conniving southerners intended to take control over Kansas in exchange for a Nebraska without slavery. Such a move could appear as the latest in the slave South's long line of aggressions against the interests, rights, and honor of northern citizens. Territorial Kansas soon hosted a miniature civil war between slavery partisans (many from Missouri to the east) and antislavery settlers. In light of the territory's ongoing voter fraud and intimidation, concludes one historian, "the notion of popular sovereignty as a means to defuse the slavery debate" became "nothing more than a hollow shell."[45]

The fallout from Douglas's Kansas-Nebraska Act included the final disintegration of the national Whig Party and the organization of various local and state anti-Nebraska coalitions into a new Republican Party committed to the geographic containment of slavery and the creation of a free-soil West. The Republicans came close to winning the presidency in 1856 despite the appearance of a third major candidate in former president Fillmore, who ran on the ticket of the nativist and anti–Roman Catholic American Party (the Know-Nothings) and won support from a rump convention of Old Whigs. The Republicans still captured all but five northern states, leading to many southern threats that a Republican victory would be grounds for disunion.[46]

In 1857, Douglas broke decisively with President Buchanan when he attempted to impose the proslavery Lecompton Constitution on both Congress and the clear majority of free-soil settlers in territorial Kansas. Douglas knew that Buchanan's policy not only made a mockery of popular sovereignty but further weakened the already crippled northern Democracy in electoral contests against Republicans.[47] In 1858, Douglas barely managed to retain his Senate seat against Lincoln's challenge by attempting to plant his political feet on "what he called the 'middle ground' between the 'dangerous extremes' of the Northern abolitionist and the Southern disunionist." Lincoln and Douglas did not shrink from employing the distortions and misrepresentations that typified frontier politics. Like most Republicans, Lincoln considered the Supreme Court's 1857 *Dred Scott* ruling an unwarranted obiter dictum that effectively rendered slavery, contrary to the Constitution and the Founding Fathers' intentions, a national institution of property rights sanctioned by the federal judiciary. And the court decision seemed a flagrant part of something akin to a conspiracy to reestablish the legitimacy of slavery even in the free states. Douglas saw the notion of a fearsome proslavery conspiracy as the fanciful creation of Republican strategists pursuing northern votes. Even if the Supreme Court had proclaimed chattel bondage a species of property recognized by the Constitution and therefore legally entitled to protection in all the territories, this abstract property right "necessarily remains a barren and worthless right," as Douglas said in the spring of 1857, "unless sustained by appropriate police regulations and local legislation."[48]

During the first session of the Thirty-sixth Congress, which had been elected in the fall of 1858, southern politicians opposed and often blocked a number of measures sponsored by Republicans and by some northern Democrats: a homestead act that slaveholders feared would populate the territories with far too many antislavery Yankee farmers, protective tariffs that would privilege northern manufacturing interests, a northern route for the transcontinental railroad, and legislation helping to create agricultural and mining colleges with grants of federal lands to the states. When a homestead bill made it to the president's desk, Buchanan's veto lent support to charges that he was a pawn of the Slave Power. As James M. McPherson observes, these issues "provided the Republicans with vote-winning issues for 1860." When Douglas joined Buchanan in calling for the annexation of slaveholding Cuba, the Republicans had additional ammunition, while most northern Democrats "kept a low profile." The Democratic caucus removed Douglas as chair of the Committee on Territories, and Jefferson Davis lambasted him with "scorn and indignation" for absolutely refusing to support a federal slave code in the national domain in the wake of *Dred Scott*.[49]

In December 1859, Douglas identified militant abolitionist John Brown's ill-conceived attempt to spark a slave rebellion by raiding Harpers Ferry (situated in a hilly, nonplantation part of northern Virginia) as the "natural, logical, inevitable result of the doctrines and teachings of the Republican party."[50] The following year, Douglas's long-standing goal of becoming the nation's chief executive was frustrated by Lincoln and the Republicans. Yet Douglas proved to be the only genuinely national candidate in the 1860 election, campaigning vigorously in both the North and the South. He alone among the four candidates received electoral votes from both slave and free states (albeit only from Missouri and New Jersey). During the campaign, he helped ensure his poor showing south of the Mason-Dixon Line and thereby helped guarantee that the election of 1860 became two different contests: Douglas versus Lincoln in the free states, Bell versus Breckinridge in the slave states.

In late August 1860, Stephen and Adele Douglas visited the Virginia port city of Norfolk, arriving by steamship from Baltimore. Addressing a large crowd from the courthouse steps, he declared that he had come "to see if there is not some common principle, some line of policy around which all Union-loving men, North and South, may rally to preserve the glorious Union against Northern and Southern agitators." He paused midway through his speech to read a slip of paper, on which were written two questions posed by a local elector pledged to Breckinridge. The first was, "If Abraham Lincoln be elected president of the United States, will the Southern states be justified in seceding from the Union?" Douglas replied, "To this I emphatically answer NO." He acknowledged the inherent and inalienable right to revolution whenever a grievance becomes too burdensome to be borne, as expressed in America's iconic Declaration of Independence. However, he also believed that secession would not and could not be justified until a president had committed some overt act that violated the U.S. Constitution. Douglas then responded to the second question: "If they, the Southern States, secede from the Union upon the inauguration of Abraham Lincoln, before he commits an overt act against their constitutional rights, will you advise or vindicate resistance by force to their secession?" In other words, would he support what most southerners termed military coercion against seceded states? The assembled crowd shouted "No!" Yet Douglas did not hesitate to disagree openly, to indicate his willingness to endorse some kind of coercion against disunionists. "I think the President of the United States, whoever he may be, should treat all attempts to break up the Union, by resistance to its laws, as Old Hickory treated the Nullifiers in 1832." Douglas's "Norfolk Doctrine" became widely known and widely denounced in the South and clearly diminished his support in the upper part of the region. Douglas received less than 10 percent of the popular vote in the Old Dominion, while Breckinridge received just under 44.5 percent and Bell garnered 44.66 percent. Douglas reiterated the thrust of the Norfolk Doctrine on 30 August while standing outside the North Carolina State Capitol in Raleigh next to a statue of George Washington. William Woods Holden, Democratic editor of the city's *North Carolina*

Standard, denounced the Illinoisan's "coercion speech." Holden previously had encouraged backers of Breckinridge and Douglas to join forces behind a fusion ticket that might prevent disunion, but after Douglas's speech, Holden endorsed Breckinridge.[51]

Following Lincoln's victory, Douglas, along with numerous leaders in the Upper South, insisted that southerners had no short-term reason to fear the new president because he would be hamstrung by a Democratic Senate, an anti-Republican House, and an essentially Democratic Supreme Court. Americans had no cause to destroy "the best government of which the history of the world gives example." Douglas believed, in Johannsen's words, that "the crisis stemmed from a conspiracy of southern leaders . . . to destroy the Union he loved so well." In other words, a cabal of traitorous Democratic fire-eaters had engineered the first separate-state secessions. During the secession winter, the senator threw himself into a variety of congressional efforts to effect some kind of compromise that would halt the secessionist avalanche and restore the Union without civil war. He served on the important Senate Committee of Thirteen appointed by Vice President Breckinridge. When Lincoln called for U.S. troops to subdue the unconstitutional War of the Rebellion against federal authority begun at Charleston, Douglas endorsed the Republican president's staunch Unionism because his understanding of the interrelations among slavery, state's rights, and the Union was ultimately closer to Lincoln's than to that of Jefferson Davis. Indeed, Douglas met with the president for some two hours the night before Lincoln made public his proclamation of coercion against treasonous disunionists, promising unequivocal support for the coming civil war. "There are but two parties," Douglas said, "the party of patriots and the party of traitors."[52]

The Little Giant's address to the Illinois General Assembly in late April, just weeks before his death, expressed poignant laments. He had worked for more than two decades on behalf of a "prosperous, happy, and united country on both sides of the Potomac." Now, with his heart "filled with sadness and grief," he had to witness "a war of aggression and extermination . . . being waged against the government established by our fathers." He had "prayed and implored for compromise" as long as there appeared to be "a hope of peaceful solution." Now it was time for every man to stand with the new federal administration against disunion, a "crime against constitutional freedom, and the hopes of the friends of freedom throughout the world." Insofar as "any of the partisan questions are involved," he still "stood in equal, irreconcilable, and undying opposition both to the Republicans and Secessionists." However, in the present crisis, "convictions of public duty" mandated setting aside all party organizations and creeds to ensure "obedience to the constitution and the laws of the country."[53]

A powerful current in American culture has always glorified idealistic politics above partisanship. Indeed, some recent scholars have argued that "antipartyism" was a persistent element of the political discourse of both early national and antebellum America. It is hardly surprising, then, that after Fort Sumter, free northerners and southerners alike called for "the suspension of party politics" in favor of nonpartisan cooperation during wartime. In 1863, German American Unionist Francis Lieber composed a nationalist pamphlet whose title could have been as easily chosen by a Confederate as by a Unionist: *No Party Now but All for Our Country*. "The most distinctive institutional development of Northern wartime politics," notes historian Adam I. P. Smith, became "the creation of the Union Party," which nominated Lincoln for reelection on a ticket with firm Unionist and former Tennessee Democrat Andrew Johnson. A "strong antiparty political culture" also infused the convention that organized the Confederacy. Many delegates wanted to purge their fledgling republic of partisan politics and factional divisions and believed that the authors of the U.S. Constitution had sought to implement the same goal. "By drawing elaborate parallels between the Confederate and American revolutions," George Rable has suggested, "Southerners staked a historical claim for their announced goal of perfecting the work of the founding fathers." Because the Confederate Constitution provided that the new country's president serve a single six-year term, the South did not experience a national political contest analogous to the Union's 1864 campaign.[54]

The 1860 campaign had featured a surfeit of partisanship, both party and sectional. Both Breckinridge and Bell posted far better showings in terms of the Electoral College than in terms of popular vote. Douglas's nearly 1.4 million popular votes yielded only twelve electoral votes, whereas Breckinridge's 850,000 votes captured seventy-two electoral votes from eleven slave states. If southerners saw Lincoln as the northern sectional candidate, most northerners perceived Breckinridge, scion of one of the most important political dynasties in American history, as a southern sectional candidate.[55] Yet many voters in the slave states saw Breckinridge not as a proslavery secessionist but as desperately trying to preserve the federal Union on terms that acknowledged the South's interests, rights, and honor.

Forty-two-year-old Iowa farmer and handyman Michael Fleenen Luark was representative of most American citizens in 1860 for at least two reasons. He was always concerned about the weather and its effects on crops, and he was one of the 60 percent of the nation's voters who did not support Lincoln.

A Virginia native who moved to Indiana at age four, Luark lived the life of "the quintessentially mobile American," as Lewis O. Saum has concluded.[56] Luark also lived in Illinois and Iowa before he responded to the midcentury siren of mining booms in the Far West, relocating to Colorado and California. By the mid-1850s, he resided in Washington Territory, coming back to Iowa with his family before the Civil War and then returning to the Pacific Northwest in 1861.

On 6 November 1860, "the day for Presidential, State, County and Township Elections," Luark recorded in his diary that he dispensed with some "little chores" before taking "two pair of cattle and the two wagons" and going to Lewis, Iowa, to cast his ballot. There, Luark saw "a good gathering but all things passed away very amicably." He then "drove wagon to Grove City" to finish a plastering job, the sort of work he frequently performed to earn supplemental income. For U.S. president and vice president, Luark selected "Stephen A Douglas of Illinois and Herschel Johnson of Tennessee, Regular Democratic Nominees," over "John C. Breckinridge of Kentucky and Joseph Lane of Oregon the Southern or ProSlavery (calling themselves the Union) Party." In 1848, President Polk had appointed Lane, a North Carolina native, as the first governor of the Oregon Territory. Lane, described by Johannsen as "a born leader and a man of consuming ambition" and as "a man of great principle [who] nevertheless exhibited a political self-interest that was common to frontier areas," had reached the Pacific Northwest by way of Kentucky and Indiana. Like Breckinridge, Lane served as a regimental officer in the Mexican War and emerged a popular hero. Lane spent eight years as the Oregon Territory's congressional delegate before winning election to the Senate as a Democrat when the territory achieved statehood in 1859. On the Kansas question, Lane sided with President Buchanan, who supported the Breckinridge-Lane presidential ticket.[57]

Third on Luark's list of presidential candidates came "John Bell of Tennessee and Edward Everett of Boston, Mass. American or Know-Nothing Nominees." They would have been disappointed to have been so directly identified with the nativist party, since they bore the official imprimatur of the Constitutional Union Party, which sought to transcend sectional tensions, and preferred to be seen as Old Line Whigs and devoted Unionists. Four years earlier, however, they had supported Fillmore's American Party candidacy, which was also endorsed by the frayed remnants of the Whig organization, including John Crittenden of Kentucky, Henry Clay's successor in the Senate. On the eve of the Civil War, to paraphrase Daniel Walker Howe, Bell and Everett qualified as elderly moderates in a time of political polarization. A Tennessee native and Nashville lawyer, Bell had acquired many slaves, along with a substantial stake in iron mining and manufacturing, through his 1835 marriage to widow Jean Erwin Yeatman. He served seven terms in the U.S. House, including a stint as speaker beginning in 1834, followed by two terms in the Senate. As of 1856, he and his wife owned some 160 slaves, many of whom manufactured iron in north-central Tennessee's Cumberland River Valley. Some may have mined coal in Kentucky for delivery to those iron foundries. In 1860, Bell appeared to be the Volunteer State's closest approximation to Clay, the late Unionist compromiser. Upper South Whigs Bell and Clay, unlike the southern Democrats, had favored federal promotion of diversified economic development and took cautious, moderate stances on the crucial issues of geographic expansion and slavery in the territories. During Senate discussions over what became the Compromise of 1850, Bell had been one of seven Whigs and six Democrats appointed to a special Senate Committee of Thirteen, chaired by Clay, to consider various proposals and amendments. Among them was Bell's plan for maintaining a temporary balance of free and slave states by having Texas set its western boundary at the Trinity River. (Under the terms of the Lone Star State's 1845 annexation, its territory could be subdivided into as many as four additional states.) Another southwestern state could thus enter the Union, presumably with slavery, thereby balancing California's admission as a free state. However, Bell was far less flamboyant and assertive than the Kentuckian, and his proposal apparently received no serious consideration. Another Upper South Whig, Congressman David Outlaw (once described as "the misnamed mild North Carolinian"), complained in a July 1850 letter to his wife that the Tennessee senator "is so cautious a man" that "he advances a proposition, and then commences qualifying" until "there is scarcely anything left of the original thought."[58]

Everett provided geographical balance on the Constitutional Union ticket. Everett was one of the antiabolitionist "Cotton Whigs" who had organized the party in Boston in early December 1859, less than a week after John Brown was hanged for treason. A Boston Brahmin par excellence and widely celebrated as a distinguished orator, Everett had served as professor and president at Harvard College, as governor of Massachusetts, and as minister to Great Britain under Presidents Harrison and Tyler and secretary of state under Fillmore. Like many other chief executives of the free states during the mid-1830s, Everett had denounced vocal abolitionists as "incendiaries." Elected to the U.S. Senate in 1853, he spoke out against the Kansas-Nebraska Act but absented himself during the vote, arousing such consternation among his constituents that he resigned after just fifteen months.[59] Another prominent organizer of the new Constitutional Union Party, Boston businessman Amos Lawrence, hoped that the organization would help northerners "learn to distinguish between hatred of slavery and hatred of the South" even as voters in the South would reject extremist proslavery fire-eaters. Constitutional Unionists would include men "who honor and cherish the Union—who mean to maintain the Constitution of the United States and faithfully carry out all its requirements and obligations."[60]

A Deep South analogue to the Cotton Whigs of Massachusetts was the remarkable concentration of affluent, cosmopolitan, and nationalist-minded slaveholders found in Mississippi's Natchez District, below Vicksburg. Here and in the Yazoo Delta above the city lived affluent and genteel bankers, doctors, investors, lawyers, and merchants, most of whom owned land and slaves and many of whom called themselves Unionists or conservatives. These men, generally far more pragmatic than doctrinaire, included northern-born entrepreneur Stephen Duncan and attorneys William Sharkey and Josiah Winchester. They had both family and business connections with the Northeast, and they, like Unionist conservatives in the Upper South, understood that secession and war could bring chaos and destruction to commercial activities dependent on the Mississippi, Missouri, Ohio, and Potomac Rivers. As the *Vicksburg Whig* insisted in January 1860, the South's peculiar institution enjoyed greater security within the Union than without it, and "disunion will sound the knell of Negro slavery in America."[61]

Duncan, the wealthiest of the "Natchez nabobs," owned some 25,000 acres divided into at least fifteen different plantations, worked in 1860 by more than twenty-two hundred black slaves who were "conservatively worth $1.7 million." He had moved to the Natchez District in 1808, at the age of twenty-one, after graduating from Pennsylvania's Dickinson College and studying medicine at the University of Pennsylvania in Philadelphia. "His identity was complex and ever-changing," observes biographer Martha Jane Brazy. His dual identities as a slaveholding southern grandee and a businessman with northern interests "merged and meshed into a complex hybrid." At least since Nat Turner's revolt, Duncan had feared that the ongoing growth of the slave population increased the possibility of serious insurrections. Rather than becoming a proslavery ultra who insisted that the peculiar institution be defended as a positive good and given legal protection in the federal territories, he argued privately for a nationalist agenda whereby protective tariffs for manufactures would encourage diversification of the South's economy and supply revenues to aid in the gradual emancipation of slaves and their colonization outside the United States. During the 1850s, however, he came to see free-soil Republicans as sectional rather than national partisans who threatened "not only to *interfere with slavery* in the States, *but to break it up by all means—destroy the welfare of the whites.*" Although Duncan lambasted both northern and southern ultras as responsible for the sectional crisis, the weight of his investments in the Lower Mississippi Valley drove him to side with the Confederacy. In a June 1861 letter to his sister, he referred to northerners as "your people, [who] seem determined to . . . subjugate" the South."[62]

The Constitutional Union ticket carried Bell's Tennessee (along with adjacent Virginia and Kentucky) but lost Everett's Massachusetts to Lincoln and Duncan's Mississippi to Breckinridge. The three Middle and Border South states that awarded their thirty-nine electoral votes to Bell and Everett had smaller percentages of slaves and slaveholders than did those in the Lower South as well as closer proximity to and more social interactions and business relations with the free states and their citizens. After Lincoln's election, Unionist conservatives argued, as historian William C. Harris has written, that their states should "adopt a 'watch and wait' policy toward the Republican administration." In the words of congressman and future governor Zebulon B. Vance of North Carolina, who supported Bell and Everett in 1860, Lincoln should receive "a fair trial as president" to save the Union from "disruption or destruction" if possible.[63]

Bell, Everett, and prominent supporters such as Vance harbored no illusions that they could win the Electoral College. Their hopes required that the Republican nominee fail to win all of the crucial states in the border North (Pennsylvania in particular), which would throw the election into the House of Representatives. If Bell could place third in the number of electoral votes, he might become the House of Representatives's intersectional, compromise, conservative choice. But although the Constitutional Unionists placed third in the Electoral College, Lincoln won virtually all the free state electoral votes and thus the presidency. Moreover, since Bell had concluded his senatorial career in 1859, he could not contribute during the secession winter to the failed congressional effort to broker a sectional compromise.

One outspoken if idiosyncratic supporter of Bell and Everett was Knoxville's William Gannaway Brownlow, who voiced unmitigated hatred for both secessionists and abolitionists. A belligerent preacher and journalist with a "scathing wit," he devoted much time and energy to castigating his many perceived enemies by "skewering them rhetorically." A native of southwestern Virginia orphaned at age eleven, Brownlow became a Methodist preacher after experiencing a born-again conversion during the Second Great Awakening in the 1820s. "Parson Brownlow" traveled through much of southern Appala-

1860 presidential candidates dividing the national map. On the left, Lincoln and Douglas struggle over the free states; Breckinridge takes the South; and Bell, on the high chair, attempts to preserve the Union with a pot of glue. (From Albert Shaw, Abraham Lincoln: His Path to the Presidency, *2 vols. [New York: Review of Reviews, 1929])*

chia as a circuit rider before settling in East Tennessee, where he established a newspaper, *Brownlow's Knoxville Whig*, in 1849. Whereas early-nineteenth-century revivals in the free states might produce some abolitionist immediatists, born-again converts in the South, like Brownlow, could become fiercely proslavery yet firmly Unionist. Prominent among the "pet causes" Brownlow promoted in his sermons and his newspaper were, according to historian Stephen B. Ash, "Methodism (the one true faith, according to the Parson), Whiggery (Henry Clay was his idol), temperance (Brownlow was a strict teetotaler), slavery (ordained by God and good for blacks as well as whites), and the federal Union." During the 1860 campaign, Brownlow's *Whig* claimed that Bell promoted "the honor, interest and welfare of the whole country" and that his election would "produce quiet and prosperity—and an end to this villainous agitation." After the election, Bell and Brownlow concurred that the Republican victory alone did not present sufficient cause for disunion and that state secession was not a constitutional right. On 15 November, Brownlow spoke for many southerners, including much of Appalachia, when he took aim at the secessionist argument that with a Republican in the White House, the South would be "exposed to all the wiles and infamy of an Abolition Government." This position could not be accepted "as legitimate in fact or in reason." How could advocates of immediate disunion be so certain that President Lincoln would "execute the purposes of Abolitionism?" Brownlow continued, "This he cannot do under the solemn oath to be administered at his inauguration. And who will say that he intends taking that oath with treason in his heart and perjury on his tongue? We have no right to judge of Lincoln by anything but his *acts*, and these can only be appreciated *after* his inauguration." Like Everett, Brownlow proved a decidedly firmer Unionist than did Bell. The candidate as well as most of his supporters in the South revealed themselves as decidedly conditional Unionists well before the organization of the Confederacy. In a letter published in December, Bell acknowledged that Republican antislavery agitation undermined "domestic tranquility" and "is well calculated to raise expectations among slaves and might lead to servile insurrection in the Southern States." Although he remained "resolved to adhere to the Union," he refused to declare "*that in no possible contingency* would I consent to a separation of the States." Bell seems to have hoped for a while that both Kentucky and Tennessee could maintain a policy of armed neutrality between the United States and the Confederacy, but after Fort Sumter and Lincoln's call for troops swelled secessionism in Middle and West Tennessee, he announced that "he was for standing by the South, all the South, against the unnecessary, aggressive, cruel, unjust, wanton war which is being forced upon us." In mountainous East Tennessee, a region with fewer slaves and plantations than the state's central and western counties, loyalty to the Union remained strong, and Parson Brownlow continued to decry disunion as reckless treason and secessionists as both traitors and potential tyrants. Vance followed Bell's path in the aftermath of Sumter. By the time the Tar Heel State's convention adopted an ordinance of secession on 20 May, Vance had already organized the Rough and Ready Guards to defend the cause of southern independence.[64]

Brownlow's former political enemy, Democratic Tennessee senator Andrew Johnson, became his antisecession and anti-Confederate political ally. Johnson, a native of North Carolina, had moved to Greenville in the 1820s and opened a tailor shop. Like Brownlow, Johnson was a resolute defender of bondage for blacks, and he would prove the only loyal senator from a seceded state. President Lincoln appointed Johnson military governor of occupied Tennessee in 1862; two years later, he won election as Lincoln's vice president on the National Union (Republican) ticket. Confederate officials arrested and imprisoned Brownlow in Knoxville toward the end of 1861 on a charge of treason. He refused to take the oath of allegiance to the Confederacy and was subsequently turned over to the Union military occupying Middle Tennessee.[65]

Brownlow expressed far less suspicion of Lincoln's Republicanism than did Luark. Like many northerners who cast ballots for Douglas or Breckinridge, Luark viewed "Abraham Lincoln of Illinois and Hannibal Hamlin of Maine" as "the Abolition or (So Called) Republican Nominees." Hamlin, like Lincoln a Whiggish attorney, had opposed the gag rule when he first took a congressional seat in 1843, and his "exceptionally swarthy skin" encouraged Negrophobes to label him part black African. Elected to the Senate in 1848, he opposed political nativism more openly than Lincoln but still came relatively late to the Republican Party.[66] Lincoln captured Iowa with more than seventy thousand votes (almost 55 percent of the ballots cast, mirroring his overall percentage in the free states). Although Douglas placed a respectable second in Iowa with more than 43 percent of the ballots cast, the Republican received more votes in Iowa, as he did throughout the North, than did all three of his opponents combined.[67]

On the last day of 1860, Luark predicted that "from present indications before the close of another year there will be some startling developments in our Political History." Prominent among the alternatives was "a Dissolution of the Union and Civil War with all its train of horrors." Another, far preferable alternative was a manageable "family quarrel among the states, a compromise and a reconciliation." Many other people north and south seem to have shared this fond hope, though Luark acknowledged that it was fading since "South Carolina has withdrawn from the Union already and taken the most ultra measures in regard to the matter." On New Year's Day 1861, Luark noted that Lincoln would be president for four years beginning on 4 March: "He being the representative of a new Political Party (the Republican) built upon the [remains?] of the old Whig Party and embracing most of the ultra sectional elements of the North. Its foundation is the Abolition Party and I predict that Lincoln's Cabinet will be composed of the most ultra sectional Abolition men of the North." Luark mistakenly included the incoming secretary of state, William Henry Seward, among this group: "Should such be the case and his administration commence with any ultra demonstration in regard to this [vexed?] Slavery question then farewell to our beloved Union of States." However, should Lincoln conduct the government "with a just discrimination[,] then all may be well."[68]

Toward the end of January 1861, Luark noted that "the whole country is on the edge of dissolution and Civil War." As a loyal Douglas Democrat, he saw the fault lying with the Republican Party and its recent electoral triumph. On 21 February, he cited newspaper reports that Georgia, Alabama, Florida, Mississippi, and Louisiana had "withdrawn from the Union and formed a Southern Confederacy with Jefferson Davis at the head as President." This wave of secession and the new Confederacy represented the "first fruits of the Republican triumph in Nov. last." On 20 April, Luark reported, "War has commenced at Charleston S.C. some days ago. So our Glorious Union of States is dissolved and Civil War is the result. Such is the first fruits of the first triumph of Abolition Politics."

A southern version of Luark's dismay can be found in the diary of Basil Armstrong Thomasson, a yeoman farmer in North Carolina's western Piedmont. Born near Winston-Salem in what is today Forsyth County and raised in adjacent Yadkin County, Thomasson married and purchased a seventy-two-acre farm in Iredell County, where he died in September 1862 at age thirty-three. The 1860 census reports that slaves comprised just over 27 percent of Iredell's population, but only 20 percent of the residents in Thomasson's immediate neighborhood were not free, and only fifteen of eighty-six households owned slaves. Unlike his neighbors, Thomasson was well-read, kept a diary, worked part-time as a schoolteacher during the winter months, and expressed dislike for the subordination of blacks and women. At the same time, he was clearly typical in that he never owned a slave but prized his independence and self-sufficiency despite his hardscrabble existence.

Thomasson's diary shows his devotion to his family, whose members' health and well-being were constantly threatened by illness. He was also a devout evangelical Christian, "for along with the members of his family he believed that this life was merely a journey to a better place . . . eternal life with God." At the same time, he possessed an optimistic and often clever outlook on life and a passionate interest in public education. He disapproved of slavery and loved the Union. His first explicit commentary on sectional political issues appears in a diary entry from late December 1859, in the aftermath of John Brown's raid at Harpers Ferry: "O! who can tell what will take place in these United States during the year 1860. The enemy of all that's good seems to be stretching every nerve for the destruction of the Union." Yet rather than voting for Douglas or Bell, Thomasson cast his ballot for "J. C. Breckenridge & Joseph Lane." Most Upper South Breckinridge supporters seem not to have openly advocated secession if Lincoln won the election. The Kentucky Democrat won the Tar Heel State with just over 50 percent of the vote; Bell followed close behind with just under 47 percent, and Douglas was a distant third with less than 3 percent.[69]

In late January, two-thirds of the North Carolina General Assembly approved a referendum on the question of calling a state convention to consider secession. According to one printed address in favor of the convention and ultimate disunion, supporters of southern rights maintained that the victorious Republicans had promised to use the federal government "not only to deprive us of political equality with them, but eventually in their fulfillment of policy to pull down the whole social fabric of the South and leave us the trembling victims of incessant alarms from negro insurrections and servile wars." Lincoln and the Republicans would establish a military despotism, destroy slavery, and recognize black freedmen "as the social and political equal of the white man." In February, North Carolina voters rejected the call for a state convention by a margin of only 661 ballots, one of them cast by Thomasson. At the end of March, Thomasson noted, "Every mail brings us some bad news—news of disunion and war." He believed that "all men ought to love and do all they could to keep peace," and he viewed the destruction of the Union and civil war as "folly." In the aftermath of Fort Sumter, North Carolinians voted again, this time agreeing to call a state convention, but Thomasson subsequently showed no interest in volunteering to fight for North Carolina or the Confederacy.[70]

Breckinridge, whom the North Carolina Unionist Thomasson supported but the Iowa Unionist Luark saw as the candidate of the "Southern or Pro-Slavery (calling themselves the Union) Party," was the grandson of John Breckinridge, a Virginia native who became a prominent slaveholder and Jeffersonian Republican politician in central Kentucky. After serving four years in the U.S. Senate, he served as attorney general under President Jefferson beginning in 1805, becoming the first cabinet appointee from the trans-Appalachian West. The oldest boy among the children born to him and his wife, Polly Cabell Breckinridge, was Joseph Cabell Breckinridge, known as Cabell. A year after graduating from the College of New Jersey (now Princeton University) in 1810, Cabell Breckinridge married Mary Clay Smith, daughter of the school's president. Their son, John Cabell Breckinridge, was born in January 1821.

Cabell's brother, Robert Jefferson Breckinridge, served as pastor of Lexington's First Presbyterian Church and taught at Danville Theological Seminary. His somewhat flexible approach to biblical revelation did not rest on "strict literalism," but reflected the influence of what has been called "common-sense literalism." This mode of interpretation attempted to blend the Calvinist and Reformed emphasis on a literal reading of the text with, in the words of Luke Harlow, "a commonsense approach to Scripture inherited from the Scottish

Enlightenment" that emphasized the laws of nature as a supplemental conduit of divine revelation. Apparently unlike most white Christians in the late antebellum South, Rev. Breckinridge concluded that the form of slavery sanctioned in Christian Scripture differed from the South's peculiar institution, which thus did not enjoy explicit divine sanction. Moreover, the employment of slave labor to raise hemp or tobacco in the Bluegrass State seemed far less productive—and more risky, given the free states just across the Ohio River—than the employment of slaves to grow cotton or sugar in the Deep South. Following the lead of Henry Clay, Robert Breckinridge actively promoted the politics of gradual emancipation and colonization for Kentucky. Any real progress toward the colonizationist vision was stymied in 1849–50, when the commonwealth's voters overwhelmingly approved what historian Harold Tallant calls "the most strongly proslavery constitution yet written in the United States." The Frankfort convention that composed the document included a very pointed passage in the appended bill of rights declaring that "the right of property is before and higher than any constitutional sanction; and the right of the owners of a slave to such slave, and its increase, is the same, and as inviolable as the right of owner, of any property whatsoever." The passage represents a proslavery version of the "higher law" doctrine that would soon be adapted to a more famous antislavery interpretation of the U.S. Constitution presented by Whig senator William Henry Seward of New York.

The 1849 motion to incorporate a proslavery "higher law" passage into Kentucky's state constitution came from nativist lawyer Garrett Davis of Bourbon County, who in late 1861 became a loyal Unionist U.S. senator, thereby testifying to the power of proslavery nationalism in the Border South. Yet most free Kentuckians professed to view slavery as what Tallant terms a "necessary evil," a perspective that permitted them to attack and defend it at the same time. Robert Breckinridge, owner of thirty-seven slaves in 1860, thus condemned abolitionists as "public enemies" propounding heretical "immediatism" and the "horrid doctrine" of racial "amalgamation." In a fast day sermon delivered on 4 January 1861, he confessed to knowing "of no way" that black bondage in the cotton states could "be dealt with at all." Yet Kentucky and its Border South neighbors should hold back from making common cause with more southern and secessionist slave states: joining them would only make the Bluegrass State subservient to "the supreme interest of cotton." Becoming a servant to King Cotton would also introduce among white Kentuckians "some millions more of African cannibals." This racial hyperbole reflected Breckinridge's concern that a new southern confederation organized by secessionists would reopen the African slave trade. This development failed to materialize, in part because the founders of the Confederacy did not want to alienate potential allies among the states of the Upper South, which sold and exported slaves to the Lower South. At the 1849 Kentucky State Convention, delegate William C. Bullitt, representing Jefferson County, which included Louisville, had argued that Kentucky need not worry about having too many slaves: the market demand for slaves from cotton and sugar plantations to the south, aided and abetted by the commonwealth's easy access to that market via the Ohio and Mississippi Rivers, held the slave population down "to a healthy point."[71]

John Cabell Breckinridge graduated from Centre College in Danville, Kentucky, before turning eighteen and then spent the winter of 1839 as a graduate student at the College of New Jersey. He subsequently enrolled in the second-year law class at Lexington's Transylvania University. Toward the end of February 1841, he received his law degree and was admitted to the Kentucky bar. Like Stephen Douglas, Breckinridge decided to seek his fortune and identity in what was then known as the West. He settled in Burlington, Iowa, seat of Des Moines County, on the Mississippi River about sixty miles above the Missouri state line. Like many frontier lawyers, he and his partner advertised themselves as "General Agents for the purchase and sale of real estate."[72] By 1843, Breckinridge had become active in local politics as a Van Buren supporter.

During a visit to Lexington later that year, Breckinridge met and courted "a petite young woman of some financial means," Mary Cyrene Burch, from nearby Georgetown. Her relatives included owners of slave plantations in the cotton states as well as Kentucky. The couple wed in December, months after Breckinridge had returned to the Bluegrass State and become a junior partner in the firm of Bullock and Breckinridge. In the 1848 presidential election, he, like Douglas, endorsed Democratic nominee Lewis Cass of Michigan, a proponent of popular sovereignty in the territories. Unlike Douglas, the Kentuckian served in the Mexican War, commissioned a major with the state's Third Regiment.

Breckinridge subsequently served a term in the state legislature, and he and thirty-seven other Democrats pooled resources to establish a newspaper, the semi-weekly *Lexington Kentucky Statesman*. The 1850 census identifies him as the owner of four slaves. During the public discussions preceding the passage and signing of the Compromise of 1850, Breckinridge spoke on behalf of Democratic resolutions that Congress had no authority "to interfere with the institution of slavery" in the federal territories or in the District of Columbia, much less the states. Even so, in October of that year he spoke at a bipartisan Union barbecue in honor of the compromise measures and Henry Clay's sponsorship of the initial omnibus bill, lauding Clay's "lofty eminence" "high above the platform of party." Breckinridge then voiced his conventional American understanding of the iconic term "honor" when he identified Clay as the recipient of a "priceless honor"—that is, "the admiration of the present and coming ages" for his courageous, eloquent, and patriotic "defense of our beloved Union, the last best hope of freedom and of mankind. Nobly has he won the honor—long may he wear it."[73] Northern Whig Abraham Lincoln could have enthusiastically applauded this salute to his political hero.

In 1851, Breckinridge upset a Whig incumbent and won the first of two terms as a Democratic congressman representing Clay's home district. Breckinridge backed popular sovereignty in 1850 but two years later expressed support for the traditional Calhounite argument that slaveholders had a constitutional right to carry all their property—including black human chattel— into all of the federal domain. This position was becoming increasingly standard proslavery constitutional fare. It seemed to accord with the state's rights argument that the western territories, having been gained through the diplomatic or military efforts of all the states, were the common property of citizens in all the states, free or slave. It also fit with a strict interpretation of the Constitution and the Fifth Amendment. Even so, Congressman Breckinridge actively supported Senator Douglas's popular sovereignty stance and Kansas-Nebraska Act. Breckinridge spoke in favor of the Kansas-Nebraska legislation because he hoped it would settle the hotly contested issue of slavery expansion and because it suggested that the final, authoritative decision in the debate over the status of slave property in the territories should come from the federal judiciary.

Into this 1854 speech, the Kentuckian interjected an arguably gratuitous personal attack on a one-term Democratic congressman from New York City, Francis B. Cutting, who had suggested referring the Kansas-Nebraska bill to a Committee of the Whole. (Cutting wound up voting with Breckinridge for the bill when it passed the House in May by a vote of 113 to 100.) The two men engaged in the elaborate etiquette that accompanied an affair of honor. "The Kentuckian chose rifles at sixty paces," reports historian James Klotter. "His opponent insisted on pistols at ten." After a total of fifteen notes written by Breckinridge, Cutting, and their seconds, a duel was avoided and the honor of both principals preserved by mutual concessions "reciprocating the sentiments of regret that any misunderstanding should have taken place."[74]

The Kentuckian declined to seek a third term in the House in favor of returning to "an increasingly lucrative legal practice." Such employment would enhance Breckinridge's ability to expand his purchase of real estate in the West as "an investment in the future of his country for the future of his children."[75] A few years earlier, Douglas had alerted the Kentuckian to the potential profits from investments in land near Chicago. Breckinridge's agent reported in the spring of 1854 that real estate prices in the Chicago area were already too high for land speculation and recommended that he consider better prospects in Minnesota, northern Iowa, and northern Wisconsin.[76] Yet numerous prominent Kentuckians found themselves irresistibly drawn to real estate investments and business opportunities in and around the Windy City. In October 1858, the *Chicago Press and Tribune* observed, "Our city has shared largely" in the "emigration of talent, and also of capital" from the "noble State" of Kentucky. Indeed, "in all the walks of business you will find Kentuckians among the shrewdest and most successful operators."[77]

In 1856, John Cabell Breckinridge became Democrat James Buchanan's vice presidential running mate, with supporters campaigning for "Buck and Breck." In March 1857, the thirty-seven-year-old was inaugurated as the youngest vice president in U.S. history. In 1860, he became a candidate for the presidency on the southern Democratic platform that in the aftermath of the *Dred Scott* decision, Congress had a constitutional obligation to protect the legal security of slavery in the territories, "not immediately but only if and when later necessary."[78] That is, if the lower federal courts failed to follow the Supreme Court's lead in upholding slaveholders' right to carry their slave property into all the national territories, Congress would bear responsibility for adopting a federal slave code, legislation designed to guarantee the security of slave property in the territories.

Breckinridge gave only one public speech during the 1860 campaign, speaking for some three hours on 5 September before a crowd estimated at between eight and fifteen thousand on the grounds of Ashland, the late Henry Clay's estate just outside Lexington. Breckinridge refused to answer or discuss the accusation that he owned no slaves. (Although he had been a slaveholder in 1850, he apparently was not in 1860, having sold his home and taken up residence in Lexington's Phoenix Hotel.) Insisting that he and his supporters merely endorsed the principles set forth by the Supreme Court in the *Dred Scott* case, he vehemently denied having any intention or desire to break up the federal Union. "I presently challenge the bitterest enemy I have had on earth, to point out an act, to disclose an utterance, to reveal a thought of mine hostile to the constitution and union of these States." He simply wanted to protect the Union and Constitution as interpreted by the country's highest judicial tribunal. To his mind, the Republicans were promoting disunion by supporting the deprivation of the southern states' constitutional rights.

However, Breckinridge's profession of Unionism and personal stay-at-home campaign captured far less national and regional attention than did the many high-profile speeches delivered on behalf of the Breckinridge and Lane campaign by forty-six-year-old William Lowndes Yancey, perhaps the most influential of all secessionist fire-eaters. A native of South Carolina, Yancey moved to Alabama and in 1858 teamed up with ultra Virginian Edmund Ruffin to organize the League of United Southerners, a secessionist pressure group. At the 1860 Democratic National Convention, held in Charleston, Yancey had led the delegations of Alabama and other cotton states on a walkout to protest the Douglasite Democrats. Famous for his oratory, Yancey was politically shrewd enough to know, in the words of William Freehling, that at times "an extremist had to bend toward the middle in order to lure moderates toward the extreme," which for him meant disunion as soon as possible. Promising that with the election of Breckinridge "would come safety and equality in the Union," explains Eric Walther, Yancey traveled to Memphis in mid-August 1860 to launch "an unprecedented, haphazard, and electrifying speaking tour of the country." Yancey's stumping on Breckinridge's behalf confirmed Douglas's observation that although "all the Breckinridge men" could not be labeled disunionists, there is "not a disunionist in America who is not a Breckinridge man."[79]

Breckinridge won most of the slave state electoral votes but still suffered his first and only defeat in a campaign for elective office. Breckinridge issued no public statements during December 1860, hoping that the impending crisis could be defused. On 18 December, the Senate approved a motion by Breckinridge's Kentucky friend, Democratic senator Lazarus Powell, calling for a special Committee of Thirteen "to consider that portion of the President's message relating to the disturbances of the country." Two days later, South Carolina began the wave of secessions. The same day, Breckinridge, in his role as the Senate's presiding officer, appointed a number of impressive men to the Committee of Thirteen, which took center stage in ultimately unsuccessful efforts to settle the nation's "disturbances." In February, Breckinridge presided over the official tabulation of Electoral College votes. He was not among the six delegates who represented the state of Kentucky at the Washington Peace Conference in February.

The Kentucky state legislature determined that Breckinridge should return to the Senate after Hamlin became vice president. In late March and early April, Breckinridge supported the idea of a border-state convention to mediate between secession and Union, but it failed to materialize before Fort Sumter and Lincoln's call for troops. Proclaiming loyalty first and foremost to his native state, Breckinridge endorsed Kentucky's initial stance of neutrality between the United States and the Confederacy. After first Confederate and then Union troops violated this neutrality later in 1861, Breckinridge became a Confederate general and then Jefferson Davis's last secretary of war. When the conflict ended, Breckinridge returned to Lexington.

It is testimony to the dilapidated intersectional vision of the second party system and to the power of sectional polarization in 1861 that all of the four southern politicians examined in this chapter proved themselves highly conditional Unionists by their support for the Confederate cause. In contrast, the two northern politicians discussed here endorsed Lincoln's staunch Unionism.

5 Jefferson Davis, Horace L. Kent, and the Old South

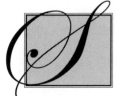enator Jefferson Davis of Mississippi, like most political leaders in the Lower or Cotton South, began the secession winter of 1860–61 as a hesitant disunionist but came to endorse the decision to quit the Union as regrettable but necessary. He hoped that the U.S. government would let the seceding states depart in peace and avoid an internecine war. In this stance, Davis seems clearly to have spoken and written what the great majority of disunionist southerners thought and hoped on the eve of the Civil War. For this reason and for the obvious reason that he became the Confederacy's first (and only) president, Davis's life story before the secession crisis provides a valuable window on the historical evolution of the Old South, setting the stage for a more wide-ranging analysis of his region's economy and society. This analysis addresses some substantial differences between the Upper and Lower Souths and discusses some individual citizens—in particular, a Virginia slaveholding merchant, Horace L. Kent, and his employee, Robert Granniss—to help illuminate those differences.

Jefferson Davis's father was Georgia native Samuel Emory Davis, probably born in 1756 and soon orphaned. After fighting against the British as a teenager during the American Revolution, Samuel Davis became proprietor of a two-hundred-acre land grant in Wilkes County and married Jane Cook of South Carolina in 1783. By the mid-1780s, his estate had grown to more than four thousand acres, though most remained uncleared, and by 1787 he owned his first slave, Winnie. In 1793, he and some of his wife's relations responded to the lure of the fabled and fertile lands in trans-Appalachian Kentucky, just separated from Virginia as an independent state. After several years there, Samuel settled his family in the southwestern part of the state in what later became Todd County. He owned a second slave by 1801. Seven years later, forty-eight-year-old Jane gave birth to her tenth child in twenty-three years. Given the first name Jefferson in honor of the Virginian then serving as president, the boy received as his middle name Finis, Latin for "the end": Jane clearly intended that he would be her last child.

Jefferson Davis spent his first two years on his father's tobacco and horse farm, housed in "a double log cabin with two large rooms on either side of a covered passageway, the classic dogtrot design," in the words of biographer William J. Cooper Jr. Samuel then moved his family again, this time south to what in 1812 would become the state of Louisiana. Samuel and Jane soon moved one last time, east to Wilkinson County in the southwestern corner of the Mississippi Territory, which became a state in 1817. Samuel built his final home, Poplar Grove, near the village of Woodville. As of 1820, he owned nearly four hundred acres and eleven slaves. Although he and Jane could read and write, according to Cooper, "nothing suggests that any of their first nine children had any more contact with formal schooling than they did." But young Jefferson Davis attended academies (preparatory schools), first Roman Catholic St. Thomas College in central Kentucky; then Jefferson College near Natchez, Mississippi; and finally the new Wilkinson County Academy, where the boy studied for five years under John Shaw, an erudite and demanding Bostonian.[1]

Samuel's eldest son, Joseph, had worked as a storekeeper's apprentice in Kentucky and then read law in Kentucky and Mississippi. By the 1820s, he "had become a prosperous attorney in Natchez as well as a substantial land-owner." When Samuel encountered financial problems in 1822, Joseph helped out by buying the family farm. Jefferson later remembered his brother as "my beau ideal when I was a boy" and as his "mentor and greatest benefactor." In 1823, Jefferson enrolled at Transylvania University, the nation's oldest college west of the Appalachian Mountains. The next year, his father died, and young Davis received an appointment to West Point, receiving his commission as a cadet from Secretary of War John C. Calhoun of South Carolina.

Jefferson Davis was accompanied to West Point by James Pemberton, a personal slave inherited from his father, in accordance with U.S. Army policy. While at the U.S. Military Academy, Davis penned his first known observation about North-South differences, in the process revealing something about his upbringing as a genteel young southerner. In January 1825, Jefferson wrote to request some money from his oldest brother, now his surrogate father, be-cause his monthly stipend as a cadet was inadequate for "the company I keep. The Yankee part of the corps find their pay entirely sufficient[,] some even more, but these are not such as I formed an acquaintance with on my arrival . . . nor are they such associates as I would at present select, enough of this as you have never been connected with them, you cannot know how pitiful they are." He graduated from the academy in 1828, ranked 23rd academically in his class of 33, apparently because he had difficulty with math and physics. Among the 208 members of the corps of cadets, he was ranked 163rd for per-sonal conduct, reflecting what historian Paul Escott has described as such "high-spirited behavior" as "long hair at inspection," "firing his musket from the window of his room," and "using spirituous liquors."[2] Davis later spoke with great pride of his training at West Point, telling members of Congress that "an uneducated officer"—one without either the sort of training he had received at the U.S. Military Academy or "a liberal education" at another institution—would likely prove unable "to command efficiently" units of artillery, an arm of the military "in the use of which so much science is involved."[3]

Davis's military service included accepting the surrender of Sauk chieftain Black Hawk in the Old Northwest. The various units of the Illinois militia mustered against Black Hawk had included Abraham Lincoln. Davis, a second lieutenant, resigned his commission in 1835, eleven days following a court-martial ruling that he had been guilty of "insubordination" but not in a manner blatantly "subversive of good order and military discipline."[4] He returned to Mississippi with a new bride, Sarah Knox Taylor, whom he had married in Kentucky after meeting her while stationed in what is now Wisconsin. "Knoxie" was the daughter of Lieutenant Colonel Zachary Taylor, Davis's commanding officer at Fort Crawford. The newlyweds contracted malaria while visiting some of his relatives in Louisiana, and Sarah died just three months after the wedding. Her grief-stricken husband turned for solace to reading in government and history, conversations with his older brother, and occasional hard labor. Davis again served under Taylor's command in 1846–47 during the Mexican War, and Taylor won election to the U.S. presidency in 1848.

At Davis Bend on the Mississippi River, south of Vicksburg, Joseph Davis owned some five thousand acres that he had purchased in 1818, between eight and nine hundred of which apparently represented Jefferson Davis's share of their late father's estate, although title remained in his older brother's name. This land, thick with cane and briers, became Brierfield plantation, just downriver from Joseph's Hurricane. Joseph also accompanied Jefferson to a Natchez slave market and loaned him funds sufficient for the purchase of ten slaves to begin work on the new estate, beginning Jefferson Davis's involvement with the interstate slave trade. In 1850, as Congress debated a proposed ban on slave trading within the District of Columbia, Davis, then a U.S. senator, told his colleagues that he saw nothing about the Washington slave trade that warranted censure. In November of that year, addressing the citizens of Mississippi's Lowndes County, he described the new legislative ban as "offensively discriminating against a particular species of property, placed by the Constitution on at least an equal footing with other property."[5]

Davis's slave purchases continued at least until late 1857, when he instructed Payne and Harrison, his factor in New Orleans, to buy a "lot of negroes." Until Pemberton's death in 1850, he and Joseph Davis managed plantation operations at Brierfield. Jefferson Davis subsequently employed many white overseers but never found one equal to Pemberton. Joseph Davis's remarkable and entrepreneurial slave manager, Ben Montgomery, at times attended to Brierfield. According to Cooper, Jefferson Davis's behavior as a slaveholder reflected "a combination of self-interest and the precepts of evangelical Protestantism" that had shaped so much of the nation during the early 1800s. "Self-interest taught that decent care of valuable property resulted in healthier and more productive laborers."[6] Scottish native Thomas Affleck, a planter in Adams County, Mississippi, made the same point in his popular plantation management book, *Cotton Plantation Record and Account Book*, which included a frequently reprinted essay on "The Duties of an Overseer." The piece advised that the principal component of "a fine crop" was "an increase in the number and a marked increase in the condition and value of the negroes."[7]

Christianity, as preached from many pulpits in the late antebellum South, instructed masters to view their slaves as perpetual children entrusted by God to fatherly stewardship—that slaveholders should treat their minions as members of an extended family. This message informed what has been called "the slaveholding ethic and religious mission to the slaves."[8] If, as one Davis biographer has observed, "something in his make-up needed deference," then the injunction to fatherly Christian stewardship reinforced Davis's need to receive deferential behavior from inferiors, who would be expected to respond with dutiful gratitude to his beneficence and concern for their well-being. His slaves "preferred either Baptist or Methodist services, the two denominations favored by slaves as well as whites everywhere." For his immediate family, Davis employed an Episcopalian chaplain.[9]

Although Davis's parents were Baptists, his boarding school exposure to Roman Catholicism promoted "ecumenical thinking," which helps explain his opposition in the 1850s to the anti-Catholic "clap-trap of Know-Nothingism" and the nativist American Party. After his second marriage in 1845, "he cleaved to his wife's Episcopal faith."[10] He thus preferred a traditional and liturgical Protestant denomination that did not experience a formal North-South schism during the Civil War era. His slaves preferred the less liturgical, more emotive and improvisational Baptist and Methodist denominations, which endured sectional splits during the mid-1840s. Of course, where white preachers often highlighted the enslavement of pagan Canaanites by the ancient Jews and St. Paul's emphasis on the duties that slaves and masters owed each other, slaves much preferred hearing about the Hebrews' Exodus from slavery in despotic Egypt and Jesus' comforting promises to the poor and downtrodden. Historian Mitchell Snay has demonstrated how the North-South denominational schisms of the 1840s served as "harbingers" of political disunion during the secession crisis, concluding that in the slave states, white Baptists, Methodists, Presbyterians, and Episcopalians "differed little in their approach to such sectional issues as slavery, abolition, and protection of Southern rights." Clergy in these churches saw "a dangerous closeness between abolitionism and infidelity" and portrayed southern Christianity as "the bastion of religious conservatism." Conservative evangelicals in most of the South emphasized that the most important Christian struggle took place in the individual Christian soul and spirit rather than in the realms of political and social controversy. Southern evangelicals thus tended to stress "the help-lessness of the moral individual to alter social arrangements," among them the gaps between rich and poor, male and female, white and black, free and slave.[11]

However, Jefferson Davis and his second wife, Varina, were decidedly less evangelical than many other masters, mistresses, and slaves. As religious historian Albert Raboteau has made clear, the more evangelical churches and denominations promoted an ecstatic mode of "revivalistic, inward, experientially oriented religion" that could and did occasionally foster "religious mutuality between white and black Christians [that] included personal recognition and respect." The "conversion experience" constituted "the core of the evangelical piety" shared by some masters and slaves, and this experience could provide slaves "with a sense of individual value and a personal vocation that contradicted the devaluing and dehumanizing forces of slavery." Christianity, as understood and practiced among slaves, therefore could contribute to what historical sociologist Wilma Dunaway has termed the "construction of a counter-hegemonic religion." In some cases, religious faith could inspire acts of rebellion, like that led in 1831 by literate slave preacher Nat Turner in Southside Virginia. Far more frequently, faith helped slaves "to assert and maintain a sense of personal value—even of ultimate worth," according to Raboteau. This identity and the nurturing provided by extended slave families and a realistic appraisal of the white power structure do much to explain the infrequency of violent slave rebellions in the Old South even as the slaves created what David Blight terms "a culture of resistance amidst oppression."

As Raboteau points out, however, there is no definitive way of determining "how many slaves were doubters, agnostics, or atheists," and "it is clear that some saw Christianity as meaningless, a sham, and a white man's religion—a fact which should temper generalizations about the piety of all slaves."[12]

In 1845, by which time he owned some seventy slaves, Jefferson Davis married Varina Banks Howell, age nineteen and almost nineteen years his junior. Joseph Davis, who had introduced Varina's father to her mother and served as best man at their wedding, also arranged Varina's 1843 introduction to Jefferson. Her father, New Jersey native William Howell, had settled in Natchez after military service in the Great Lakes campaign during the War of 1812. As a partner in the mercantile firm of Sprague and Howell, he prospered until the financial panic of 1837 and subsequent depression brought a rude end to the "bloated abundance" of the Flush Times in the cotton-growing Old Southwest. The bust relegated Howell's family to what biographer Joan Cashin calls "the fringes of the planter gentry." Yet Varina, like Mary Todd in Kentucky, received a more extensive formal education—including two terms at a select school for young ladies in the northern metropolis of Philadelphia—than was typical among even elite women in the slave states, just as Jefferson Davis's level of education surpassed that of most of his planter peers and far exceeded that of Abraham Lincoln. One historian describes Varina Davis as "a Victorian woman" who upheld "the decorum of society" and "condemned any display of sex" while displaying witty grace as an accomplished hostess.[13] As Jefferson Davis's wife, observes Cashin, Varina came "to love beautiful clothes as an expression of femininity" and as a symbol of "social status." Like the great majority of married Victorian American women, Varina Davis generally deferred to her husband's will and priorities; his understanding of "the supreme importance of duty gave first priority to politics, while hers focused on family." Like most plantation mistresses, Varina Davis learned that supervising the clothing, medical care, and perhaps the meals of slaves on the plantation could demand a great deal of her time and energy, although their labor provided her with a relatively high degree of leisure and freedom from hard or dirty manual labor. At the same time, Davis proved an atypical plantation mistress by developing extensive expertise with the new midcentury technology of the sewing machine. She muffled her occasional reservations about slavery and accepted the region's "extreme version of the double standard that prevailed in the rest of the country." White women pretended not to know or resigned themselves to the fact that white males fathered large numbers of illegitimate children, free whites and mulatto slaves, the latter sometimes conceived during sex forced on bondswomen. No evidence suggests that either Jefferson or Joseph Davis had any slave offspring, although Joseph, whom Varina called a "libertine," had several white children born out of wedlock.[14]

Soon after his second marriage, Jefferson Davis won election to the U.S. House of Representatives as a Jacksonian Democrat, although the rich alluvial soils and high cotton lands near the Mississippi River nurtured far more Whig than Democratic politicians.[15] His mainstream Democratic hostility to the Bank of the United States is evident in his March 1844 letter to Ohio senator William Allen: "I had but cannot find a speech of yours [from the 1830s] showing that the U.S. Bank loaned at a time which indicated the purpose, more money to members of Congress than the amount of their pay—can you send me a copy of that speech?"[16]

After Congress declared war on Mexico in 1846, the future Confederate president did not formally resign from the House of Representatives until he had commanded (with the rank of colonel) the First Mississippi Regiment of volunteers at the Battle of Monterrey. Pemberton was left in charge of operations at Brierfield. James Green, a personal slave on loan from Joseph Davis, accompanied the colonel to Mexico. In 1847, Jefferson Davis was wounded during the Battle of Buena Vista, returned home to Mississippi, and received a gubernatorial appointment to the U.S. Senate. He needed crutches to stand while taking the oath of office in Washington, and while in the Senate, he suffered intense eye inflammation probably caused by a viral infection that led to deterioration of the cornea and blindness in his left eye. He experienced a partial recovery but endured another serious attack in 1858 and surgery the following year. In subsequent photographs, his damaged left eye is turned away from the camera.

In the Senate, Davis supported traditional Democratic policies of strict construction, state's rights, and low tariffs. He also argued consistently that the Founding Fathers had acted under the premise that property rights in human beings warranted the same respect as did all other property rights. In August 1849, in the midst of congressional debates over the status of slavery in the Mexican Cession, Davis wrote, "We rely on the Bible as authority for the establishment of slavery among men, and on the Constitution for its recognition throughout the United States."[17] This single sentence seems a condensation of the basic ideological differences between proslavery southerners and antislavery northerners.

Beginning in the early 1830s, explained Davis, American abolitionism had organized to promote "the antislavery agitation which disturbs the fraternity and peace of the Republic." He continued, "Fanatics and demagogues have inflamed popular passion . . . fed by sectional pride . . . among the masses of the North." Davis saw the current effort to exclude slavery from the Mexican Cession as "a sectional discrimination, alike violative of our constitutional rights, and offensive to our feelings for the institution we inherited, with the arrogant alternative of submission or compulsion."[18] Davis interpreted the Constitution as providing special recognition and protection to slave property as "coextensive with the supremacy of Federal laws, its existence subject only to the legislation of the sovereign States possessing powers not drawn from, but above, the Constitution." The Mississippian followed the lead of South Carolinians John Calhoun and Robert Barnwell Rhett in propounding "what came to be known as the common-property doctrine." Because the Constitution and the creation of a republican federal government had been approved by the states through state conventions, territory acquired by the U.S. government belonged to the states, and the federal government governed such territory as an agent for all the states, slave as well as free. However, Davis, like Presidents Franklin Pierce and James Buchanan during the 1850s, did not see this common-property doctrine as implying that the federal government should show any hesitation about acquiring Cuba and its slave plantations from Spain just because citizens in a majority of states—that is, the free states without slaves—opposed the sugar-growing Caribbean island's incorporation into the United States.

Despite Calhoun's and Davis's protestations in the Senate, the Compromise of 1850 provided for California's swift admission to the Union as a free state. This development particularly galled those proslavery southerners still smarting over the effective exclusion of their peculiar institution from the Oregon Country gained in 1846 after negotiations with the British overlords of Canada. Furthermore, such southerners believed that slaves could be put to productive and profitable labor alongside free white workers in mines and factories, citing as proof the gold mines at Dahlonega, in northern Georgia, which had opened in 1836 and at which slaves comprised three-quarters of the workforce. Stated Davis in 1850, "The production of rice, sugar, and cotton is no better adapted to slave labor than the digging, washing, and quarrying of the gold mines of California."[19]

Lawyer and politician Henry Wise, owner of nineteen slaves and four hundred acres on the Eastern Shore of Virginia, saw in California gold mines a highly lucrative source of additional demand for slave labor not needed on unproductive or worn-out fields in the Old Dominion. A bondsman worth a thousand dollars there might fetch three to five times as much in California. Wise and numerous other Upper South slaveholders found quite appealing the opportunity not only to sell their slaves at such high prices but also to gradually remove the state's black population and do away with slavery there. "Wise believed," according to biographer Craig Simpson, "that the loss of California" cost Virginia and other Upper South states "a last, golden opportunity" for emancipation "at a profit." Other Virginians, among them planter-physician Richard Eppes, reached a different conclusion about the future of slavery in the Tidewater counties of the Old Dominion. In the fall of 1860, Eppes identified various "causes of depression of Landed property in Lower Virginia" that could be overcome if "improved farming by judicious investment of capital in manures & machinery" became more common among planters, who needed to pursue "economy, industry[,] close application of farming as a profession, [and] inculcation & practice of sound principles of the improvement and management of landed property." Such improvement of the soil required "increasing or rather retaining negroes to cultivate it," reversing the current exodus of slaveholders and slaves to the cotton states. Hence, the success of agricultural improvement in eastern Virginia necessitated "the removal of the exciting causes now shaking our Union to its very Foundations." The prospect of an antislavery Republican victory in November 1860 was "leading to insecurity of property thereby checking the investment of capital to improve the naturally poor soil of Lower Virginia." For Eppes, therefore, the Upper South did not want or need new territory, but its agriculture might not survive the election of a Republican president.[20]

In the process of securing the Democratic nomination for his congressional seat in 1845, Davis had outpolled Dr. William Gwin, a graduate of Kentucky's Transylvania University. A Tennessee native, Gwin had acquired several Mississippi plantations with some two hundred slaves. At an 1845 Vicksburg ball honoring Calhoun, Varina Davis was outraged when Gwin's wife, Mary, wore a black velvet dress cut so low that it exposed her bosom to leering men, among them Calhoun's son, with whom she danced. Davis wrote soon thereafter, "It made my blood run cold and I felt like kicking them both out of the room for daring to conduct themselves in such a manner before innocent girls." Jefferson Davis later helped resolve a dispute between Gwin and Congressman Jacob Thompson before it led to a duel. In 1849, Gwin decided that moving to California offered the best hope of realizing his burning ambition for a seat in the U.S. Senate. Soon after arriving in California, he determined that the gold diggings could be worked efficiently with enslaved laborers, a point that Davis made repeatedly in 1850. Yet Gwin realized that hardworking white miners wanted manual labor to remain respectable and honorable; they certainly did not want to compete in the mines with black slaves. Political ambition therefore dictated that he stand against the legalization of bondage in his adopted state. Gwin nevertheless emerged as the leader, explains historian Leonard L. Richards, of "a coalition of Southern-born politicians" who became the influential "Chivalry faction" within California's dominant Democratic Party. The doctor won two elections to the Senate, where he usually "thought and voted like a typical Deep South Senator." When the Republican Party's 1856 nominee, John C. Frémont, went down to defeat in five free states, he lost California by the largest margin, winning barely 19 percent of the vote. In 1859, Gwin and the Chivalry faction came remarkably close to having southern California, with less than 10 percent of the population, become a separate slave state. In the following year's election, Lincoln took California despite receiving only 32.3 percent of the popular vote (a lower percentage than in any other free state), edging Stephen A. Douglas's 31.7 percent.

Gwin as well as California's other senator and its two congressmen revealed their southern sympathies by campaigning for Breckinridge, who received 28.4 percent of the state's ballots. In Washington, D.C., the Gwins owned a palatial mansion that contained furnishings worth some seventy-five thousand dollars. The night before the Davises left the capital after his resignation from the Senate in January 1861, the two couples conversed until three in the morning. After 4 March, Gwin, now a former senator, spoke with William Henry Seward on behalf of commissioners from the Confederacy, telling the conciliationist secretary of state that the Confederate leaders were "ready to accept war" if negotiations over Forts Sumter and Pickens broke off. When California remained loyal to the Union, Gwin returned to Mississippi until the fall of Vicksburg, thereafter working on behalf of the Confederacy in France and Mexico.[21]

After passage of the Compromise of 1850, Davis gave up his Senate seat to make a bid for the Mississippi governorship. Despite his defeat the following year, his combination of military and political experience led to his 1853 appointment as secretary of war under newly inaugurated Democratic president Franklin Pierce. That Pierce and Davis had overlapping agendas had become clear when Pierce strongly supported the annexation of slaveholding Texas in 1845. Three years earlier, Pierce had resigned his seat in the U.S. Senate to earn a higher income by practicing law in New Hampshire, his home state. His legal work there catered increasingly to corporations and mill companies. After supporting the expansionist Polk's victory in February 1845, Pierce was appointed district attorney for New Hampshire. He attended the state's Democratic Party convention, which adopted an expansionist but not proslavery resolution that represented the stance of most New Democrats and Young Americans nationally: "That the annexation of Texas, by widely extending the domain of this republic—by strengthening our means of defense in war, and greatly increasing our resources in peace—without adding to the numbers of the enslaved—without increasing the relative political powers of the slaveholding interest of our country—will guaranty the blessings of a republican government to millions of patriotic and kindred beings who might otherwise be reduced to become the oppressed and unprivileged subjects of European despotism."[22]

As secretary of war, Davis favored a southern route for the first transcontinental railroad, as the Gadsden Purchase of 1853 suggests. (Its construction would be delayed until after the secession crisis, when Republicans in Congress encountered no opposition to a northern route.) Davis also gave strong support to the Kansas-Nebraska Act of 1854, arranging a meeting with Douglas that secured Pierce's endorsement, as well as to American acquisition of slaveholding Cuba. "Davis had always been his own man, by nature more autocratic than collegial," according to one biographer. While secretary of war, "he became noted for his unwillingness to delegate, and for a compulsion to do everything himself." Nonetheless, he proved himself what Escott terms a "hardworking and competent" cabinet officer, "keeping his contentious nature largely in check." Despite a tendency to self-righteous anger, Davis had developed a degree of "formidable self-control" that would serve him well during his trying tenure as president of the Confederacy. Like Lincoln, Davis seems to have been "plagued with melancholy or 'morbid sensibility,'" concludes Lynda Casswell Crist. However, in response to criticism, "Lincoln tended to self-deprecation," whereas "Davis was thin-skinned." This sensitivity seems to have contributed to what another historian terms his often "poor judgment about human beings," which became more evident over time.[23]

In 1856, Davis discreetly lobbied the Mississippi legislature for another stint in the U.S. Senate, his efforts reflecting what one scholar has described as "Victorian-era sensibilities" that "inhibited self-promotion."[24] He resumed his seat in March 1857, siding with President Buchanan on the proslavery Lecompton Constitution for Kansas and pressing the case for some sort of federal guarantee to slaveholders in the territories. During a speaking trip to the Northeast, Davis pleaded his warm attachment to the Union, while back home in Mississippi he voiced more secessionist sentiments. According to biographer William C. Davis, Jefferson Davis's "repeated enunciation of the abstract right of secession branded him a disunionist in the eyes of his Northern foes," while "any expression of fondness for the old Union made him equally despised by the ultra fire-eaters of the South." After Lincoln's election, the Mississippian tried to steer a cooperationist middle course between immediate secessionists and hesitant or delaying conditional Unionists. He acknowledged the Black Republican victory as a "declaration of hostility" against the South yet promoted Mississippi's "readiness to cooperate" with other slave states in pursuing "whatever measures" they deemed appropriate. He sought to sidestep the question of whether an overt act of aggression by the Republicans should precede a state's formal decision to secede, simply insisting that he could never accept any military coercion directed against a state by the federal government.[25]

In 1860, Davis told the Senate that blacks constituted a "subservient race," their enslavement in the South serving as "the substratum on which the white race is elevated to its true dignity." He defined "the condition of slavery among us" as "but the form of civil government instituted for a class of people not fit to govern themselves." This definition is all the more interesting in light of the family legend, originated decades after the Civil War by Varina Davis and Joseph Davis's granddaughter, that slaves on both Brierfield and Hurricane plantations participated in their own government through juries of black peers that tried every slave accused of violating plantation rules and imposed punishment that could be reduced only by the master's intervention. According to one biographer, "The picture Davis painted of the tranquil and happy plantation life of white and black together really existed on Davis Bend, however much it may have been a dream world elsewhere." A subsequent biographer offers a more cautious conclusion: "That such a fascinating system of slave management run by two such prominent individuals in such an accessible location completely escaped notice [by contemporaries] is puzzling."[26]

In 1853, antislavery Swede Frederika Bremer wrote about witnessing a comparable phenomenon while visiting a plantation on St. Simons Island owned by a respected Georgian, probably James Hamilton Couper. Bremer had heard Couper, the owner of four different Sea Island plantations and the eldest son of an indentured servant from Scotland who became a wealthy merchant, described as "a reformer, who had introduced trial by jury among his slaves, with many educational institutions, to prepare them for a future of liberty." Like Thomas Jefferson, Couper allegedly saw persons of African ancestry as deficient in the capacity for abstract reasoning but nevertheless looked ahead to the eventual emancipation of his fifteen hundred slaves, followed by their colonization somewhere outside the United States, where they could enjoy the blessings of self-government. Yet Bremer reported finding in Couper "merely a disciplinarian, with great practical tact, and also some benevolence in the treatment of Negroes." According to Elizabeth Fox-Genovese and Eugene D. Genovese, Bremer simply "did not understand that slaveholders defended their system precisely as one that blended self-interest with moral demands for humane treatment of labor." In 1856, Couper, like Lincoln, finally abandoned the dying Whig organization but moved in the opposite political direction, endorsing Democratic nominee Buchanan as "the most sound and conservative" bulwark against "the Black Republican party." Although Couper opposed Georgia's secession in 1861, "once the die was cast he was as loyal a Southerner as could be found and supported the cause with all he had, particularly with his five sons."[27]

To James Couper and Jefferson Davis, as to most free Americans in the Lower South (along with many in the Upper South and some in the free states), the fact that a Republican had won the presidency in 1860 on a platform of firm geographical containment of slavery appeared ominous, even apocalyptic. Such would have been the case even in the absence of the widespread belief that the new party's leaders, including Lincoln, were in reality abolitionists poorly concealed behind a guise of Unionist moderation, as northern Democratic newspapers and politicians often said. For the first time, the nation had elected a president who had repeatedly voiced clear antagonism to chattel slavery, labeling it a "great social, moral and political evil." Because he had won the presidency without receiving a single electoral vote from a slave state, he had no substantial political debts or obligations south of the Mason-Dixon Line and the Ohio River. Most white southerners saw the election of such a man to the nation's highest office, occupied for most of its history by slaveholding southerners, as a form of degradation, an affront to their interests, rights, and honor.

It is difficult to avoid generalized labels such as "the South" and "white southerners" when studying the antebellum region. Yet historians have become increasingly cognizant that in 1860 neither the fifteen slave states nor the eighteen free states constituted an economic, social, or political monolith. Indeed, intraregional variations—differences among and even within individual states north or south—at times appear as historically significant as intersectional differences between states where slavery was legally established and those where it was not.

When considering political orientation on the eve of the Civil War, it is helpful to view both the slave South and the free North as divided into subregions or tiers on a roughly north-south continuum. The Old South can be seen as encompassing three subregions: the least disunionist border states; the more disunionist middle states; and the most disunionist states of the Deep

South. Moreover, individual states across the country experienced strong internal divisions between areas intensely hostile to political antislavery as well as radical abolition and areas more focused on the dangers of disunion and secession. Virginia, the most populous slave state, split between 1861 and 1863 into a loyalist trans-Allegheny west and a Confederate east. Similarly, the most populous free state, New York, experienced tensions in 1860–61 between strongly antislavery Upstate and a greater New York City metropolis sympathetic to the South, although the Empire State became firmly Unionist after the Fort Sumter episode.

More emphatically than any other scholarship on the slave South, the two volumes of William Freehling's *The Road to Disunion* demonstrate the importance of understanding the differences and divisions among the South's three principal subregions. The southernmost tier includes the seven Cotton or Deep South states, extending from South Carolina west to Texas, that seceded between Lincoln's presidential victory and his inauguration four months later. Freehling's intermediate tier, the Middle South, comprises Virginia, North Carolina, Tennessee, and Arkansas, all of which withdrew from the Union after Lincoln's call for troops in April. The northernmost tier, the Border South, included those slave states that never seceded from the Union—Delaware, Maryland, Kentucky, and Missouri. The Middle and Border South states were and often still are denominated the Upper South. Four of these states—North Carolina, Tennessee, Kentucky, and Virginia—encompass almost all of mountainous southern Appalachia and experienced serious internal conflict during the Civil War. In Freehling's words, "The farther north the southern state, the cooler the clime, the fewer the slaves, and the lower the relative commitment to perpetuating slavery." A Charlottesville, Virginia, newspaper made the same point more coarsely in late November 1860: "Give the latitude, and you can give the figure at which the negrometer stands." But "the thermometer cannot settle accurately a moral question."[28]

It makes analytical sense to include in the category of the Border South during the secession crisis a fifth state that did not exist as a separate entity until 1863. Most residents of what would become West Virginia had stronger connections with Pennsylvania and Ohio via the Ohio River Valley than with the easternmost Tidewater and Piedmont divisions of the Old Dominion. Within antebellum Virginia, the social, economic, and cultural differences between the more mountainous counties and the more plantation-friendly eastern counties had been obvious and palpable for decades. "The tidewater and the tobacco regions made up Old Virginia," explains William Shade; these eastern counties were "closely wed to slavery and the plantation system." The upcountry western counties beyond the Blue Ridge Mountains, especially those west of the valley between the Blue Ridge and Alleghany Mountains, had many more slaveless farmers and far fewer slaveholding planters than did Old Virginia to the east. Intrastate political tensions over legislative apportionment, white manhood suffrage, taxes on slave property, and state expenditures on internal improvements had dominated the Virginia Constitutional Conventions of 1829–30 and 1850–51. At the second convention, western reformers, aided by outspoken allies Henry Wise from the Eastern Shore and John Minor Botts of Richmond, brought political democracy to the Old Dominion by assuring elitist conservatives that "majority rule would not endanger the economic interests of the planters." Democratic reforms accelerated "the passing of planter hegemony" in Virginia politics even before the Civil War.[29]

Antebellum North Carolina and Tennessee manifested analogous internal divisions. However, Virginia, with its geographical division into an eastern Chesapeake region and a western region linked to the Ohio River, offers the most dramatic example of a slave state whose internal conflicts shaped the course of the secession crisis and the Civil War. After the Old Dominion made its contested and reluctant decision to join the Confederacy in the spring of 1861, the western trans-Alleghany counties, with help from Union armies, seceded from the Old Dominion and constituted an independent West Virginia. Given the firmly Unionist attitudes of most future West Virginians during the secession crisis, which contrasted with the provisional or conditional Unionist stance of most eastern Virginians, and given that the Old Dominion became the only state to experience permanent internal disunion during the Civil War, it makes sense to locate the imminent reality of West Virginia within the Border South prior to the war. Doing so helps to clarify the divisions within the Upper South between the reluctantly secessionist states of the Middle South and the ultimately loyal states of the Border South. Thus, in 1860–61, Virginia was the only slave state that included sections of both the Border and Middle Souths.

Virginia's internal diversity at the beginning of the Civil War also reflected the presence of both greater manufacturing capacity and a larger network of cities than existed in any other Confederate state. In fact, the Old Dominion alone contained almost as much industry as did all seven Deep South states. As David Goldfield has emphasized, Virginia's eastern regions possessed "the most extensive rail network in the South, which urban and rural allies pieced together though numerous legislative battles," and these railroads made possible "far and away the most advanced urban network of any state that joined the Confederacy."[30] Because of Virginia's cities, industry, population, and history, the Confederate government moved its capital from Montgomery, Alabama, to Richmond, situated just below the falls of the James River. Virginia's capital city straddled the point of contact between the upriver boundary of the Tidewater and the downriver boundary of the Piedmont. The terminus of five railroads as well as the James River and Kanawha Canal, it became the Confederacy's most industrial city.

Richmond's population grew rapidly from just over 27,500 in 1850 to nearly 38,000 a decade later. Almost 38 percent of the city's residents (14,275 people) were African Americans, more than 11,500 of them enslaved. Owners hired out many slaves to employers in the commercial, manufacturing, and transportation sectors of the economy. On the one hand, slave hiring provided rural slaveholders with surplus labor a means of earning money and perhaps of disciplining and dispatching difficult servants. On the other hand, hiring out could encourage independence and initiative among enslaved workers, even as it also compromised and contradicted planters' widespread patriarchal self-perception.[31]

Among the Virginians who looked to Richmond as a market for hiring out slaves was Colonel Robert E. Lee. After the death of his father-in-law in 1857, Lee returned from his military posting on the West Texas frontier to serve for twenty-six months as the executor of George Washington Parke Custis's heavily indebted and dilapidated properties in eastern Virginia, which included several plantations and almost two hundred slaves. The career U.S. Army officer and future Confederate general understood, in the words of a recent biographer, that "the key to enhancing productivity" was slave labor, "and productivity was what Lee needed in order to make the property solvent." By 1859, the younger and stronger slaves had been removed from Arlington plantation, just across the Potomac River from Washington, D.C., because they brought the highest rates of hire. Lee transferred half a dozen slaves south to Richmond and in July 1858 instructed an agent to "dispose of them at the end of the year to the best advantage." A year later, he wrote to his son that several slaves hired out in Richmond had been "put to your service and mine and much to your mother's relief." During the coming year, he advised, "it may be better to hire them all out. Their presence [at Arlington] seems to be of no advantage."[32]

Virginians owning more African Americans than they could employ productively at home might also sell surplus chattel to traders in Richmond, who supplied the market for bond labor for the Deep South's cotton and sugar plantations. The threat of sale could serve as a disciplinary tool, and the decision to sell could reflect an owner's calculation that a slave had become too difficult to keep. In November 1859, the month after John Brown's aborted raid at Harpers Ferry, Richard Eppes confided to his diary that he had arranged for "Dickinson & Hill Auctioneers of Slaves" to sell Bins, a twenty-one-year-old male, for $1,495: "It is truly a painful thing to sell a really troublesome negro but it must be done for the good of the others or discipline & good management will disappear from the estate."[33]

Eppes and other affluent planters in eastern Virginia also pondered buying Deep South lands suitable for cotton or sugar cultivation and sending surplus slaves to work those fields. Perhaps Eppes had in mind the example set by his distant relations resident in the Piedmont, John Hartwell Cocke and his son, Philip St. George Cocke, who had established cotton plantations in Alabama and Mississippi. In July 1860, Eppes visited Richmond and met a planter named Haskell from Abbeville, South Carolina—probably Charles T. Haskell of Home Place plantation, owner of 160 slaves in the Abbeville District. Eppes seriously considered Haskell's recommendation, based on his son's experience with a plantation near Pine Bluff, Arkansas, to purchase "bottom lands on the Arkansas River."

When the Virginia Secession Convention opened in Richmond in February 1861, the only delegate to whom the 1860 census ascribed the ownership of more than one hundred slaves in a single county was fifty-four-year-old James Coles Bruce of Halifax County, in the southern Piedmont. Bruce told his fellow delegates that after returning to Virginia from a visit to New Orleans in 1844, "I advised my friends who were also large planters to carry a portion of their negroes South, where their profits were great, and not keep them here where our profits were small. To show my sincerity in the belief, I went to Louisiana, and became a cotton and sugar planter."[34]

While affluent planters such as Bruce, Cocke, and Eppes looked to the cotton South for profitable investment opportunities, the diversified city of Richmond attracted migrants from both abroad and the free states. In addition to the nearly two-fifths of Richmond's residents who were free or enslaved African Americans, 13 percent of Richmond's 1860 population had been born outside the United States, a number that had grown by more than 160 percent since 1850. The number of northern-born whites also nearly doubled during the decade, testimony to strong business, social, and family connections between eastern Virginia and the Northeast. In the judgment of Democratic editor John Moncure Daniel of the *Richmond Examiner*, the city was "overrun with yankees and German societies."[35] Two such Yankees, merchant Horace L. Kent and his young employee, Robert Granniss, illuminate antebellum eastern Virginia's strong business, cultural, and social connections with the Northeast as well as the power of Unionist sentiment in the state. At the same time, the large slave population of most Tidewater and Piedmont counties determined that the great majority of free eastern Virginians embraced conditional rather than staunch Unionism, which proved to be, in James M. McPherson's words, "a perishable commodity."[36] When forced to choose between siding with the Confederacy and providing troops to coerce it, eastern delegates to the Virginia State Convention in April voted overwhelmingly in favor of secession. The older and more established of the two Yankees sided with the Confederacy, while the younger returned to his roots in metropolitan New York.

Whigs more than Jacksonian Democrats had supported government promotion of "internal improvements" (i.e., railroads and canals) and diversified economic development. In 1860, therefore, Virginia's major eastern cities—Richmond, Norfolk, Alexandria, and Lynchburg—remained centers of Whiggish sentiment, though former Whigs referred to themselves as the Opposition. Whereas two-party competition had faded in the Lower South a decade earlier, the survival in Upper South states of anti-Democratic Opposition organizations, supported by former Whigs and nativist Know-Nothings, helped to restrain the secessionist fever that swept the cotton states after Lincoln's election. "Most Richmond business and professional men," writes Marie Tyler-McGraw, realized that disunion "would be financially disastrous and politically unwise."[37] Much of the city's commercial and financial life involved connections with major northeastern ports, especially New York City. The general trend of antebellum American and transatlantic commerce had brought "the increasing dominance of New York over all other" U.S. ports. The city's merchants handled more than two-thirds of the nation's import trade, and its shipping carried well over a third of the country's exports, up from less than a fifth in 1815. That year, Richmond and Norfolk had captured a respectable 11.5 percent of U.S. exports, a figure that fell to a paltry 1.3 percent by 1860.[38]

Richmond's burgeoning dry-goods businesses had especially strong connections with metropolitan New York and southern New England. Exemplifying those ties was Kent, who was born in Suffolk, Connecticut, in 1804 and moved to Richmond at the age of seventeen. According to Samuel Mordecai's 1860 reminiscence, Kent built "the splendid store of Kent, Paine, & Company, the first specimen in Richmond of the Broadway style of" department store.[39]

Such emporiums had been pioneered by Alexander Turney Stewart, who immigrated from Belfast, Northern Ireland, to Manhattan in 1818. Five years later, after inheriting five thousand dollars, he opened a small dry-goods store on Broadway just north of City Hall Park. His business prospered and by 1837 occupied a five-story, double-width building at 257 Broadway. He developed a mail-order business by placing advertisements in newspapers nationwide, and his policy of accepting only cash rather than extending credit enabled him to survive the 1837 financial panic and the subsequent depression. Indeed, he took advantage of other people's business troubles, buying up "great amounts of distressed merchandise from bankrupt wholesalers . . . , emerging as one of the city's first millionaires." He drew his clientele "from among the expanding company of middle-class and working women who developed a taste for bargain-priced imported textiles." In 1846, Stewart paid sixty-five thousand dollars for the northeast corner of Broadway and Chambers Street, where he opened a huge new store that became known as the Marble Palace. The interior featured a large circular central court with a domed skylight. Customers were encouraged to stroll leisurely around the selling floors, inspecting goods atop polished mahogany counters and marble shelves. Items were organized into nineteen departments within the store, and every object was tagged with a set price, so that women need not engage in unseemly haggling with young male salesclerks. Newspapers hailed him as "Stewart the Great" and "King Stewart." Before the Civil War, his business was the nation's largest importer and the world's largest dry-goods retail establishment, taking in some nine million dollars a year.[40]

Kent brought Richmond a scaled-down four-story model of the Marble Palace and became a prominent member of the city's elite. Owner of six slaves by 1850, Kent and his family lived in a fashionable and "imposing mansion" at 12 East Franklin Street. The house was constructed with two stories in 1845, and at some point Kent added a third story and an iron veranda probably ordered from New York; according to an architectural historian, "The pattern of this ironwork is unlike any we have encountered in Virginia or Maryland" and resembled "the veranda of the Harper House on Gramercy Park in New York City." His brother, James S. Kent, followed Horace to Richmond, also becoming a dry-goods merchant and slaveholder. James purchased an Albemarle County farm, Rougement, where he lived with his New York–born wife, and some of their ten daughters and three sons. Horace Kent gained the friendship and respect of his mercantile peers, including leading merchant and slaveholding patron of the arts Mann Satterwhite Valentine Sr.[41]

In 1847, when the state legislature awarded a charter to extend what became known as the Central Virginia Railroad west to Charlottesville, Kent held the office of secretary of the commissioners who solicited subscriptions for the stock and helped persuade the city council to take as much as two hundred thousand dollars in stock. In 1852, Richmond merchants, recognizing that most imports came by way of ships landing at northern ports, called a meeting of the members of the state's mercantile community to discuss promoting direct trade between foreign countries and ports on the James River. Horace Kent was elected vice president of the gathering, and he subsequently became president of the Richmond Board of Trade, crossing the Atlantic to encourage "direct trade" between England and Virginia. He and R. B. Haxall, a member of a prominent Richmond family that owned and operated one of the country's largest flour mills, persuaded the city council to appropriate thousands of dollars to refurbish market stalls "to better accommodate buyers and sellers" in the downtown commercial district. Kent's Board of Trade also attempted to arrange improved coordination among incoming railroads, ship arrivals, and teamsters so that goods would not languish on railroad platforms and wharves.[42]

In the aftermath of John Brown's raid on Harpers Ferry, public opinion in Richmond and much of the state became preoccupied with internal security. Although conservative Republicans such as Lincoln and Seward denounced Brown's illegal violence, white Virginians became increasingly likely to take seriously secessionist fire-eaters' claims that the Republican Party included Brown supporters who favored invading the South and fomenting a race war. After his capture, Brown told Wise, now Virginia's governor, and Lee, commander of the troops that had stormed the firehouse at the Harpers Ferry armory, that they "might dispose of me very easily . . . but this question is still to be settled—this negro question I mean—the end of that is not yet." Lee described Brown's effort to foment a slave insurgency as "the attempt of a fanatic or a madman that could only end in failure."[43]

Despite Brown's short-term failure, his raid promoted much anger, fear, and resentment in the white South, and its repercussions extended through the election year and the secession winter. One account of Richmonders' reactions to Brown's raid comes from Robert A. Granniss, a New York native who worked as a clerk in Kent's retail emporium. The eighteen-year-old Granniss had moved to Richmond in September 1858 and apparently used his father's business connections to obtain a job with Kent, Paine, and Company. He lived in a boardinghouse near the governor's mansion and frequently dined with the Kent family, becoming a friend of Horace's son, Charles. Granniss also courted one of the "radiantly lovely" Kent daughters, Emma, although he failed, at least in part because Horace Kent deemed her too young for Granniss's overtures. He made "his debut into Richmond society" and frequently attended St. Paul's Episcopal Church, "the most aristocratic church in the city," where the members were "all highly respectable."

In late October, Granniss learned of the "riot" at Harpers Ferry, describing it as "an attempt on the part of the Abolitionists to excite the negroes to revolt." The story dominated the newspapers through mid-November, and over the weekend of 19–20 November, "the whole city was in confusion" because Governor Wise received telegraph dispatches about an anticipated "attack from Abolitionists to rescue Old Brown. The result was the ringing of the alarm, troops assembled from all parts of the city." On Sunday night, the city's "outskirts were patrolled by detachments of the Lancers," as some residents feared "an insurrection among the negroes." Granniss's boardinghouse roommate, Horace Baldwin, mustered with the Richmond Grays, while Granniss joined a new militia, B Company, attached to the First Regiment of Virginia Volunteers. Its members elected him fourth sergeant. His enlistment expenses totaled forty-two dollars, almost half of the hundred-dollar raise awarded him by Kent effective January 1860. However, his "military glory" proved short-lived; by 10 December, "the excitement [had] pretty much died out." Granniss received promotion to third sergeant in June 1860, and in December, after Lincoln's election but before South Carolina's secession, his company received a new name, the Richmond City Guard.[44]

Public pressure in Richmond to speak out in defense of southern rights nevertheless remained intense, especially after a county court's conviction of the "brilliant self-publicist" Brown for treason and his hanging on 2 December in Charlestown elicited many paeans to his selfless martyrdom from the free states. Though Kent was a decidedly Whiggish Unionist, he endorsed a January 1860 memorial to the General Assembly to make Virginia "independent of the Northern and Eastern States of this Confederacy." Citing the "evident hostility of the Free Soil-States" and "their plain determination to subject the Slave States to the despotism of a sectional majority," the signers proposed several economic reforms, including taxes on imports and manufactures from the North. To help encourage more direct trade with Europe, they asked for state bonuses and tonnage duties that would build up Virginia's commercial merchant marine. "More a call for Southern economic independence than a secessionist screed," according to one scholar, "the memorial still contained strongly sectional language" and of course state's rights rhetoric. The memorial received support from most Richmond merchants and prominent manufacturers, including Joseph Reid Anderson of the Tredegar Iron Works and tobacco manufacturer James H. Grant.[45]

Business in the city remained good. On a single day in April, Kent, Paine, and Company sold twenty thousand dollars worth of merchandise and Granniss worked until four o'clock in the morning, two hours past the normal closing time. In his free time, the young clerk made a point to visit the city's famous sights, including St. John's Church, located on Church Hill, east of the Capitol, and Hollywood Cemetery in the western suburbs, where he "saw the grave of ExPres Monroe." Hollywood had become the city's premier tourist attraction after the transfer of James Monroe's body from New York City to a newly constructed tomb in his home state in 1858. In the late 1840s, Horace Kent and two other New Englanders had been among the approximately twenty-five city leaders who raised $4,675 to purchase the nearly forty-three acres, Harvie's Woods, that became Hollywood Cemetery, and Kent joined the new cemetery's five-member board of trustees. Initially, said a city newspaper, it was to be called Mount Vernon Cemetery, "a second Mount Auburn," following the example set by the country's first parklike necropolis designed to serve an urban area, which had been dedicated in 1831 and was located on seventy-two acres in Cambridge, Massachusetts, along the Charles River four miles from Boston. The initiative for the Hollywood project originated with two of the city's longtime business acquaintances, entrepreneur Joshua Jefferson Fry and William Henry Haxall, manager of his family's successful flour mills. The two men met by chance in Boston in the spring of 1847, visited Mount Auburn, and decided to create just such a burial retreat in Richmond. Situated atop a steep granite bluff overlooking the falls of the James River, Hollywood offered views of the downtown skyline; just to the south, at the base of the bluff, lay the James River and Kanawha Canal, with its wide towpath. The canal was never extended beyond the Appalachian Mountains and thus never captured any Ohio Valley commercial traffic for Richmond, while the Erie Canal funneled traffic from the Great Lakes to New York City, and the Baltimore and Ohio Railroad later connected Wheeling and the Ohio River to Baltimore. However, the canal brought some grain and other produce from the Shenandoah Valley and southwestern Virginia to Richmond and carried return goods back to its terminus at Buchanan in Botetourt County.[46]

"In the 1850s," observes historian Ernest B. Furgurson, "Richmond's biggest business was not tobacco, flour, or iron, but slaves."[47] They were available for purchase as well as rental. Soon after his arrival in Richmond, during an October 1858 walk through the downtown commercial district, Granniss "passed through a negro auction and stepping in I behold a fellow being sold. A fine negro boy was standing on the platform and waiting to be knocked down to the highest bidder." The boy, with his trousers and shirt sleeves rolled up, "was ordered to step down on the floor and a space being cleared he walked from the stand to the door about 20 feet and back. Like a horse his 'action' was shown. He was then ordered to stand still and his teeth were examined and his chest and head." The boy "sold for $1100 and odd. A large price for a boy 14 yrs. old." Granniss "left the scene thoroughly disgusted with the 'peculiar institution.'" According to historian Greg Kimball, "Granniss, from a society where selling was a way of life, was not prepared to confront the inspection of a human being for sale as a commodity."[48]

On the eve of the 1860 presidential election, Granniss correctly observed, "A dissolution of the Union would play sad havoc among the merchants here." He could not determine whether the Old Dominion would go for Constitutional Unionist John Bell or southern Democrat John Breckinridge. Both Granniss and Kent supported Bell, whose most vocal supporter in Richmond was Botts, a former Whig and substantial slaveholder, who has been described by recent historians as "stubborn [and] self-righteous," "mercurial, honest, and ruthlessly opportunistic," "a populist tribune of imposing ambition," and the creator of "a powerful urban machine that vaulted him to influence in state affairs." According to Elizabeth Varon, Botts became "the standard bearer of Richmond Unionism, positioning himself as a mediator between the sectional extremes of northern radical abolitionism and Deep South disunionism, and fancying himself heir to his political idol, the 'Great Compromiser' Henry Clay."[49] Clay was also Lincoln's political hero, and the Republican Party adopted a version of the American System associated with Clay's Whigs.

Secessionists in the Old Dominion saw the 1860 election and its aftermath as a test of whether the South was, in the words of fire-eater Edmund Ruffin, to "remain free, or to be politically enslaved—whether the institution of negro slavery, on which the social & political existence of the south rests, is to be secured by our resistance, or to be abolished in a short time, as the certain result of our submission to Northern domination."[50] If free southerners accepted Lincoln's election and the prospect of slavery's exclusion from U.S. territories (as promised in the Republican Party's platform), then they would lose the self-assertive independence associated with the citizens of a republic and instead become passive subjects of "submission," "subjugation," and "utter degradation." They would thereby be dishonored, publicly shamed as unworthy of both their own self-esteem and respect from their fellow citizens.

Richmond's citizens voted by a 2-to-1 margin for Bell and the Constitutional Union ticket, which carried the state as a whole by only 156 votes. (Less than 1 percent of Virginia's voters—concentrated in northwestern counties, especially the panhandle situated between the Ohio River and Pennsylvania, but including some in the counties along the Potomac River—cast ballots for Lincoln.) A great majority of voters in eastern Virginia supported Bell or Douglas. These votes apparently mean that before Lincoln's antislavery victory, residents of the eastern part of the state saw the peculiar institution in the Old Dominion as safer within the existing Union than outside it as one of the northernmost slave states in a potential new confederacy. In that position, runaway slaves would be able to reach free soil relatively easily, but the Fugitive Slave Act would no longer facilitate their return. Representing northern Virginia's Fauquier County, Robert E. Scott proposed a referendum whereby the state's voters could choose between secession and the convening of a border state conference that would seek a cooperative solution to the problem of maintaining the Union on terms consistent with the security of southern slave society. Charlestonian George W. Summers, a Whiggish western Virginian slaveholder and longtime proponent of gradual emancipation linked to mandatory colonization of the state's slaves, became the leading spokesman for Unionism at the state convention that gathered in Richmond on 13 February 1861. In retrospect, the strongly conditional nature of Unionist loyalty in eastern Virginia was foreshadowed by Botts's failure to win a seat at the convention. In fact, Botts never held elective office after a losing race for Congress in 1849. Although at most 50 of the 152 convention delegates endorsed disunion at the time of their election, the conditional Unionist plurality voted for secession after the events at Fort Sumter.[51]

In late December 1860, after South Carolina's secession, Granniss noted that "the country is in a very distracted state" of "gloom and depression." His personal outlook also soon became gloomy and depressed, and he turned to Divine Providence for hope: "God grant that it may be peace." After Emma Kent brought an emotional end to their relationship in early January, Granniss resigned from the Richmond City Guard, and on 14 March 1861, he recorded that Lincoln's "inaugural address created no little excitement. It foreshadows coercion of the seceded states," now comprising "a nation called the Confederate States of North America. Lincoln's policy is coercive." By 9 April, "obstinacy on both sides" meant that "the nation seems upon the eve of Civil War." In the middle of the month, after the surrender of Fort Sumter, Granniss declared, "Mr. Lincoln's policy is coercive and Va will secede from the Union," and he recognized that conflict had become unavoidable: "From the North there comes a stern determination to support the Federal Government." For his part, however, he could not "be expected to bear arms against home and kindred."[52]

Robert E. Lee similarly could not countenance the prospect of taking up

arms against "my native state" and extended family. He did not support secession, considered the movement "nothing but revolution," and endorsed
the Crittenden Compromise as deserving "the support of every patriot." But
neither the Republican nor the southern members of the Senate's Committee
of Thirteen supported the compromise, and in late April, the Virginia State
Convention offered Lee command of all military forces in the newly independent Old Dominion. He accepted. According to biographer Elizabeth Pryor
Brown, "Lee may have succumbed, as did J. E. B. Stuart, to the urgency for
action before 'the southern army will be drawn and you will have the place of
the laggard'" rather than an honorable position of command. In any event,
Lee became one among the approximately three-fifths of U.S. officers from
Virginia who resigned their U.S. commissions, although a few, like Dennis
Hart Mahan, refused to take either side in the coming conflict. Of the U.S.
Army's 1,080 officers, some 300 left with the seceding states.[53]

By 13 May, Granniss had left Virginia and returned to his family in New
York. Although he and a fellow clerk had "feared no personal difficulty" in
Richmond, they deemed it "not unlikely that we should if the worst came be
compelled to enlist in the Southern forces and fight against our own friends
and kindred." He turned twenty-one in late July, entering "manhood with
no very animated prospects, out of employment." He subsequently landed a
five-dollar-a-week job as a clerk in "the Wire business," "a miserable pittance"
compared to what he had received in Virginia.[54]

Kent remained in Virginia, ostensibly loyal to the Confederacy. However,
he and other former Unionists, including Elizabeth Van Lew, gave money to
the pastor of Second Presbyterian Church, the Reverend Thomas Moore, for
federal prisoners held at Libby Prison and Castle Thunder. During Reconstruction, Kent became a prominent moderate Republican—that is, as Varon
has put it, he "accepted black suffrage but did not countenance social equality
between the races."[55] One of his daughters, probably Emma, apparently had
ardently supported the Confederate cause, and at his death, he left her emancipated slaves and worthless Confederate bonds whose face value came to a
quarter of a million dollars, commenting in his will, "I could continue the list
to the extent of more than half a million dollars, but the above will suffice—
she will see what the effect of secession has been, but for which I could have
left my children a handsome competency." However, because Kent had stood
by Confederate Virginia, his 1872 obituary in the *Richmond Dispatch* recalled
him as among the city's "most valued merchants and citizens—a man of ster-
ling worth and integrity and a Christian gentleman." In 1904, Granville G.

Valentine acquired Kent's home on East Franklin Street. Valentine was the grandson of Kent's merchant friend, Mann S. Valentine Sr., and the son of Mann S. Valentine II, the founder of the Valentine Museum, whose focus after 1930 became the history of Richmond. The new owner made significant alterations to the building's architecture, but a mid-twentieth-century observer noted that although the structure had lost "the letter of its original architectural character, the Kent-Valentine house has kept that more elusive quality, the spirit of a vanished period."[56]

The white citizens of Kent's Old Dominion, minus the counties that became West Virginia, committed themselves to the cause of Confederate independence from 1861 to 1865. However, the crops raised by agricultural slaveholders in the states of the Upper South—wheat, tobacco, and hemp—were no more distinctively southern in 1860 than were corn or hogs. The westernmost of the border slave states, Missouri, had joined the Union in 1819. Although cotton was raised in the southeastern part of the state, Missouri did not belong to the Cotton Belt, which enjoyed between 40 and 50 more frost-free days per year than the 175 or so such days that were the norm in Missouri. By the 1840s, Missouri, as much western as southern, had become "the most exposed of the slave hinterlands," surrounded on three sides by free states and with four-fifths of its acreage above the confluence of the Ohio and Mississippi Rivers. Even so, Missouri produced some fiercely proslavery secessionists, among them David R. Atchison, son of a Kentucky farmer with a few slaves. In the western reaches of Missouri, Atchison became a bachelor lawyer, circuit judge, U.S. senator, and owner of a single slave. The Compromise of 1850, he declared, did not give the South "equal and exact justice, but we escaped dishonor and degradation." During the mid-1850s Atchison became a leader of the "Border Ruffians" determined to bring Kansas into the Union as a slave state. Missouri's strongest support for slavery and disunion tended to come out of the centrally located Little Dixie area in the Missouri River Valley, where farmers found they needed fewer than ten slaves to raise a variety of food crops in addition to hemp and tobacco. Little Dixie's "largest and most successful slave trader" was John R. White of Howard County, whose net profits averaged more than 27 percent, "far above the 10 percent earnings slaves returned in agriculture." Little Dixie was home to fire-eater Claiborne Fox Jackson, a Kentucky native whose life tells a story, in the words of biographer Christopher Phillips, of "complete calculation, a quest for dominance over others, whether political or personal." At the beginning of the Civil War, Jackson saw Lincoln's troops as engaged in "military coercion" of the slave states and urged Missouri to take up "the Struggle for Liberty." Missouri, led by its decidedly antislavery metropolis of St. Louis, remained in the Union.[57]

Border state areas such as Missouri's Little Dixie, Kentucky's Inner Bluegrass, and southern Maryland can be seen as part of an Old South characterized by the distinctly southern combination of large-scale commercial agriculture with a racially defined form of unfree and capitalized labor. The South's peculiar institution encompassed those of perceived African heritage (as opposed to European ancestry) who were legally denominated chattel slaves. First and foremost, the institution of the slave plantation made Dixieland seem to some observers, then and today, far more akin than was Yankeedom to the aristocratic and hierarchical landed societies of feudal Europe. In the slave states, a quarter of the free residents belonged to slaveholding families, a third of the population was enslaved, and most of these slaves worked productively in plantation agriculture. In the free states, not even 2 percent of the population was black, and chattel slavery had all but disappeared.

In the states that seceded from the Union as well as in those portions of the border slave states that clearly sympathized with disunion and the Confederacy, plantation proprietors and their allies in the learned professions wielded great influence. According to historian Christopher Clark, in the free states and crucial parts of the border states that remained loyal to the Union (especially the cities of Baltimore, Louisville, and St. Louis), comparable influence was wielded by "merchants, bankers, in some cases manufacturers, and in many cases the lawyers who constructed the commercial system and worked at making it function." Because nonagricultural businessmen had assumed important leadership roles in the free states, they could contribute immensely to the northern war effort. The South's elite provided significantly less industrial capacity and management expertise to the Confederate military.[58]

Nevertheless, most slave states had promoted the growth of effective and stable banking systems in the aftermath of the nationwide financial panic of 1837. Two decades later, another panic brought far less stress to southern banks, even after New York banks suspended specie payments (that is, refused to redeem their paper notes for gold and silver) in October 1857. Continued strong European demand for cotton, a steady rise in cotton exports from 1857 to 1860, and most southern railroad companies' ongoing success at showing profits and paying dividends to shareholders encouraged optimism about the economic prospects for an independent southern nation. Nonetheless, most southern bankers appear to have understood that they depended on northern banks, concentrated in the far more diversified and urban Northeast, "to remain solvent if they were to maintain specie payments." Largely for this reason, the great majority of southern bankers wanted to avoid damaging their contacts and relationships with northern financiers. According to historian Larry Schweikert, "knowledgeable businessmen and bankers" in the slave states seem to have "believed the war would be over within a short period of time and that normal relations would resume." Prior to the secession crisis, "southern banking had made monumental strides toward furnishing a solid banking structure capable of promoting economic growth."[59]

Southern business interests understood that slave labor could be and was employed effectively in industrial enterprises, as in Richmond's iron foundries and tobacco processing facilities. Yet in 1860, large slaveholders owned only 12 percent of the South's manufacturing stock. This figure does not reflect the high level of investment by members of the agricultural elite in the region's rapidly expanding railroad network during the preceding decade. David Goldfield reports that twenty-one of the twenty-six largest rural stockholders in several Virginia railroad companies were farmers, four practiced law, and one was a physician. "Their average real property holding was $24,000, placing them in the top three percent of real estate wealth in Virginia." Moreover, "their average slaveholding was of plantation size—twenty-eight."[60] Looking south and west from the Old Dominion, Jefferson Davis's Magnolia State had a remarkable number of diversified investors, particularly in the counties around Natchez and Vicksburg. As William Shade has concluded, it seems highly improbable that "any group of [antebellum] Americans" could have been "more cosmopolitan in their tastes and connections" than were the "Natchez nabobs."[61]

Richard T. Archer, a Virginia native and William and Mary graduate who moved to Mississippi in 1824, observed nine years later, "I shall probably be rich. . . . Land rises very fast in value here." By 1860, he owned five plantations in Claiborne and Holmes Counties and at least 432 slaves. In the early 1850s, he described black chattel as "property peculiar in kind and of a magnitude that it is almost the sole basis of Southern prosperity and happiness." He considered himself the "Son of a Rebel of 1776" and a traditional republican disciple of the state sovereignty principles expressed in the Virginia and Kentucky Resolutions of 1798. To his mind, the "the Constitution was an experiment" and had not been designed to be "perpetual." As secretary of war in the 1850s, Jefferson Davis described Archer as "an extreme man [with] little attention and no support" as well as a man "of high personal respectability, and greater tenacity of purpose." Archer contemptuously dismissed those who rejected his fire-eating secessionism as "submissionists," citing in particular the "large slaveholders of Adams County," near Natchez. At the time Archer, like Davis, belonged to the minority of affluent planters in the Delta-Loess counties of western Mississippi who had been Democratic rather than Whig partisans. Despite his intense proslavery sectionalism, Archer was a rather cosmopolitan businessman. In October 1856, he wrote happily from New York City to his wife, Ann, that he had been reelected to the board of directors of the Southern Pacific Railroad, in which he owned almost six thousand shares, expecting them to be worth a hundred dollars each before the end of 1857. During May 1858, in the aftermath of the financial panic of 1857, however, he informed his eldest son, Abram, "I expect we will be swindled out of all that we have invested in the SPRR Co."[62]

Economic historians Fred Bateman and Thomas Weiss have suggested that even if a "planter ethos" that emphasized land and slaves as sources of wealth and status had not caused "the region's comparative advantage" in large-scale, staple-crop agriculture to be "overindulged," the Old South's "factor endowment"—the amount of land, labor, capital, and entrepreneurship that a state or in this case region can exploit for manufacturing—"would have still led to an industrial sector . . . small relative to that of the" Northeast. Another economic historian, William Parker, explains that the nineteenth-century international economy "arranged itself with heavy concentrations of industry in Northwestern Europe and the Northeastern United States," in part because almost all the new transportation techniques developed between 1770 and 1870, especially the railroad and the oceangoing steamship, "promoted the geographical concentration of industry." Nonetheless, slave state investments in manufacturing enterprises grew at the substantial rate of 64 percent during the 1850s, although free state investments, already far larger, grew at 83 percent. The Middle South town of Petersburg, Virginia, appeared to be "a thriving industrial center (by southern standards at least)," according to economic historian Howard Bodenhorn; in manufacturing output, it ranked fifth among slave state cities but only forty-ninth nationally.[63]

Scholars should be cautious about exaggerating what economic historian Stanley Lebergott has termed the "seigneurial pleasures" derived from slaveholding over its "monetary return." Thirty-four-year-old fourth-generation North Carolina planter Edwin Michael Holt responded to the collapse of cotton prices after the financial panic of 1837 by borrowing money and traveling to the Northeast to purchase machinery for a small spinning mill. This mill, later known as the Alamance Factory, was "built on his family's land along the Haw River in rural Orange County." According to biographer Bess Beatty, "After 1837 the Holts were fundamentally capitalists committed to industrial development." Edwin's seven sons "became successful industrialists in their own right." Edwin's slaves, of whom he owned fifty-one in 1860, "helped construct the mill buildings and mill houses and they may have worked in the dye house, but there is no evidence that they ever tended the spindles and looms." All of those who worked the machinery apparently were white, and three-quarters were female. Beatty concludes that Holt "needed all of his slaves to perform myriad agricultural and construction tasks." Daniel Pratt, a New Hampshire native who lived for fourteen years in Georgia before moving to Alabama in 1833, took a very different tack. Responding in part to the post-1837 depression, he established a gin factory in 1839 and later incorporated the Prattville Manufacturing Company to produce cotton osnaburg. In January 1858, Pratt purchased a nearby plantation with thirty-two slaves. His biographer asks, "Was Pratt attempting further to solidify his position as a landowner and slaveowner with this purchase in 1858? The answer is much simpler. Pratt, first and foremost a businessman, probably saw a seemingly good investment opportunity and grabbed it."[64] During the 1850s, the search for good investment opportunities also led a good many Border South slaveholders, including Kentucky attorney William Waller, to speculate in real estate in the burgeoning midwestern metropolis of Chicago. Waller was unusual, however, in responding to Lincoln's election by selling his land and slaves near Maysville and moving with his family to the Windy City.

Whence came the Old South's character as a plantation and slave society? Yale professor Ulrich B. Phillips, a Georgia native, opened his at one time popular and influential *Life and Labor in the Old South* (1929), "Let us begin by discussing the weather, for that has been the chief agency in making the South distinctive."[65] Climate, geography, and staple or cash crops such as tobacco, rice, cotton, sugar, and hemp unquestionably played an important role in the region's development. But more recent scholarship by economic historians Robert Fogel, Michael Tadman, Gavin Wright, and others has provided a more sophisticated understanding of how race-based slavery as an institution of capitalized labor interacted with geography and climate to shape the South's economic and social history.[66] For example, as Wright explains, the slaveholding elite "had little to no interest in encouraging flows of migrants into the region," which "would tend to depress the wages of labor generally" and thereby depress the value of slave chattel as capitalized workers.[67]

A plantation system based on slave labor, tobacco, and rice had firmly rooted itself along the southeastern coast during the eighteenth century. The birth of the Cotton Kingdom in the 1790s extended the slave plantation's sway westward into what became the Gulf States as slaveholders responded to the

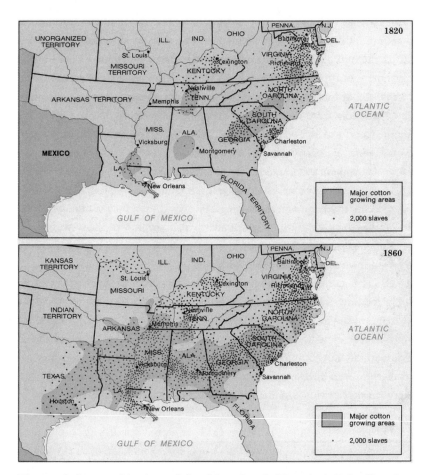

The spread of cotton cultivation and slave labor, 1820–60 (From Arvin D. Smallwood and Jeffrey M. Elliot, The Atlas of African-American History and Politics *[Boston: McGraw-Hill, 1998]; © The McGraw-Hill Companies, Inc.)*

impressive growth of the British textile industry and in the transatlantic demand for cotton. Chattel slavery proved both profitable (because investments in slave labor were quite lucrative, though less so than riskier investments in alternative ventures such as factories) and viable (in the long-run sense that slaveholders garnered capital gains from biological reproduction among slaves and hence were economically better off not manumitting infant slaves).[68] Between 1800 and 1860, as the cultivation of upland, short-staple cotton expanded beyond the piedmont plains of South Carolina and Georgia south toward the Gulf of Mexico and west across the Mississippi River, the monetary value of cotton output per hand increased about fivefold, and the average price of a prime field hand tripled.[69] Although the South's average per capita income (free and slave) remained far behind that of the North in 1860, per capita incomes in the slave states had risen by 39 percent over the preceding twenty years, compared to 29 percent for the free states and 33 percent for the nation as a whole during that period.[70] A recent observation by Kenneth Pomeranz seems particularly relevant to the Old South: "Where production and elite incomes can be increased by driving bound laborers harder and/or bringing unused land under the plow, elites are not very likely to invest in attempts to develop new production processes."[71]

After Congress closed the foreign slave trade in 1808, entrepreneurial farmers settling in new territories and states had to either migrate with their slaves or purchase new laborers transported from older states to the east or north. At least 60 percent of slave movements between states involved interstate sales, leaving at most 40 percent as part of forced migrations with owners. As Lacy Ford has explained, speculators and traders "not only helped create a regional market for the Old South's primary source of liquid capital, chattel slaves, but in the process enhanced the efficiency and productivity by helping distribute labor to its most profitable use."[72] David Lightner argues that even as antislavery constitutional attacks on the interstate slave trade waned during the 1850s, proslavery concerns that federal authorities could construe and employ the Constitution's Commerce Clause to attack the interstate commerce in black chattel waxed. In fact, Republican Party leaders included some prominent radicals whom McPherson has aptly termed "abolitionists in all but name," including many proponents of regulating or even prohibiting the interstate slave trade as well as repealing the 1850 Fugitive Slave Law and abolishing slavery in the District of Columbia. Though conservatives such as Lincoln, Seward, and Tom Corwin of Ohio did not endorse such radical measures, southern fears of Republican ultras doubtless played an important role in fueling secessionist sentiment after Lincoln's election.[73]

Walter Johnson's work has helped to provide a better appreciation of how slaves could understand their bodily commodification as marketable and auctionable property. By manipulating their personas in the presence of prospective purchasers, they might exert occasional influence on the conditions or even the likelihood of sale.[74] At the same time, most masters' actions demonstrated that they did not hesitate to buy or sell slaves when profit or convenience was at stake. Slave traders could serve as convenient scapegoats for the most unseemly side of what antislavery women saw as "the divisive, immoral, and home-wrecking influence of slavery."[75] Yet members of the planter elite seldom shunned or ostracized well-to-do slave traders and speculators, with the exception of what historian Steven Deyle has termed "the lowest fringes," which included "those whom everyone despised: kidnappers, thieves, and crooks." In 1857–58, former slave trader John Armfield played a crucial role in helping to organize and fund the establishment of the University of the South at Sewanee in eastern Tennessee, a project that "had long been the dream of Episcopal Bishops Leonidas Polk of Louisiana and James Otey of Tennessee."[76]

A notable facet of the unseemly traffic in slave bodies was the "fancy trade," the sexualized commodification of light-skinned and mulatto girls, who might sell at prices several times higher than the going rate for females expected to work in the fields. John Hunt Morgan of Lexington, Kentucky, who became a legendary Confederate cavalry officer, learned from his mother's family that "property ownership was the key to honor," or gentlemanly reputation; from his father's family, he learned about the manly martial virtues' importance to that same honor. In 1848, after serving as an officer in the Mexican War, Morgan married Rebecca Bruce, daughter of Sanders Bruce, a partner in a Lexington hemp business. With financial help from his mother, Morgan bought sixteen slaves to rent to hemp manufacturers. In 1853, he and his brother became partners in a hemp factory on West Main Street. By 1859, he owned thirty-three slaves, and the hemp factory also hired both free blacks and other slaves. Morgan also became involved with slave trader Lewis Morgan, a noted purveyor of light-skinned "fancy girls."[77]

Historian Brenda Stevenson has carefully researched the differences between black and white family structures that reflect the impact of the slave trade. Her work on Loudoun County, Virginia, not far south of the Potomac River and Harpers Ferry, leads to the conclusion that under slavery, "the black family differed profoundly from that of the European American southerners." Far more than the families of free whites, the families of slaves "were not nuclear and did not derive from long-term monogamous marriages." Slave marriages had no standing in law because such sanction would have limited slaveholders' control over their chattel. Instead, the slaves' "most discernible ideal for kinship organization was a malleable extended family" within which children tended to live in matrifocal nuclear families. Furthermore, since most male and female slaves alike performed hard labor, "gender-differentiated roles that were so prevalent in white families and also lauded in many free black, nuclear-core families" usually did not operate among slaves.[78]

Since the 1960s, much scholarly debate has concerned whether southern slave plantations and northern free-labor factories qualified as two distinct species of the complex and protean historical genus "capitalism."[79] All sides in this debate seem to agree that the slave states were characterized by their blend of slave-based commercial agriculture and family farms, while the free states, in the words of economic historian Stanley Engerman, "had a commercial agriculture based on family farms" alongside "a developing industrial sector based on wage labor."[80] John Majewski suggests that contentious debates about whether the slave South was capitalist have overshadowed a more concrete and historical question: "Why did the North and the South develop differently?" Focusing on Cumberland County, Pennsylvania, and Albemarle County, Virginia, Majewski concludes that eastern Virginia failed to develop a large commercial metropolis that could provide investors, traffic, and passengers for major transportation projects, especially "intersectional trunk lines" linked to towns and markets in the Ohio Valley. Although Virginians during the decade before the Civil War "invested in more miles of railroad per capita than did Pennsylvanians" and the Old Dominion's government purchased more than 60 percent of the stock of the Virginia Central Railroad, which ran through Albemarle Country, the Virginia General Assembly never overcame the intrastate town rivalries that pitted "Richmond, Norfolk, Petersburg, and Lynchburg in a battle for commercial supremacy." In contrast, in the late 1830s, Philadelphia financiers delivered most of the capital invested in the Cumberland Valley Railroad, which linked Cumberland County to the state capital, Harrisburg, on the Susquehanna River. The Pennsylvania Railroad, whose corporate financing came from either Philadelphia capitalists or city governments, subsequently integrated the Cumberland Valley Railroad and other systems into major trunk lines that extended to Chicago and beyond. But Virginia failed to develop a metropolis comparable to Philadelphia primarily because of the state's combination of staple-crop commercial agriculture and slavery, which encouraged "the growth of largely self-sufficient plantations that limited population density and town growth," thereby severely stunting the intrastate market for manufactured goods. "Philadelphia's densely populated countryside" provided both foodstuffs to the metropolis and a market for the products of the city's workshops and factories and thus "spurred industrialization well before the arrival of interregional railroads."[81]

This conclusion echoes a judgment familiar to British economic historians, who contend that the prominent port city of Bristol began to fall behind its rivals, Liverpool and Glasgow, during the eighteenth century because it lacked "an extensive hinterland" that underwent "rapid economic and demographic growth."[82] At the same time, Majewski's work illuminates the need to distinguish clearly between the microeconomic profitability of individual slave plantations for their proprietors and the macroeconomic impact of plantation agriculture and slavery on antebellum southern society. As Morton Rothstein has observed, it is one thing to discuss "whether slavery was on the whole profitable for individual plantation entrepreneurs," as in eastern Virginia, and another to discuss "whether a society which encouraged and protected slavery did not inescapably create institutions and barriers to long-term growth" of the kind experienced by southeastern Pennsylvania.[83] Pennsylvania-born Thomas Green Clemson was John C. Calhoun's son-in-law, an expert agronomist, and a mining engineer who willed most of his land and money to a state agricultural college (now Clemson University) in 1889. Clemson called slaves a drag on diversified economic development but an excellent investment all the same, "the most valuable property in the South . . . the basis of the whole southern fabric."[84] On the eve of the Civil War, Clemson's perspective informed the actions of both Mississippi native and planter-politician Jefferson Davis and Connecticut-born Virginia merchant Horace Kent.

6 Abraham Lincoln, Henry Waller, and the Free-Labor North

When Abraham Lincoln began to appear to be a serious contender for the 1860 Republican presidential nomination, the editor of the *Chicago Tribune*, Joseph Medill, sent reporter Jon Locke Scripps to the Illinois state capital, Springfield, to gather information for a brief campaign biography. (On the day of Lincoln's inauguration, the entrepreneurial editor wrote to the president's political ally, Senator Lyman Trumbull, that he hoped Scripps would receive a patronage appointment as the new postmaster of Chicago. "If Mr. Scripps has it," Medill pointed out, "the country postmasters of the Northwest would work to extend our circulation.")[1] Borrowing a line from a favorite poem, Thomas Gray's "Elegy Written in a Country Churchyard," Lincoln told Scripps that his early life could "be condensed into a simple sentence: 'the short and simple annals of the poor.'" In this instance, Lincoln's penchant for self-deprecating humor served him well in driving home a potent and positive political message. Throughout his political career, Lincoln liked to paint himself as embodying the American dream of substantial, even dramatic upward social mobility from humble, modest beginnings—what one historian has termed "the embodiment of the American success story." During his first, unsuccessful run for a seat in the Illinois state legislature in the early 1830s, he had portrayed himself as "humble Abe Lincoln" from "the most humble walks of life." During the 1860 campaign, Republican boosters portrayed him as the "Rail Candidate for President" and the "People's Candidate for President"; his political persona appeared to embody the cult of the self-made man. The phrase "self-made man" seems to have been introduced to American parlance by Lincoln's political hero, Kentucky's Henry Clay, during a Whiggish paean to industrial entrepreneurs in 1832. Clay, according to two biographers, had "a genius for self-dramatization" and "nurtured the pretense of great poverty in his youth" for the political reason that "the ideal of the 'self-made man' added considerable luster to his reputation in the minds of his contemporaries" during the era of Jacksonian democracy for white men.[2]

Lincoln's formidable Democratic opponent, Senator Stephen A. Douglas, could also portray himself as a self-made man of the West. However, whereas Lincoln had been born in a slave state, moved north into Indiana as an adolescent, and then settled permanently in Illinois as a young man, Douglas had been born in New England, moved west to New York as an infant, and then moved to Illinois as a young man on the make. Moreover, as a politician, Douglas always spoke for the Democracy, while Lincoln espoused Clay's Whig gospel before joining the new Republican Party in the mid-1850s.

Another Kentucky native and Whig disciple of Clay who eventually made his home in Illinois was attorney Henry Waller, born and raised among the Bluegrass State's genteel slaveholding elite and therefore even less of a self-made man than Clay. However, after Waller opened a law office in Chicago during the mid-1850s as first the Whig and then the nativist Know-Nothing organizations collapsed, he did not convert to the Republican creed. During the 1858 Illinois Senate race, he campaigned for Douglas's reelection and against Lincoln. Two years later, Waller again supported Douglas over Lincoln, this time for the presidency.

The many opportunities for upward social mobility available to free men on the eve of the Civil War largely reflected the simple fact that the United States had a huge temperate land mass and, relative to industrializing countries in western and central Europe, a small population. In 1860, the U.S. population numbered only 31.5 million, and only one-sixth of the American people lived in communities of 8,000 or more people. The slave states generally had a relatively less temperate and more subtropical climate, fewer towns and cities, and less economic and social diversity than did the free states. Many families north of the Mason-Dixon Line and most of those north of the Ohio River and west of the Appalachian Mountains continued to make their living in agriculture and husbandry. Yet 60 percent of the North's labor force worked at non-agricultural occupations, compared to only 16 percent in the South. While one-third of northerners lived in towns and cities, only one in eight southerners did so. Moreover, by 1805, every northern state had abolished bondage or at a minimum begun the process of dismantling slavery, with New York and New Jersey bringing up the rear.[3] In the free states, manual labor enjoyed decidedly greater dignity and respect among well-to-do citizens, at least in their public pronouncements. Rapid urban growth in parts of the antebellum North accelerated the enlargement of the mercantile and salaried middle classes, whose status involved their freedom from the necessity of dangerous and dirty hard labor. By the mid-1850s, the country's greatest metropolis, New York City, counted nearly 14,000 clerical workers alone. With these newer middle classes came the nascent "distinction between 'blue-collar' or manual and 'white collar' or nonmanual work."[4] Even so, as Eric Foner has noted, "The dignity of labor was a constant theme of ante-bellum northern culture and politics." And this principle was directly linked to "the assumption that the major responsibility for a person's success or failure rested with himself, not society."[5] Northerners tended even more than southerners to glorify the frugal and hardworking man from a modest background who rose in society as a business entrepreneur or the practitioner of a learned profession. The North's free-labor version of the American dream, its vision of upward social mobility from anonymous poverty to acclaimed respectability, could be embodied in men such as Lincoln, although Lincoln's vision that every white wage laborer could rise into the ranks of the independent middle or professional classes became more problematic with the late-nineteenth-century rise of big business and national labor unions, fruits of the nation's accelerating pace of industrialization and urbanization.

In March 1860, Lincoln invoked his personal story during an address in New Haven, Connecticut, that helped prepare the political ground for his run for the Republican presidential nomination. He recounted his devotion to the gospel of hard work and argued that black men should also have the opportunity to better their condition in a free society: "When one starts poor, as most do in the race of life, free society is such that he knows he can better his condition; for he knows that there is no fixed condition of labor, for his whole life. I am not ashamed to confess that twenty-five years ago I was a hired laborer, mauling rails, at work on a flat boat—just what might happen to any poor man's son! I want every man to have the chance—and I believe a black man is entitled to it—in which he can better his condition—when he may look forward and hope to be a hired laborer this year and the next, work for himself afterward, and finally to hire men to work for him! That is the true system."[6] For Lincoln and most citizens of the free states in the 1850s, the glory and pride of their republican and democratic society was the absence of a permanent substratum of dependent, much less enslaved, manual laborers, which in turn testified to the dynamism and productivity of the North's free-labor economy.

Apologists for antebellum slavery, mostly southern but some antiabolitionists in the North, mainly Democrats, took exception to this self-congratulatory free-labor perspective, especially as celebrated by the antislavery Republicans. Slavery apologists might point to the northern reality of propertyless and degraded "wage slaves," especially in northeastern factories and among newer immigrants to America.[7] According to an Indiana Democrat in early 1860, Republicans who belittled black bondage "can see no slavery in the bound apprentices, and in the busy din of fourteen hours in the factories of the North."[8] Probably the best known among southern proslavery attacks on "free" wage labor during the 1850s came from a self-educated and idiosyncratic Virginia lawyer, George Fitzhugh, whose writings Lincoln read and pondered. Though Fitzhugh was the scion of one of Virginia's first families, his family's plantation had been sold off in the 1820s, and he practiced law in the small Tidewater town of Port Royal. Those inclined at the time to dismiss him as a toady for the Slave Power might have pointed to his appointment under President James Buchanan to a minor position in the office of U.S. attorney general Caleb Cushing of Massachusetts, a noted southern partisan among northern Democrats. The widely known New Orleans periodical *DeBow's Review* published more than one hundred of Fitzhugh's articles, prominent among them the 1857 essay "Southern Thought," in which he argued that intellectuals in the slave states "must justify the slavery principle, justify slavery as natural, normal, and necessitous" because of the protection against the impersonal exploitation that impoverished and heavily taxed laborers experienced at the hands of capitalists in "densely settled countries, where lands are monopolized by the few." Though populous and industrializing England had long since emancipated its workers from unfree forms of labor such as serfdom, in the absence of chattel bondage, "there must be white slavery, else the white laboring class are remitted to slavery to capital, which is much more cruel and exacting than domestic slavery" as practiced in the South. Fitzhugh suggested that "excluding Russia," where serfdom was not abolished by tsarist decree until 1863, "the South is the only conservative section of civilized Christendom." England and western Europe had developed "slavery to capital," which created "slaves without masters," or "wage slaves"—that is, de facto bondspeople whose employers, unlike slave owners, had no vested and personal interest in the slaves' well-being.[9]

Although Fitzhugh argued for color-blind slavery in articles and books published during the 1850s, at the Virginia Constitutional Convention of 1850–51, and during the secession crisis, the Virginian emphasized the exceptional advantages of the South's racially defined system of bondage.[10] In the decade prior to the outbreak of war, few southern writers proved willing to endorse Fitzhugh's argument for color-blind enslavement, since it so directly contradicted the mainstream proslavery argument that the racial enslavement of a black underclass promoted in the South a stable form of egalitarian republicanism among all whites, rich and poor. George Frederick Holmes, a migrant academic and essayist, responded to Fitzhugh's *Sociology for the South; or, The Failure of Free Society* (1854) by agreeing that "the serf of the feudal ages was more happily situated than the labouring freeman of today." Yet Holmes declined "to go so far as Mr. Fitzhugh and maintain that nothing but slavery can be right." At the same time, Holmes praised Fitzhugh's efforts "to refute the arrogant pretensions, and neutralize the vain malignity of those who introduce the presumption of the exclusive righteousness of the free labor system as a ground for the denunciation of slave communities."[11]

Religiously intense northerners, among them individuals as different as Roman Catholic conservative Orestes Brownson and liberal Baptist Francis Wayland, were wont to note that the American creed of democratic individualism for white men entailed the dangers of extravagant self-indulgence, a dearth of social benevolence, and irresponsible liberty. Wayland, who became president of Brown University in Providence, Rhode Island, at the age of thirty-one, has been described as "the leading Protestant moralist of antebellum America," though he is generally less well known to religious historians today than the more charismatic evangelicals Lyman Beecher and his son, Henry Ward Beecher, and Charles G. Finney. During the mid-1840s debates over slaveholding and slavery that caused a sectional rift among the nation's Baptists, Wayland engaged in a polite but substantive debate, conducted in long letters and published in many editions, with the Reverend Richard Fuller of Beaufort, South Carolina, a slaveholder. Although Fuller denied that he could or should be considered an abolitionist, he believed that slavery should be accounted "a moral and social evil" because it violated both the sentiments expressed in the Declaration of Independence and Jesus' admonition to love one's neighbor as oneself. Wayland's textbooks, *The Elements of Moral Science* (1835) and the *Elements of Political Economy* (1837), went though many editions and, according to historian Mark Schantz, "provided guidance to college students for decades," especially on the question of how "to reconcile the pursuit of piety and the drive for wealth." This problem presented itself in free as well as slave societies. Although Wayland can be seen as a rabid disciple of classical, free market economics who viewed the pursuit of individual wealth and the accumulation of private capital as essential to economic and social progress, he denounced speculators (those who became rich by rapidly buying and selling property without adding any real value to it through their labor) for their "tendency to foster a spirit of avaricious worldliness," which in turn promoted "practical atheism." Like many evangelical preachers, Wayland saw divine judgments in the economic crises sparked by the financial panics of 1837 and 1857–58. The legitimate pursuit of profit could too easily become "an excessive avidity for the rapid accumulation of property"; the "unhallowed passion for wealth" could become "too strong for the control of moral principle, nay of religion." As punishment, God brought the collapse of business and economic ruin. God's Providence held sway over the natural law of business cycles.[12]

Most citizens in the free states evinced far less anxiety than did Wayland about the consequences of an "unhallowed passion for wealth." And they seem to have believed, as did Lincoln, that business proprietors and the laborers they employed had fundamentally similar interests. For skilled, native-born, frugal, and temperate workers, "wage labor was to be merely a way station en route to economic independence. If jobs were lacking, agricultural expansion in the West would provide a new route to realize their independence."[13] Hence the United States was destined to avoid serious class conflict between labor and capital. There would be no high wall in America between capitalist employers and permanent proletarians (wage-earning and almost propertyless laborers). At midcentury, across the Atlantic, Karl Marx and Friedrich Engels were predicting ongoing immiseration for the working classes in rapidly industrializing areas of western Europe. And some evidence indicated incipient proletarianization in New York City and other parts of the Northeast in 1860–61. However, as Anne Rose points out, the great majority of pre–Civil War wage earners did not see themselves as part of a discrete and self-conscious working class: "Not all who aspired to middle-class status achieved the prosperity they sought. But whether a working class with distinctive views emerged during the antebellum period is much less certain. Perhaps it is most accurate to say that many urban manual laborers were aware of their social distance from men in nonmanual occupations but that they had yet to develop a coherent, critical social ideology of their own."[14]

This judgment certainly does not mean some wage earners in textile and footwear manufacturing, which was concentrated in industrializing portions of New England, did not engage in work stoppages and strikes that involved substantial anger and serious criticism of their employers. And what did a free-labor propagandist like Lincoln say to such striking workers? In New Haven, Lincoln referred to a contemporary strike, the largest in the nation's history to that point, centered in Lynn, Massachusetts, the hub of the U.S. shoe industry. Neither striking cordwainers nor manufacturers understood at the time that the Lynn labor conflict marked the demise of the older putting-out system, which had existed for half a century, and the victory of the more impersonal factory system, which would emerge full-blown less than a decade after the Civil War, when shoe workers became machine operatives tending technology in large factory buildings.[15] Over many years prior to 1860, the men and woman who made shoes had experienced an intensifying work pace brought on by partial mechanization of the manufacturing process. In particular, sewing machines, invented in the 1840s and widely deployed by the middle of the following decade, led to the concentration of workers in large central shops, forerunners to factories, and the concurrent displacement of slower handwork done in the homes of small farmers or in modest "ten-footers" (shops known by that name because they were often ten-foot squares). "The ten-footers were physical remnants of an earlier phase of the business when both master and journeyman labored together under the same roof," explains historian Paul Faler. "However, with the demise of the masters and their replacement by manufacturers, the masters either became journeymen and remained in the shop to work in the customary manner or abandoned the ten-footer for the central shop." Even as improved transportation systems and technology (plank and macadamized roads, canals, steam railroads) had fostered expanding, more distant markets for basic commodities and manufactured goods, new manufacturing techniques promoted greater division of labor and more efficient modes of production in proto-industrial communities. Shoe manufacturing in eastern and central Massachusetts became, in the words of one scholar, "a highly competitive industry" in which bosses felt they had constantly to seek cost reductions, "and the largest cost was labor." More and more Lynn employers forwarded by roads and railroads "parcels of materials prepared in the central shop" to laborers living and working outside the town "who would assemble the parts at cheaper rates than workers in Lynn."[16]

In the aftermath of the recession that began in 1857 and brought large wage cuts and rising unemployment rates, Lynn workers organized the Journeymen Cordwainers Mutual Benefits Society, and its spokesmen urged their peers throughout New England "to combine in self-defense." In early February 1860, the Lynn Society issued its schedule of acceptable wage rates even as a new slump in the shoe business was under way. Many journeymen pledged to withhold their labor from employers who refused to accept the published wage rates. The new Lynn Mechanics' Association walked off the job on Washington's Birthday (22 February) after marching to the central shops and turning in their lasts. The strikers invoked the radical rhetoric of the working-class movement from a quarter century earlier, before depression and immigration had effectively destroyed the early unions. They identified themselves as mechanics and producers while acknowledging their dependence on bosses: the principle that "the laborer is worthy of his hire" should impel manufacturers to show respect for workers as the ultimate source of value and wealth. Invoking the libertarian rhetoric of 1776, they likened employers to English King George III and other despots and called on fellow workers to "sink not to the level of slaves." One speaker told New Englanders that they did not need to see slaveholders to find "labor's oppressors," since those in Lynn were intent on "drawing the chains of slavery and riveting them closer and closer around the limbs of free-laboring men." Alonzo Lewis, a poet and teacher as well as a strike leader, composed a "Cordwainers' Song" frequently sung by the workers that began,

> Shoemakers of Lynn, be brave!
> Renew your resolves again;
> Sink not to the state of slave,
> But stand for your rights like men!

Faler observes that "racism was widespread in Lynn"; "most citizens . . . referred to blacks as niggers, and it is doubtful if one could find a single shop in Lynn with a black cordwainer." Some shoemakers no doubt joined in a crowd that protested and attacked an English abolitionist lecturer, George Thompson, and forced him to flee Lynn. However, according to Faler, the shoemakers were really provoked by "the failure of most abolitionists to condemn wage slavery and grant that a similarity existed between chattel slavery in the South and the wage system in the North." The workers found it "especially galling . . . to see manufacturers 'enjoying the titles of honest, honorable, and benevolent men,' while treating their workers 'like so many old and broken down southern slaves.'"

When Lincoln spoke in New Haven on 6 March, the strike was near its peak, and he told his listeners,

> *I am glad to see that a system of labor prevails in New England under which laborers* CAN *strike when they want to, where they are not obliged to work under all circumstances, and are not tied down and obliged to labor whether you pay them or not! I* like *the system which lets a man quit when he wants to, and wish it might prevail everywhere. . . .*
>
> What is the true condition of the laborer? I take it that it is best to leave each man free to acquire property as fast as he can. . . . Up here in New England, you have a soil that scarcely sprouts black-eyed beans, and yet where will you find wealthy men so wealthy, and poverty so rarely in extremity. There is not another such place on earth! I desire that if you get too thick here, and find it hard to better your condition on this soil, you

may have a chance to strike and go somewhere else, where you may not be degraded, not have your family corrupted by forced rivalry with negro slaves.[17]

Lincoln thus suggested that the gospel of free labor in the Northeast and its goal of propertied and honorable independence required access to free-soil farmland elsewhere. In other words, underpopulated western territories closed to slavery were necessary to ensure that wage earners in the industrializing Northeast—a region with a "thick" population—continued to have opportunities for upward social mobility into the ranks of independent landowners. Ironically, Lincoln's free labor argument in 1860 mirrored Fitzhugh's proslavery logic of 1857. Fitzhugh recognized that slavery to capital—the phenomenon of slavery without masters endemic to "densely settled countries"—would "never be felt at the North, until our vast possessions in the West are peopled to the Pacific, and a refluent population begins to pour back upon the East."[18]

The shoemakers' strike eventually involved at least ten thousand workers and perhaps twice that number in eastern Massachusetts; at the strike's peak in early March, at least forty thousand people attended workers' meetings and parades. At that time, notes Faler, "female shoe binders greatly augmented the strikers' ranks in Lynn when they voted . . . to strike for their own price list." Although the strikers' ultimate success depended on their ability to prevent or reduce substantially the manufacture of shoes, the majority wanted to avoid violence and professed respect for the sanctity of private property. The desire to avoid violence was strongly reinforced by the arrival of one hundred special deputies from Boston, Salem, and South Danvers to supplement Lynn's police force and by the activation and arming of the Lynn Light Infantry (one of two militia companies of the Fourteenth Regiment based in Lynn). Most strikers did not and would not employ force to prevent the manufacturers from transporting materiel and stock out of Lynn to other communities of workers. In April, therefore, the owners eventually won a combination standoff and war of attrition.[19]

One of the most important labor-management disputes in the Old South had occurred thirteen years earlier in Richmond, Virginia, which would become both the capital city and the most industrialized city in the Confederate States of America. The conflict arose during Joseph R. Anderson's two-year tenure managing both the older Tredegar and the newer Armory iron mills. Anderson believed that he could reduce his labor costs by introducing slave workers as skilled puddlers at the Armory Iron Company. The skilled white workers at the Tredegar mill had previously accepted slaves who worked at less skilled positions, but the threat of enslaved black puddlers caused free white puddlers at both ironworks to announce their intention to strike "to prohibit the employment of colored people" throughout the mills. Whereas New England's striking shoemakers received some support from the Massachusetts and Connecticut press, both of Richmond's major newspapers, the Democratic *Enquirer* and the *Whig*, backed Anderson's refusal to accept any of his striking workers' demands and his insistence that they vacate any housing rented from the firms. To accept the workers' demands, stated the *Enquirer*, would render property in slaves "utterly valueless." Moreover, after dismissing the strikers, Anderson took them to court on the grounds that they had combined illegally to exclude slaves from his mill: "Such combinations are a direct attack on slave property; and if they do not originate in abolition, they are pregnant with its evils." In other words, while New England's shoemakers would later accuse their bosses of designs to enslave free workers, the boss in Richmond condemned his striking ironworkers for being akin to abolitionists in their disrespect for slaveholders' property rights.

Nevertheless, the strikers lost both disputes. Although the mayor's court in Richmond dismissed Anderson's case, the former ironworkers did not recover their jobs. "It is to be hoped that the case may operate as a warning," wrote the *Enquirer*, "and that nothing may again occur to disturb the regular current of business." In 1848, after the strike, the Armory Iron Works employed thirty-nine slaves, while the number of slaves at the Tredegar Iron Works had grown from forty-one to seventy-eight. According to Anderson, the labor of these slaves enabled him "to compete with other manufacturers." But as the Tredegar works expanded dramatically during the 1850s, Anderson's firm drew additional skilled workers primarily from the ranks of artisans born in the North or Europe. In 1860, the plant employed more than seven hundred free white workers and only eighty bondsmen (twenty-eight of them owned by Anderson, others rented at an annual rate between 10 and 15 percent of their market value). Slave labor thus added stability to Anderson's workforce while helping to avoid labor strikes, but it did not enable Tredegar to overcome the "glaring weakness" of "a pitifully inadequate raw materials base" in Virginia. Anderson's ironworks consumed more pig iron than was produced in all sixteen of the state's blast furnaces. During the last quarter of 1860 and the first quarter of 1861, for every ton of Virginia metal puddled by the Tredegar rolling mills, the plant processed four tons of northern pig iron, most of it from Pennsylvania, where anthracite furnaces were replacing the sort of "antiquated charcoal stacks" generally used in the Old Dominion.[20]

Lincoln, like other observers in the free states, argued that white workers such as those at Tredegar necessarily became "degraded" by both competition and proximity with black slave labor.[21] Northern wage earners who moved west in search of greater independence and income certainly preferred not to compete against enslaved blacks in either agriculture or manufacturing. When the Kansas-Nebraska Act of 1854 opened the northern stretches of the Louisiana Purchase to slavery under the contested principle of popular sovereignty, Lincoln focused at first less on the wickedness of slavery and more on the perfidy of those who had dared to overturn the long-established Missouri Compromise of 1820, which had excluded slavery from what became the territories of Kansas and Nebraska. During the late 1850s, his inclination to extol free labor in the North and the western territories while lambasting the morality and side effects of slavery in the South became more pronounced. He presented himself as the guardian of the Founding Fathers' antislavery convictions and of constructive (as opposed to extreme) precedents by pointing to the wisdom of earlier federal legislation, beginning with the Northwest Ordinance of 1787, followed by the exclusion of slaves from abroad in 1808, and extending to the Missouri Compromise. In both 1787 and 1820, the federal government had limited the geographical expansion of slavery to create ample room in the territories for "the homes of free white people." George B. Forgie has argued that Lincoln and other antebellum leaders wanted to win honorable fame for themselves by accomplishing something as glorious as the founding of the American republic, even though their accomplishment might destroy the republic as created by the Founding Fathers—revered men who had made substantive constitutional and legislative compromises on the issues of slavery and slavery expansion. As Don E. Fehrenbacher and Robert W. Johannsen concur, Lincoln's ambition "drove him hard" in the 1850s, yet "it was an ambition leavened by moral conviction."[22]

This moral conviction led the Illinoisan to condemn slavery as a "monstrous evil" that violated the American creed of 1776. Although this creed posited a body of natural rights that Jefferson delineated only in part (that is, "among them, life, liberty, and the pursuit of happiness"), these rights clearly encompassed a man's "liberty," or right to elevate himself economically and socially in "the pursuit of happiness." However, if a man in the free states remained a lifelong wage-earning laborer, would he therefore appear to be deficient in both ambition and independence and therefore incapable of enjoying the full measure of the freedom and liberty available to a worthy American citizen? Lincoln had suggested as much in a September 1859 address at the Wisconsin State Fair in Milwaukee: "If any continue through life in the condition of the hired laborer, it is not the fault of the system, but because of either a dependent nature which prefers it, or improvidence, folly, or singular misfortune."[23] Lincoln's ascent from hired laborer to successful attorney and presidential candidate bespoke his own ambition, discipline, and intelligence while glorifying the northern free-labor society that had nurtured his rise.

Lincoln's story and political stance raise the question of whether the free states offered more upward social mobility than did the slave states. Most scholars seem to agree with Susan-Mary Grant's judgment that "wealth in both sections was concentrated in the hands of a few, and they tended to hang on to it; consequently, vertical mobility was similar, that is, infrequent, in both North and South."[24] This evaluation applies only to the free population and does not take into account the enslaved third of the South's residents. Although historians have uncovered some rare instances where black southerners born slaves became free people of substance before or even without leaving the slave states, their paths to freedom depended on largesse extended to them as children of white masters and female slaves.[25] To white Americans in the free-labor North, such racial amalgamation appeared to be one of the most degrading and objectionable aspects of the South's peculiar institution. To northerners, Lincoln's ascent seemed representative of the opportunities available to white manual laborers in their region, including those, like his, whose families had left the slave South.

Lincoln's paternal grandfather, Abraham, a militia captain during the American Revolution, owned thousands of acres of good farmland in Virginia's Kentucky County (created in 1776) when he died at the hands of Indians in 1786. Under Virginia's law of primogeniture, his eldest son, Mordecai, inherited Abraham's estate. Semiliterate Thomas Lincoln, eight at the time of his father's death, acquired manual skills as a carpenter and cabinetmaker before obtaining a modest farm in Kentucky's Hardin County just before the birth of his son, Abraham. His hardworking wife, Nancy Hanks Lincoln, gave birth to the baby in a log cabin near Hodgenville, Kentucky, on February 12, 1809. In 1814, Thomas Lincoln, respectable though hardly affluent, ranked fifteenth on the county's list of ninety-one taxpayers. Lincoln, a good storyteller, was active in the Baptist Church; that this denomination at the time included some critics of slavery has led some biographers to suggest that antislavery sentiment influenced his 1816 decision to leave Kentucky for Indiana. However, Lincoln's principal reason was "problems with titles to all three of the farms he owned in Kentucky," which were common under "the cumbersome Virginia land system." When Thomas and Nancy Lincoln moved their family across the Ohio River to the formally free-soil Old Northwest after the War of 1812, it represented at the time not so much "a move from south to north," in the words of one historian, "as a move from east to west, or more precisely, from west to west-er."[26] Although Abraham Lincoln probably did not imbibe strong antislavery convictions from the Calvinistic, hard-shell Baptist church to which his family belonged, he may well, as George M. Fredrickson has suggested, "have derived his fatalism, his sense that there was an inscrutable Providence at work over which human beings had little or no control, from this early religious influence."[27]

In 1818, after the Lincolns established a farm at Pigeon Creek, Indiana, Nancy Lincoln died, leaving behind nine-year-old Abraham and his sister, age eleven. Thomas Lincoln returned to Kentucky to find another wife. He chose a widow, Sarah Bush Johnston, who had three children of her own. Despite the disruptions, Abraham grew to manhood with his self-confidence nurtured by the genuine devotion of two mothers. Although he received less than a year of formal schooling, he became an avid reader, with access to a small family library that included the Bible, *Pilgrim's Progress*, *Aesop's Fables*, and Parson Weems's heroic *Life of Washington*. He also seems to have yearned for independence from what Lincoln later called "parental tyranny" and a scholar has termed "familial indentured servitude." According to biographer Michael Burlingame, "Because [Abraham's] father treated him like a slave," the two became estranged, and the future president "empathized with the bondsmen."[28] After doing chores on the farm, young Abraham's services might be rented out to neighbors. As he grew older, he took jobs farther away, selling firewood to Ohio River steamboats and taking a flatboat of goods downriver for sale in New Orleans.

On the eve of his twenty-first birthday, Lincoln helped his family move farther west to another small farm on the Sangamon River in Macon County, Illinois. At the time, Illinois was attracting a flood of settlers with Kentucky roots. Lincoln made another commercial flatboat trip to New Orleans, moved to the hamlet of New Salem in 1831 to work as a store clerk, and enlisted and twice reenlisted in the Illinois militia, serving briefly and uneventfully in the Black Hawk War of 1832. Already burning with political zeal and ambition, he made an unsuccessful though impressive 1832 run for the state legislature. He proclaimed his support for a Bank of the United States, protective tariffs for the nation's "infant industries," and federally funded "internal improvements" (in particular navigational enhancement of the Sangamon River). "My politics are short and sweet, like the old woman's dance," is an early example of the folksy and clever humor that became his political trademark. Though he lost the election, he continued efforts to leave behind his youthful life of hard physical labor, though he never lost his ingrained sympathy for the working man. As he once said, "I have always thought that the man who made the corn should eat the corn."[29] That same year, he became co-owner of a short-lived general store. Lincoln also continued his reading, devouring Shakespeare's plays, Edward Gibbon's *Decline and Fall of the Roman Empire*, and Thomas Paine's attack on conventional religion in *The Age of Reason*. Despite Lincoln's support for the emerging Whig Party, he received an appointment as postmaster in New Salem for three years during Democrat Andrew Jackson's administration. Supplemental income came from work as an assistant land surveyor.

In 1834, he again ran for the state legislature, winning the first of four terms. In this campaign, he kept quiet about his support for Clay and the threefold American System that he had endorsed so openly two years earlier. During his first legislative session, he began to study law, borrowing books from a supportive Springfield lawyer and purchasing a used copy of the reigning textbook, *Blackstone's Commentaries on the Laws of England*. At the close of the legislative session, he returned to his job as postmaster and continued reading law. Later that year, his first true love, Ann May Rutledge, died, sending him into his first bout with serious depression, what he would call his "hypo." In the Illinois legislature, he supported the building of a canal to link the Chicago and Illinois Rivers.

Although Lincoln clearly held antislavery views, he did not broadcast them, largely because Illinois qualified, in the words of one scholar, as among "the most negrophobic of all the Northern states."[30] Like his hero, Clay, Lincoln disliked radical agitators on both sides of the slavery question and hoped for eventual success of a cooperative and gradual colonization movement. In 1837, a year after being admitted to the state bar, he took up residence in Springfield and joined in a law partnership with fellow Whig John Todd Stuart. Lincoln campaigned hard on behalf of Stuart's 1838 candidacy for a seat in the U.S. House of Representatives, in which Stuart barely defeated Stephen A. Douglas. Lincoln subsequently represented the state's Whigs in debates with Douglas, then the chair of the state Democratic Party, foreshadowing their far more famous debates during the 1858 senatorial campaign.

Stuart, like Lincoln's subsequent two law partners, was a Kentucky native, as was Lincoln's best friend, Joshua Speed, who came from a prominent Louisville family and was temporarily serving as proprietor of a general store in Springfield when they met in 1837. The three women in whom Lincoln seems to have felt romantic interest all hailed from the Bluegrass State as well. He met the last of them—the cultured, fashionable, and witty Mary Ann Todd—in Springfield in 1839, when she was visiting her sisters and the sizable network of expatriated Kentuckians there. They married after three years of roller-coaster courtship.[31] Biographer William C. Harris opines that although "the moody, introspective, emotionally withdrawn Lincoln was far from an ideal husband," his "periodic bouts of depression" seem to have become "less severe after his marriage."[32] Scholar Lynda Casswell Crist concludes that Mary Lincoln became the same kind of emotional rock to her husband that Varina Davis became to Jefferson Davis; the two "smart, capable, willful women . . . were their husbands' closest confidants, advisers, and helpmates." A different interpretation has come from Burlingame, who believes that if Lincoln had found his wife "a more sympathetic soul, he might not have devoted so much time and energy to politics and thus would probably not have attained the presidency."[33] Mary Lincoln's father, Robert Smith Todd, was a slaveholding merchant and landowner in Lexington and a friendly neighbor of Henry Clay, to whom Abraham Lincoln may have been introduced. Mary Lincoln's connections to Kentucky would make the Civil War years in the White House at least as much a trial for her as for her husband.[34]

During the 1840 presidential campaign, which concluded with Whig William Henry Harrison's defeat of incumbent Democrat Martin Van Buren, Lincoln served as a member of the Illinois state Whig committee. Honest Abe's highly partisan speeches of 1839–40, like those of most politicians, "routinely exaggerated the opposition's threat to the republic and to constitutional liberties," in Harris's words. Lincoln lambasted Jackson's destruction of the Second Bank of the United States and Van Buren's support for an "independent subtreasury" system of federal depositories that operated separately from state-chartered banks. For Whigs, the Bank of the United States had promoted what James Simon terms "a mutually beneficial alliance between the private business community and the federal government." The economic depression that followed the panics of 1837 and 1839 demonstrated that the Democrats' despotic attacks on the national bank earlier in the decade had "undercut the strength and stability of the national economy." At the same time, in a speech delivered at Tremont, in central Illinois, Lincoln showed he was not above the race-baiting that infected so much political discourse in both the North and the South. The *Sangamon Journal* reported Lincoln's "disclosure of President Van Buren's vote in the [1821] New York [Constitutional] Convention in allowing Free Negroes the right of suffrage." As would always be the case throughout his antebellum career, Lincoln the politician recognized the voters' overwhelming hostility to the notion of political and social equality between the races even as he declared that "the institution of slavery was founded on both injustice and bad policy." Yet he also insisted that the Constitution protected slavery in the states where it already existed. The clients for whom he provided legal representation included Robert Matson, a Kentucky slaveholder who sued for the return of his slaves after they had made their annual sojourn as laborers on their master's Illinois farm. Massachusetts abolitionist Wendell Phillips subsequently denigrated Lincoln as "that slave hound from Illinois." To Lincoln's mind, the promulgation of abolitionist doctrines promoted "mobocratic" and violent lawlessness and tended "rather to increase rather than to abate" the evils of human bondage. In response to abolitionist calls for emancipation in the federally governed District of Columbia, Lincoln maintained that Congress could implement this policy only if the District's citizens endorsed it and slaveholders received cash compensation.[35]

In March 1847, Lincoln became the only Whig member of the Illinois delegation in the U.S. House of Representatives. Even though a U.S. victory in war with Mexico appeared likely, Lincoln did not hesitate to attack President James K. Polk for his role in provoking war by sending U.S. troops into territory claimed by both Mexico and the new slave state of Texas. Lincoln believed that Texas would not have been annexed so precipitously in 1845, the Mexican War would not have commenced, and sectional divisions would not have been exacerbated had Clay won the 1844 election. If the political abolitionists in New York had supported the moderate and responsible Kentuckian, Lincoln wrote in the fall of 1847, "Mr. Clay would now be president, whig principles in the ascendant, and Texas not annexed."[36] Although Lincoln did not speak out in the House during the fierce sectional debate over the Wilmot Proviso, he voted repeatedly in favor of Pennsylvania Democrat David Wilmot's motion that slavery be excluded from any new territory acquired as a result of the Mexican War. The future president seems not to have appreciated either then or later the intense feeling of so many free southerners that federal action against the spread of slavery into new territories posed a real threat to the safety and security of the slave states. He certainly did not think that congressional containment of slavery, if couched within promises not to disturb the peculiar institution in those states where it already existed, could lead to disunion.

In 1848, after the emergence of the Free-Soil Party, Free-Soil–Democratic coalitions won one of Ohio's seats in the Senate for Salmon P. Chase and one in Massachusetts for Charles Sumner. Both opposed the Compromise of 1850 as too favorable to the Slave Power. After the Kansas-Nebraska Act of 1854, Chase and Sumner became chieftains of the new Republican Party. Also in 1848, Lincoln campaigned for the victorious Whig presidential candidate, Zachary Taylor, touring New England during the fall on his behalf. Having agreed in 1846 that he would serve only a single term in the House and support another Whig for the seat in the 1848 congressional elections, Lincoln turned down the offer of appointment as governor of the new Oregon Territory and returned to Springfield and his law practice in the spring of 1849. Lincoln's political ambition for what he later termed "the honors of official station" nonetheless continued to burn brightly.[37] He remained active in Whig political circles, defending the party's unsuccessful 1852 presidential nominee, Winfield Scott, against Democratic charges that the Whig Party in the North, while claiming to be above sectionalism, was actually abolitionist.

That same year, two years after Clay's death, Lincoln delivered a eulogy in the state Hall of Representatives at Springfield, praising Clay's role in the Compromises of 1820 and 1850. Like most Americans of the time, Lincoln believed and hoped that the 1850 compromise measures had "settled forever" the issue of slavery in new American territories. He knew that popular acceptance of its provisions was essential to maintaining the Whig Party as a viable national and therefore conservative political force. In retrospect, the compromise measures constituted what David M. Potter terms "a truce, perhaps, an armistice, certainly a settlement, but not a true compromise" in the sense of "an agreement between adversaries."[38]

Stephen A. Douglas, who had been indispensable in shepherding the several parts of the 1850 compromise through the U.S. Senate, unintentionally played a crucial role four years later in bringing both Lincoln and sectional tensions over slavery back to the forefront of American politics. The fallout of his Kansas-Nebraska Act included the final disintegration of the national Whig Party along with the organization of various local and state anti-Nebraska coalitions into a new Republican Party committed to the geographical containment of slavery. Republican successes in a number of October 1855 state elections won over two prominent antislavery Whigs in New York, Senator William Henry Seward and his indispensable ally, editor Thurlow Weed. Seward became Lincoln's principal rival for the 1860 Republican presidential nomination. Despite Seward's efforts to tone down his antislavery rhetoric, many delegates attending the 1860 Democratic National Convention saw him as more tainted by both antinativism and abolitionist radicalism than was Lincoln and thus less likely to capture the border free states along the Ohio River. Seward had also been closely linked to the New York political machine operated by the crafty and manipulative Weed, and the senator had a powerful enemy in the nation's most influential Republican newspaper editor, Horace Greeley of New York City. During the secession winter, Seward proved more open than Lincoln to compromise on the crucial issues of slavery in the territories and the status of Fort Sumter, even as the New Yorker sought to establish himself as the de facto premier of Lincoln's administration in his post as secretary of state. At the other extreme within Lincoln's cabinet was a figure whom Allan Nevins has called one of "the true-blue implacables," Secretary of the Treasury Salmon P. Chase.[39]

By early 1856, the establishment of rival territorial governments in Kansas—a proslavery administration at Lecompton and an antislavery government at Lawrence, the latter declared illegal by President Franklin Pierce—led to a national opposition convention that drew delegates from several different groups: antislavery Whigs and anti-immigrant Know-Nothings, Free-Soilers and anti-Nebraska Democrats, plus those radicals already willing to be labeled Republicans. The February meeting established a national party committee that created "the most significant political product of sectionalism," inviting support from "everybody opposed to the Pierce administration, the repeal of the Missouri Compromise, and the admission of Kansas as a slave state."[40] The Republicans came close to winning the presidency in 1856, taking all but five northern states and eliciting many promises in the South that election of a Republican nominee would provide grounds for disunion.

In 1855, Lincoln remained reluctant to abandon the Whig Party, even though its national organization was collapsing and his hope of being elected a Whig U.S. senator by the Illinois legislature that year proved futile. Many Whigs had already abandoned the party for the nativist American Party or the antislavery Republican Party, but Lincoln found Know-Nothing prejudice against Catholic Irish and Germans distasteful, although he prudently kept his hostility to nativism quieter than did Seward. Lincoln also saw too much extremist and fanatical hostility to slavery and slaveholders among the earliest Republicans. In August 1855, he wrote, "I think I am a Whig but others say there are no Whigs and that I am an abolitionist. I now do no more than oppose the extension of slavery." In early 1856, Lincoln became the only prominent politician to attend a meeting of anti-Nebraska editors to lay the groundwork for an anti-Nebraska Illinois state convention. In May, Lincoln also attended the convention in Decatur that established the "Anti-Nebraska party of Illinois" and finally committed to joining what would soon be called the state's Republican Party.

Until the Kansas-Nebraska Act of 1854, Lincoln seems to have believed that the majority of Americans remained committed on the subject of slavery to what he believed had been the Founding Fathers' intentions. That is, most people believed that slavery constituted a regrettable reality inherited from the colonial era and that the Constitution obligated the new nation to uphold slavery in those states where it already existed. Even so, the federal government could and should take forceful measures to limit slavery's spread and thereby place it on the road to gradual, peaceful, and voluntary extinction at the hands of each slave state's own citizens. However, the Kansas-Nebraska Act convinced Lincoln that the leadership of the Democratic Party was determined to reverse the Founding Fathers' intentions. As early as October 1854, he delivered an anti-Douglas speech in Peoria, Illinois, that, according to Harris, "clearly identified the Springfield lawyer as the leader of the anti-Nebraska forces in the state." He began to downplay his public support for traditional Whig economic and financial policies and to focus on opposition to slavery expansion. He decried "the monstrous injustice of slavery itself" and the indifference of northern Democratic leaders such as Douglas to its expansion. This indifference only supported charges from critics of the U.S. experiment in constitutional and republican liberty that Americans were in fact hypocrites. Because the nation's Democratic leadership had abandoned the antislavery precedents set by the Northwest Ordinance of 1787 and the Missouri Compromise of 1820, controversy over the future of slavery would threaten the Union's existence.

In 1856–57 came Buchanan's election and inauguration. The doughface Democrat interjected his opinions and preferences into deliberations taking place among Supreme Court justices about the proper ruling in an important case dealing with slavery. Almost immediately after Buchanan's inauguration in March, Chief Justice Roger Brooke Taney presented the Court's ruling that the Constitution prohibited the exclusion of slave property from any federal territory by either Congress or its dependent territorial governments. Lincoln, always the calculating if principled politician, hesitated to use the freighted phrase "Slave Power" in public, probably as part of his ongoing efforts to distinguish his position from that of more radical antislavery men. But in his 1858 senatorial debates with Douglas, Lincoln posited the existence of an obvious tendency toward the nationalization of slavery, of a movement toward another judicial ruling that not even a long-established free state could exclude slavery, thereby making slavery "perpetual, national and universal." Indeed, he believed that the Kansas-Nebraska Act was but "the beginning of a conspiracy for that purpose." In his view, Pierce, Buchanan, Douglas, and Taney "all understood one another from the beginning, and all worked upon a common *plan* or *draft* drawn up before the first lick was struck."[41] This dubious charge, which Lincoln admitted he could not prove, made for effective political propaganda throughout the free states.

Lincoln and Seward expressed analogous objections to the *Dred Scott* decision and the ongoing mini–civil war between antislavery and proslavery forces in Bleeding Kansas. At the beginning of his campaign against Douglas, Lincoln delivered his famous "House Divided" speech. Four months later, in Rochester, New York, Seward delivered an equally provocative speech, positing the existence of "an irrepressible conflict between opposing and enduring forces [that] means that the United States must and will sooner or later become either entirely a slave-holding nation or entirely a free-labor nation."[42]

Seward had made another antislavery address in 1850, five years before abandoning the waning Whig Party to join the new Republican organization. During the debates over the Compromise of 1850, the New Yorker proclaimed the principle that the U.S. Constitution devoted "the national domain . . . to union, to justice, to defense, to welfare, and to liberty." However, he continued, "there is a higher law than the Constitution," a law of liberty that seemed to challenge the insistence of Garrisonian abolitionists as well as proslavery Calhounites that slavery was both recognized and protected by parts of the Constitution. According to Seward, the higher law would not finish its work until the people of the South complied, "yielding in your time, and in your own manner, indeed, but nevertheless yielding to the progress of emancipation."[43]

Both Lincoln and Seward believed that the federal government possessed the constitutional authority to prevent the spread of slavery into new states and territories and that the geographical containment of slavery would advance the "progress of emancipation." Most thoughtful Americans, including Jefferson Davis and other proslavery southerners, accepted the apparent Malthusian reality that slavery would eventually disappear when the wages paid to free laborers fell below the costs of maintaining slaves, a time that would arrive when population density reached a certain level. Lincoln and Davis could agree that the peculiar institution would wither and eventually die if it could no longer expand south and west. However, Davis and other slaveholders feared what would happen in the slave South at some point between the geographical containment of black bondage and the beginnings of a responsible and honorable program of emancipation—responsible and honorable because citizens in the slave states would favor it and because it would involve a gradual process including financial compensation and mandatory colonization. Would the immediate fallout from political containment of slavery's geographical expansion be sharp declines in the market value of owners' huge investments in slave property? Would these declines be accompanied by increasing agitation from abolitionist fanatics, encouraging violent and vengeful slave rebellions and leading either to a war of racial extermination or to degrading racial amalgamation? In the 1850s, Davis felt constrained to press John C. Calhoun's case for some kind of federal guarantees to assure that all national territory remained open to slaveholders and their black chattel. The Supreme Court provided him with a contested judicial guarantee in its 1857 *Dred Scott* ruling, but just over three years later, the presidency was captured by a candidate who had denounced the decision and intended to pursue its reversal by all means available to him under the Constitution.[44] The staunch Unionist Lincoln, like fire-eating Alabama secessionist William Lowndes Yancey, seems to have appreciated wealthy slaveholders' fierce determination to preserve the huge monetary value of their investments in human chattel. However, unlike Yancey, Lincoln failed to appreciate how the election of a Republican president pledged to the geographic containment of slavery could elevate slave state anxieties about property and race to the point of disunion.

During the 1850s, northern Whigs and later Republicans generally seem to have invoked racial epithets against black Americans less often than did Democrats from either the North or the South. However, some Whigs were intensely Negrophobic. Oregon Whig David Logan wrote in the mid-1850s, "The Whigs are all dead out here—they call themselves the *Republican party*—which means negro worshippers." He continued, "I can't go to the Locofocos and I'll see the Republicans to the Devil before I'll vote with them. I don't know exactly what I am exactly, but anything but an abolitionist." Logan had migrated to Oregon in 1849 after fighting in the Mexican War. Like Lincoln, Logan was a Kentucky native, and his father, Stephen T. Logan, was Lincoln's law partner for a few years. In 1859, David Logan barely lost election to the U.S. Senate from Oregon as what he called "a popular Sovereignty–non intervention Republican," appealing to Douglasite Democrats for votes.[45]

Logan's defeat, along with the time and effort then required to travel by land or sea from the Pacific Northwest to the Great Lakes, encouraged Oregon's Republican leadership to approve two relatively idealistic and radical notables from the Northeast as delegates to the party's 1860 national convention in Chicago: Massachusetts's Eli Thayer, famous and infamous for his promotion of the New England Immigrant Aid Society and its sponsorship of free-soil settlers in territorial Kansas; and editor Horace Greeley of the

New York Tribune. Such men represented a potent wing of the Republican Party, in the words of one scholar, because they "still reflected the idealism of the crusade against slavery" and its commitment to "a general program of nineteenth-century liberal reform" that drew sustenance from aspirations and ideals held by most northern evangelicals and many in what might be termed the professional middle classes. Yet even Greeley, who served on the platform committee, understood that his party could not succeed "on a square slavery issue" and needed to win support from the growing numbers of "pragmatic and conservative Republicans," who often spoke for the interests of manufacturing and interstate commerce.[46] In 1860, Lincoln proved to be the candidate best suited to building the necessary bridge between idealists and pragmatists.

During the late 1850s, Lincoln repeatedly professed what was usually called the conservatism of his opposition to slavery—what today would likely be labeled moderation as opposed to radicalism. On the eve of the 1860 Republican convention, Lincoln highlighted his conservative stance, writing, "I agree with Seward in his 'Irrepressible Conflict,' but do not endorse his 'Higher Law' doctrine."[47] Lincoln did not deem it necessary or politic to appeal to a higher or divine moral law to take a constitutional and political stand against slavery expansion. As for the peculiar institution in the existing slave states, the citizens of those states would make the decision for gradual and compensated emancipation in their own time and on their own terms, and Lincoln clearly endorsed the colonizationist expectation that freed slaves would have to enjoy their natural right to freedom outside the United States, in Africa or in Latin America. This stance reflected what he called in a September 1858 debate with Douglas "a physical difference between the white and black races which I believe will forever forbid the two races living together on terms of social and political equality." The antebellum Lincoln emphatically rejected both contemporary forms of color-blind radical abolitionism: the antipolitical and religious moralism of William Lloyd Garrison and the younger Frederick Douglass, who viewed the Constitution and American partisan politics as corrupted beyond redemption by the sin of slavery; and the political abolitionism of the Liberty Party and the later Douglass, who came to believe that the Constitution empowered the federal government to act against slavery everywhere in the Union. Lincoln claimed that he, like the Founding Fathers, saw slavery in the Old South as a regrettable reality whose expansion could and should be arrested, thereby putting it on the long and gradual road to what he called "ultimate extinction." But the South's peculiar institution could not and should not be disturbed where it was already rooted. Citizens in the existing slave states should have no fears that he intended black ex-slaves to live among them.

"In Lincoln's mind white prejudice was so deeply ingrained that it precluded the possibility of racial equality," concludes historian James Oakes. "By massaging the racial prejudices of northern voters Lincoln allowed them—or enough of them—to overcome their resistance to his strong antislavery message."[48] Most of his political opponents could not grasp or would not concede that he could condemn the injustice of slavery yet refuse to endorse political and social equality between blacks and whites. His political adroitness and clever command of the spoken word served him well in responding to accusations that he really supported black political and social equality with whites. And his responses not only affirmed that blacks and whites shared a common humanity but also helped to rebuff the expectations of color-blind abolitionists that he should favor racial equality. As he declared, "I protest, now and forever, against the counterfeit logic which presumes that because I do not want a Negro woman for a slave, I do necessarily want her for a wife." After laughter and cheers from his audience, Lincoln continued, "God made us separate, we can leave one another alone and do one another much good thereby. There are white men enough to marry all the white women, and enough black men to marry all the white women, and in God's name let them be so married." In 1859, responding to a private query about his thoughts on the subject of the Illinois law against interracial marriage, Lincoln reportedly said, "The law means nothing. I shall never marry a Negress, but I have no objection to anyone else doing so." He then went on, "If a white man wants to marry a Negro woman, let him do it, if the Negro woman can stand it." Although Lincoln spoke out harshly in 1858 against full equality for free blacks in the North, Harris concludes that he "never again made a blatant racist appeal," though he continued to advocate colonization of freed blacks until 1863.[49]

But what constituted "a blatant racist appeal"? In March 1860, Lincoln assured the audience in New Haven that if slavery could be geographically contained, migrating workers who sought greater economic opportunities in the West would "not be degraded, not have your family corrupted by forced rivalry with negro slaves." It was not clear, however, whether white settlers in territory open to slavery would experience greater degradation because they had to compete against slave labor per se or black slave labor in general. To nearly all southerners and northerners alike, including Lincoln, black slaves appeared to lack the capacity for genuine respect and honor; again, it seems well-nigh impossible to separate the relative degrees of degradation associated with African physiognomy and enslaved status.[50] The degradation associated with blackness would survive the end of slavery but could never be dissociated from the fact that almost all Africans had come to America in chains.

To many white southerners, the victorious Republican in 1860 embodied the combined challenge of virulent antislavery in political league with the accelerating demographic and economic power of the free states vis-à-vis the slave states. If the most powerful symbol of progress in midcentury America was the steam railroad, then the new transportation technology was transforming northern society more quickly and thoroughly than it was the Old South. Indeed, Lincoln's professional and political ascent in the 1850s was closely linked to the rapid expansion of railroad and telegraph lines in the Old Northwest and hence to that region's growing transportation and communication connections with the Northeast. His legal practice had depended on many minor cases with small fees that had involved circuit riding to local and state courts. By the middle of the decade, his practice had become more focused on litigation involving Illinois's expanding railroad network. Lincoln's breakthrough case came at the beginning of the decade, when he represented the Alton and Sangamon Railroad, which he termed "a link in the great chain of railroad communication that shall unite Boston and New York with the Mississippi," and the Illinois Supreme Court ultimately endorsed his argument. "The decision, subsequently cited in twenty-five other cases throughout the United States, helped establish the principle that corporation charters could be amended in the public interest," concludes biographer David Donald, and "established Lincoln as one of the most prominent and successful Illinois practitioners of railroad law."[51] Lincoln's legal work was fully in accord with traditional Whiggish principles as articulated by Clay in his support of the American System of internal improvements that would link communities, states, and sections into a harmonious and healthy U.S. economy. Federal land grants dated back to legislation creating the state of Ohio in 1803, when the U.S. government promised to donate 5 percent of proceeds from the sale of public land to help build public roads. More generous canal grants went to Illinois and Indiana, but they too were dwarfed by land grants to railroads.[52]

Geography and topography do much to explain why the states above the Mason-Dixon Line and the Ohio River experienced the impact of the antebellum transportation and industrial revolutions far more dramatically than did most southern states. Connecting the Northeast and Old Northwest via transportation infrastructure projects across the northern Appalachians proved relatively easy compared to what was involved in constructing roads, canals, and railroads across the more formidable Appalachian ranges of the Upper South. Well before the dawn of the railroad age, New York State's construction of the Erie Canal from 1817 to 1825, "making use of the sole natural break through the Appalachian barrier," gave Hudson River traffic access to the interior Great Lakes. The canal also encouraged the construction of other canals connecting Lake Erie to the Ohio River, although "nothing could compare with the Erie Canal" in tons of freight carried.[53] The Erie Canal and later railroads that paralleled its route promoted both settlement of the Midwest and the emergence of New York City as the nation's commercial entrepôt. Constructing an east-west canal or railroad connecting the Atlantic ports of Savannah or Charleston to the Old Southwest at Montgomery or Vicksburg would also have been relatively easy, but the Gulf coastal plain and the navigable rivers that flowed southward into the Gulf of Mexico through that plain provided access to Atlantic commerce and limited the demand for interstate canals or railroads in the Lower South. During the late antebellum years, river traffic made New Orleans and Mobile the region's major ports for shipments of cotton. The North's more integrated system of transportation by water and later rail, together with the ongoing expansion of commercial activity and the growth of manufactures employing wage labor in the Northeast, further promoted the free states' higher rates of population growth, immigration, and urbanization.

The economic development of the free states both east and west of the Appalachian Mountains cannot be sharply separated from economic activity in the slave states. The Ohio and Mississippi River Valleys facilitated intersectional linkages, as in the shipment of midwestern pork to cotton plantations. More dramatically, cotton from the slave South, most of which was bound for European markets, constituted the most valuable American export, accounting for well over half the total. Yet the preponderance of the overseas as well as domestic cotton trade was conducted by mercantile and financial firms based in the northeastern port cities. Businessmen in the Northeast, particularly in the commercial centers of Boston, New York, and Philadelphia, learned to exploit what one historian has called the "insight that fortunes were to be made as readily in handling goods as from producing them."[54]

Moreover, during the 1840s and 1850s, many of the ships that carried cotton bales to northwestern Europe returned filled with immigrants, bringing new arrivals to port cities in New England and the Mid-Atlantic. Many

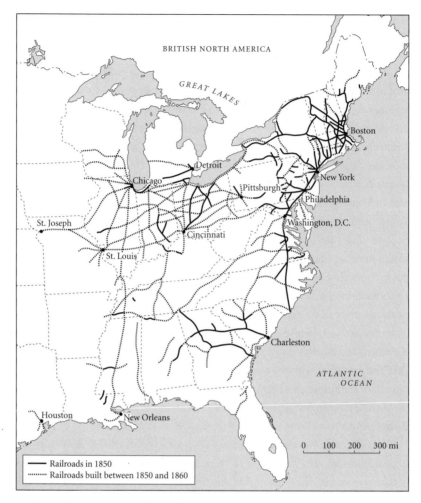

Railroads, 1850 and 1860

of these newcomers moved inland, where they established farms and found work in mills, thus not only providing manual labor but also driving up the market value of land and services. Northern businessmen and professionals therefore had strong incentives to attract migrants, a goal that could be promoted by encouraging state and local governments to use their public borrowing authority to build or subsidize transportation infrastructure and other public improvements, such as schools.

The average free resident of the slave states was 50 percent wealthier than the average resident of the free states in 1850, and high cotton and slave prices during the subsequent decade drove that figure up to 80 percent by 1860.

But as Gavin Wright explains, "The accumulation of *nonslave* wealth by the southern economy was 40 to 45 percent below the northern standard." In particular, farm value per acre was more than twice as high in the North.[55]

The 1840s brought the free states two crucial economic and social developments that indirectly but powerfully encouraged North-South sectional differences. First, as Christopher Clark makes clear, a variety of forces, including northeastern industrialization, rising European immigration, the spread of railroads, and secular as well as religious arguments against direct physical coercion and compulsion of human labor, encouraged and accompanied "a steady increase in the importance of wage labor in the North." According to Clark, "Wage work, once regarded as disreputable and a mark of dependence unless undertaken as a temporary expedient by independent farmers, artisans, or their sons, was beginning a profound shift in respectability. By the late 1840s it would emerge as one archetype of an ideal 'free labor' system."[56] For Lincoln and his Republican allies, free wage labor was worthy of respect and honor because and if it enabled ambitious men to elevate themselves into the ranks of propertied men no longer dependent on earning wages.

Second, the Northeast's emerging mercantile, financial, and industrial clout became more closely linked to the agrarian Midwest, primarily because of the growing east-west trade, facilitated by older canals, newer railroads, and the telegraph lines that ran alongside railroad tracks. Midwestern railroads by and large were not built ahead of demand, and most were profitable almost immediately. Rail lines in the 1850s were usually built to serve existing farm regions, as in Lincoln's Illinois.[57] Interregional linkages encouraged greater political support first for federal as well as state aid to transportation improvements and then for higher federal tariffs on some imported goods (such as iron). Democrats as well as Whigs came to endorse legislative boosts to economic development with the goals of promoting a more integrated national market, increasing domestic production, and raising the standard of living. Reaching these goals would promote national security in the event of war.

In 1850, Illinois contained only 110 miles of railroad, less than could be found in South Carolina and three other slave states. By 1860, Illinois had 2,868 miles of railroad, trailing only Ohio; Indiana ranked fifth, after New York and Pennsylvania. Of the eleven lines that served Chicago the longest, at some 705 miles, was the Illinois Central, which was unusual in that it ran north-south rather than east-west. The funding of this railroad testified to the fact that Democrats as well as Whigs had come to favor government support for internal improvements that would stimulate economic development. In

1851, the promoters of the Illinois Central had estimated the cost of the road at $16.5 million, more than double the total investment in all Illinois manufacturing at the time. Such large sums had already been raised to finance canal construction, after the model of the Eriè Canal. About three-quarters of the $190 million invested in canals had come from public funds—that is, tax monies and revenue from bonds sold by state and local authorities. Yet many ambitious canal projects in the free states, like the Pennsylvania Main Line and the Wabash and Erie, had become financial busts, making both state and local governments leery of such commitments. The Illinois Central was exceptional in its goal of linking Chicago with New Orleans and Mobile (by a sister line), and trans-Appalachian interests in Congress, led by Douglas and his fellow senator, William King of Alabama, with support from New York and Boston investors, in 1850 won the passage of the first federal act awarding land grants in support of railroad construction. In accord with the widely accepted emphasis on state's rights, the land grants went to the states of Illinois, Alabama, and Mississippi, which in turn passed them on to the railroad companies. Congress made several more such land grants before the Civil War, the largest going to Iowa in 1856 for four east-west lines across the state. Republicans' aggressive support for such federal aid helps to explain why the party had already captured Iowa's legislature and why the Hawkeye State voted overwhelmingly for the Republican presidential nominees in both 1856 and 1860. Giving railroads land allowed the companies to underwrite construction costs with land sales and gave them access to well-established mortgage markets rather than forcing reliance on the nascent private bond and equity markets.

During the middle of the nineteenth century, as historian Peter A. Coclanis has succinctly explained, "the 'networked' Northeast not only played a key role in the development of the interior of the United States, particularly the 'Old Northwest' . . . and the Great Lakes region, but also began incorporating this area into what would later become the industrial core of America, the quadrant east of the Mississippi River and north of the Ohio River." According to another economic historian, the Old Northwest "began its industrial ascent" in the iron and machine-building industries yet still remained overwhelmingly agricultural, with more than 70 percent of U.S. manufacturing concentrated in New England and the Middle Atlantic, especially New York, Pennsylvania, and New Jersey. New England and the Mid-Atlantic demonstrated "the precocious growth of a true business-industrial culture" that would reach maturity during the decades following the Civil War.[58] The South had sufficient industrial capacity in 1860 to rank "among the world's leaders in railroad mileage and cotton textile production per capita" yet still lagged well behind the North. According to the 1860 census, the slave states had a third of the nation's population but produced only 10 percent of its manufacturing output and contained but 11 percent of its manufacturing capital. In these categories, the South trailed not only New England and the Mid-Atlantic but also the Midwest.[59]

The Old Northwest between the Appalachian Mountains and the Mississippi River stood at the forefront of railroad construction during the generally prosperous 1850s. U.S. mileage soared from about 3,300 in 1840 to just under 9,000 a decade later to more than 30,000 in 1860. Most important, the early 1850s saw the completion of four trunk lines, paralleled by telegraph lines, connecting the mercantile and industrializing Northeast with the trans-Appalachian West, and all four subsequently bolstered the Union cause. The New York Central and the Erie reached Lake Erie, while the Baltimore and Ohio extended from Baltimore to Wheeling, Virginia, and the Pennsylvania connected Philadelphia and Pittsburgh. In addition, the Baltimore and Ohio was eventually extended to St. Louis, and the Pennsylvania absorbed a 468-mile route between Pittsburgh and Chicago, the emerging regional metropolis. During the 1850s, lines radiated out from Chicago, among them the 180-mile Chicago, Rock, Island, and Pacific, which completed the first bridge across the Mississippi River in 1856 and employed Lincoln in lawsuits against rival steamboat interests.

As of 1861, however, no bridge crossed either the Potomac or the Ohio River. In fact, the southeastern port cities of Norfolk, Wilmington, Charleston, and Savannah had not developed direct rail connections with the Ohio River Valley, in part because of the high construction expenses imposed by mountainous Appalachian geography and rivalries among the cities competing for commercial opportunities. In short, the nation's late antebellum railroad systems tied together the Northeast and the Old Northwest much more successfully than they did the North and the South or the Upper South slave states east and west of the Appalachian Mountains. The absence or presence of such connections, in turn, helped set the historical stage for the outcomes of the 1860 election, the secession crisis, and the Civil War.

By 1860, writes historian George Rogers Taylor, Chicago had assumed its "place as the greatest railroad center in the world." It had become the world's "greatest primary grain port" as well as its "leading lumber market" through the efforts of entrepreneurial capitalists taking advantage of the city's location on an important water corridor and land bridge, which connected "two different ecosystems, the timber-rich forests of northern Wisconsin and Michigan and the woodless prairies" so favorable for raising grains. By 1852, iron rails and horses reaching into Chicago's midwestern hinterlands brought more wheat to the city than the combined traffic carried in wagons and canal boats between Chicago and the Ohio and Mississippi River Valleys. Farmers grew more wheat for market in large part because of the mechanical reaper that Cyrus McCormick had developed in the Valley of Virginia before locating his manufactory in Chicago in the late 1840s. By 1851, "McCormick's four-story brick factory was one of the first industrial concerns in the city and by far the largest, employing about 120 men, and much of its machinery was driven by a thirty-horsepower [steam] engine that locals considered one of the marvels of the age."[60]

Wheat was brought into the city by rail and shipped out by boat on Lake Michigan. These grain ships passed lumber boats moving south to Chicago, whence the lumber was shipped by canal and rail to farmers. Donald L. Miller explains that during the 1850s, the Chicago Board of Trade established "the world's first modern commodity exchange, a place where commodities, such as grain and hogs, are marketed in the same way that stocks and bonds are marketed on a stock exchange."[61] Just as farmers in western Pennsylvania decades earlier had marketed their grains in condensed and more potable form as liquor, midwestern farmers marketed corn in the form of hogs. As a contemporary observed, "What is a hog, but fifteen or twenty bushels of corn on four legs?" During the Civil War, Chicago replaced Cincinnati as "Porkopolis, the capital of western meatpacking."[62]

In 1856, the Illinois Central began regular service to Cairo, at the junction of the Ohio and the Mississippi. Because other railroads extending west from Chicago had reached the eastern banks of the Upper Mississippi, river trade that had previously gone to St. Louis could be rerouted by rail to Chicago. Boosters of the Windy City thus "began calling the Illinois Central 'the St. Louis cutoff.'" In 1854–55, Lincoln, probably with research assistance from his law partner, William Herndon, had argued the case of *Illinois Central Railroad v. the County of McLean* before the Illinois Supreme Court. The justices eventually accepted Lincoln's argument for the constitutionality of the state legislature's favoring the railroad by exempting its property from local taxes. Having received a retainer of $250, Lincoln then brought a successful suit against the railroad for the very high fee of $5,000 but was nevertheless hired by the company to handle subsequent cases.

In 1858, a newspaper observed that southern Illinois had been opened to "middle state and New England ideas" by the railroad, which had begun to transform the "political physiognomy" of the area. As an example, the paper cited Jonestown, located "a mile and a half from the railroad. The station is called 'Anna' and is as large as the town itself. The station is Republican, the town is Democratic."[63] Formerly Whiggish lawyers, entrepreneurs, and land speculators who had connections to railroads in the free states—like Lincoln in Illinois and William Penn Clarke in Iowa—usually gravitated toward the Republican Party. However, the Democratic Party also included very important railroad promoters. Among the increasing number of Iowa Democrats interested in better communication with markets east of the Mississippi, enthusiasm for the new transportation technology trumped the traditional Jacksonian suspicion of what one governor called "the sometimes oppressive monopolizing tendencies of powerful corporations." Support for railroad corporate charters frequently translated into support for the chartering of more banking institutions within the state.[64] Illinois's Douglas had won election to the Senate in 1846 on a platform "calling for the federal government to cede public lands to the state, as it had with the Illinois and Michigan Canal project, to help pay for construction of a Central Railroad running north and south across Illinois and extending all the way to the Gulf of Mexico." In September 1850, the new telegraph technology carried word from Washington to Chicago that Whig president Millard Fillmore had signed the bill to create the Central Railroad. The Illinois Central would enrich both Chicago and the group of boosters for whom Douglas spoke (including John Wentworth and money men in the Northeast), who invested in land within and near the city where the railroad was likely to build. At the same time, the Illinois Central was part and parcel of "Douglas's nationalistic vision of a stupendous railroad system that would bind together large sections of the country and kill off growing sentiment in the South for separation." Ironically, his hopes for sectional reconciliation were negated by congressional approval of Douglas's Kansas-Nebraska Act, which he had expected would help him realize his ambitions for both the presidency and a transcontinental railroad that would connect the East and West Coasts—by way of Chicago, of course.[65]

During the 1850s, southerners as well as northerners felt the powerful lure of investments in the interconnected sectors of railroad projects and real estate. Investors saw that communities that might be served by rail lines—particularly towns likely to become important rail junctions—offered fertile fields for speculative plays in real estate, especially if the railroads might become linked to a prospective transcontinental line. Douglas encouraged his political allies, among them Kentucky's John C. Breckinridge, to consider investing in the Chicago area even before passage of the Kansas-Nebraska Act. Although Breckinridge had no attention of leaving the Bluegrass State, other Kentuckians from slaveholding families moved north to Chicago during that era to pursue what they perceived as business opportunities better than those available south of the Ohio River. Indeed, in October 1858, the *Chicago Press and Tribune*, a Republican newspaper, observed that "in all the walks of business you will find Kentuckians among the shrewdest and most successful operators."[66] These entrepreneurial Kentuckians included several men related to the Breckinridge clan, among them brothers James and Henry Waller, attorneys and sons of prominent bank cashier William S. Waller and Catherine "Kitty" Breckinridge Waller.

Younger brother James Breckinridge Waller practiced law first in Bowling Green and then in Lexington. An ardent Whig admirer of Clay, James first visited the Windy City in 1849 and soon began making investments there. James and his family moved permanently to the shores of Lake Michigan in 1858, two years before Henry and his family joined them. Henry Waller, a graduate of West Point and also an attorney, had served a term in the Kentucky state legislature during the 1840s as a Clay Whig. He apparently made his first visit to Chicago in 1853, when he seems still to have retained deep roots in the Bluegrass State. In that year, he joined a new law partnership with John G. Hickman in Maysville, on the Ohio River, and won unanimous election as president of a company established to build the Maysville and Lexington Railroad. Waller's interest in and commitment to the success of this venture and his travels beyond the borders of Kentucky in pursuit of financial support for the nascent rail line simultaneously reinforced and reflected his growing appreciation for Chicago's status as the emerging railroad and mercantile hub of the Midwest. Writing home in March 1853, he enthused that Chicago presented "one of the finest fields for speculation in the world." He continued,

> The whole great northwestern country around, is of unexampled fertility, and developing with a rapidity hitherto unknown in any age or country. Most of this vast country is tributary. So Chicago is the natural point where are to be received, and where are to be distributed, the grand aggregate of production and articles of consumption. The great natural advantages conferred on Chicago by its convenient harbor on a great lake, in the midst of a great country, have been increased, and are still to be increased to a tenfold degree by the concentration upon her of mighty systems of railroads, reaching though Cleveland, Pittsburgh & Wheeling to the great Atlantic Cities, New York, Philadelphia & Baltimore on the East; to New Orleans and Mobile on the Gulf; to Iowa & Minnesota on the North West;

and through Rock Island and Council Bluffs, along a branch of the great [transcontinental railroad] to the Pacific. Some of these roads are already completed and others in a rapid state of organization & construction, to the number of fifteen. There is no difficulty in making railroads here; the country is so level, that to grade and prepare them for the iron, the dirt has simply to be thrown up from the small parallel ditches to the centre. The profits they pay are enormous. Under the influence of such advantages, which are being developed from day to day, the growth of Chicago is without precedent, and must so continue.[67]

A few days later, Waller reported that he had already made a "splendid investment" in a pair of lots: twenty acres outside the city limits, at $275 per acre, for himself and his brothers James and William, and forty acres within the city, at $1,000 per acre, for the "Maysville Company." And Henry Waller intended to make three more purchases before returning to Kentucky. The pull of burgeoning business investments and opportunities became so powerful that in 1855 he established a Chicago residence and became a partner in the law firm of Waller, Caulfield, and Bradley, though his wife, Sarah Bell Langhorne Waller, known as Bell, and children remained on the family's Kentucky farm.[68] Henceforth, Waller's financial hopes centered first and foremost on profits from his real estate investments. After the financial panic of 1857 deflated his speculative bubble, he had increasing difficulty maintaining two residences while mustering the funds to pay taxes and interest on money borrowed for his investments. Although Waller continued to practice law in Chicago until after the Civil War, by 1859 he had become "heartily tired of the law" and believed that "my property now needs all my attention." That same year, he waxed eloquent about what later adherents to the Weber thesis would see as a close connection between Calvinist theology and worldly success. "Consider what a noble character is a Christian merchant," he wrote during April 1859. "With a perfect reliance upon the Divine word—and with the law of God in his heart—he deals uprightly with all, and secures at once the blessing of God and the confidence of man. What better guarantee of success can mortal man have or hope for?" Indeed, "the business man needs religion as much as any other human being; and it will advance his true interests more than any other thing under heaven."

By 1858, both Henry and James Waller had transformed their earlier Whiggish Unionism into outspoken support for Stephen A. Douglas. In the absence of the formerly Whig opposition to the Democracy that remained a powerful political presence in the states of the Border and Middle South,

Henry Waller saw Douglas's version of popular sovereignty as the only feasible alternative for his Unionism to the unacceptable Republican demand for slavery's geographical containment. On 22 October 1858, in Chicago's Light Guard Hall, Waller delivered a speech "on the Dred Scott Decision and Other National Issues Involved in the Senatorial Canvass in Illinois," subsequently published as a pro-Douglas pamphlet. Introducing himself as "what is now called an Old Line Whig," Waller maintained that "of all the forms and subjects of agitation, the agitation of slavery has ever been regarded by the Whig party as the most fearful." And this agitation had been fueled by the Republican Party's assertion that Congress could exclude slavery from a territory, a position maintained even after the *Dred Scott* decision. In fact, because "Congress can no more prohibit or establish slavery in a territory than in a State," insisted Waller, "the doctrine of Mr. Lincoln is impracticable in our system of government, is radical in its tendencies, and must be revolutionary in its results." In contrast, the incumbent Illinois senator, Douglas, "deals with the subject of slavery with the wise circumspection which distinguished the fathers of the republic, and all the great national men of our own times." How? The Illinois Democrat "plants himself upon the fundamental right of every political community," including federal territories, "to determine and control its own domestic institutions in its own way."[69]

While working on behalf of the "wise" Douglas and against the "revolutionary" Lincoln, Waller received regular complaints from his wife about both his extended absences from Kentucky and their straitened finances. During May 1860, Bell wrote, "Oh darling this debt is so terrible, it overshadows me in your absence, more than when you are with me." The next month, she reported, "I had not money to pay the harvest hands." She lamented that even during Waller's brief visits home, he seemed "so hurried and occupied." Divine Providence seemed to have decreed that she bear alone "the responsibility of my domestic life," so that her husband would not suffer "a sacrifice of your interest, and business." In mid-October, she conceded that Chicago "is bound to be the great city of the north west." By this time, Waller realized that Lincoln would win the election, that his victory made "secession and civil war almost inevitable," and that Kentucky would likely become contested ground. Bell advised Henry to "ask the guidance of a higher power . . . and God will lead you in the right way." The right way, they agreed, stretched north to the great city on Lake Michigan.

After Lincoln's election, Henry Waller sold his Kentucky farm and moved his entire family, including his widowed mother, to Chicago. Ultimately, all four Waller brothers and their families took up residence in the Windy City, where the clan gained far greater prominence than it had enjoyed south of the Ohio River.[70] In November 1860, his sister, Kate, married to a physician and planter in Louisiana's East Carroll Parish, expressed her thoughts about the move: "I think the unpleasant part of living in Chicago will be the difficulty of keeping servants but Bell is such a good disciplinarian she may have less problems than other persons." However, given what both brother and sister saw as the imminent "dissolution of the Union," she saw the potential servant problem as being "not so great as the disadvantages of living on the border, and I think your property is worth much more now than it will be for a long time again." Henry Waller agreed, as he later recalled: "I had made investments [in Chicago]; my sons were growing up & I thought would have a better field here in this rapidly rising city & energetic population; the war was coming on; I could not neglect my interests here; and I could not live separated (as I had done for some time) from my family during the portentious [sic] times coming upon the country. So I sold out suddenly, before the storm burst and prices went down[,] and brought my family here in safety."[71]

Prior to the move, Waller had pondered the servant issue and decided to bring north one of the family's slaves, Emily, even though doing so would make her free. He explained the plan in a letter to his mother, whom Emily had long served as a cook: "Now, Mother, we shall need a good cook, when we go to Chicago, more than anything else; and if you are willing, and if Emily is, we would like to have her in place of a white cook—paying for her just what we would have to pay for a white servant. If Emily were to move she would be free you know, just as she would have been had she gone to New York [with another member of the family]; and therefore the hire we pay her, would I presume have to be satisfactory to her." Because Emily was a good cook and had a positive relationship with his mother, Henry thought that the former slave could continue to be a valuable domestic servant working for wages as a free woman. Such flexibility of attitude may help explain his success as a businessman and attorney in Chicago.

Although none of Chicago's rail links with New York City operated under unified management until 1868, the midwestern city's emergence as a regional railroad hub reflected the accelerating economic importance of trade between the Northeast and the Midwest. By 1860, this commerce was significantly affecting Gotham's commercial activities and highly influential business community. Since the early nineteenth century, the Deep South's expanding Cotton Kingdom and the slave labor that made it possible had been the predominant source of profit for New York City's mercantile elite. As Sven Beckert has written, "It was, above all, New York's intense commitment to cotton that helped it decisively leave Philadelphia, Baltimore, and Boston behind." Because most of Manhattan's merchants and bankers played the role of middlemen in the Atlantic economy between the South and Europe, they tended to support compromises between the North and the South and therefore gravitated toward the Democratic Party during the middle and late 1850s. Upstate New York provided Lincoln with his narrow 1860 margin of victory in the Empire State.[72] The Republican ticket won 54 percent of the state's 675,000 ballots, while the northern Democracy took the remainder. In New York City, however, Lincoln received just 35 percent of the nearly 96,000 ballots, though that figure represented a "huge improvement" over the Republicans' 22 percent showing in 1856. The Republicans' effectiveness in minimizing the fallout from city Democrats' race-baiting is demonstrated by the fact that Abraham Lincoln and Hannibal Hamlin won their victory on the same day that a constitutional amendment to extend suffrage to free blacks went down to a resounding defeat. In the words of historian Debby Applegate, during the decade before the Civil War, "the epithet 'nigger' was far more commonly heard in New York than in the South."[73]

At the same time, as Beckert points out, "Western commerce" began to challenge the "exalted role" that trade with the South played for New York City, "a slow-moving shift whose political repercussions were only just being felt on the eve of the Civil War."[74] Increasing numbers of merchants and bankers were becoming involved in the exchange of finished goods for western agricultural commodities that the railroads encouraged. Together the New York and Erie Railroad (completed to Dunkirk on Lake Erie in 1851) and the Hudson River Railroad (opened to Buffalo in 1853) sustained the overwhelming advantage that New York City had enjoyed since the completion of the Erie Canal in 1825 in the movement of western produce to eastern cities. By the late 1850s, Gotham was handling half again as much rail tonnage as Philadelphia and Boston combined. According to historians Edwin G. Burrows and Mike Wallace, "The city adroitly positioned itself with respect to three of the most dynamic regions of the nineteenth-century global economy — England's manufacturing hinterlands, the cotton-producing slave South, and the agricultural Midwest — and it prospered by shipping cotton and wheat east while funneling labor, capital, manufactured and cultural goods west."[75]

During the summer and early fall of 1860, New York merchants and financiers could not fail to notice, as historian Roy Franklin Nichols has pointed out, that farmers from the Old Northwest expected a bumper harvest; buyers for the region's merchants and businessmen flocked to New York to place orders. In contrast, drought conditions in much of the Lower South meant that many planters would not have their bank balances replenished by heavy cotton sales, and southern debts held by the city's creditors might not be paid off. In response, wondered merchants, "Should the wishes of the South no longer be so much consulted? Were not East-West connections the ones to be cultivated thenceforth?" For the year, New York City received $161 million worth of goods from the West, just about the value of that year's cotton crop. New York and other merchants involved in the western trade were certainly sympathetic to the Republican Party's call for aggressive federal funding of internal improvements and could learn to make common cause with those up-and-coming manufacturers who favored both internal improvements and protective tariffs.[76]

Many workers agreed with manufacturers that the two groups constituted common members of the producing classes. They often claimed superiority to nonproducers (such as merchants, bankers, and planters who lived off the physical labor of others) and were drawn to the sort of free-labor arguments espoused by Greeley, Lincoln, and other Republicans. New York's richest manufacturer, artisan become millionaire Peter Cooper, like Lincoln, seemed to embody the American dream of dramatic upward social mobility, although Cooper rose by managing businesses rather than providing them with legal services. And his dramatic ascent made him atypical among the wealthiest New Yorkers of the time. According to the 1856 tax records, about 70 percent of those New Yorkers whose wealth was assessed at more than one hundred thousand dollars had inherited substantial fortunes.

Cooper was the son of a "struggling merchant" and at age seventeen was apprenticed to a maker of coaches. In his early twenties, he went to work in a Long Island factory that made cloth-shearing machines. After the War of 1812, he opened a retail grocery in Manhattan and began investing in real estate. In 1821, he bought a glue factory; under his management, the company sold a high-quality product for less than the cost of comparable European imports. In 1828, he invested in a large tract of real estate near the Baltimore waterfront. The discovery of iron ore deposits on the land led to Cooper's establishment of the Canton Iron Works, which in turn designed and manufactured the first successful steam engine produced in the United States—the new Baltimore and Ohio Railroad's Tom Thumb. After selling out in 1836 for Baltimore and Ohio stock, Cooper established a trio of New Jersey businesses: a Camden iron mine, a blast furnace at Phillipsburg, and a factory producing wire, wrought iron, and railroad tracks in Trenton on the Delaware River, easily accessible to anthracite coal from Pennsylvania. The Trenton ironworks delivered track to the Camden and Amboy Railroad and in

1854 produced the country's first structural iron. Cooper's son, Edward, and son-in-law, Abram Hewitt, further enlarged the business by "combining the whole process of iron manufacture from ore to finished product in one enormous complex, employing over two thousand workers." As Cooper's business interests indicate, the island of Manhattan became the hub of an industrial belt and subregional economy that included other adjacent manufacturing centers, notably Brooklyn (ranked fifth in the country) and Newark (sixth). Yet in the mid-1850s, Manhattan industries employed an estimated one of every fifteen people who worked in the country's manufacturing sector.[77]

Cooper dressed simply and for most of his life employed only two household servants, well under half as many as were engaged in the average upper-crust Manhattan home. He disdained the ostentatious display of wealth and provided his children with vocational training—handicrafts for his boys and housekeeping, cooking, and sewing for his daughter. He was prominent among those upper-class New Yorkers—"overwhelmingly manufacturers, lawyers, and western merchants," according to Beckert—who joined the state's Republican Party within a year of its founding in September 1855. He abandoned his lifelong affiliation with the Democracy primarily because he did not think that the Slave Power should direct federal government affairs. Artisans become industrialists such as Cooper were far more likely to associate with the Republican Party in the 1850s than were merchants and financiers such as department store magnate Alexander T. Stewart and banker Alexander August Belmont.

Lincoln became president-elect in November 1860 in large part because he could articulate and at the same time embody the vision of America as a dynamic economy and just society based on both free labor and opportunities for upward social mobility. This man from the Midwest expressed the same assumptions held by prominent northeastern Republicans. Those Republicans, through the Young Men's Central Republican Union, invited Lincoln to speak in New York City at the end of February 1860. The Central Republican Union, founded in 1856, took as its purpose promoting "a series of political lectures for the enlightenment of busy citizens," as Benjamin Thomas has noted. However, "actual leadership of the organization was vested in a group of veteran Republican politicians intent on thwarting Seward's aspirations to the presidency." When Lincoln received the invitation, the most prominent western alternative for the 1860 Republican nomination was Ohio governor Salmon P. Chase, who appeared too radical for conservative Republicans.

The *New York Tribune*'s Greeley was prominent among Seward's political enemies and a "senior adviser" in the Young Men's Central Republican

Union. In 1860, the *Weekly Tribune*, which reprinted articles from the daily publication, reached a circulation of two hundred thousand, making it probably the most widely read newspaper not only in America but in the world.[78] Greeley's *Tribune*, along with Henry J. Raymond's *New York Times*, had become the Republicans' principal national print organs, with the *Times* appealing to more moderate party members. The Whiggish Greeley, like former Democrat Cooper, had joined the Republicans soon after the founding of their state organization in late 1855. His ideal society was composed of prosperous and literate free men, a vision that contrasted with the economic and cultural stagnation he saw in southern slave society and that helps to explain his promotion of various "social justice 'causes.'" In 1853, he posed a powerful rhetorical question to the delegates attending a meeting of the World Temperance Association: "Ought law to conform to public sentiment, or ought law to be based upon essential righteousness, and then challenge a public sentiment to act in conformity therewith?" This moralistic stance won him credit for encouraging the New York legislature to pass the 1855 Act for the Prevention of Intemperance, Paupers, and Crime. "An intensely self-absorbed person whose emotions lay close to the surface," in the words of one historian, Greeley propounded an antislavery rhetoric that was at times so moralistic and pugnacious that journalistic and political opponents tarred him with the radical brush of abolitionism. Like Lincoln, Greeley had served a single term in the House of Representatives during the 1840s but continued to harbor political ambitions. In the process of denying Seward the Republican Party's presidential nomination, Greeley might also undermine the power of the Weed-Seward Albany Regency in state politics and perhaps enhance his own chances of winning a seat in the U.S. Senate.[79]

The *Tribune* welcomed Lincoln to New York with a biographical sketch that portrayed him "as "emphatically a man of the People, a champion of Free Labor, of diversified and prosperous Industry, and of that policy which leads through peaceful progress to universal intelligence, virtue and freedom." Lincoln would not disappoint sympathetic editors such as Greeley and William Cullen Bryant of the *New York Evening Post*. As historian Richard Current has emphasized, Lincoln's speech before a crowd of some fifteen hundred people at Cooper Union won him "the attention and respect of eastern Republicans and greatly increased his eligibility for the presidential nomination." Essentially, concludes Harold Holzer, the address constituted "a subtle but unmistakable preconvention campaign speech" that "bristled with barely contained indignation over the moral outrage of human slavery." Many historians thus have misconstrued the Cooper Union speech as conservative.

Instead, it represents "an ingenious attempt to make Republican principles appear unthreatening to moderate Northerners by identifying them with historical doctrine."[80] If Lincoln's argument involved identifying the containment and ultimate extinction of slavery as the legacy or historical doctrine of the Founding Fathers, then it might in fact warrant the label "conservative" in the literal sense of aiming to conserve something from that legacy deemed worthwhile. But conservatism, like most -isms, is a slippery concept for which full-blown, fleshed-out definition always depends on historical context. Lincoln challenged a fundamental conservative belief held by the overwhelming majority of free Americans, north and south, that the Declaration of Independence's notion of "all men" being "created equal" did not apply to people with black skin and African ancestry.[81] Proslavery conservatives went a step further, insisting that white Americans cease condemning slavery and instead follow the Founding Fathers' example of substantial and evenhanded compromise when dealing with the present as well as future security of the South's peculiar institution.

Lincoln's address had initially been slated to take place at Henry Ward Beecher's Plymouth Church in Brooklyn; however, before the candidate's arrival on Manhattan Island, the venue was shifted, without his knowledge, to Manhattan's Cooper Union for the Advancement of Science and Art. Cooper Union, a recently constructed "sparkling brownstone behemoth" on Seventh Street, at the southern edge of Midtown Manhattan, and named for benefactor Peter Cooper, contained the country's best auditorium, though it could not accommodate as large an audience as could Beecher's church. Beecher, ordained in 1838 as a New School Presbyterian, had left the more hierarchical Presbyterian polity for the relative autonomy of Congregationalism in 1847, when he accepted the pastorate of the new Plymouth Church in Brooklyn Heights. This community attracted so many New England refugees and transplants that it became known as Little Boston; it seemed to have been conceived by a marriage between "New Yorker entrepreneurship and Yankee conscience." Working in tandem with wealthy merchant and powerful trustee Henry Chandler Bowen, Beecher "built Plymouth Church into one of the few institutions in America that was popular, prosperous, and unapologetically antislavery." Church activists raised money to purchase slaves from bondage, and the building served as a way station on the Underground Railroad. Lincoln attended services at ten o'clock in the morning on 26 February 1860, taking a ferry to Brooklyn from Manhattan. He may well have heard Beecher preach about the qualities of a gentleman, "a man that has truthfulness and honor, and is so trained in them that they govern him spontaneously, and are a second nature to him." Lincoln greatly respected Beecher and according to one historian saw in him "an anointed spokesman for middle-class America." If Lincoln took a critical yet moderate antislavery stance in politics, Beecher assumed an analogous religious position, making antislavery respectable and responsible, even though both men on occasion employed immoderate language against the peculiar institution that antagonized and alienated those with investments in or sympathy for black bondage or a stable union. While radical abolitionists denounced the great majority of Christians for betraying Christ's true message by tolerating slavery as a regrettable but intransigent evil, Beecher tended to express the more positive perspective that America's churches and congregations, like the U.S. Constitution and the nation's politics, could be reformed and turned against slavery. As one biographer has concluded, "Beecher's determination to negotiate his way to liberty for all Americans without ripping apart the bonds of loyalty to the past appealed to a generation of Americans searching for a revolution that would not destroy" their cherished vision of the venerable Founding Fathers and the Constitution. Beecher and Lincoln reassured their fellow citizens "that they could embrace healthy change without burning their bridges to the past."[82]

About a week before Lincoln departed from Illinois, his presidential prospects received a significant boost from the influential *Chicago Press and Tribune*, which endorsed him first and foremost because he could carry Indiana and Illinois along with pro-tariff Pennsylvania and New Jersey. The twelve-hundred-mile trip from Springfield to New York required nearly three days and nights, and Lincoln had to take five different trains. While he was in New York, the president of the New York Central Railroad, Erastus Corning, supposedly called on the Illinoisan in his room at the Astor House hotel and offered him ten thousand dollars a year to become the railroad's lead attorney. Lincoln's son, Robert, who pursued a well-compensated career as a railroad executive, believed that the story was untrue: occupancy of the White House would bring Abraham Lincoln not only far more fame than would any success as a railroad lawyer but also an annual salary of twenty-five thousand dollars, "two and one half times what the New York Central allegedly had in mind."[83]

Tickets for Lincoln's Cooper Union address cost a modest twenty-five cents, the same fee Niblo's Saloon charged for an evening performance of George Christy's famous minstrel show, which specialized in songs and farce performed in blackface. The address, "one of the longest, best prepared, and most important speeches he ever made," bespoke extensive historical research in constitutional and political history, most of it in the well-equipped Illinois state law library across the town square from his Springfield office.[84] According to Holzer, the Cooper Union address "deserves to be recognized as the final round in the Lincoln-Douglas debates" begun in 1858. In September 1859, the country's leading literary magazine, New York's *Harper's New Monthly*, had published a copyrighted essay, "The Dividing Line between Federal and Local Authority: Popular Sovereignty in the Territories," by Douglas, who was also well versed in legal and constitutional history. According to Douglas's biographer, the essay was "long and tedious, written in a turgid style that lacked the vibrancy of his speeches." Douglas sought to discredit not only the Republican position that Congress and the courts could and should keep slavery out of the American territorial domain but also the insistence by fellow Democrats overly sympathetic to slaveholders that the Constitution obligated federal protection of the peculiar institution in the national domain. His attempt to gild the thoroughly pragmatic political lily of squatter sovereignty with the gold of constitutional theory and historical precedents only provoked much "indignation and protest" in the South as well as a powerful antislavery rebuttal from Lincoln, which he delivered in the form of his Cooper Union speech.[85]

The Republican began by contending that "the thirty-nine framers of the original Constitution" plus "the seventy-six members of the Congress which framed the [first ten] amendments thereto do certainly include those who may be fairly called our fathers who framed the Government under which we live." This phrase, which Lincoln used repeatedly in the speech, had been introduced by Douglas in his *Harper's* piece. According to Lincoln, no political father argued prior to 1800 that his understanding of the Constitution "forbade the Federal Government to control as to slavery in the federal territories." The Republican Party, he insisted, only followed the Founders' genuinely conservative lead in identifying slavery "as an evil not to be extended, but to be tolerated and protected only because of and so far as its actual presence among us makes that toleration and protection a necessity." Lincoln thus could deny the southern charge that he and the Republicans were simply sectional.[86]

In response to free southerners' claims that they were "conservative," Lincoln defined the term as "adherence to the old and tried, against the new and untried" and countered, "you are unanimous in rejecting and denouncing the old policy of the founders." He denied that "a single Republican" had been "implicated" in John Brown's 1859 raid on Harpers Ferry and painted Brown's "peculiar" plan as "an attempt by white men to get up a revolt among slaves in which the slaves refused to participate." In fact, "Republican doctrines and declarations are accompanied with a continual protest against any interference" with slaves and slaveholders in the South. Like their political fathers, Republicans declared their "belief that slavery is wrong; but the slaves do not hear us declare even this." Lincoln displayed a substantial degree of either ignorance or disingenuousness about exactly what slaves heard or understood about contemporary American politics, arguing that they "would scarcely know there is a Republican party" if southerners had not misrepresented party members as committed to "insurrection, blood and thunder among the slaves." Lincoln seems not to have understood, as Frederick Douglass had written five years earlier, that "ignorance is a high virtue in a human chattel; and as the master studies to make the slave ignorant, the slave is cunning enough to make the master think he succeeds."[87]

Lincoln attempted to reassure white southerners with words that failed for at least two reasons. First, he contradicted most slaveholders' strong preference for portraying the interactions between masters and slaves as akin to the affectionate but often strained relations between parents and children in a patriarchal family. At the very least, insisted Virginia senator Robert M. T. Hunter in a January 1860 speech subsequently published as a pamphlet, "the happiest relation which you can establish between [the Negro] race and the white, is that of master and slave."[88] Second, Lincoln reminded white residents of the South that the members of their immediate families lived with the constant threat that one or more disaffected slaves might perform desperate and perhaps fatal acts of retaliation. "Occasional poisonings from the kitchen, and open or stealthy assassination in the field, and local revolts extending to a score or so, will continue to occur as the natural results of slavery; but no general insurrection of slaves" after the Haitian model "can happen in this country for a long time." Lincoln seems not to have understood that free southerners tended to see a ban on slavery expansion as leading to higher black population density in the existing slave states, which would not only reduce the monetary value of slave chattel but also hasten the day when a "general insurrection" might become feasible. He tended to focus on the hope that geographical containment of the peculiar institution would lead slaveholders to become more open to programs of gradual and compensated emancipation coupled with colonization. In short, Lincoln could not really understand how the white South's post–Harpers Ferry preoccupation with insurrections might connect to the question of slavery's territorial expansion. Instead, he suggested that southerners would be satisfied only if northerners would "cease to call slavery *wrong*, and join them in calling it *right*." If the free states submitted on this moral issue, asked Lincoln, would they be obliged to permit bondage "to spread into the National Territories, and to overrun us here in these Free States?" After his election in November, Lincoln made much the same point in a pre-Christmas letter to Georgia congressman Alexander Stephens, a prominent conditional Unionist who became vice president of the Confederacy: "You think that slavery is *right* and ought to be extended; while we think it is *wrong* and ought to be restricted. That I suppose is the rub. It certainly is the only substantial difference between us."[89] However, Lincoln did not make explicit to Stephens his strong suspicion that the Slave Power wanted to nationalize bondage by making it legal in the North.

What of the recent *Dred Scott* decision? According to Lincoln, only "a bare majority of judges," each for his own reason, had supported a decision "mainly based upon a mistaken statement of fact—the statement in the opinion that 'the right of property in a slave is distinctly and expressly affirmed in the Constitution.'" Furthermore, he noted, as soon as "this obvious mistake" was brought to the attention of the justices, "is it not reasonable to expect that they will withdraw the mistaken statement, and reconsider the conclusion based upon it?" With that, he did away with the constitutional interpretation most favored by defenders of slavery, claiming, in effect, that the intentions of the nation's Founding Fathers had been misconstrued and even warped by Democratic logic, whether the northern version of Douglas's popular sovereignty or the southern version adopted by Chief Justice Taney.

Lincoln's Cooper Union address, along with eleven subsequent speeches in three New England states, indeed broadened his appeal as a Republican alternative to Chase and Seward. Lincoln seemed more conservative or moderate on the subject of slavery and therefore less liable to being linked with the extremist violence of John Brown and far more likely to carry the states of the Lower North, especially Pennsylvania, Indiana, and Illinois. He also appeared more acceptable to nativists who had voted for Fillmore in 1856 as well as to Protestant German Americans.

The Republican National Convention gathered in May in Chicago's new Wigwam, a huge structure combining the characteristics of a barn and a tent that was designed to accommodate ten thousand persons. The first order of business was a party platform. Its seventeen planks denied to both Congress and any territorial legislature the authority "to give legal existence to slavery" but denounced Brown's "lawless invasion" and deleted the 1856 platform's inflammatory references to polygamy and slavery as "twin relics of barbarism." Republicans took aim at the corruption rampant in Buchanan's Democratic administration by calling for an end to "the systematic plunder of the public treasury."[90] Party members also made the requisite rhetorical commitment to the "inviolate" rights of the states, though those rights did not include secession. The platform avoided taking stands on controversial issues that divided conservatives and radicals—that is, the 1850 Fugitive Slave Law, the status of slavery (rather than the slave trade) in the nation's capital, and the question of colonizing/deporting free blacks. The new party endorsed several measures favored by Old Line Whigs, including federal support for transportation projects, free land or homesteads for settlers in the western territories, and an implicitly upward "adjustment" of tariffs "to encourage the development of the industrial interests of the whole country." Lincoln could not or would not acknowledge that his election on this conservative platform might prompt a slave state to secede from the Union.[91]

After his nomination in May, Lincoln made no campaign speeches and wrote no letters for publication. In late October, Kentucky Unionist George Prentice, editor of the *Louisville Journal*, requested that Lincoln provide a public letter "setting forth your conservative views and intentions," thereby taking away "from the disunionists every excuse or pretext for treason." Although Republican victories in northern state elections had already made it probable that Lincoln would capture the Electoral College and the presidency, Prentice was particularly concerned with bolstering Unionist loyalty in the Upper South. Lincoln quickly responded, "If I were to labor a month, I could not express my conservative views and intentions more clearly and strongly, than they are expressed in our [party] platform, and in my many speeches already in print, and before the public."[92]

Toward the end of November, the *New Orleans Daily Crescent* opined that Lincoln was taking the advice of "his Abolition allies" and remaining "mute as an oyster—what might be called eloquently silent."[93] In an era when the older tradition of handwritten letters and the newer telegraph technology constituted the only direct means of long-distance communication, Lincoln sought through a large personal correspondence to mediate the tensions between his party's radical and conservative wings. While antislavery radicals spoke out zealously against Slave Power demands for concessions on the issue of slavery expansion, conservatives tended to focus on matters more tangential to the peculiar institution, such as tariffs and internal improvements. Lincoln understood the tactical advantages of maintaining an ambiguous silence, knowing that "delaying announcements on both patronage and secession enabled him to retain the loyalty of both his party's dueling factions." As historian Philip Shaw Paludan has suggested, Lincoln believed that his party "needed unity as desperately as the Union did."[94]

Some contemporary observers suggested that Lincoln should have offered public reassurances to southerners fearful of his presidency, a perspective with which historians have concurred. On 21 November, the *St. Louis Daily Missouri Republican* argued that Lincoln should make "new pledges and new guarantees," especially with regard to enforcement of the Fugitive Slave Law. The fifteen slave states had suffered serious "indignities" at the hands of the eighteen free states and now demanded their "respect."[95] According to one recent biography of Lincoln, a "reaffirmation of his conservatism and his goodwill toward the South" might have fortified an already robust Upper South Unionism. In addition, such assurances "might have made a difference in the course of secession in states like Georgia, where voters were divided." In particular, he could have done "more to reassure anxious southerners that he would not use his patronage powers to place hard-line Republicans in federal appointments in the slave states."[96] Although he wrote a Whiggish Unionist in North Carolina in mid-December that when dispensing "patronage in the slave states . . . I do not expect to inquire for the politics of the appointee, or whether he does or not own slaves," he nonetheless declined a request to make a public statement to this effect. Perhaps Lincoln thought that if he acquiesced, he would have to repeat another point—one that southerners would not find reassuring—made in the same "strictly confidential" letter: "On the territorial question I am inflexible." Perhaps he also did not want to make public such statements as the one he included in another "confidential" letter written around the same time: "Mr. Lincoln is not pledged to the ultimate extinction of slavery."[97] Lincoln probably meant that those exact words, which he had in fact used earlier, did not appear in the Republican Party platform, and hence he was not officially "pledged" to them. At the same time, he likely had no desire to disavow the phrase before the northern public. In any event, whether the South Carolina elite would have heard and believed calming assurances of "his conservatism and his goodwill toward the South" is certainly debatable, as is how much Lincoln could have done to stanch disunionism in the Cotton or Lower South, where he appeared to be "diabolic abolitionism personified."[98] Moreover, Lincoln's silence seems to have done less than the imminent prospect and then the reality of the Southern Confederacy to place the Upper South between a rock and a hard place in early 1861. And Lincoln's silence made little difference in the Border South, where dislike or distrust of Republicans coexisted quite easily with the same feelings toward fire-eating secessionists.[99]

Most Republican Party leaders seem to have supported Lincoln's "prudence (or what is called a 'masterly inactivity')" before what they saw as hyperbolic secessionist bluster. They had heard such threats before, and they constituted treason. The Sunday before the 1860 election, Henry Ward Beecher's sermon had mocked those who feared that a Republican victory would spark secession: "Take my word for it—all the barking will be done before the election and there will be no biting afterwards." "The power of the slave interest in Washington is broken," he contended, and "the crisis is over."[100]

Two weeks after Lincoln won the election, New York governor Edwin Morgan wrote that offering comforting words to the slave interests would, "instead of *appeasing* . . . only create an appetite for *more*." In Illinois, governor-elect Richard Yates, a spokesman for the amorphous plurality of Republican "moderates," declared that "the American people cannot be coerced by insolent threats of secession or disunion. . . . Let us know whether the millions of freemen of this nation are to get on their knees to Slavery at every Presidential election." As historian Russell McClintock suggests, Yates's statement "tapped the heart of the Republicans' mass appeal—the need to defend American liberty and self-government from the dominance of the Slave Power." In the process, Yates "appealed to northerners' manly pride to resist Southern intimidation."[101]

While the president-elect received advice to stand firm against secessionist threats, Henry Waller urged a peaceful compromise solution to escalating sectional hostilities. In the late 1850s, he had won some renown as an outspoken Douglas supporter, yet after Lincoln's election, when Waller perceived that his native Kentucky would be trapped in the vise of escalating North-South sectional conflict, he sold his property in the Bluegrass State and moved his family to the western shore of Lake Michigan. Like Douglas in Washington during the secession winter, Waller worked in Chicago for the Crittenden Compromise, often speaking on behalf of those who had voted for Douglas in the presidential election. The city had given 10,697 votes to Lincoln and 8,094 to Douglas, far more than Bell's 107 and Breckinridge's 87.[102]

The 7 January 1861 *Chicago Press and Tribune* identified "Henry Waller, Esq." as one of seven featured speakers who addressed "The Citizens Meeting," a "Grand Rally at Bryan Hall" the previous Saturday evening. In the aftermath of South Carolina's secession, the paper suggested that all of the speakers endorsed "The Constitution, Union, and Enforcement of the Laws" as well as "Patriotism Not Party." It announced that Chicago "Is For the Union" and "Endorses Major [Robert] Anderson," then holding onto his position at Fort Sumter. The meeting's presiding chair, "S. S. Hayes, Esq.," voiced his understanding "that the gathering had assembled irrespective of party for an expression of views as to our national affairs, and our determination to sustain the Union and the Executive." However, Waller's remarks elicited many negative responses from the audience, which seemed to include numerous Republicans.[103]

"I stand here as a representative of Old Kentucky," Waller began. After paying his "compliments" to Anderson, who, Waller noted, was a Kentuckian, he invoked the memory of Henry Clay in 1850 by asking, "Who was it poured the oil that allayed the perils of a former crisis like this? A son of Kentucky." Waller then noted that "Kentucky has again spoken in the Senate," referring to the Crittenden Compromise. The newspaper reporter heard someone shout, "We won't endorse him," and others made "cries of 'No concession.'" Waller responded, "This is not the tone of the fathers who laid the foundation of our nation with their blood. . . . We have reached the time when all the politicians and demagogues that have afflicted the nation are to be swept off like weeds upon an ocean billow, and that billow is to come from the bosom of the people. We must take hold of the question itself and look for some feasible remedy." When he asked, "How is this to be done?," someone shouted, "Put down the rebellion." Waller disavowed partisanship: "I am no Democrat, no Republican; I was a Whig, that's past, I am now *a patriot at large.*" After hearing cheers, he continued. "Kentucky has suffered more in one year than South Carolina in fifty. You say you can have 'no concession for traitors'; have you concession for those who are patient and faithful to the Union?"[104]

Waller claimed that in Republican eyes, "all this impending trouble has sprung from the repeal of the Missouri Compromise," and he "was against that repeal. Now I cannot see how the Republican side [can] object *to a restoration of that compromise,*" as Crittenden proposed. Members of the crowd responded with "cries of 'Never'; 'No Sir'; 'No extension of slavery.' Cheers." Waller went on: "Now I want peace. I want to save the country. It can only be achieved by speaking out on practical questions." He insisted that if the Missouri Compromise line were "restored," it would give "the North more territory in proportion to her population than the South[,] therefore she ought not to object," eliciting "confusion, cheers, cries of 'No,' 'No.'" Waller then posed another hypothetical: "Suppose the crisis threatens as it does a shedding of blood. If it comes to that *there are fifteen states on one side and eighteen on the other.*" A voice declared, "And we'll lick 'em like the devil, too." The chair rebuked the audience for excessive noise.[105]

Waller then presented another scenario: "Now suppose in the struggle the North *takes fifteen conquered provinces; they will be no longer sovereign states.* You want to reach that?" Then came shouts of "No, No." He appealed to his listeners' pride and their prejudices: "You will have freed four millions of blacks and enslaved eight million whites. Then let us pause. I appeal to you in the spirit of the fathers who based their Constitution on *concession*. Can you not rise up to their spirit?" Then came an appeal to the crowd's courage and sense of fairness: "You are not afraid of the Southern [seceding] States, but will not quietly and fairly hear the border States, with the olive branches in their hands? You are in the majority. Can't you afford to be magnanimous? Cannot you have the spirit of it? The border States say, *'Strike — but hear.'*"[106]

Waller closed with a plea that "Mr. Crittenden's proposition" be included among the formal resolutions adopted by the rally's attendees, citing his "desire that this meeting do something practical—that the Missouri Compromise be restored and embodied in the Constitution of the United States." But the audience responded with more "cries of 'No, No.'"[107]

Waller's speech failed to persuade most of his Chicago listeners that Crittenden's proposed amendment would justly and peacefully preserve the Union. Border state efforts to head off a civil war—in particular, Kentucky's fruitless claim to neutrality between the United States and the Confederate States—similarly came to naught in 1861. And in this way, Lincoln and Waller, two native Kentuckians who began their political careers as devoted disciples of Whig Unionist Henry Clay, wound up at odds and opposing one another on the eve of the Civil War.

7 Keziah Goodwyn Hopkins Brevard and Sojourner Truth

Faith, Race, and Gender

*P*rivate diaries, at least those not subsequently edited by the diarist with a view to publication, are more likely to offer genuinely candid expressions of the author's feelings and judgments at the moment than are letters and speeches composed by politicians for colleagues or the electorate. Such is the case with the extraordinary diary kept by Keziah Goodwyn Hopkins Brevard, a pietistic Christian and slaveholding widow in South Carolina during the secession crisis. Her journal reveals much about the life and thoughts of a highly independent woman living and working on a plantation, often in the company only of black people.[1] Brevard's account demonstrates how a woman could manage plantation affairs quite well without a white man's presence and supervision, even as she held to Victorian assumptions about the proper gender roles assigned to genteel men and women.[2]

Kizzie was one of five children born to Keziah and James Hopkins, although only two of their daughters survived childhood. She also had three stepsiblings from her mother's first marriage; one of them, James Hopkins Adams, served as governor of South Carolina for two years in the mid-1850s. A daughter of privilege, Kizzie Hopkins received a first-rate education for a young woman in the Old South, attending both a local school and the Columbia Female Academy. She and her sister, Caroline, married a pair of North Carolina brothers, Joseph and Theodore Brevard. Caroline died in childbirth; Keziah and Joseph had no children before his death in 1842, following recurring mental and physical disorders. Her mother had died two years earlier, and her father passed away two years later, leaving his entire estate to his surviving daughter, with four men serving as trustees. Her father's Sand Hills home place, situated about ten miles east of Columbia in the Carolina Piedmont, became Kizzie's principal residence. She never remarried, personally running the farm and slaves at Sand Hills and hiring overseers to manage her other properties. She enlarged the Sand Hills house and purchased a townhouse in Columbia, probably seeking to increase her social outlets. Yet she spent most of her time directing affairs at Sand Hills, demonstrating

Keziah Goodwyn Hopkins Brevard (Courtesy of Dr. Edward D. Hopkins Jr.)

what John Hammond Moore, the editor of her diary, terms "a competent, no-nonsense mind capable of making decisions, formulating plans, and carrying them out." As much as any male head of a farming household, she valued her rural domain as a source of independence. She seems to have found "the responsibility of managing a large agricultural operation . . . more appealing than giving parties and making small talk over tea and cakes." According to the 1850 census, Keziah Brevard owned two farms in Richland County, together comprising twenty-six hundred acres and 180 slaves. During the 1850s, she purchased large amounts of real estate in the Lower Richland area, even as some of her neighbors "departed to try their luck in Florida, Texas, and other far places."[3] By 1860, she had more than doubled her landholdings to some six thousand acres, and she owned 209 slaves.[4]

Unlike Senator Jefferson Davis, Brevard lived close to many of her slaves during most of the secession winter, and her diary testifies to her constant struggle with "the morality of slavery and secession." Where Davis had been raised a Baptist but became an Episcopalian, Brevard was nominally a Presbyterian and was "not disposed to unite" with either Baptists or Episcopalians, although she contributed to a local Methodist mission. Like many plantation owners, concludes Moore, Brevard "wanted desperately to be respected and even loved by those she owned and often tried to cultivate their affection." She wrote, "Make my servants (those who labor for me) to know thee & love thee is one of my constant prayers." Yet "like most wealthy people," Moore notes, she was "accustomed to having her own way in all matters." When her "servants" did not behave as she expected and wished, they became "impudent," a fault that, as Frederick Douglass explained, "was one of the commonest and most indefinite in the white catalogue of offenses usually laid to the charge of slaves."[5] Brevard admitted her occasional lack of patience with the slaves, as when she confided to her diary in 1861, "I have sinned this day grumbling with my poor negroes. I ought to have more patience." She frequently expressed concerns not only about her sins but also about those of the nation, wondering whether God wanted to break up the Union as retribution for past sins. A population degraded by sin, she mused, "is a curse to a country." She prayed, "Lord Jesus save us from degradation—let us draw nearer & dearer to all that is beautiful & good in thy sight." She contrasted godliness, which would ensure the soul's salvation after death, with worldliness. Early in September 1860, she wrote, "These are perilous times—perilous because we do not love God as we should." Nations received mercy from God "so soon as they turn to him in sincerity and truth." However, she asked, "have we not as a people made riches our God—I feel it is ever a sin with me."[6]

Although the sin of worldliness afflicted both sections of the country, Brevard saw antislavery northerners as positively evil and wicked. "Those Northern cut throats—Oh Change their wicked hearts. . . . [H]ow can a southerner love those whose highest glory would be to know that we are exterminated, to give place to a people far inferior—I wish every vessel that would go to Africa to bring slaves here—could sink before they reached her soil." She could not abide "the fanatics of the No[rth]—think they are doing God service to destroy us & our property." On 13 October 1860, she penned, "It is time for us to show the rabble of the North we are not to be murdered in cold blood because we own slaves." Enslaved blacks had been "transmitted down to us & what can we do with them?—free such a multitude of half barbarians in our midst— no—no—we must sooner give up our lives than submit to such a degradation." At Harpers Ferry in late 1859 John Brown came "to cut our throats because we held property we could not do otherwise with."

Brevard reported that many of her bondswomen "are of the lowest caste— making miserable their own fellow servants by meddling with the husbands of others—I am not excusing the males, but in the world they are not so degraded by such conduct as the females." She lamented, "Oh I wish I had been born in a Christian land & never seen or known of slaves of any colour. A degraded population is a curse to a country. Negroes are as deceitful and lying as any people can be—Lord give me better feelings towards them." She talked about selling an "impudent" slave and wanting "to get rid of all my bad negroes," and she supported the colonization of freed blacks.[7]

After learning on 9 November that Abraham Lincoln had been elected president, she wrote, "I do pray if there is to be a crisis—that we all lay down our lives sooner than free our slaves in our midst." Almost a week later she declared, "I wish Lincoln & Hamlin could have died before this & saved our country dissolution—the South ought to go out of the U[nion]—as it is—Northern abolitionists hate us so they ought to be glad we are not part of them. . . . I hate their principles—I go as much for Patriarchal feelings for my or our blacks as any one does—but I do not go for mixing the two races." She insisted, "We are attached to our slaves—they are as our own family & would today have been a happy people if Northern fanaticism had not warred against us." Toward the end of November, she confessed, "It is dreadful to dwell on insurrections—many an hour have I laid awake in my life thinking of our danger." She pointed to the threats of poisoning and arson, more subtle than overt and violent resistance but still terrifying. Since "we are in the very midst of our enemies . . . we can never be safe with them in our midst." On 10 December, she expressed hatred for northern abolitionists because they wanted slaves to become "assassins, the selfish & envious sons of Satan."[8]

Early in the new year, she expressed the hope, common in both the North and the South, that God's Providence would bring about reconciliation between the sections. "In my heart I was opposed to breaking up this beautiful union of ours—but I must act for my home, the home of my forefathers for three generations." Southerners wanted an end to "Northern fanaticism—we want *the love of Christ in our souls* [so] that we love the brethren & do unto others as we would have others do to us." Later that month and again in February, she noted a James Henley Thornwell's Thanksgiving Day sermon delivered the previous November. Thornwell, a Presbyterian who taught at South Carolina's Columbia Theological Seminary, was known as the "Calhoun of the southern church" and has been described as the region's "ablest theologian." According to historian Paul Conkin, Thornwell "defended the servitude of blacks in the South as the best solution given their situation. Nothing in the Bible condemned such servitude (it did place responsibilities on both master and servant), and plenty of biblical examples seemed to provide a type of endorsement. But Thornwell really tried to convert slavery into nothing more than a form of employment and set such high standards for masters (they had to protect black marriages, teach blacks to read, and instruct them in the Christian faith) that slave owners found his strictures little better than those of the abolitionist, particularly when Thornwell tried to get state laws to reflect such high moral demands." Thornwell's preaching meshed with both Brevard's brand of religiosity and her strongly prejudiced condemnation of interracial sex as degrading and sinful. "I consider the vast body of slaves little above brutes—I am sorry to think it—*but I believe it*. Many white faces in this land of light sin high in the presence of God setting our poor negroes degraded examples—I thank the Heavenly father I have never had a son to mix my blood with *negro* blood—Oh such a sin would [be] & is disheartening to Christian Mothers."[9]

Near the end of February, Brevard wrote, "I hope the South will shew herself honorable through this strife—God will not prosper if she is deceptive." She infused the traditional notion of honor with the more modern, perhaps bourgeois virtue of honesty. Anticipating the new president's inaugural address, she observed that within "a few short days . . . we shall hear from Lincoln's lips what we may expect—if he makes war on us the whole body of men No. & So. should rise against him & make a blow at the man himself who would dare to bring such trouble on this land won by the blood of our forefathers from British encroachments." Lincoln and his friends "are black republicans, our enemies—they must have dreadful hearts to wish to cut our throats because we are sinners—as if they were pure and undefiled—no surer sign of what deceivers they are than to see how self conceited they are—God can punish every sinner & will do it." Brevard asked, "What is the South contending for—she is or has to work against a set of fanatics—who would glory in shedding every drop of white blood."[10] She repeatedly expressed her conviction that Republicans intended to destroy her community and its way of life.

A diary entry from early April, after the organization of the Confederacy but before the attack on Fort Sumter, expressed her sorrow that "our once strong country is now severed and I believe forever—for I see no disposition in the stubborn North to yield any thing from advantage—& the South thought she could make the North succumb to her." Brevard subsequently declared, "I do despise the principles of the Northern Republicans." Apparently referring to politicians both North and South, she wondered, "Why are they stubborn about the forts if they have any thoughts of reconciliation?" She could not "believe the South did right to break up our Union." Her diary

*Sojourner Truth
(Courtesy of the
Library of Congress)*

ends on 15 April with news that "Mr. Edmund Ruffin fired the first shot on Ft. Sumter. O Lord let the N. & S. now compromise and shed not more blood."[11]

Although Sojourner Truth was also a woman, her take on the secession crisis represents very different religious, racial, gendered, and sectional perspectives from those of Brevard. The story of Truth, a former slave living in the North, provides much information about the legacy of slavery and the enduring power of intense racial prejudice above the Mason-Dixon Line.

According to historian Margaret Washington, Truth was "the most notable and highly regarded African-American woman in the nineteenth century."[12] She experienced a less dramatic version of the substantial upward social mobility from humble beginnings embodied in and celebrated by Lincoln. However, her story shines a very different kind of light on the nineteenth-century gospel of success. As biographer Nell Irvin Painter has explained, Truth's life evolved in three grand stages: from chattel slavery to Christian evangelism to public advocacy for both abolition and woman's rights.[13]

Sojourner Truth entered the world when slavery was still an important institution in parts of northern society, particularly in New York and New Jersey. As of 1800, well over two-thirds of New York's almost seventeen thousand black persons were still enslaved. Serious consideration of abolition had not begun in the Empire State until after the American Revolution, and New York did not officially endorse gradual emancipation until 1797, with supplemental legislation adopted in 1809 and 1817.[14] According to the first law, slaves born after 4 July 1799 had to serve long periods of contractual or indentured servitude—twenty-five years for females and twenty-eight years for males. This was precisely the kind of gradual emancipation that Lincoln expected to take place in the southern states, with full freedom not granted until as long as a century after the geographic containment of slavery went into effect. Yet most people living in the northeastern states tended to downplay or overlook the fact that slavery remained an important institution in some states north of the Mason-Dixon Line well into the nineteenth century.[15] In the 1830s, when abolitionists began aggressively to campaign against the South's peculiar institution, chattel slavery had only recently disappeared from the Empire State, leaving some former slaves subject to temporary bondage as well as racial prejudice.[16] At the same time, some northern owners of slaves inherited from the colonial era, like some slaveholders in the Chesapeake states of Virginia and Maryland, did not hesitate to sell human property to the expansive cotton South, even though New York law prohibited selling slaves to states where slavery would remain legal after 1827. Many white northerners—usually men on the make who married heiresses in the slave states—also became affluent planters and southern sympathizers.

Truth began life in Ulster County, New York, in 1797 as Isabella, the youngest of twelve or thirteen children born to Elizabeth and James Baumfree, slaves of Colonel Johannes Hardenbergh Jr., and grew up speaking Dutch. The colonel belonged to the local slaveholding elite, though by the standards of wealthy southern planters, he owned but a modest number of human chattel. According to the 1800 census, Ulster County had a population of 29,554, of whom just over 10 percent had African ancestry (about the same percentage as in New York City). Under the terms of the 1797 law, slaves born before 4 July 1799 would be freed when they reached age thirty, and Isabella Baumfree spent that time living and working amid the rural and small-town communities of the Hudson River Valley below Albany, the same area that nurtured Martin Van Buren. Her parents lived in a state of semi-independence in a cottage and farmed some of Colonel Hardenbergh's often hilly land. They also endured the sales of some of their adolescent children, including Isabella, who was sold to an English-speaking farmer after Hardenbergh's death when she was nine.

Isabella Baumfree was sold twice more by 1810. The final purchaser, John Dumont of Kingston, paid about seventy English pounds (roughly two hundred dollars today) for her, and she spent the next sixteen years with the Dumont family, working in fields that produced mediocre wheat and wool suitable for homespun yarn and doing household labor. In the process, she gained a command of spoken English, though she remained illiterate.

John and Sally Dumont abused Baumfree both physically and sexually, though the beatings she received were hardly unusual for slaves north or south. According to Painter, Baumfree "accepted the patriarchal order in which she lived and blamed herself," assuming "that submission to Dumont was the same as being true to God" and responding to her master's beating "by identifying with him." Although sexual exploitation of female slaves by male masters was widespread, Baumfree was unusual in that she experienced sexual abuse at the hands of her mistress and came to despise Sally Dumont. Olive Gilbert, the amanuensis to whom Sojourner Truth later dictated her autobiography, may well have been reluctant, "from motives of delicacy," to provide any details about this abuse. However, Truth had at least one practical reason to mention it only obliquely. Concerned about her credibility before the public, she feared that her experiences had been "so unaccountable, so unreasonable, and what is usually called so unnatural" that "uninitiated" readers would not believe her story.[17]

In 1815, Baumfree married another slave, Thomas. According to New York law, their children were legitimate but would remain in bondage even after the parents became freedpeople, so two of Truth's five children, Elizabeth and Sophia, did not become free until 1850 and 1851, respectively. According to Painter, Truth's marriage to a fellow slave "seems to have conformed to the working-class model of people attached to one another without the romantic gloss of what middle-class people prize as love."[18] Although the Dumonts evidently subjected Baumfree to "sustained and multifaceted abuse of the sort that destroys self-esteem and distorts reality," she found in one brand of Christianity a pronounced freedom from fear and sense of personal empowerment.[19] In 1826, the year before she was to become legally free, Baumfree's God instructed her to set out from Kingston on her own with her infant daughter, Sophia. Only a few miles away, in Wagondale, she found a sympathetic antislavery couple, Isaac and Maria Van Wagenen, who paid Dumont enough money to keep Baumfree for the final year of her enslavement. Isabella then took the last name Wagenen. In 1827, she participated in the founding of Kingston Methodist Church and became part of the holiness and perfectionist movement within the Methodist denomination in the northeastern states.[20] Wagenen's new faith and freedom seem to have empowered her, along with financial help from Quakers and a pair of Dutch lawyers in Ulster County, to achieve an unusual legal victory through the courts. In 1826, the Dumonts had sold her son, Peter, then only five or six years old, to an in-law in New York City. He had soon illegally been resold to a planter in Alabama. "Although intimidated and naïve," reports Painter, Wagenen "entered a complaint with the Ulster County grand jury." In the spring of 1828, young Peter was returned to New York state, bearing scars and back lacerations that caused his mother to exclaim, "Oh, Lord Jesus, see my poor child."[21] Wagenen's embrace of freedom and liberty had a markedly spiritual dimension that was missing from Lincoln's far more secular free-labor gospel. His prewar condemnations of slavery appealed to the natural rights principles of the Declaration of Independence rather than to the evangelical Protestantism and egalitarian Christianity favored by abolitionist immediatists such as William Lloyd Garrison and the future Sojourner Truth.

In the late 1820s, Wagenen left Ulster County for New York City, spending four years working for and living rather ascetically with the family of a perfectionist Methodist merchant, James Latourette, on Bowery Hill. At Zion African Church, she found her long-lost older sister, Sophia, and their brother, Michael. As a participant in revivals at Methodist camp meetings, she displayed the inspirational magnetism of a preacher, effecting miraculous conversions. Wagenen adopted a religion that would probably be identified today as Pentecostal, with its emphasis on the Holy Spirit's power to break forth in people's lives. According to Conkin, "All aspects of modern Holiness churches and much of modern Pentecostalism were present in early Methodism."[22] God's spirit could inspire a personal holiness that rejected the evil physical temptations of this world. "Pentecost traditions," explains Margaret Washington, "included the evocation of a 'Holy Wind' that would rush through the heart, provoking tongues of fire, speaking in tongues, and spiritual telepathy."[23] These "gifts of the Spirit" recalled the precedent of the Apostles at Pentecost, fifty days after Jesus' resurrection, according to the New Testament Book of Acts. Yet Wagenen's conversion, like that of many slaves in the Old South, also seems to have tapped into African aesthetic and spiritual traditions.

As with most believers of Pentecostal persuasion, her faith involved a conviction that the world would soon end with Christ's Second Coming and God's final judgment of sinful humankind. Though Wagenen had not yet heard her summons to preach against slavery and patriarchy, some variations on the theme of apocalyptic millenarianism appealed to abolitionists black and white—among them David Walker and Theodore Dwight Weld—who looked to a day of divine vengeance on the evil injustice of slavery. Visions of racial conflict derived from slavery motivated many antebellum Americans, inspiring abolitionists, for whom slave rebellion and "racial bloodbath" would represent the "wages of sin,"[24] as well as more moderate opponents of slavery who advocated gradual emancipation and colonization as the proper path to avoid the horrors of race war.

Boston Unitarian Theodore Parker was a militantly abolitionist opponent of the Slave Power who became one of the "Secret Six" who provided financial backing to John Brown. Parker had no doubts about Anglo-Saxon racial superiority, writing in 1859 that slavery must end in the United States to prevent the "Africanization of America." The same demon also haunted William Henry Holcombe, a slaveholding physician in Tensas Parish, Louisiana. Brooding about the Republican Party's threat to the slave South shortly after Lincoln's election, Holcombe penned a pamphlet, *The Alternative: A Separate Nationality or the Africanization of the South* (1860), soon reprinted as an article in Richmond's *Southern Literary Messenger*. Negrophobia was far more constant, intense, and pervasive among whites in the South than in the North, but not because southerners were necessarily more "racist." African Americans constituted a third of the population in the fifteen slave states, with much higher percentages in many parts of the Lower South. In the stressed imaginations of many free southerners, black slaves' savagery (or at least lack of civilization) could not help but fan the fires of white dread at the prospect of angry resentment and violent retaliation. "According to the present rate of increase, in fifty years the negroes of these [slave] states will amount to twenty millions," explained Holcombe. "Suppose them to be restricted to their present area. Suppose them in addition to be free. Imagine the crime, the poverty, the barbarism, the desolation of the country."[25]

Decades earlier in New York City, the newly converted and free Isabella Van Wagenen found a kindred spirit in the well-to-do, pious, and philanthropic Elijah Pierson, becoming his live-in housekeeper. A former businessman who founded the Mt. Carmel Church in expectation of the imminent "great and dreadful day of the Lord," Pierson was a reformist enthusiast associated with another philanthropic businessman, Arthur Tappan, who helped Garrison found the American Antislavery Society in 1833. In the same year, Wagenen followed Pierson into the authoritarian and patriarchal "kingdom" of the self-proclaimed Prophet Matthias, commanded by God to take control of this world before its righteous destruction. Matthias beat Wagenen "for the infraction he considered abominable in women: insubordination."[26] Although he claimed the power of subduing the devil, who caused bodily illness, Matthias failed to save Pierson from death in 1834 after a series of seizures and was tried for poisoning the man. Although the prophet was acquitted, he spent four months in prison for whipping his disobedient daughter and contempt of court. When Matthias left New York state, Wagenen returned to domestic work in New York City.

On 1 June 1843, she heard the Holy Spirit call her to assume the name Sojourner Truth and to flee the "wicked city," a "second Sodom" to be destroyed by fire and brimstone. She became an "instrument of God" "whose self-proclaimed mission was to 'sojourn' the land and speak God's 'truth.'"[27] During this year, the dispensational, premillennial movement known as Millerism reached its peak, only to lose steam when William Miller's precise dates for the apocalypse—originally 21 March 1843, then the same day a year later, and finally 22 October 1844—passed without Christ's return and the Day of Judgment. As Painter suggests, Truth likely was "a Millerite Second Adventist expecting the imminent second coming of Christ."[28]

After leaving New York, Truth joined a Massachusetts utopian cooperative community, the Northampton Association for Education and Industry, where she worked in the laundry. Among the association's more postmillennialist reformers, who believed that God intended believers to purge the world of its most grievous and manifest evils before the Day of Judgment, Truth began in earnest another conversion, this time to a feminist form of antislavery. The Northampton community, which was dissolved in 1846, owed much to another reformist businessman, George W. Benson, a former lawyer from Brooklyn whose sister had married William Lloyd Garrison in 1834. Like Garrison, Benson had become radicalized on the subject of slavery largely because of the racist hostility to blacks shown by New England's antislavery colonizationists.

At Northampton, Truth came to know another, much younger former slave, Frederick Douglass, who had fled Maryland for New England, had taken a new name, and was about to become the most famous black man in America. Douglass, striving to become an eloquent stylist in English prose as well as speech, wrote that Truth struck him as "a genuine specimen of the uncultured Negro," caring "very little for elegance of speech or refinement of manners." Yet he also recognized that her "quaint speeches," with their "strange compound of wit and wisdom, of wild enthusiasm and flint-like common sense," held great appeal for more refined audiences. Ironically, according to Painter, "Truth's close associates during her adult life," apart from her children, were in fact "middle-class white people of education, if not always of standing."²⁹

After Douglass's first autobiography, published by Garrison's American Antislavery Society in 1845, became something of a sensation, Truth began dictating an account of her life to a female abolitionist and fellow member of the Northampton Association. Garrison helped Truth arrange for the book's initial publication in 1850 and advertised it in *The Liberator*. With the failure of her utopian community at the end of 1846, Truth remained in Northampton and moved into her first home, which she purchased with the help of a three-hundred-dollar mortgage from Samuel L. Hill, one of the founders of the Northampton Association. Revenues from the sale of her volume enabled the fifty-seven-year-old Truth to pay off the mortgage in 1854.

The *Narrative of the Life of Sojourner Truth*, in Painter's words, signifies its author's "first step in a deliberate representation of self" as "a person worth reading about in her own life." It concludes "not with indictment, but with the Christian forgiveness of a slaveholder." The occasion for this tale of forgiveness came with a visit that Truth made in 1849 to her daughter, Diana, in New York. Diana had remained with John Dumont, and Truth became convinced that Dumont had been transformed. "A slaveholding master turned into a brother!" she wrote. "Poor old man, may the Lord bless him, and all slaveholders partake of his spirit."³⁰

By the time Lincoln made his unsuccessful run for the Senate in 1858, in the process striving mightily to distance himself from color-blind abolitionists, Sojourner Truth had worked for years as an orator proclaiming both color-blind abolition and woman's rights. She seemed little interested in political complexities and identified with the Garrisonians, as opposed to politically more realistic antislavery proponents who declined to identify opposition to slavery with the even more suspect movement for woman's rights. In 1854, Garrison publicly burned a copy of the U.S. Constitution, insisting that genuine Christian principles mandated his viewing the document as "a covenant with death, and an agreement with Hell." The nation's founding document, he argued, was hopelessly degraded by passages upholding the heinous sin of slavery. To redeem itself from the stain of guilt by association with southern sinfulness, Garrison called on the North to separate from the United States.³¹

In November 1850, Truth and Douglass spoke before the Rhode Island Antislavery Society. While condemning the new Fugitive Slave Act, Douglass reiterated Garrison's call for northern political separation from the damned slave South—"No union with slaveholders." In her brief remarks, Truth confessed that "she did not know anything about politics—could not read the newspapers—but thanked God that the law was made—that the worst had come to worst; but the best must come to best." During the winter of 1851, she went on a speaking tour through western New York and Ohio in the company of Garrison and abolitionist Englishman George Thompson. According to Painter, Truth's speeches seldom dealt with political issues, instead drawing on her work as a rural slave to romanticize farm labor as "the embodiment of real work." She recounted her experiences to demonstrate that a woman could work just as hard and productively on the farm as a man. Because "I could work as much and eat as much as a man (when I could get it)," Truth argued, she deserved the same freedom and the same pay as a man. However, Truth seems never to have spoken the phrase so often attributed to her: "Ar'n't I a woman?"[32] According to an unreliable account published by Frances Dana Gage in 1863, Truth uttered these words at a woman's rights convention in Akron, Ohio, in 1851:

> "I tink dat, 'twixt de nigger of de South and de womin at de Norf, all talkin' 'bout rights, de white men will be in a fix pretty soon." . . .
>
> "Dat man ober dar say dat womin needs to be helped into carriages, and lifted ober ditches, and to hab de best place everywhar. Nobody eber helps me into carriages, or ober mudpuddles, or gibs me any best place!"
>
> And raising herself to her full height, and her voice to a pitch like rolling thunder, she asked, "And ar'n't I a woman? . . . I have ploughed, and planted, and gathered into barns, and no man could head me! And ar'n't I a woman?"[33]

However, at this point few citizens in the free states had much interest in the plight of working women, black or white. The rapidly growing Republican majority, conservatives and radicals alike, was far more concerned about the Slave Power and its designs.

Truth does not seem to have embraced antislavery politics until the outbreak of the Civil War, when, according to Painter, she "stopped denouncing slavery and started discussing the war and Union. For the first time in her life she became the political partisan of a secular power." She visited northern Indiana to attend a pro-Union rally at the Steuben County Courthouse in June 1861. There she encountered heckling from prejudiced northerners, some of them Copperheads sympathetic to the Confederacy, who were far from pleased with what they saw as a northern war with the South over "Niggers." She addressed the crowd, reportedly delivering some of her most profound lines: "It seems that it takes my black face to bring out your black hearts: so it's well that I came. . . . You are afraid of my black face, because it is a looking glass in which you see yourselves."[34]

Although Truth became a public supporter of Lincoln's war for the Union, the two did not meet until October 1864, in Washington, D.C. By this time, the War of the Rebellion had also been a war against slavery for some two years, thanks to the combined influences of a longer and more brutal war than expected, slaves fleeing their owners and seeking refuge behind Union lines, and the Lincoln administration's need for more fighting men. Truth, now living in Battle Creek, Michigan, had been impressed when Lincoln signed the District of Columbia Emancipation Act in 1862 and was then thrilled when he issued the Emancipation Proclamation on 1 January 1863. In a letter published in the *National Antislavery Standard* in February 1864, she announced, "I believe the Lord means me to do what I want to do, viz; to go east in the Spring." She wanted "to see the freedmen of my own race" as well as the "first antislavery President." With financial help from friends and escorted by a grandson, Samuel Banks, she left her home and traveled east. En route, she visited friends and gave speeches in support of Lincoln's reelection campaign. In Boston in August, she chatted with the much younger and shorter Harriet Tubman, like Douglass a former slave from Maryland, who had earned the nickname "Moses" by guiding more than two hundred runaway slaves north toward freedom. Both women had done hard labor on farms, had lost husbands and found nonfarm employment as domestic help, and "laid claim to a deep spiritual connection with God." Although neither could read or write, both became great storytellers, though Tubman proved far more reluctant than Truth to speak in public. Tubman was more skeptical about Lincoln's motivations and more realistic than Truth about the ongoing power of anti-black prejudice and discrimination. Many years later, Tubman confessed that her original judgment of Lincoln had been too harsh: "I'se sorry now that I didn't see Master Lincoln and thank him."[35]

Lucy Colman and Elizabeth Keckly arranged Truth's audience with the president. Colman, a white woman from Rochester, New York, knew Truth through their shared work as lecturers on behalf of abolition and woman's rights. Keckly, a former slave from Virginia, had won renown as a Washington dressmaker whose clients included Varina Howell Davis. Keckly had become Mary Todd Lincoln's personal attendant and dressmaker, qualifying as a "genteel & intelligent" individual among "colored persons." Keckly and Colman knew one another from their involvement in the Ladies' Contraband Relief Association, founded prior to the Emancipation Proclamation, when official U.S. government policy still viewed escaped slaves as a form of property seized from the enemy. After emancipation, the organization, now known as the Freedmen and Soldiers Relief Association, continued to operate a camp on Seventh Street in the District of Columbia, later the site of Howard University. The association helped persuade the War Department to establish a Freedmen's Inquiry Commission, which in turn recommended establishing the Freedmen's Bureau in the spring of 1865.

Colman accompanied Truth to the White House on 29 October 1864. According to Truth's account of the meeting, Colman introduced her to the president as "Sojourner Truth, who has come all the way from Michigan to see you." Lincoln rose from his desk to greet her, clasped her hand, and bowed, saying, "I am pleased to see you." Then Truth told Lincoln that when he became president, "I feared you would be torn to pieces; for I likened you unto Daniel, who was thrown into the lion's den; for if the lions did not tear you to pieces, I knew it would be God that had saved you; and I said if He spared me, I would see you before the four years had expired. And He has done so. And I am now here to see you myself." She praised him "as the best president who has ever taken the seat." Lincoln replied, "I expect you have reference to my having emancipated the slaves in my proclamation." Several earlier presidents, particularly George Washington, "were just as good and would have done just as I have done if the time had come. If the people [south of the Potomac] had behaved themselves, I could not have done what I have; but they did not, which gave me the opportunity to do these things." Truth thanked God and his Providence "that you were the instrument selected by him and the people to it." When she confessed to not having heard of the Illinoisan "before he was talked of for president," he smiled and said, "I had heard of you many times before that." Lincoln showed her a Bible presented to him "by the colored people of Baltimore." Truth recalled, "I was never treated by any one with more kindness and cordiality than were shown to me by that great and good man. . . . He took my little [autograph] book, and with the same hand that signed the death-warrant of slavery, he wrote as follows: 'For Aunty Sojourner Truth. Oct. 29, 1864. A. Lincoln.'" As she took her leave, evidently taking no offense at being addressed as "Aunty," the president "arose and took my hand, and said he would be pleased to have me call again."[36]

Colman later published a far less positive account of the meeting that Painter adjudges "closer to prevailing attitudes and scholarly appraisals of Lincoln's racial consciousness." Colman introduced the elderly black woman as "my friend, Sojourner Truth, a woman widely known, not only in our country, but abroad." The president then became tense and uncomfortable, addressing Truth as "Aunty," "as he would his washerwoman," and bristling when Truth praised him as the great emancipationist president. Colman thought it wise to escort Truth quickly from the room because Lincoln "believed in the white race, and not in the colored, and did not want them put on an equality."[37]

Truth and Colman thus provided very different reports about their meeting with Lincoln, leading to the question of just how Lincoln thought about race and slavery. The issue carries scholars onto the controversial terrain of Lincoln's personal racial attitudes, all the more problematic because Lincoln was "so famously 'shut-mouthed' and deliberate in his choice of words."[38]

Lincoln's initial encounter with Frederick Douglass sheds some light on the subject. Douglass was escorted to the White House by Kansas senator Samuel C. Pomeroy. When Douglass entered the president's unpretentious upstairs study, Lincoln rose to shake the abolitionist's hand, saying, "Mr. Douglass, I know you. I have read about you, and Mr. Seward has told me about you." Douglass recalled "not the slightest shadow of embarrassment from the first moment," characterizing his reception from Lincoln "just as you have seen one gentleman receive another." Lincoln blamed his hesitancy on matters related to slavery and black Union troops on "all the hatred which is poured on the head of the Negro race in America." According to historian James Oakes, Douglass's recollection of their conversation "confirms how sensitive Lincoln was to the prejudices of white Americans, even if he himself did not share those prejudices."

Both Oakes's version of the meeting and the one provided by historian William McFeely recognize Lincoln as a calculating politician who was always concerned about his listeners' perceptions and responses and who thus presented somewhat different personas to different audiences. Scholar Jennifer Fleischner wonders whether the president might have been less comfortable with Truth in 1864 than with Douglass in 1863 because she was "neither mixed-race, genteel, nor male." According to McFeely, Lincoln was conversing with two white men, former Wisconsin governor Alexander Randall and Joseph T. Mills, just prior to meeting Douglass. Seeing Douglass awaiting his appointment, Mills asked Lincoln jokingly whether Douglass had converted the president to a positive view of miscegenation. "That's a democratic mode of producing good Union men," Lincoln responded playfully, "& I don't propose to infringe on the patent." The president subsequently told Randall and Mills more earnestly, "My enemies condemn my emancipation policy. Let them prove by the history of this war, that we can restore the Union without it." McFeely points out that the president "had only two private conversations with Douglass—and none with other black leaders, except for the famous meeting with *creole de couleur* gentlemen from New Orleans just before the president's death, in which the franchise of black leaders like themselves was discussed." Furthermore, "the president sought almost no counsel from his black constituents with respect to the postwar problems of the freedmen."[39] Then, as earlier, Lincoln attached far greater importance to the health and preservation of the Union and its white citizenry than to the well-being and opinions of African Americans.

At the same time, his relative dearth of overt racist attitudes and demagoguery and his openness to changing personal views about black soldiers and citizenship show Lincoln to have been far more flexible and progressive than the great majority of white Americans north and south. His ongoing attempt to tread a middle path between Negrophobes and egalitarians was evident in his last public speech, delivered on 11 April 1865. He explained to radicals among his fellow Republicans why he preferred only limited or qualified suffrage for black Louisiana males when the state was readmitted to the Union: Although it was "unsatisfactory to some that the electoral franchise is not given to the Colored man, I would myself prefer that it was now conferred on the very intelligent and on those who serve our cause as soldiers."[40] In 1865, such an outlook qualified as extremely progressive.

8 President Buchanan, the Crittenden Compromise, President Lincoln, and Fort Sumter

*A*ge sixty-six at his election in 1856, James Buchanan was, in the words of Jean H. Baker, "almost as old as the United States, a point of pride throughout his life." Few presidents in American history have drawn on such long and varied experience in Washington—certainly not his Republican successor, Abraham Lincoln, whose experience in national government encompassed but a single term in the lower house of Congress during the late 1840s. Yet Buchanan was deficient in the qualities of political shrewdness and capacity for personal growth that distinguished Lincoln. The Pennsylvania Democrat had repeatedly sought his party's nomination for the presidency since 1844, when he helped derail former president Martin Van Buren's attempt to win a third nomination after his failed reelection bid in 1840. Despite Buchanan's courtly manners, fastidious dress, and rather distinguished appearance, concludes historian William Gienapp, the fifteenth president proved "plodding and unimaginative" and "isolated himself from dissenting views." At the same time, "Old Buck" impressed others as "a kind man, firmly religious, decent, and extraordinarily courteous."[1]

In early 1857, as Buchanan prepared for his inauguration, he wrote to Virginia senator John Y. Mason, a fellow Democrat, that the new administration's "great object" would be "to arrest, if possible, the agitation of the slavery question at the North and to destroy sectional parties." In other words, he would seek to weaken the popularity of free-soilism in the North and the clamor of abolitionists against southern slavery and slaveholders. Yet the fires of northern antislavery continued to be fanned by high winds from what many knew as Bleeding Kansas and Bleeding Sumner. Buchanan paid the conventional if genuine tribute to dependence on God's will by adding, "Should a kind Providence enable me to succeed in my efforts to restore harmony to the Union, I shall feel that I have not lived in vain." Nonetheless, God's favor did not shine on his efforts, which more often than not exacerbated the sectional tensions he intended to abate. Indeed, his first ten months in the White House, beginning with the Supreme Court's announcement of its decision in the *Dred Scott* case, "encompassed a political crisis which proved to be decisive in the coming of the Civil War," Kenneth M. Stampp has concluded. In the spring of 1858, the Buchanan administration's stubbornness and unsavory tactics contributed to "a crushing defeat" for southerners in Congress. The House, instead of approving a fraudulent as well as proslavery Lecompton Constitution, voted 120–112 for a substitute motion to resubmit the document to Kansas voters, who subsequently rejected it by a 6–1 ratio.[2] Also in 1858, Buchanan vetoed a homestead bill giving 160 acres of public land in the West to each free settler five years after he occupied it. (During the previous session of Congress, a homestead bill had handily passed the House, but as president of the Senate, Vice President John C. Breckinridge broke a tie by voting against the measure.) Because the 1858 homestead measure received support from free state Democrats in the Midwest, Buchanan's veto "played into the hands of the Republicans," who had argued that the Slave Power would prevent passage of such a free-soil bill. As David M. Potter points out, southerners "recognized that no one could establish a plantation on 160 acres, but the lure of free land might attract immigrants who would add to the already great preponderance of the free-state population."[3] Buchanan's sympathies for white southerners and his political "march of folly" did much to assure an 1860 presidential victory for the candidate of the same northern antislavery party that Buchanan's Democracy had barely managed to defeat four years earlier.

In early December 1860, the lame-duck House and Senate convened in Washington, remaining in session until the inauguration of Lincoln and Vice President Hannibal Hamlin on 4 March and grappling unsuccessfully with sectionalism and secession. On 3 December, Buchanan delivered his fourth and final annual message to both houses of Congress. The opening section made clear his proslavery brand of Unionism: "The long continued and intemperate interference of the northern people in the question of slavery in the southern States has at length produced its natural effects"—the formation of "sectional" and "hostile political parties." Like most white southerners, Buchanan saw "the incessant and violent agitation of the slavery question throughout the North for the last quarter century" as having "at length produced its malign influence on the slaves, and inspired them with vague notions of freedom." Hence "a sense of security no longer exists around the family altar," a disquieting, even terrifying prospect among slaveholders and their partisans.[4]

Nevertheless, Buchanan insisted, "How easy it would be for the American people to settle the slavery question forever, and to restore peace and harmony to this distracted country." He pointed to the *Dred Scott* ruling as having upheld the state's rights and proslavery argument that "the question of whether slavery shall or shall not exist" within the limits of a federal territory could be decided only when and where the "people" resident in a territory had elected "a convention of delegates" and that convention met "for the purpose of framing a constitution preparatory to admission as a state into the Union." The Court had thereby rejected the antislavery and northern interpretation of popular sovereignty, according to which a territorial legislature could determine whether to endorse or exclude slave labor. The federal judiciary had essentially endorsed the understanding of the late John C. Calhoun and his disciples, including Jefferson Davis. Buchanan, having invoked the ruling of the Taney Court, pointed to the personal liberty laws in northern states as "most palpable violations of constitutional duty," since legislation mandating the return of runaway slaves "has been the law of the land from the days of Washington until the present moment."

Yet, the president declared, state secession was not a legitimate constitutional remedy for the South's substantial grievances. Reiterating the stance taken in 1833 by slaveholding president Andrew Jackson of Tennessee, Buchanan insisted that the United States "was intended to be perpetual, and not to be annulled at the pleasure of any one of the contracting parties." However, unlike Old Hickory, Buchanan believed that the right of southerners to resist "the tyranny and oppression of the federal government . . . cannot be denied." That is, the South's white male citizens retained the inherent right of revolution. Even though South Carolina had not yet adopted an ordinance of secession, every one of the federal officials within the Palmetto State—all the district judges, district attorneys, and marshals—had resigned, leaving federal authority there effectively "demolished." The president declared, "The Executive has no authority to decide what shall be the relations between the federal government and South Carolina." Since he would certainly not engage in "a naked act of usurpation" of power by the executive branch, Buchanan proclaimed his "duty to submit to Congress the whole question in all its bearings."[5] But Buchanan's transfer of responsibility to Congress was accompanied by the president's clear determination that the federal government had no "power, by force of arms, to compel a state to remain in the Union," because "the power to make war against a State is at variance with the whole spirit and intent of the Constitution." In short, Buchanan's Constitution permitted neither secession nor coercion, a stand that alienated both firmly Unionist Republicans and southern disunionists.

If the federal government resorted to coercion, said Buchanan, the outcome would be a "fraternal conflict" in which "a vast amount of blood and treasure would be expended." Such a civil war would render "future reconciliation between the States impossible" and thereby "destroy" the U.S. republic, "the grandest temple which has ever been dedicated to human freedom since the world began." Most Americans north and south seem to have agreed. His proposed solution to the apparent sectional impasse involved the convening of a national constitutional convention to consider amendments to the Constitution that would render chattel bondage in the existing slave states and in the territories more secure and enhance the federal government's commitment to returning fugitive slaves to their masters.[6] "The most realistic part" of this proposal, concludes Potter, "was its recognition of what had really caused southern disaffection—not a concern for territorial abstractions or constitutional refinements, but rather a pragmatic fear that continued propagandizing on the slavery issue would lead to slave insurrection."[7]

On 5 December, Buchanan recognized clearly that Republicans "say there is a contradiction between my opinion that the states cannot constitutionally secede & a denial of the power to compel them to remain in the Union. Not in the least!" The president's duty was simply to execute federal laws "until this is impossible with the means in his power."[8] In mid-December, he issued a presidential proclamation that reflected the widespread inclination to invoke powerful religious sentiments to calm rising political ferment. The nation should set aside 4 January as a day of fasting and prayer: "Let us humble ourselves before the Most High," imploring "Him to remove from our hearts the false pride of opinion that would impel us to persevere in the wrong for the sake of consistency." Instead, Americans should "yield a just submission to the unforeseen exigencies by which we are now surrounded." As in 1857, Buchanan again summoned "an omnipotent Providence" to "overrule existing evils for permanent good."[9] Most Americans seem to have entertained the same prayerful hopes.

The outgoing president's underlying Unionism became more pronounced and assertive as the New Year approached, and the stiffening of his administration became manifest in Buchanan's 8 January message to Congress. He declared that "the Union must and shall be preserved by all constitutional means." His cabinet no longer included Secretary of the Treasury Howell Cobb of Georgia or Secretary of War John Floyd of Virginia, both sympathetic to disunion (and, in Floyd's case, prone to fraud and embezzlement). They had been replaced by firm Unionists. Attorney General Jeremiah Black, another Pennsylvanian, succeeded the doltish Lewis Cass of Michigan as secretary of state. Black's friend, Edwin Stanton, also from Pennsylvania, took over the

Justice Department, and Kentuckian Joseph Holt became secretary of war. On 1 January, Georgia senator Robert Toombs, a future Confederate secretary of state, sent a warning telegram to an Augusta newspaper that encouraged Governor Joseph E. Brown to have state troops seize U.S. Fort Pulaski, at the mouth of the Savannah River: "Mr. Holt of Kentucky, our bitter foe, has been made Secretary of War. Fort Pulaski is in danger. The abolitionists are defiant."[10] Under the influence of Black, Stanton, and Holt, on 5 January the administration dispatched an unarmed, two-deck coasting steamer (nearly 230 feet in length, built by Cornelius Vanderbilt in 1852) from Pier 29 in New York Harbor, loading the *Star of the West* with supplies and some two hundred soldiers belowdecks. Its goal was to strengthen the "defensive position" of the federal forces holding Fort Sumter in Charleston Harbor. However, *Star of the West* took fire from South Carolina guns at Fort Moultrie and on Morris Island. Though undamaged, the merchant ship reversed course and returned to sea as Major Robert Anderson's guns at Fort Sumter remained silent. "As always in such incidents," note J. G. Randall and David Herbert Donald, "each side considered the other the aggressor."[11]

At this point, Buchanan had sufficient justification to order a military response against South Carolina for its aggressive and hostile attack on the U.S. government. Provocative taunts continued coming from hotspur fire-eaters. Texas senator Louis Trezevant Wigfall, who remained in the Senate until the popular referendum on secession in Texas, declared in Congress on 2 March, "Your flag has been insulted; redress it, if you dare. . . . We have dissolved the Union; mend it if you can; cement it with blood; try the experiment." Wigfall did not appreciate how many Yankees and Unionists honored the Stars and Stripes as what Stephen A. Douglas called the "emblem of peace and union, and of constitutional liberty." Palmetto State widow Keziah Goodwyn Hopkins Brevard offered a more measured, less bombastic slaveholding response to the *Star of the West* incident on 10 January: "We have never invaded Northern rights—all we want is *right* in its plainest sense."[12]

Historian Russell McClintock argues persuasively that after the *Star of the West* incident, given "the emotional climate in the North" as manifested at Unionist meetings and state legislatures across the free states, almost all Republicans and many Democrats there would have rallied behind a patriotic summons to defend and uphold the U.S. government's authority and honor. Yet the president chose to maintain the standoff in Charleston to avoid military conflict and civil war. His administration also agreed to a truce with Florida authorities over the status of Fort Pickens in Pensacola Harbor on the Gulf of Mexico, the only other significant U.S. military installation in the

South still under federal command. Like Sumter, the fortification was situated on an island, and just as Major Anderson had evacuated Fort Moultrie in mid-November for his island redoubt, so Lieutenant Adam Slemmer and his smaller garrison at the Pensacola Naval Yard had fled to Santa Rosa Island on 4 January. Slemmer's move came one day after he received orders from army commanding general Winfield Scott to do his "utmost" to prevent capture of the harbor's four forts. Two days later, soldiers from Florida seized the base, even though the Sunshine State did not officially secede until 10 January. In contrast to Sumter's relatively exposed position well inside Charleston Harbor, Fort Pickens lay at the "outer mouth" of Pensacola Bay, and the Buchanan administration ordered ships with hundreds of soldiers aboard to stand ready just outside the bay's mouth. Fort Pickens "could be defended by the fleet or reinforced at any time."[13]

President Buchanan seems to have increasingly focused on avoiding any act that might provoke armed conflict while hoping to leave office without giving up any more federal property in the South. After Fort Sumter submitted in mid-April, he became and remained throughout the war a solid Unionist. Supporting the federal draft but not the Emancipation Proclamation, he "never understood northern feelings against slavery" and always insisted that he felt "no regret" for his actions as president. In her recent biography of Buchanan, Baker evinces much the same hostility to the Pennsylvanian as did fervent northern Unionists during the secession crisis, noting his "favoritism" toward and "partiality for the South." Had Buchanan's administration pursued "a vigorous reaction to the secession of South Carolina" and "a strong reaction to the taking of federal property throughout the cotton states," he "would have staunched the departure of others." Even so, Baker's judgment seems more measured than the indictment of Buchanan by Congressman Thaddeus Stevens, a Pennsylvania Radical Republican, who called the president a "slave of slavery" and a traitor.[14]

One study of northern public opinion during the secession winter offers a decidedly more empathetic evaluation of Buchanan as "more in touch than his fellow Northerners with the daunting complexity of the situation and the profound inadequacy of the Constitution to meet the crisis."[15] But those sensitive to complexity and ambiguity can be paralyzed by it. Those whose principles or visions simplify or transcend the details of ambiguity and complexity seem better equipped to act firmly and decisively. Lincoln seems to have held two such principles: first, that the slave states ought to acknowledge, at least tacitly, that slavery was regrettable, should be contained, and needed to be put on a long path to gradual termination; and second, that peaceable secession was both impossible and unacceptable. However much observers may admire strongly principled politicians, they do not prove particularly good at predicting the long-term consequences of their firm decisiveness. Lincoln's stance simply could not be squared with that of firm disunionists such as Wigfall. "The grievance is not about the Territories. That is not it," the fire-eating Texan told the Senate on 2 March. "It is the denial that slaves are property, and the Declaration that the Federal Government has a right to settle that question." Wigfall also insisted, "We do not desire war; we wish to avoid it." But war could be avoided only by "an amendment to the Constitution declaring that each state has the right to secede—which is admitting the right of self-government to the people of each one of these sovereign States."[16] Wigfall and Lincoln sincerely believed that their different judgments reflected the correct interpretation of the Founding Fathers' legacies as set forth in both the Declaration of Independence and the Constitution.

If Republicans understood southern threats of disunion as attempts to coerce northerners into making concessions, for southerners, "coercion" meant Republican threats that federal force might be wielded to maintain the Union. Republicans spoke about the importance of "defending the Constitution and enforcing the laws," and even Douglas acknowledged that government by definition "*is* coercion," in the sense that it must both command and enforce obedience to preserve itself from degradation and destruction. White southerners occasionally expressed fears that their own degradation and destruction might come from a centralized, consolidated central government under Republican rule. Even before Lincoln's inauguration, disunionists insisted that Republicans would not relent in their "crusade," according to the Texas State Convention's rationale for secession, to "trample upon our rights" and to effect "the ruin of the slave-holding States." Some persons sympathetic to the South during the winter of 1860–61 hoped that after the mere threat of secession had become the palpable reality of seceded states, Republicans might become more amenable to substantive compromise on the crucial issue of slavery in the territories. Many southerners could not really believe that the free states would support the use of military force against seceded states. Many northerners expressed reluctance to employ force against the Confederacy: "But a few weeks ago, my State, so far as I am advised, considered that the greatest calamity that could befall this country was secession," said Democratic senator Henry M. Rice of Minnesota in response to Wigfall on 2 March, "but I believe they now consider a civil war to be a greater calamity than secession. We will do all that we honorably can to keep the southern states with us; but if they are determined to leave us, they must go in peace."[17]

The Senate Committee of Thirteen appointed in December 1860 by Vice President Breckinridge included a number of what Potter has described as "political chieftains" and became the most important body within the federal government striving to contain the secession movement and restore the broken Union.[18] Although Breckinridge's Kentucky friend, Lazarus Powell, chaired the committee, its de facto leader was another Kentuckian, Whiggish septuagenarian John J. Crittenden. Since the beginning of his long federal political career in the late 1810s, Crittenden had cultivated a reputation as "a calming nonpartisan leader," in the words of biographer Thomas E. Stephens. On the Committee of Thirteen, Crittenden hoped to achieve the kind of Unionist fame and glory heaped on Henry Clay after the Compromise of 1850. The analogous House Committee of Thirty-three, chaired by veteran Whig-Republican Thomas Corwin of Ohio, appears, in Potter's words, "for the most part a roster of forgotten names." Nonetheless, the committee urged the adoption of a constitutional amendment to assure the slave states that slavery within their borders was forever secure against federal interference.[19] The Republicans on the weightier Senate Committee of Thirteen included William Henry Seward of New York, who had lost the 1860 Republican nomination to Lincoln and now seemed open to discussing sectional compromise. According to James M. McPherson, Seward "had abandoned the irrepressible conflict to become chief of the conciliationists.[20] Douglas, the preeminent northern Democrat, at first denounced both Republicans and disunionists as dangerous radicals, insisting that only his version of popular sovereignty provided the common ground on which responsible, conciliatory conservatives in both sections could unite to save the Union.

Jefferson Davis became the most important of the southern Democrats on the Committee of Thirteen. The entire committee accepted his proposal that it make no recommendation to the Senate unless supported by a majority of votes among both the five Republicans and the other eight committee members (seven of them Democrats). According to Potter, this procedural rule not only reflected Calhoun's principle of the necessity for concurrent majorities within two strongly opposed factions but also invited failure. Such a rule would have "spelled defeat" for the two packages of compromise legislation approved in 1820 and 1850. An analogous compromise during the secession winter would have been based on Crittenden's proposed six amendments to the Constitution and four supplementary resolutions. Potter adjudges that only one of these ten items—a partial modification of the provisions of the 1850 Fugitive Law—"could be considered a concession to the antislavery element, a fact lending credence to Republican complaints that the whole thing was not a compromise but a surrender." Seward and most Republicans followed Lincoln's firm lead, seeing the proposed amendment restoring the Missouri Compromise line "in all the territory now held, or hereafter acquired" by the United States as representing an abject abandonment of their party's founding principle. At his death in 1850, Calhoun had dreamed of such an amendment, which would have prohibited "slavery or involuntary servitude, except as punishment for a crime," north of the 36°30' line of latitude, while mandating that to the south, "slavery of the African race" would be "recognized as existing, and shall not be interfered with by Congress, but shall be protected as property by all the departments of the territorial government during its continuance." Potter concludes that throughout the secession winter, Republicans rejected this solution to the territorial question "most emphatically" and southerners demanded it "most insistently." Most Republicans insisted on closing future acquisitions beyond the Southwest to slavery. In late January, New Jersey's *Newark Daily Advertiser* captured the essence of the position dominant in Republican ranks: Crittenden's willingness to apply the 36°30' line to all future U.S. territories "strikes so squarely at the leading principle of the Republicans that they refuse to go to that length—especially as they foresee that the acquisition of Mexico, Central America, and the [Caribbean] would place the slave power forever in the ascendant."[21]

The *New Orleans Daily Delta* had expressed the dominant Lower South position on 1 November: giving up on a principle—like "the question of Southern rights in the territories"—would mean "submission to Black Republican domination and despotism."[22] Had not the Supreme Court's 1857 *Dred Scott* ruling stipulated that slave property should receive due recognition and security in all of the national domain? Even so, Davis and the other cotton state senator on the Committee of Thirteen, Georgia's Robert Toombs, initially indicated their willingness to endorse Crittenden's solution to the crucial territorial question as long as the committee's Republican members did likewise. Since the Republicans would not accept the proviso to apply the agreement to future territories, Davis and Toombs also voted in the negative during the committee's December negotiations. According to historian William J. Cooper Jr., southerners "desperately wanted a settlement on terms that would salvage southern rights and honor." But because the "new Republican chieftain, Abraham Lincoln, stood ramrod-straight on the territorial issue," congressional Republicans, too, stood fast. "Lincoln knew little of the South" and "was fundamentally ignorant of his southern political foes." Had the president-elect been better informed, he would have recognized that southern senators including Davis and Louisiana's Judah P. Benjamin "were not radicals." Yet "they were receiving ferocious pressure from their states, where the fervor for secession dominated public opinion." The committee's 7–6 vote against Crittenden's territorial proposal reflected its members' earlier endorsement of the Calhounite principle that a motion would not be forwarded to the whole Senate unless it commanded a "dual majority" among Republican and Democratic appointees.[23] Too many northern Republicans and southern Democrats would not run the risk of appearing submissive. The Republicans found precious little common ground with southern Democrats and their disappearing northern allies.[24] Sectionalized understandings of exactly what constituted essential interests, rights, and honor seem to have precluded constructive communication and compromise. Furthermore, many northerners seem to have believed that southerners were bluffing, exploiting the threat of long-term disunion simply to force concessions favorable to the Slave Power, while many southerners could not believe that the Republicans would resort to military force to maintain the Union. On 31 December 1860, the Committee of Thirteen reported its inability to reach agreement on a recommendation to its senatorial colleagues. Although Crittenden determined to have his compromise package reach the floor of the Senate, the entire body effectively rejected it on 18 January by a 25–23 vote, though futile efforts to broker and adopt a comparable compromise continued through the rest of the congressional session. In February in the House of Representatives, moderate Illinois Republican William Kellogg sincerely worked on behalf of a compromise whose centerpiece was a constitutional amendment providing that the 1820 Missouri Compromise line be applied to all the territories then owned by the United States. Republican voters in his congressional district condemned Kellogg for his willingness "to submit to the dictation of a Slave Oligarchy" and for having "sold himself to the slave power for a very small sum."[25]

After South Carolina's state convention in mid-December provided the expected jump-start to separate-state secession, Lincoln and congressional Republicans received much strong advice to compromise on the territorial issue in the interest of preserving the Union. Peter Cooper and other conservative New York City Republicans traveled to Washington and pleaded for support of the Crittenden Compromise. So too did Whiggish, Oppositionist Unionists from the Border and Middle Souths, who came to think they had a sympathetic and powerful insider in Seward as the incoming secretary of state. Yet even before the presidential election, Crittenden had inadvertently shown how difficult sectional negotiations would prove during the secession winter. He had supported Douglas against Lincoln in both the Illinois Senate contest of 1858 and the presidential election two years later. Speaking in Louisville in August 1860, Crittenden had predicted that "the mere fact of Mr. Lincoln's election," even in the absence of "an act positively offensive or injurious to any interest of the country," would "keep the country agitated and unhappy, if not create an opposition and resistance to the government itself." In fact, the Kentuckian feared that a Lincoln victory would result in more aggressive northern opposition to slavery and thereby "cause still greater dangers to the peace and security" of the slave states. Though hardly a proponent of disunion, Crittenden identified a powerful rationale for secession in the wake of Lincoln's victory.[26]

Lincoln faced a genuine dilemma.[27] If he and his party refused to give in on the crucial issue of slavery in the territories, more white southerners would probably accept the necessity of disunion. At the same time, a compromise on the most important plank in the Republican Party's platform would probably appear to be a surrender to the Slave Power, splitting the still-fragile party into acrimonious factions. The more conciliatory Seward understood that loyalty to the Union was more conditional in the South than the hard-line Lincoln realized. Yet the president-elect understood better than his future secretary of state that, as McClintock has written, "the core of Republican strength lay in its dual commitment to restricting the reach of the Slave Power and maintaining the purity of the West." Although Lincoln seemed willing to accept a proposal from the House Committee of Thirty-three that left territorial New Mexico (which in 1860 had barely twenty slaves) open to slavery, on this score he was honoring the Compromise of 1850, just as he had been willing to honor the Compromise of 1820. In addition, he may well have thought that slavery would never take root in the arid Southwest. However, Republicans refused to support the New Mexico plan unless southerners bowed to the admission of Kansas as a free state, as the overwhelming majority of its residents clearly wished. In turn, most House Republicans voted against a supposedly ironclad Thirteenth Amendment to the Constitution that purported to prevent the federal government from ever taking steps against slavery in the existing states. Although Lincoln gave the amendment passive support, opposition from most congressional Republicans lent credence to white southern fears that Lincoln's party contained too many potential abolitionists. Even so, the two-fifths of Republicans who voted for the proposed amendment provided the two-thirds vote necessary to initiate the process of state ratification, which was derailed by the Civil War.[28] In one of the great ironies of the 1860s, the Thirteenth Amendment ratified at the end of 1865 provided for the conclusive end of chattel bondage in the United States.

After the Confederacy's establishment in February 1861, staunch and conditional Unionists in the Upper South maintained their alliance until mid-April and thereby prevented additional state secessions, working assiduously if unsuccessfully to achieve peaceful reunion. South Carolina's *Charleston Mercury* lamented on 14 February that the Upper South seemed prepared to accept even less than the provisions in the failed Crittenden Compromise. In contrast, exclaimed the *New York Tribune* on 7 March, "Here are eight of the fifteen slave states declaring that they wish and mean to stay in the Union, and not follow the defeated and bankrupt [Democratic] officeholders into the abyss of secession and civil war."[29] Raleigh's *North Carolina Standard* had succinctly summarized the mind-set of most citizens in the Upper South at the beginning of December: "There is only one evil greater than disunion and that is the loss of honor and Constitutional right." However, in the interim, "our honor as a people is still untarnished—our Constitutional rights, so far as the federal government is concerned, are still untouched." Should that change, North Carolinians—slaveholders and nonslaveholders alike—would be ready to embrace disunion. "But not now!" North Carolina could wait and see as long as its rights were "not assailed" and remaining in the Union was compatible "with safety and honor to ourselves."[30]

For nearly a month after his inauguration, Lincoln continued to play a version of the delaying game that the Buchanan administration had initiated after the initial wave of separate-state secessions. Clearly misunderstanding the highly conditional character of most white southerners' commitment to the United States, he and Seward hoped that secession could be quarantined in the Deep South and the eight loyal slave states kept in the Union. The president seemed to believe that with time and calm, the majority of citizens in the slave states would feel a resurgence of their deep-seated Unionist sympathies, temporarily repressed by the fear-mongering of fire-eating hotspurs. In this scenario, southern Unionism, like an incoming tide, would drown most of the ugly disunionism that had appeared when the waters receded.

As Lincoln ultimately recognized, he committed what could have been a serious public relations blunder near the end of his journey from Springfield to Washington for his inauguration. The president-elect had "remained stubbornly oblivious to concerns about his safety," in the words of Harold Holzer, until Alan Pinkerton, "a Scottish-born sleuth," convinced Lincoln that "a mob of Secessionists" had engaged in "a well-planned conspiracy to murder" him outside Baltimore's Calvert Street railroad station as his party changed trains. Lincoln agreed to make "secret trips" through Philadelphia and Baltimore to meet the Baltimore and Ohio engine that was to pull his sleeping car into Washington. However, his sudden, clandestine arrival in the District of

Columbia appeared to smack of cowardice, embarrassed some Republicans, and triggered "a barrage of deeply wounding personal criticism." One Marylander stated, "How unfortunately Mr. Lincoln was advised! How deplorably did he yield to his advisers!" New York's *Albany Atlas and Argus* suggested that his "Underground Railroad" journey reflected his fear of "ass-ass-in-nation." A Louisville newspaper even charged that he and his wife had exchanged clothing and that Lincoln had made his clandestine trip through Baltimore in a dress, offering "an eerie preview of the libels" that Jefferson Davis faced after his flight south from Richmond to Georgia in 1865. Cartoonists in 1861 mocked Lincoln as an effeminate cross-dresser wearing a "big shawl." Lincoln later acknowledged that the secret trip had been "one of the grave mistakes in his public career." Nonetheless, he recouped some of his losses by having a dignified "pictorial rebuttal" taken at Mathew Brady's gallery on Pennsylvania Avenue; the image was "quickly mass produced" on *cartes de visites*, which "had suddenly become a national collecting rage for display in family albums."[31]

Several days after his arrival in Washington on 23 February, the president-elect may have seriously considered abandoning Fort Sumter in return for a decision by delegates at the Virginia State Convention, then meeting in Richmond, to end their sessions and go home. He reportedly told elderly Virginia senator William Cabell Rives, "If Virginia will stay in, I will withdraw the troops from Fort Sumter," and several days later he quipped to a European diplomat that "a state for a fort is no bad business." If Lincoln did in fact ponder such a strategy, what Seward labeled "the violent remonstrances from the north and east against the abandonment of Fort Sumter" seemed to reinforce the president's awareness that evacuation would likely exacerbate the divisions within Republican ranks, just as the appearance of Republican capitulation to Confederate demands risked encouraging the boldness of secessionists throughout the South.[32]

After the failure of the Crittenden Compromise and especially after Lincoln's inauguration, the fundamental sectional fissure became quite simple. Most white southerners saw the prerogative of each slave state to separate itself from the Union and become an independent republic as simply not open to question, however regrettable that separation might be. It made no real difference whether the rationale for disunion was constitutional secession or the inalienable right of revolution. Lincoln and his Republican allies saw disunion as unacceptable and insisted on the permanence of the United States, the perpetuity of the Union created by the Founding Fathers.[33] Moreover, the Republican Party had captured the White House according to the explicit terms of the Constitution, and after the election Lincoln and his associates did nothing in violation of the nation's fundamental compact. Secession therefore constituted a clearly unprovoked and unjust rebellion. The party's leaders accused disunionists of having decided to abandon and ruin the glorious United States only because the Slave Power no longer controlled the executive branch. Most free state citizens wondered what the president-elect could possibly have done to southern rights that would warrant seven Lower South states' decision to quit the United States. Northerners saw no palpable reason for the February organization of the independent Southern Confederacy other than the establishment of a stronger bargaining position for demanding northern capitulation to reconstructing the Union on decidedly proslavery terms. Some Republicans, including Lincoln, understood that in the Upper South and especially in the border slave states, the majority of citizens could not condone the idea that any state had the right to withdraw from the Union simply because its citizens refused to accept the results of a presidential election.

Fernando Wood, the Democratic mayor of New York and spokesman for some of the city's businessmen who engaged in profitable commercial and financial dealings with the South, suggested an unlikely secessionist "fantasy" under which the metropolis would secede from both New York State and the Union and become an independent "free city," analogous to Bremen or Hamburg in the German Confederation.[34] The overwhelming majority of New Yorkers seemed to have applauded the sentiments expressed by Lincoln in his February 1861 speech in the city: "There is nothing that can ever bring me willingly to consent to the destruction of this Union, under which not only the great commercial city of New York, but the whole country has acquired its greatness."[35] Indeed, a week after Confederate guns opened fire on Fort Sumter, Wood reminded a crowd at Union Square of a brash vow, made before a very different crowd outside the Exchange Hotel in Montgomery, Alabama, while Sumter was under attack. The Confederate secretary of war, Leroy Pope Walker, had boasted that his country's flag would fly atop the U.S. Capitol dome by 1 May and soon thereafter even atop Boston's Faneuil Hall. But Wood told his listeners that "before that banner can fly over Faneuil Hall," it would have to be "carried over the dead body of every citizen of New York." Wood's rhetoric did not help him gain reelection to an unprecedented fourth term as mayor in the fall of 1861, when he was defeated by a Republican, but he did win election to the House of Representatives a year later.[36]

Echoing Mississippi's argument for refusing submission to the North, Boston's *Daily Atlas and Bee* emphatically rejected on 1 February 1861 the inclination to compromise and conciliation associated with "the mercantile mind," so influential in northeastern port cities involved in trade with the South: "Submission to traitors NEVER!" Far to the west, St. Paul's *Daily Minnesotan* asked rhetorically on 19 January whether the North should accept slave state secession and disunion. Answering in the negative, the newspaper declared that the issue boiled down to "resistance and submission. We have chosen resistance to the encroachment of the slave-power."[37] Toward the end of his February trip from Springfield to Washington, Lincoln made much the same point, albeit with less militant rhetoric, delivering a speech before the New Jersey legislature that was widely republished: "I shall do all in my power to promote a peaceful settlement of all our difficulties . . . but it may be necessary to put the FOOT DOWN FIRMLY." These words elicited "loud, long cheers" from his listeners.[38] Lincoln thus concisely expressed most northerners' ambivalent feelings. The citizens of the free states seemed to be demanding some blend of a conciliatory spirit with honorable firmness, feeling that some concessions should be made to the slave states while still upholding the U.S. government's authority and dignity.[39]

From the perspective of most Republicans and some northern Democrats, Lincoln had antagonized the more radical elements among the Republican antislavery coalition by saying that the Fugitive Slave Act of 1850, the object of so much resentful opposition in the free states, ought to be enforced. He had publicly condemned fiery abolitionist John Brown after his violent attempt to ignite a slave insurrection at Harpers Ferry, Virginia, in the fall of 1859. Archetypal secessionist fire-eater Edmund Ruffin had witnessed Brown's hanging in Charlestown for treason. A modern description of Ruffin as playing the "dour" role of "a biblical patriarch dispensing justice with fire and brimstone" is equally appropriate for John Brown.[40] Lincoln had expressed little patience for radicals and ultras of any persuasion, whether in the guise of abolitionist immediatists or fire-eating disunionists. He had repeatedly insisted that as president, he would possess neither the constitutional authority nor the personal inclination to interfere with the peculiar institution in those states that already recognized and enforced human bondage.

Yet Lincoln had labeled chattel slavery a "monstrous evil," implying that free southerners must be "evil" for defending it. Most slaveholders could not reconcile Lincoln's protestations of conservatism with the insulting denunciations issued by other, far more obviously radical Republicans. In February 1858, Illinois congressman Owen Lovejoy, running for reelection with strong backing from his good friend, Lincoln, delivered a speech, "Human Beings, Not Property," that was printed widely in central Illinois newspapers. Lovejoy

Lincoln raises the U.S. flag in Philadelphia, February 1861. (Courtesy of the Library of Congress)

declared that slavery "skulks under and behind the sovereignty of the States, beyond the reach of the Federal Government." Yet a system of property rights in human beings "has no moral right anywhere. . . . I affirm that it has not the sanction of natural or revealed religion, or of the Constitution." However, since the *Dred Scott* decision, the "demon of slavery . . . has grown bold, and defiant, and impudent. It has left its lair, lifted its shameless front toward the skies, . . . and mutters its blasphemies about having the sanction of a holy and just God." Most white southerners saw northerners' apparent willingness to endorse or at least tolerate such statements not only as dangerous threats to the stability of slavery as the essential foundation of their economic and social interests but also as insults to their fundamental rights and honorable reputations as Americans. In February 1861, Virginia's Sherman Clemens met with the president-elect and described him as "an abolitionist of the Lovejoy and Sumner type." Such statements are hardly surprising in light of the fact that a Democratic newspaper in Lincoln's hometown, the *Springfield State Register*, had blamed Republican Party leaders for Brown's raid: "Their open-mouthed treason, which culminates in precisely such outrages as that at Harper's Ferry, is but the logical sequence of the teachings of Wm. H. Seward and Abraham Lincoln."[41]

Few northern congressmen were as fiercely and outspokenly abolitionist as Lovejoy and Stevens. However, most northerners and a few southerners seem to have concluded that slavery was an unjust and regrettable system that at least had to be localized; perhaps this step would put it on the gradual road to distant and peaceful extinction. Ever since the terms "slavery" and "enslavement" had become metaphors or tropes in eighteenth-century politics for the result of tyranny's victory over liberty, northerners had perceived chattel slavery as increasingly incompatible with republican and natural rights principles, especially as they achieved a kind of cultural fusion during the Second Great Awakening. Moreover, the Founding Fathers had clearly intended to limit the spread and permanence of chattel slavery, as evidenced by the Northwest Ordinance of 1787, adopted under the Articles of Confederation and reaffirmed by the first Congress convened under the Constitution, and the Constitution's provision allowing abolition of the foreign slave trade after twenty years. At the same time, a decided majority of citizens in the free states, imprinted with the Negrophobia so characteristic of nineteenth-century America, clearly hoped that excluding slavery from the trans-Mississippi West would also mean the exclusion of African Americans. Many northerners, among them Lincoln, had even come to suspect that the political and judicial managers of the Slave Power hoped to nationalize slavery, making it constitutionally legal within the free states that had provided for its internal demise during the decades after the American Revolution.

Conversely, most southerners as well as a good many northerners found themselves somewhere on a spectrum from puzzlement to infuriation at American politicians' inability in 1860–61 to produce the same kind of compromises, sympathetic to slaveholders, that the Founding Fathers had engineered or accepted in the interests of establishing and maintaining a constitutional republic. Why could Republican leaders not show more respect for the property rights of slaveholders and more sympathy for their racial prejudices and anxieties? Faced with the hard reality of secession and disunion, many free southerners supposed, northern politicians might come to their senses and return to the compromising spirit evidenced in 1787 and 1820. Most southern whites, contrary to the fanatical rantings of self-righteous abolitionists, had no doubt that the institution of slavery found clear support in both the Bible's Old and New Testaments. At the same time, many elite and scholarly southerners really believed that their patriarchal system of domestic servitude was preferable to the exploitative wage slavery evident in northern cities and factories. The institution of slavery even seemed to have undergirded the personal dignity, exemplary character, and leadership skills that had distinguished Founding Fathers such as George Washington and Thomas Jefferson.

At the beginning of the secession crisis, therefore, white southerners feared that Black Republicans were out to gain complete political dominance over the South, hem in and then destroy slavery, promote racial equality, and impose degradation and dishonor on the region's white population. A Republican administration posed fearful and intolerable threats to southern interests, rights, and honor. At the same time, Republicans believed that the federal government had been too long dominated by the Slave Power. After the northern electorate voted in 1860 to curtail the Slave Power's influence, conniving secessionists seemed intent on destroying the Union now that they could no longer dominate it. The North's and the nation's interests, rights, and honor would not permit such destruction.

Lincoln took the presidential oath of office on 4 March facing Chief Justice Roger Brooke Taney, the Marylander whose opinion in the *Dred Scott* decision four years earlier had so infuriated the Illinoisan and his party. The new president's inaugural address reiterated his respect for state's rights as he understood them by quoting from one of his published speeches: "I have no purpose, directly or indirectly, to interfere with the institution of slavery in the States where it exists. I believe I have no lawful right to do so, and I have no inclination to do so." The original draft of his inaugural address had included clear challenges to the new Confederacy, among them his intention to "reclaim the public property" in the South already seized by disunionists. However, at the urging of his Illinois friend Orville H. Browning, Lincoln deleted this provocative promise, though he also made clear his determination not to abandon southern federal forts still in Union hands.

Lincoln also toned his address down a bit by accepting Seward's suggestions to say nothing that would preclude the possibility of a new constitutional amendment providing explicit protection to slavery where it already

Northern and southern views of Lincoln's inaugural address, in what may have been Thomas Nast's first published political cartoon (From Albert Shaw, Abraham Lincoln: His Path to the Presidency, *2 vols. [New York: Review of Reviews, 1929])*

existed and to omit the qualifier "unless you first assail *it*" after "the government will not assail *you*." From the Republican perspective, the Confederacy had indeed "assailed" the United States with its April cannonade against Fort Sumter. Seward's influence was also reflected in the eloquence of Lincoln's closing appeal to the South's Unionist loyalties, whose power he clearly overestimated: "We are not enemies, but friends. We must not be enemies. Though passion may have strained, it must not break our bonds of affection. The mystic chords of memory, stretching from every battle-field, and patriot grave, to every living heart and hearthstone, all over this broad land, will yet swell the chorus of the Union, when again touched, as surely they will be, by the better angels of our nature."[42]

After the failure of the Crittenden Compromise and especially after Lincoln's inauguration, with the old Congress adjourned and the new body not scheduled to convene until the following December, hope for a negotiated settlement faded. On Inauguration Day, Buchanan received and passed on to Lincoln a disturbing report from Major Anderson: Not only would the army garrison have to abandon Fort Sumter in a few weeks because of dwindling provisions, but the commander and his officers agreed that "the only way to relieve Sumter successfully would be to land a large army on Morris Island and sweep away its batteries." General Scott reported that it would be impossible to prepare such a military force in time and thus saw "no alternative but a surrender."[43] Upper South Unionists, evidently encouraged and supported by both Secretary of State Seward and Senator Douglas, continued their repeated warnings that any federal military action against the Confederacy would ignite a bloody civil war. Proponents of this view saw war as the greatest danger to the possibility that the seven Confederate states might return to the Union. The new president avoided bald threats or overt military actions against the secessionist rebels, hoping against hope that the new Confederacy would not long survive without additional slave states from the Upper South.[44] Perhaps not until 27 March did Lincoln finally receive "reliable firsthand testimony" that "no attachment to the Union" could be found in South Carolina or any of the Confederate Gulf States. The testimony and report came from Stephen Augustus Hurlburt, a Charleston native and thirty-year resident who had moved to Illinois to practice law and briefly returned to Charleston at Lincoln's request, ostensibly to visit his sister and brother-in-law. Lincoln also received what proved to be badly flawed military advice from Navy captain Gustavus Fox, who argued that a complex naval expedition could relieve Anderson's garrison at Sumter. An inexperienced administrator, the president at times acted, in the words of one historian, "so hastily and clumsily that he made several critical mistakes." They included dispatching Ward Hill Lamon to evaluate the situation in Charleston Harbor: the assessments provided by Lamon, one of Lincoln's law partners and his frequent bodyguard, proved far less acute and adroit than did those of Hurlburt.[45]

By the time April arrived, Lincoln knew that the prospects for peaceful restoration of the old Union were fast receding and that war was likely. Anderson wrote another despairing report, read by Lincoln on 4 April, that the garrison's food supplies would be depleted in about a week. Convinced of his constitutional duty "to hold and protect the public property of the United States, and to enforce the laws thereof," the president, with a split cabinet vote of 3–2, dispatched a supply expedition under Fox to prevent Fort Sumter's surrender. The fort had to be kept in Union hands even if, in the words of Allan Nevins, "relief meant war,"[46] though neither Lincoln nor the great majority of Americans in either section anticipated the long and bloody war that followed. As McClintock puts it, Lincoln thought he had only two alternatives, to "relieve Sumter or recognize disunion," and the latter option represented "our national destruction."[47] Yet when war began, neither he nor Jefferson Davis wanted responsibility for firing the first shot. Each knew that observers on both sides of the Atlantic would perceive whichever side did so as the aggressor, and such appearances might well decide whether Upper South states remained in the Union or joined the Confederacy. Lincoln gained the upper hand primarily because he insisted that his immediate purpose was only to reprovision Fort Sumter and because authorities in Charleston and Montgomery learned about the relief expedition long before the ships arrived off the South Carolina coast. Indeed, on the day of Lincoln's inauguration, former senator Wigfall wired a warning from Washington to Charleston: "Inaugural means war. There is strong ground for belief that reinforcements will be speedily sent. Be vigilant." Although Wigfall was premature, Confederate commissioners in Washington a month later sent cables south identifying preparations "in the War and Navy Departments." Just before receiving notification directly from Lincoln that a relief expedition was coming, Governor Francis Wilkinson Pickens and General P. G. T. Beauregard had Sumter's mailbag seized from the post office and read Anderson's 8 April official report. Appended to that report was a "heart-felt prayer," addressed personally to his friend Lorenzo Thomas at the office of the adjutant general in Washington. It included a confession that Anderson's "heart is not in the war which I see is to be commenced."[48]

Lincoln had long interpreted the Founding Fathers as providing inspiration to and rationale for his conservative antislavery stance. The Confederate leadership, by initiating a cannonade against Fort Sumter in mid-April, made it possible for Lincoln to appear a conservative president who had no choice other than a martial response to outrageously aggressive and treasonous rebels. Although he lost half of the eight Upper South states to the Confederacy in the process, he united the free states in a patriotic and defensive "War of the Rebellion."[49]

On 8 April, Jefferson Davis in Montgomery received a dispatch from Beauregard: "Authorized messenger from Lincoln just informed Governor Pickens and myself that provisions would be sent to Sumter peaceably, otherwise by force." Davis immediately responded that the fort "must be completely" isolated from the delivery of provisions. The next evening, he held a lengthy cabinet meeting. At that meeting, according to reports decades after the war, Secretary of State Robert Toombs initially said, "The firing upon that fort will inaugurate a civil war greater than any the world has yet seen; and I do not feel competent to advise you." The discussion continued while Toombs paced the floor; he then suddenly turned to Davis and prophesied, "Mr. President, at this time, it is suicide, murder, and will lose us every friend at the North. You will wantonly strike a hornet's nest which extends from mountains to ocean, and legions, now quiet, will swarm out and sting us to death. It is unnecessary, it puts us in the wrong; it is fatal." The next day, the secretary of war, Walker, wired Beauregard in Charleston that he should demand the evacuation of Fort Sumter and that if this demand were refused, he should "proceed, in such manner as you may determine, to reduce it."[50]

Beauregard waited three days to begin an artillery bombardment of the island fortress. The Confederate staff had not yet completed placement of troops and equipment on the occupied islands around Charleston Harbor— what the general called his "circle of fire." During the thirty-four-hour Confederate cannonade on 12–13 April, Confederate batteries fired a total of 3,341 rounds, more than three times as many as issued from Sumter's guns. That no soldier on either side died during the exchange demonstrated to Anderson that "there is a higher power over us."

Union private Daniel Hough, the war's first official casualty, was killed after the bombardment ended. As part of the evacuation agreement, Beauregard permitted Anderson to fire cannon in salute to the U.S. flag. During the fifty-gun salute, Hough was ramming gunpowder into a cannon muzzle when the gun fired prematurely, blowing off his right arm at the shoulder. Less than two hours later, Hough's body lay in a grave dug on Fort Sumter's parade ground.[51] Also fatally injured in the explosion was Private Edward Gallway, who died in a Charleston hospital and was buried in a city cemetery. Gallway may have been the youngest member of Anderson's garrison, and he was among the two-thirds of the approximately 13,000 enlisted men in the U.S. Army who were immigrants; half of them, including Gallway, were Irish.[52]

Just before Beauregard's official representatives had reached a final agreement with Anderson for Fort Sumter's transfer to Confederate authorities, an unofficial and self-appointed spokesman for the general took it upon himself to initiate negotiations. Newly commissioned colonel Louis Trezevant Wigfall, one of the general's aides, saw the fort's huge flag go down. He commandeered a skiff and, accompanied by three slaves and Private William Gourdin Young (a nephew of secessionist leader Robert Gourdin), had the boat rowed out to the island fortress. With a white handkerchief waving at the tip of his sword, Wigfall told the commanding officer, "You have defended your flag nobly, Sir. You have done all that it is possible to do, and General Beauregard wishes to stop this fight. On what terms, Major Anderson, will you evacuate this fort?" The major stated his terms, and Wigfall departed to inform Beauregard. Shortly thereafter, the general's three official emissaries

(Stephen D. Lee, William Porcher Miles, and Roger Pryor) arrived and agreed to the same conditions, including the flag salute.[53]

What had happened to Fox's naval relief expedition? His four ships had departed New York City for Charleston on 8 and 9 April. The *Baltic*, with Fox aboard, arrived at the rendezvous point outside Charleston Harbor just before dawn on 12 April, immediately prior to the beginning of Beauregard's cannonade at daybreak. Yet three shallow-draft tugs intended to run supplies to Sumter across the harbor sandbars never arrived. And Captain Fox did not know until he reached Charleston that the newly commissioned *Powhatan*, the U.S. Navy's "most powerful warship," had been assigned to a fleet sailing for Fort Pickens. Seward had initiated the assignment and had it confirmed by the president, though without the knowledge of either Fox or Secretary of the Navy Gideon Welles. It is an astounding "improbability," observes Nelson Lankford, that "two naval expeditions were being readied in New York without knowledge of each other." Fox later confessed that Confederate guns would have made short work of the vessels at his command. However, during the evacuation, his ships were enlisted to carry north the soldiers of Anderson's garrison.[54]

Lincoln assumed his position as commander in chief of the armed forces, with constitutional authority to "suppress insurrections," and called for seventy-five thousand volunteers from the loyal states to put down the overt "rebellion" against the United States commenced in Charleston Harbor. The U.S. president invoked his authority (under Article II, Section 3 of the Constitution) to "take care that the laws shall be faithfully executed." Congress had many decades earlier passed legislation to enable the call-ups. The Militia Acts of 1795 and 1807 supplemented Article I, Section 8, which authorized the commander in chief to summon militia "to execute the Laws of the Union, suppress Insurrections, and repel Invasions." Since Lincoln denied the constitutionality of secession and disunion, the Confederate states remained legally in the Union; the U.S. government did not prosecute war against sovereign state republics and their new confederation but instead suppressed insurrectionary rebels.[55] At the same time, Lincoln called for a special session of Congress to convene on the Fourth of July, giving the president three months to act without having to confer and negotiate with a divided legislature. His message to the special session argued that "public necessity" and public opinion had demanded executive action when Congress was adjourned; hence the Constitution's "war powers" had passed completely into the hands of the president, "trusting then, as now, that Congress would readily ratify them."

Lincoln's actions in late April had included putting into place a U.S. Navy blockade of the rebellious states. Such a step, explains historian Donald L. Robinson, had previously been viewed, "in both American constitutional law and the law of nations, as contingent upon the existence of war, which Congress alone could declare." Also, according to the almost universally held judgment of that time, Congress alone could suspend the writ of habeas corpus, yet Lincoln did so. In early May, the president expanded the small regular army from sixteen thousand to thirty-nine thousand and called for some forty-two thousand volunteers to enlist for three years. He had already approved expenditures of two million dollars by private citizens for requisitions "necessary for the defense and support of the government."[56]

Because Congress did not bestow formal legitimacy for a naval blockade of Confederate ports until 13 July, Lincoln's unilateral imposition of the blockade faced legal challenges finally settled by the Supreme Court in the 1863 Prize Cases. At issue was whether ships that had violated the blockade prior to Congress's opening in July 1861 had been lawfully seized. The justices concurred that both the blockade and the seizures were defensible only if a state of war existed but did not agree on the question of the president's authority to take war measures without a congressional declaration. By a 5–4 majority, the Court retroactively approved Lincoln's resort to acts of war because of the severity of the rebellious challenge to federal authority. In effect, the Court upheld Congress's decision to provide the president with a retroactive "explicit authorization of force," as distinct from a formal "declaration of war."[57]

Almost all Republicans and most northern Democrats saw Confederate violence against U.S. government agents, property, and authority at Fort Sumter as provoking and fully justifying the administration's bellicose response. "Once the Confederate battery in Charleston opened fire on the fort," reports one historian, "almost everyone in the North, Republicans and Democrats alike, seemed to explode with anger and appeared wild for war," joining "a bipartisan crusade to support Abraham Lincoln in crushing the rebellion."[58] Among the minority who continued to oppose coercion was Providence, Rhode Island, businessman Zechariah Allen. Allen had inherited from his father a small farm and almost one hundred thousand dollars, some of it profit from the *Nancy* and *Susannah*, two brigs engaged in the foreign slave trade that had made a number of illegal voyages out of Rhode Island in the 1790s. In 1822, Allen invested his inheritance in the construction of a textile mill and "its satellite village" and became a trustee for life of Brown University, from which he had graduated in 1813. Like most mill owners, he would not employ black laborers. Two days after the firing on Fort Sumter, he confided to his diary that the free states should consider themselves blessed by separation from the South, because "all history demonstrates that the existence of slavery has first corrupted and then destroyed every republic in which it has been admitted."[59]

After the bombardment of Fort Sumter, Confederate leaders found much less support than they hoped for in the big cities of the border slave states—Baltimore, Louisville, and St. Louis. Baltimore journalist William Wilkins Glenn, whose sympathies for the Confederate cause led to his arrest and confinement in September 1861, wrote on 13 April, "Fort Sumter fell, after nearly two days bombardment. There was great excitement in Baltimore. The general feeling however was against the action of South Carolina." Although the existence of strong sentiment in the city against Republicans and for the Confederacy would become clear later that spring, the predominant Unionism of large Border South cities and the ultimate loyalty of their states to the Union eventually cost the Confederacy dearly by compromising its economic ability to wage a long-term war against the United States. Baltimore, with a population greater than that of the largest Confederate city (New Orleans), became what William W. Freehling has termed "the Civil War hospital for Yankee railroads."[60]

Pro-Union antagonism to the Confederacy fed in part on a number of what Kenneth Stampp has labeled "mundane matters." For example, on 1 April 1861, the new Morrill Tariff went into effect, almost doubling import taxes. The Confederacy obviously would not collect such high "protective" duties for the U.S. government, instead envisioning much lower Confederate "revenue" duties, allegedly as the primary device for emancipating southern farmers and merchants from Yankee exploitation. "The tariff therefore became the challenge which, more than anything else, crystallized sentiment among Yankee businessmen in favor of applying force against the South." However, articulate defenders of coercion against traitors embellished the practical, economic benefits of maintaining the Union, offering encomiums to "patriotism, nationalism, equality, and self-government." Southern disunionists "became obstacles to national progress and prosperity, enemies of democracy and freedom, degraded defenders of an effete slave economy, and criminal advocates of treason and corruption."[61]

Notable exceptions to Stampp's generalization about northern businessmen existed, especially among northeastern manufacturers, merchants, and financiers dependent on the transatlantic or coastal trades. Edward Neufville Tailer Jr., a wealthy, well-traveled, and fashionable merchant and bank director who lived on Fourth Street in Manhattan, showed no love for the Republican Party, voting the "straight Tammany ticket" in 1859. Tailer, like the

U.S. soldiers march off to war, 1861. (Courtesy of the New York State Military Museum and Veterans Research Center, Division of Military and Naval Affairs)

"grand sachem" of New York's Democratic machine, believed that "they ought to hang all those who interfere with the rights of Southern slaveholders."[62] On 6 November 1860, Tailer wrote, "If Lincoln is defeated, confidence will be restored and prosperity will return." After Lincoln's victory, Tailer longed for some sort of peaceful compromise between the sections. On the last day of December, he noted ruefully that congressional Democrats and Republicans alike could not reach such an agreement. Early in the new year, he expressed pleasure at the "commercial confidence" inspired by pro-Union "border state resolutions." On 21 February, he declared that the United States simply could not afford to acknowledge Confederate independence. Four days later, Tailer termed Congress's passage of the Morrill Tariff "another sin by Republicans." His mercantile business was suffering, and he was selling only a few goods to Chicago and St. Louis. Yet on 15 April, he acknowledged President Lincoln's call for troops and concluded, "Every good citizen now knows but one party that of the Union, & the laws must be enforced else we are a ruined people." Tailer's patriotic resentment at Confederate aggression eventually trumped his dislike of Republican antislavery rhetoric and economic policies.[63]

On 14 April, in response to telegraph news of "the attack upon Fort

Sumter," the moderate Republican *New York Times* observed, "There is but one sentiment in this City touching the duty of the citizen at this hour to the Government. The most belligerent in tone, and resolute in their determination to stand by the Government now, at whatever cost, are the *Democrats*. On every corner, in every car, on board every ferry-boat, in every hotel, in the vestibule of every church, could be heard the remark: 'I am a Democrat, dyed in the wool. I voted against LINCOLN, but I will stand by the Government of my country when assailed as it is now by traitors.'"[64] The *New York World* concurred five days later: "Patriotic devotion is the one dominating feeling everywhere. We have, at last, thank God—and most reverently do we say it— we have, at last, a united North."[65]

Northern citizens had united, at least temporarily, to defend their perceived sectional interests, rights, and honor against the southern slaveocracy's irresponsible aggressions against the U.S. government. These slaveocrats had become secessionist after the Slave Power's influence within the Union was severely compromised by the election and behavior of an antislavery Republican president. For their part, Confederate partisans saw themselves as engaged in noble and defensive battle for their perceived rights, interests, and honor—inextricably entwined with a way of life ultimately based on black chattel slavery as a system of both capitalized labor and racial control— against the irresponsible aggressions of would-be Black Republican tyrants. Unionists and Confederates alike were convinced that Divine Providence favored their cause. Enslaved African Americans seem to have been expectant and observant, looking for an opportunity to assert their independence from white masters and mistresses.[66]

Notes

CHAPTER 1

1. See esp. Michael A. Morrison, *Slavery and the American West: The Eclipse of Manifest Destiny and the Coming of the Civil War* (Chapel Hill: University of North Carolina Press, 1997), 276.

2. See C. C. Goen, *Broken Churches, Broken Nation: Denominational Schisms and the Coming of the American Civil War* (Macon, Ga.: Mercer University Press, 1985), 3–9; Garry Wills, *Head and Heart: A History of Christianity in America* (New York: Penguin, 2007), chapter 18, "Schisms over Slavery."

3. Peter J. Parish, *The American Civil War* (New York: Holmes and Meier, 1975), 66. Parish's perspective is all the more valuable for having come from a British professor at the University of Glasgow.

4. William E. Gienapp, "The Crisis of American Democracy: The Political System and the Coming of the Civil War," in *Why the Civil War Came*, edited by Gabor S. Boritt (New York: Oxford University Press, 1996), 110.

5. The votes of the Electoral College were not officially counted and announced in Washington, D.C., until 13 February 1861. As Gienapp points out, "Under the winner-take-all principle" that determined how almost all states awarded their electoral votes, "Lincoln received 98 percent of the North's electoral votes although he won less than 54 percent of the popular vote in the free states" (ibid., 87).

6. L. E. Chittenden, *A Report of the Debates and Proceedings in the Secret Session of the Conference Convention, for Proposing Amendments to the Constitution of the United States, Held at Washington, D.C., in February A.D. 1861* (New York: Appleton, 1864), 14.

7. The inconclusive evidence available to historians suggests that Lincoln's antislavery call for containing black bondage and thereby limiting the slaveocracy's political clout appealed most strongly to the free states' younger voters—those in their twenties and thirties. The younger generation of voters in the slave states seem to have responded most positively to Breckinridge, the sitting vice president, whom they saw as most determined to defend southern rights. Even so, many exceptions to this generalization existed. There seems to be a growing and constructive interest in generational studies that identify age cohorts. See, for example, Peter S. Carmichael, *The Last Generation: Young Virginians in Peace, War, and Reunion* (Chapel Hill: University of North Carolina Press, 2005); Yonatan Eyal, *The Young America Movement and the Transformation of the Democratic Party, 1828–1861* (Cambridge: Cambridge University Press, 2007).

8. James M. McPherson, *Battle Cry of Freedom: The Civil War Era* (New York: Oxford University Press, 1988), 264.

9. Abraham Lincoln, "Proclamation Calling Militia and Convening Congress, April 15, 1861," in Abraham Lincoln, *Speeches and Writings, 1859–1865*, edited by Don E. Fehrenbacher (New York: Library of America, 1989), 232.

10. Joseph P. Reidy, *From Slavery to Agrarian Capitalism in the Cotton Plantation South: Central Georgia, 1800–1880* (Chapel Hill: University of North Carolina Press, 1992), 111.

11. McPherson, *Battle Cry of Freedom*, 276.

12. Ibid., 274–77.

13. Charles P. Roland, *An American Iliad: The Story of the Civil War*, 2nd ed. (Boston: McGraw-Hill, 2002).

14. Jean H. Baker, preface to *Mary Todd Lincoln: A Biography* (1987; New York: Norton, 2008), xiv.

15. Richard Wrightman Fox, *Jesus in America: A History* (New York: HarperCollins, 2004), 126.

16. After 1776, "the American denominations that expanded most rapidly were the ones that most successfully presented themselves as both traditionally Christian and faithfully republican"—Baptists, Congregationalists, Methodists, and Presbyterians. As of 1860, "between a third and two-fifths of Americans were members of churches," but "the rate of adherence—of people participating regularly in church life—was probably double the rate of membership" (Mark A. Noll, *The Civil War as a Theological Crisis* [Chapel Hill: University of North Carolina Press, 2006], 23, 11).

17. See esp. Wills, *Head and Heart*, 223–24, 324.

18. James M. McPherson, *What They Fought For, 1861–1865* (New York: Anchor, 1994), 6.

19. Among recent titles, see Drew Gilpin Faust, *The Creation of Confederate Nationalism: Ideology and Identity in the Civil War South* (Baton Rouge: Louisiana State University Press, 1988), esp. 19–35; Susan-Mary Grant, *North over South: Northern Nationalism and American Identity in the Antebellum Era* (Lawrence: University Press of Kansas, 2000), esp. 3–5.

20. Debby Applegate, *The Most Famous Man in America: The Biography of Henry Ward Beecher* (New York: Three Leaves/Doubleday, 2006), 224. See also Kenneth M. Stampp, *The Imperiled Union: Essays on the Background of the Civil War* (New York: Oxford University Press, 1980).

21. Maury Klein, *Days of Defiance: Sumter, Secession, and the Coming of the Civil War* (New York: Knopf, 1997), 33. In 1860, the number of postal workers approximated the number of Methodist clergy; today the ratio is about nine to one (Noll, *Civil War as a Theological Crisis*, 12).

22. David M. Potter, *The Impending Crisis, 1848–1861*, completed and edited by Don E. Fehrenbacher (New York: Harper and Row, 1976), 484.

23. Elizabeth R. Varon, *Disunion!: The Coming of the Civil War, 1789–1859* (Chapel Hill: University of North Carolina Press, 2008), introduction.

24. François Furstenberg, *In the Name of the Father: Washington's Legacy, Slavery, and the Making of a Nation* (New York: Penguin, 2006), 224.

25. See Charles Grayson Summerwell, *Adventures with the Great Seal of the Confederacy* (Tuscaloosa, Ala.: Word Way, 1998), 7–8; Gary W. Gallagher, *The Confederate War: How Popular Will, Nationalism, and Military Strategy Could Not Stave Off Defeat* (Cambridge: Harvard University Press, 1997), esp. 65.

26. Manisha Sinha, *The Counterrevolution of Slavery: Politics and Ideology in Antebellum South Carolina* (Chapel Hill: University of North Carolina Press, 2000), 210.

27. E. Brooks Holifield, *Theology in America: Christian Thought from the Age of the Puritans to the Civil War* (New Haven: Yale University Press, 2003), 502.

28. Anne Sarah Rubin, *A Shattered Nation: The Rise and Fall of the Confederacy, 1861–1868* (Chapel Hill: University of North Carolina Press, 2005), 1, 100.

29. Russell McClintock, *Lincoln and the Decision for War: The Northern Response to Secession* (Chapel Hill: University of North Carolina Press, 2008), 24.

30. Anne Sarah Rubin, *Shattered Nation*, 1, 4, 240, 244, 246–47. See also Peter Kolchin, *A Sphinx on the American Land: The Nineteenth-Century South, a Comparative Perspective* (Baton Rouge: Louisiana State University Press, 2003), 34–36.

31. James H. Moorhead, *American Apocalypse: Yankee Protestants and the Civil War, 1860–1869* (New Haven: Yale University Press, 1978); Robert H. Abzug, *Cosmos Crumbling: American Reform and the Religious Imagination* (New York: Oxford University Press, 1994).

32. Anne C. Rose, *Voices of the Marketplace: American Thought and Culture, 1840–1860* (Lanham, Md.: Rowman and Littlefield, 1995), 14–15. See also Abzug, *Cosmos Crumbling*, 192.

33. Applegate, *Most Famous Man*, 21, 243–45, 257. For a good discussion of millennialism, see Daniel Walker Howe, *What Hath God Wrought: The Transformation of America, 1815–1848* (New York: Oxford University Press, 2007), 285–89.

34. Robert M. Calhoun, *Evangelicals and Conservatives in the Early South, 1740–1861* (Columbia: University of South Carolina Press, 1988), 189–90; Noll, *Civil War as a Theological Crisis*, 81–82. A helpful biography is James Oscar Farmer Jr., *The Metaphysical Confederacy: James Henley Thornwell and the Synthesis of Southern Values* (Macon, Ga.: Mercer University Press, 1986).

35. Nonetheless, by 1860 Beecher had far outstripped northern public opinion by becoming an open advocate of woman suffrage. He learned to "shed the Calvinist inhibitions against riches, idle pleasure, and free thought" and in the process gave a powerful impetus to a more modern "therapeutic view of religion" whereby "Christianity did not exist for the glory of God, but for the pleasure and health of mankind" (Applegate, *Most Famous Man*, 247, 268, 316).

36. Moorhead, *American Apocalypse*, xii, 14.

37. Lewis O. Saum, *The Popular Mood of Pre–Civil War America* (Westport, Conn.: Greenwood, 1980), 3; Noll, *Civil War as a Theological Crisis*, 75.

38. John Rodgers Meigs, *A Civil War Soldier of Christ and Country: The Selected Correspondence of John Rodgers Meigs, 1859–64*, edited by Mary A. Giunta (Urbana: University of Illinois Press, 2006), 83. Captain Meigs was then superintending the construction of the U.S. Capitol and Washington Aqueduct. Conflict with Secretary of War John Floyd, from Virginia, over government contracts led Meigs to be sent south to Fort Jefferson, in the Florida Keys, in late December 1860. In June 1861, Captain Meigs became the very capable quartermaster general of the U.S. Army. See McPherson, *Battle Cry of Freedom*, 324–25. On 10 December, a farmer in Iowa's Hamilton County, J. H. Williams, wrote to his son, James, then in Alabama, "But dark as the storm that hvors [*sic*] on the Horizon,

I trust in Divine Providence." He expected that the storm "will pass away" and "the calm that will follow will be all the pleasanter, and better appreciated" (John Kent Folmar, ed., *This State of Wonders: The Letters of an Iowa Frontier Family, 1858–1861* [Iowa City: University of Iowa Press, 1986], 114).

39. Keziah Goodwyn Hopkins Brevard, *A Plantation Mistress on the Eve of the Civil War: The Diary of Keziah Goodwyn Hopkins Brevard, 1860–61*, edited by John Hammond Moore (Columbia: University of South Carolina Press, 1993), 92–93. A biographer has said of Leonidas Polk, the decidedly evangelical planter-priest who served as Episcopal bishop of the Diocese of Louisiana, "His emotional conversion, his emphasis on preaching the gospel, and his providential worldview reflected the typical experiences and characteristics of evangelicals" (Glenn Robins, *The Bishop of the Old South: The Ministry and Civil War Legacy of Leonidas Polk* [Mercer, Ga.: Mercer University Press, 2006], xi–xii).

40. Noll, *Civil War as a Theological Crisis*, 80–81.

41. Harry S. Stout, *Upon the Altar of the Nation: A Moral History of the American Civil War* (New York: Viking, 2006), xvi; Edward L. Ayers, *In the Presence of Mine Enemies: The Civil War in the Heart of America, 1859–1863* (New York: Norton, 2003), 6. See also Noll, *Civil War as a Theological Crisis*, chapter 5, "The Crisis over Providence"; Robert J. Miller, *Both Prayed to the Same God: Religion and Faith in the American Civil War* (Lanham, Md.: Lexington, 2007). Earl J. Hess, *Liberty, Virtue, and Progress: Northerners and Their War for the Union*, 2nd ed. (New York: Fordham University Press, 1997), provides good insights into the "ideology" of Unionist northerners in 1860–61 but does not explicitly recognize the importance of popular beliefs in divine providence.

42. "Lincoln the politician was positioning himself as the conservative defender of the nation's founding principles" (James Oakes, *The Radical and the Republican: Frederick Douglass, Abraham Lincoln, and the Triumph of Antislavery Politics* [New York: Norton, 2007], 142; see also 135).

43. Phillip Shaw Paludan, *The Presidency of Abraham Lincoln* (Lawrence: University Press of Kansas, 1994), xv.

44. Ibid., 34.

45. Oakes, *Radical and the Republican*, 136.

46. Robert V. Remini, *Henry Clay: Statesman for the Union* (New York: Norton, 1991), 740–45.

47. See the description of Ralph Waldo Emerson in Daniel Aaron, *The Unwritten Civil War: American Writers and the Civil War* (New York: Knopf, 1973), 10: "To Emerson the very notion of a broker-politician reconciling Right and Wrong was a profanation."

48. Avery O. Craven, *The Growth of Southern Nationalism, 1848–1861* (Baton Rouge and Austin: Louisiana State University Press and the Littlefield Fund for Southern History of the University of Texas, 1953), 397. Cf. the different emphasis in Allan Nevins, *The Ordeal of the Union: Selected Chapters*, edited by E. B. Long (New York: Scribner's, 1971), 184–85.

49. J. G. Randall and David Herbert Donald, *The Civil War and Reconstruction*, 2nd ed. (Lexington, Mass.: Heath, 1969), 176.

50. Roy Franklin Nichols, *The Disruption of American Democracy* (New York: Free Press, 1948), 502–5; Ayers, *In the Presence*, 417.

51. Karen Stenner, *The Authoritarian Dynamic* (Cambridge: Cambridge University Press, 2005), 17, 323. Stenner usefully distinguishes between the emphasis of authoritarians on "achieving unity" and the stress on maintaining "stability" among "conservatives," who can be "libertarian" (11).

52. For reasons suggested by Ronald P. Formisano, some political historians prefer not to label the politics of the 1790s a true "party system" analogous to that created by Whigs and Democrats in the 1830s. He cites Joanne Freeman's work in support of positing "the absence of political development in a political culture still antipartisan and dominated by gentlemen guided by an obsessive concern with personal reputation and honor" (review published in *Journal of American History* 91 [March 2005]: 1418).

53. Michael F. Holt, *The Fate of Their Country: Politicians, Slavery Extension, and the Coming of the Civil War* (New York: Hill and Wang, 2004), 128. See also Gienapp, "Crisis of American Democracy," 91.

54. Barbara Tuchman, *The March of Folly: From Troy to Vietnam* (New York: Knopf, 1984).

55. "Alexander H. Stephens's Unionist Speech, Wednesday Evening, November 14," in William W. Freehling and Craig M. Simpson, eds., *Secession Debated: Georgia's Showdown in 1860* (New York: Oxford University Press, 1992), 54, 59, 69.

56. Nevins, *Ordeal of the Union*, 184.

57. Mark Kurlansky, *Nonviolence: Twenty-five Lessons from the History of a Dangerous Idea* (New York: Modern Library, 2006), 35.

58. Gerda Lerner, *The Grimké Sisters from South Carolina: Pioneers for Woman's Rights and Abolition* (1967; New York: Schocken, 1971), 340.

59. William Bowen Campbell to Arthur Campbell Beard, 15 March 1861, Campbell Family Papers, Perkins Library, Duke University, Durham, North Carolina. See Shearer Davis Bowman, *Masters and Lords: Mid-19th-Century U.S. Planters and Prussian Junkers* (New York: Oxford University Press, 1993), 158.

60. Roger L. Ransom, *Conflict and Compromise: The Political Economy of Slavery, Emancipation, and the American Civil War* (Cambridge: Cambridge University Press, 1989), 11.

61. Michael Vorenberg, *Final Freedom: The Civil War, the Abolition of Slavery, and the Thirteenth Amendment* (Cambridge: Cambridge University Press, 2001), 6–21.

62. A recent monograph argues that even as antislavery constitutional attacks on the interstate slave trade had waned during the 1850s, proslavery concerns about them—that is, fears that the Constitution's Commerce Clause could be employed to undermine the peculiar institution—waxed during the decade before the Civil War. They played no small role in fueling secession after Lincoln's election. See David L. Lightner, *Slavery and the Commerce Power: How the Struggle against the Interstate Slave Trade Led to the Civil War* (New Haven: Yale University Press, 2006), esp. 139.

63. For a serious and sustained argument that the Civil War indeed cost far more than it was worth, see Jeffrey Rogers Hummel, *Emancipating Slaves, Enslaving Free Men: A History of the American Civil War* (Chicago: Open Court, 1996).

CHAPTER 2

1. John R. Skates, "Mississippi," in *The Encyclopedia of Southern History*, edited by David C. Roller and Robert W. Twyman (Baton Rouge: Louisiana State University Press, 1979), 825.

2. William K. Scarborough, "Mississippi, Slavery in," in *Dictionary of Afro-American Slavery*, edited by Randall Miller and John David Smith (New York: Greenwood, 1988), 484–85; James C. Cobb, *The Most Southern Place on Earth: The Mississippi Delta and the Roots of Regional Identity* (New York: Oxford University Press, 1992). What Joseph P. Reidy found in the counties of central Georgia around Macon, where three-quarters of white families owned slaves, also appears true of other Black Belt areas: "The evidence suggests that most of the well-established planters of both Whiggish and Democratic antecedents opposed secession at first. . . . Whiggish planters seem to have clung to that opposition until after the state seceded, but Democratic planters . . . and commercial interests of both persuasions broke early and advocated disunion" (*Slavery and Agrarian Capitalism in the Cotton Plantation South: Central Georgia, 1800–1880* [Chapel Hill: University of North Carolina Press, 1992], 110).

3. For a revealing exchange between an immediate secessionist and a more conservative cooperationist, both of whom condemned Republicans and defended slavery, see in particular a pair of Florida pamphlets: *Governor's Message, Transmitted to the Legislature of Florida, November 26, 1860* (Tallahassee[?], 1860), R. K. Call, *An Address to the People of Florida, from Gen. R. K. Call* (n.p., 1860), both at the Newberry Library, Chicago.

Fire-eaters tended to favor reversing the 1807 decision of Thomas Jefferson's presidential administration and the U.S. Congress to end American involvement in the transatlantic slave trade with Africa. The goal here was usually twofold: first, to make slave property more accessible and affordable to the majority of southern whites who were not slaveholders; and second, to land a proslavery counterpunch against both contemporary abolitionist critics and the Founding Fathers' legacy of apologizing for slavery as a "necessary evil" rather than portraying it as a "positive good." Most affluent slaveholders, "whose slave forces grew by natural increase and whose investment in slave property would be devalued, vehemently opposed the African trade" (Reidy, *Slavery and Agrarian Capitalism*, 92).

4. William Lewis Nugent, *My Dear Nellie: The Civil War Letters of William L. Nugent to Eleanor Smith Nugent*, edited by William M. Cash and Lucy Somerville Howorth (Jackson: University Press of Mississippi, 1977), 38. See also William L. Barney, *The Secessionist Impulse: Alabama and Mississippi in 1860* (Princeton: Princeton University Press, 1974), 205–6.

5. David M. Potter, *The Impending Crisis, 1848–1861*, completed and edited by Don E. Fehrenbacher (New York: Harper and Row, 1976), 530–33; William J. Cooper Jr., *Jefferson Davis, American* (New York: Knopf, 2000), 99, 103, 312, 318, 323, 330. James M. McPherson, *Battle Cry of Freedom: The Civil War Era* (New York: Oxford University Press, 1988), 244–46, argues that "secession fit the model of 'pre-emptive counterrevolution' developed by [European] historian Arno Mayer. Rather than trying to restore the old order, a pre-emptive counterrevolution strikes first to protect the status quo before the revolutionary threat can materialize."

6. This speech was published in pamphlet form as *Remarks on the Special Message*

on *Affairs in South Carolina, Jan. 10, 1861* (Baltimore, 1861) and is available in Jon L. Wakelyn, ed., *Southern Pamphlets on Secession, November 1860–April 1861* (Chapel Hill: University of North Carolina Press, 1996), 115–42; quotations on 133–35. Wakelyn is mistaken in his statement that "Davis supported the Crittenden Compromise over slavery in the territories" (115).

7. The powerful political impact of slaveholders' growing concerns about the market value of their slaves is central to James L. Huston, *Calculating the Value of the Union: Slavery Property Rights, and the Economic Origins of the Civil War* (Chapel Hill: University of North Carolina Press, 2003).

8. William C. Davis, *Jefferson Davis: The Man and the Hour* (New York: Harper-Collins, 1991), 305.

9. See Glenn C. Altschuler and Stuart M. Blumin, *Rude Republic: Americans and Their Politics in the Nineteenth Century* (Princeton: Princeton University Press, 2000), 106. It is testimony to "the force that 'Victorian' refinement exerted on upper- and middle-class American men both before and after the Civil War" that "whatever honors might accrue to a governor, an ambassador, or any other high public servant, were threatened by disreputable political practice — by 'the vicious life of the politician.'" The phrase "public honor" is taken from T. Michael Parrish, *Richard Taylor: Soldier Prince of Dixie* (Chapel Hill: University of North Carolina Press, 1992), 116–17, which portrays Dick Taylor's political outlook as a southern manifestation of "Whiggish conservatism, part of the plantation ideal of a hierarchical society," including the "myth" that the planter elite provided "unchallenged leadership by a beneficent ruling class."

10. Seward as quoted in Kenneth M. Stampp, ed., *The Causes of the Civil War*, 3rd rev. ed. (New York: Touchstone/Simon and Schuster, 1991), 139–40. See also Daniel W. Crofts, "Seward, William Henry," in *American National Biography*, edited by John A. Garraty and Mark C. Carnes (New York: Oxford University Press, 1999), 19:676–81.

11. Fulton Anderson hailed from Hinds County, an anti-Democratic stronghold during the previous two decades. In fact, in 1860, Hinds County voters were equally hostile to both antislavery Republicans and secessionist Democrats, awarding a decisive majority of 449 votes (out of 2,529 cast) to Constitutional Unionist nominees Bell and Everett. Anderson subsequently became one of the county's three Cooperation candidates for election to Mississippi's state convention. The label "Cooperation" indicated their preference for the slave states to engage in some kind of deliberate, interstate, cooperationist response to the threats posed by Black Republicans after Lincoln's election, a contrast to proponents of immediate separate-state secession. Anderson and his two compatriots suffered a clear defeat at the hands of less distinguished advocates of immediate secession, who received 60 percent of the popular vote. This defeat demonstrated, according to a historian of Mississippi, "the very radical swing of public opinion towards disunion after Lincoln's election." It reinforces what William Freehling has identified as "the largest generalization about secession crisis allegiance"—i.e., "the more and thicker the black belts" with substantial slave populations, "the faster and the more enthusiastically a neighborhood massed behind secessionists." See George H. Reese, ed., *Proceedings of the Virginia State Convention of 1861, February 13–May 1* (Richmond: Virginia State Library, 1965), 1:50–52; Charles B. Dew, *Apostles of Disunion: Southern Secession Commissioners and the Causes of the Civil War* (Charlottesville: University Press of Vir-

ginia, 2001), 61–63; Stampp, *Causes*, 139–40; Elizabeth Fox-Genovese and Eugene D. Genovese, *The Mind of the Master Class: History and Faith in the Southern Slaveholders' World View* (Cambridge: Cambridge University Press, 2005), 113; Percy Rainwater, *Mississippi: Storm Center of Secession, 1856–1861* (1938; New York: Da Capo, 1969), 193–94; Christopher J. Olsen, *Political Culture and Secession in Mississippi: Masculinity, Honor, and the Antiparty Tradition, 1830–1860* (New York: Oxford University Press, 2000), 189–90; William W. Freehling, *The Road to Disunion* (New York: Oxford University Press, 2007), 2:530.

12. The discussion of Eppes draws heavily on Shearer Davis Bowman, "Conditional Unionism and Slavery in Virginia, 1860–61," *Virginia Magazine of History and Biography* 96 (January 1988): 31–54; in turn, this article is based on the Eppes Family Muniments, 1722–1948, Virginia Historical Society, Richmond. When I was writing this article, I did not have access to Daniel W. Crofts, *Reluctant Confederates: Upper South Unionists in the Secession Crisis* (Chapel Hill: University of North Carolina Press, 1989), which deals with three of the four slave states that left the Union after Fort Sumter: Virginia, North Carolina, and Tennessee. On the fourth, Arkansas, see James L. Woods, *Rebellion and Realignment: Arkansas's Road to Secession* (Fayetteville: University of Arkansas Press, 1987), esp. 151: "By the spring of 1861 most white Arkansans were probably conditional Unionists." See also Donald P. McNeilly, *The Old South Frontier: Cotton Plantations and the Formation of Arkansas Society, 1819–1861* (Fayetteville: University of Arkansas Press, 2000), esp. 181–91.

13. I am indebted to Michael Parrish for bringing this point to my attention.

14. See esp. the revised version of Calhoun's address available in John C. Calhoun, *Union and Liberty: The Political Philosophy of John C. Calhoun*, edited by Ross M. Lence (Indianapolis: Liberty Fund, 1992), 469–76.

15. J. William Harris, *Plain Folk and Gentry in a Slave Society: White Liberty and Black Slavery in Augusta's Hinterlands* (Middletown, Conn.: Wesleyan University Press, 1985), 131–38; George M. Fredrickson, *The Black Image in the White Mind: The Debate on Afro-American Character and Destiny* (New York: Harper Torchbooks, 1971), esp. 61. See also George M. Fredrickson, *The Arrogance of Race: Historical Perspectives on Slavery, Racism, and Social Inequality* (Middletown, Conn.: Wesleyan University Press, 1988), 138–39, 252–53.

16. "On December 20[, 1860,] all 395 Southerners at the Jefferson Medical College in Philadelphia—over sixty percent of the student body—and those at the University of Pennsylvania Medical College resolved to 'secede' and return to the South" (Eric H. Walther, *The Shattering of the Union: America in the 1850s* [Wilmington, Del.: Scholarly Resources, 2004], 177).

17. William J. Cooper Jr., ed., *Jefferson Davis: The Essential Writings* (New York: Modern Library, 2003), 198–203.

18. Bennett as quoted in Harold Holzer, *Lincoln at Cooper Union: The Speech That Made Abraham Lincoln President* (New York: Simon and Schuster, 2004), 165.

19. See esp. John Chester Miller, *The Wolf by the Ears: Thomas Jefferson and Slavery* (New York: Free Press, 1977), 221–52.

20. Henry Cleveland, ed., *Alexander H. Stephens in Public and Private* (Philadelphia:

National, 1866), 721; Thomas E. Schott, *Alexander H. Stephens of Georgia: A Biography* (Baton Rouge: Louisiana State University Press, 1988), 334.

21. George C. Herring, *From Colony to Superpower: U.S. Foreign Relations since 1776* (New York: Oxford University Press, 2008), 225–32. Herring credits Seward with demonstrating "more than once . . . that rarest and most essential of diplomatic skills, talking tough enough to satisfy his domestic constituency and give an adversary pause while compromising when the situation demanded it" (227).

22. Frank Moore, ed., *The Rebellion Record: A Diary of American Events, with Documents, Narratives, Illustrative Events, Poetry, Etc.* (New York: Putnam, 1864–65), 1:166–75; Jefferson Davis, *The Messages and Papers of Jefferson Davis and the Confederacy: Including Diplomatic Correspondence, 1861–1865,* edited and compiled by James D. Richardson (Philadelphia: Chelsea House, 2001), 1:63–82; James A. Rawley, ed., *Secession: The Disruption of the American Republic, 1844–1861* (Malabar, Fla.: Krieger, 1990), 250–53; Cooper, *Jefferson Davis, American,* 341–42. Davis's "Message" is not included in Cooper, *Jefferson Davis: The Essential Writings.*

23. Cooper, *Jefferson Davis, American,* 619, 626; David W. Blight, *Race and Reunion: The Civil War in American Memory* (Cambridge: Belknap Press of Harvard University Press, 2001), 260. It is helpful to compare Davis's postwar denial of slavery's importance in the secession crisis with that of Richard Taylor, whose *Destruction and Reconstruction: Reminiscences of the Late War* (1879) expressed "the popular dogma that secession erupted from a sincere desire for political liberty and not for the sake of slavery" (Parrish, *Richard Taylor,* 111).

24. On this subject, see Forrest McDonald, *States' Rights and the Union: Imperium in Imperio, 1776–1876* (Lawrence: University Press of Kansas, 2000).

25. Proslavery southerners "became rigid state's righters only on a state's right to withdraw consent from all the Union's laws," concludes Freehling, "not on a state's right to hinder particular national laws" (*Road to Disunion,* 2:349). According to McPherson, "On all issues but [the 1850 Fugitive Slave Law], southerners stood for state's rights and a weak federal government" (*Battle Cry of Freedom,* 78). However, those who demanded explicit federal protection for slaves in the territories might also have wanted, in this instance, an assertive federal government.

26. Mark A. Noll, *The Civil War as a Theological Crisis* (Chapel Hill: University of North Carolina Press, 2006), 18–19, 58–59.

27. Alfred H. Kelly and Winfred A. Harbison, *The American Constitution: Its Origins and Development,* 4th ed. (New York: Norton, 1970), 359.

28. Don E. Fehrenbacher and Ward M. McAfee, *The Slaveholding Republic: An Account of the United States Government's Relations to Slavery* (New York: Oxford University Press, 2001), 208–9: "The clause written into the Constitution made interstate rendition of slaves part of the national purpose and did so in the language of legal command. Plainly, it enforced a restriction on state authority, though without specifying the means of enforcing that restriction. At the same time, there is nothing in the text or the context to indicate that it was also intended as a mandate to the legislative branch of the new government. The wording of the clause, together with its placement in a section on interstate comity (rather than among the enumerated powers of Congress), seems fairly conclusive

on that point." Finally, "discussion of the fugitive slave clause in the state ratifying conventions likewise did not reveal any expectation of it being enforced by federal statute.... By the time the Second Congress assembled in October 1791, however, a running quarrel between Virginia and Pennsylvania had set the stage for Congressional intervention," in the wake of dispute over a slave named John. He had become legally free in 1783 because his Pennsylvania owner failed to register him as required by the state's 1780 gradual emancipation law. Nevertheless, John remained in slavery and was hired out in Virginia before escaping to Pennsylvania with abolitionist help in 1788. In his 3 December 1860 State of the Union address, President Buchanan endorsed the historical necessity argument for the Constitution's Fugitive Slave Clause, declaring the doctrine "a well-known historical fact."

29. Ibid., 205–30.

30. Robert Remini, *Daniel Webster: The Man and His Time* (New York: Norton, 1997), chapter 40, "The Seventh of March Speech," 662–81. After Zachary Taylor's death several weeks later and Millard Fillmore's assumption of the presidency, Webster resigned his Senate seat and became secretary of state. See also McPherson, *Battle Cry of Freedom*, 78–80.

31. Stanley L. Campbell, "Fugitive Slave Act," in *The Oxford Companion to United States History*, edited by Paul S. Boyer (New York: Oxford University Press, 2001), 294.

32. See esp. McPherson, *Battle Cry of Freedom*, 88–91; Glenna Matthews, "'Little Women' Who Helped Make This Great War," in *Why the Civil War Came*, edited by Gabor S. Boritt (New York: Oxford University Press, 1996), 36–37.

33. Leonard L. Richards, *The Slave Power: The Free North and Southern Domination, 1780–1860* (Baton Rouge: Louisiana State University Press, 2000), 26–27. For a provocative twist on Richards's argument that something like a Slave Power did in fact exist, see Robin L. Einhorn, *American Taxation, American Slavery* (Chicago: University of Chicago Press, 2006), esp. 7–8: "The antigovernment rhetoric that continues to saturate our political life is rooted in slavery rather than liberty. The American mistrust of government is not part of our democratic heritage. It comes from slaveholding elites who had no experience with democracy where they lived and knew only one thing about democracy: that it threatened slavery."

34. Rowland Gibson Hazard, *Economics and Politics: A Series of Papers upon Public Questions from 1840 to 1885*, edited by Caroline Hazard (Boston: Houghton Mifflin, 1889), 29–31. Hazard's father had established, circa 1802 in South Kingston, Rhode Island, the Peace Dale Manufacturing Company, the area's first wool-carding and fulling mill operated by water power. By 1814, the company also spun wool and possessed perhaps the earliest power-loom weaving machine in the state. See the entry for Rowland Gibson Hazard in *National Cyclopaedia of American Biography* (Ann Arbor: University Microfilms, 1967), 9:442; Gail Fowler Mohanty's biographical sketch of a brother, Thomas Preston Hazard, in *American National Biography*, edited by Garraty and Carnes, 10:443–44. There is no mention of Hazard in William E. Gienapp, *The Origins of the Republican Party, 1852–1856* (New York: Oxford University Press, 1986); but see Myron O. Stachiw, "'For the Sake of Commerce': Slavery, Antislavery, and Northern Industry," in *The Meaning of Slavery in the North*, edited by Martin Blatt and David Roediger (New York: Garland, 1998), 39–42.

35. Here Clay clearly illustrated the differences between post-Enlightenment, post–

natural rights cultural and political values and those of classical thinkers such as Plato and Aristotle, for whom slavery was simply one aspect of "an assumed hierarchy of the natural moral order, rather than a problem demanding moral scrutiny" (Seymour Drescher and Stanley Engerman, *A Historical Guide to World Slavery* [New York: Oxford University Press, 1998], 283).

36. Henry Clay, *The Life and Speeches of Henry Clay*, edited by Daniel Mallory (Hartford, Conn.: Silas and Andrus, 1855), 2:595–600.

37. For a fine account of Bleeding Sumner, see David Herbert Donald, *Charles Sumner and the Coming of the Civil War* (New York: Knopf, 1974), 285–94. Sumner had delivered the lengthy Crime against Kansas speech on the floor of the U.S. Senate in May 1856. He had labeled South Carolina senator Andrew P. Butler, formerly a friend, as the "Don Quixote of the harlot, Slavery," for he "has chosen a mistress to whom he has made his vows, and who, though ugly to others, is always lovely to him, though polluted in the sight of the world." Sumner also denounced the immorality of the popular sovereignty solution to the controversy over slavery's expansion into western territories as advocated by Illinois Democratic senator Stephen A. Douglas, whom Summer belittled as "the squire of slavery, its very Sancho Panza, ready to do its humiliating services." Brooks, Butler's cousin, who was not known as a fire-eating proslavery extremist, then attacked Sumner on the Senate floor, striking him repeatedly with a walking stick. Seeing himself as avenging family honor against degrading insults, Brooks reported giving Sumner "about thirty first rate stripes. Towards the last he bellowed like a calf. I wore my cane out completely but saved the head which is gold." Public meetings held at almost every northern city voiced protests against the assault and sympathy for the assaulted Sumner. As Horace Mann wrote to Sumner on 27 May, "We are not only shocked at the outrage committed upon you, but we are wounded in your wounds, and bleed in your bleeding." The assault won many voters to the Republican cause on the eve of the 1856 elections, providing further evidence to the party platform's indictment of Mormon polygamy and southern slavery as "twin relics of barbarism." The battered and for many martyred Sumner did not return to the Senate chamber until 1859. See also William E. Gienapp, "The Crime against Sumner: The Caning of Charles Sumner and the Rise of the Republican Party," *Civil War History* 25 (September 1979): 218–45.

38. Hazard, *Economics and Politics*, 129–64.

39. See Nicole Etcheson, *The Emerging Midwest: Upland Southerners and the Political Culture of the Old Northwest, 1787–1861* (Bloomington: Indiana University Press, 1996), 98–116.

40. Richard N. Current, *The History of Wisconsin*, vol. 2, *The Civil War Era, 1848–1873* (Madison: State Historical Society of Wisconsin, 1976), 270–71, 291; Potter, *Impending Crisis*, 295.

41. William L. Barney, *The Road to Secession: A New Perspective on the Old South* (New York: Praeger, 1972), 200–201; Richard B. Harwell, "Longstreet, Augustus Baldwin," in *Encyclopedia of Southern History*, edited by Roller and Twyman, 732.

42. See William A. Link, *Roots of Secession: Slavery and Politics in Antebellum Virginia* (Chapel Hill: University of North Carolina Press, 2003), 97–100.

43. Steven Deyle, *Carry Me Back: The Domestic Slave Trade in American Life* (New York: Oxford University Press, 2005), 257.

44. Solomon Northup, *Twelve Years a Slave*, edited by Sue Eakin and Joseph Logsdon (Baton Rouge: Louisiana State University Press, 1968), 158. On slave skills at dissimulation, see esp. Freehling, *Road to Disunion*, 1:77.

45. William Howard Russell, *My Diary North and South*, edited by Eugene D. Berwanger (New York; Knopf, 1988), 73–74, entry for 15 April 1861.

46. Mary Chesnut, *Mary Chesnut's Civil War*, edited by C. Vann Woodward (New Haven: Yale University Press, 1981), 48, entry for 13 April 1861. See also the twentieth-century interview in Alabama with ex-slave Sarah Fitzpatrick (b. 1847), as reported in David W. Blight, "They Knew What Time It Was: African-Americans," in *When the Civil War Came*, edited by Boritt, 70–71.

47. This argument is powerfully made by Fox-Genovese and Genovese, *Mind of the Master Class*, esp. 670–71.

48. The concept of paternalism became current among historians only during the 1960s and 1970s. Although anthropologist John W. Bennett's article on the subject appears in the *International Encyclopedia of the Social Sciences*, edited by David L. Sills (New York: Macmillan, 1968), 2:472–77, there is no entry on paternalism in Julius Gould and William L. Kolb, eds., *A Dictionary of the Social Sciences*, compiled under the auspices of UNESCO (New York: Free Press of Glencoe, 1964). Nor, surprisingly, does the term receive an entry in Alan Bullock and Stephen Trombley, eds., *The Harper Dictionary of Modern Thought*, rev. ed. (New York: Harper and Row, 1988). For helpful short entries on paternalism, see David Jary and Julia Jary, eds., *The HarperCollins Dictionary of Sociology* (New York: HarperCollins, 1991), 356–57; John Scott and Gordon Marshall, eds., *Oxford Dictionary of Sociology*, 3rd ed. (Oxford: Oxford University Press, 2005), 481; Bryan S. Turner, ed., *The Cambridge Dictionary of Sociology* (Cambridge: Cambridge University Press, 2006), 432–33.

49. Eugene D. Genovese, *Roll, Jordan, Roll: The World the Slaves Made* (1974; New York: Vintage, 1976), esp. 3–7.

50. Ira Berlin, *Generations of Captivity: A History of African-American Slaves* (Cambridge: Belknap Press of Harvard University Press, 2003), 17–18. See also Shearer Davis Bowman, "Synthesizing Southern Slavery: A Review Essay," *Register of the Kentucky Historical Society* 103 (Autumn 2005): esp. 736–38.

51. Deyle, *Carry Me Back*, 208.

52. Lawrence N. Powell, introduction to Frederick Law Olmsted, *The Cotton Kingdom*, edited by Arthur M. Schlesinger (New York: Modern Library/Random House, 1984), xi–xx.

53. Frederick Law Olmsted, *The Papers of Frederick Law Olmsted*, vol. 2, *Slavery and the South, 1852–1857*, edited by Charles E. Beveridge and Charles Capen McLaughlin (Baltimore: Johns Hopkins University Press, 1981), 155, 161–64; Charles Hoffmann and Tess Hoffmann, *North by South: The Two Lives of Richard James Arnold* (Athens: University of Georgia Press, 1988), xiii–xiv, 1–9, 230–42, 252–53, 273.

54. On Morel, see Hoffmann and Hoffmann, *North by South*, xx, 166–71, 255, 268–69.

55. The indispensable work for the wartime years is Leon F. Litwack, *Been in the Storm So Long: The Aftermath of Slavery* (New York: Vintage, 1980), esp. 40–41, 63, 151, 162. The majority of slaves were "neither rebellious nor faithful" during the war but instead were "ambivalent and observant, . . . searching for opportunities to break the bonds

of dependency that bound them to their white families." Although "most body servants remained loyal and faithful attendants," some of them "calculatingly exploited the trust placed in them to desert to the Yankees at the first opportunity."

56. Link, *Roots of Secession*, 118. See also Blight, "They Knew What Time It Was," 68–69: "The role the slaves played in causing the Civil War can never be precisely determined. But collectively, by both their mere presence and their concerted actions, they exerted enormous pressure on the sectional conflict of the 1850s."

57. William W. Freehling, *The South versus the South: How Anti-Confederate Southerners Shaped the Course of the Civil War* (New York: Oxford University Press, 2001), 26.

58. Link has suggested "a conservative estimate, coming from federal census takers." During the 1850s "something like 1,000 slaves per year became runaways across the entire South" (*Roots of Secession*, 99). This is indeed a very conservative estimate; according to Freehling, "more than 5,000 runaways a year" reached the free states, "the vast majority" from the border states (*South versus the South*, 27).

59. Dwight Lowell Dumond, ed., *Southern Editorials on Secession* (1931; Gloucester, Mass.: Smith, 1964), 238–39, 265.

60. New England's anger at the Kansas-Nebraska legislation was also inflamed by the show trial of fugitive slave Anthony Burns, seized in Boston by six men two days after the adoption of the territorial legislation. See Catherine Clinton, *Harriet Tubman: The Road to Freedom* (Boston: Little, Brown, 2004), 114–15.

61. It is hardly surprising that African Americans responded quite differently. In late 1859, Baltimore "police burst into an annual ball held by free blacks of that city. They found the assembly hall filled with Brown's image emblazoned on banners and a bust of John Brown inscribed 'The martyr—God bless him'" (Walther, *Shattering of the Union*, 78).

62. Charles B. Dew, *Ironmaker to the Confederacy: Joseph R. Anderson and the Tredegar Iron Works* (1966; Richmond: Library of Virginia, 1999), 43. This stance could bolster slave state producers. Anderson and his partners continued to seek U.S. government contracts in the spring of 1861, refusing to "let their secessionist sympathies stand in the way of a profitable business deal" (75).

63. Ibid., 39–40.

64. Robert Cook, *Baptism of Fire: The Republican Party in Iowa, 1838–1878* (Ames: Iowa State University Press, 1994), 38; Edward L. Ayers, *In the Presence of Mine Enemies: The Civil War in the Heart of America, 1859–1863* (New York: Norton, 2003), 77.

65. William Kauffman Scarborough, *Masters of the Big House: Elite Slaveholders of the Mid-Nineteenth-Century South* (Baton Rouge: Louisiana State University Press, 2003), 285, 152, 287–88.

66. "Have We Exhausted Our Constitutional Remedies?," *Natchez Daily Courier*, 17 November 1860, 1–4, reprinted in *An Appeal to Thinking Men* (1860), at the Huntington Library, San Marino, California.

67. Jonathan Worth, *The Correspondence of Jonathan Worth*, edited by J. G. de Roulhac Hamilton (Raleigh, N.C.: Edwards and Broughton, 1909), 1:130–43.

68. Blight, "They Knew What Time It Was," 63–68.

69. Howard Cecil Perkins, ed., *Northern Editorials on Secession* (1942; Gloucester, Mass.: Smith, 1964), 1:200, 288.

70. Cooper, *Jefferson Davis, American*, 330.

71. This wording was hardly unique to the Old Dominion. At the end of November 1860, South Carolina's *Florence Gazette* had called for cooperation, at least among the cotton states, in quitting the federal union because "the powers granted under the federal Constitution" had been "perverted to our injury and oppression" (Dumond, *Southern Editorials*, 271).

72. McPherson, *Battle Cry of Freedom*, 235; Dale Baum, *The Shattering of Texas Unionism: Politics in the Lone Star State during the Civil War Era* (Baton Rouge: Louisiana State University Press, 1998), 80, 57–58. See also Robin E. Baker and Dale Baum, "The Texas Voter and the Crisis of the Union, 1859–1861," *Journal of Southern History* 53 (August 1987): 395–420. Ernest William Winkler, ed., *Journal of the Secession Convention of Texas, 1861* (Austin: Texas Library and Historical Commission, 1912) offers much testimony to the accuracy of Baum's analysis.

73. Donald E. Reynolds, *Texas Terrors: The Slave Insurrection Panic of 1860 and the Secession of the Lower South* (Baton Rouge: Louisiana State University Press, 2007), 200–203.

74. Scarborough, *Masters of the Big House*, 287; Freehling, *Road to Disunion*, 2:369, 361. On Unionism in the Upper South, see Crofts, *Reluctant Confederates*.

75. Freehling, *Road to Disunion*, 2:388; Cooper, *Jefferson Davis, American*, 359–60.

76. Robert W. Fogel, *Without Consent or Contract: The Rise and Fall of American Slavery* (New York: Norton, 1989), 63.

77. David Detzer, *Allegiance: Fort Sumter, Charleston, and the Beginning of the Civil War* (New York: Harcourt, 2001), 14.

78. Potter, *Impending Crisis*, 386–88; Earl Schenck Miers, introduction to Hinton Rowan Helper, *The Impending Crisis of the South: How to Meet It* (New York: Collier, 1963); Manisha Sinha, *The Counterrevolution of Slavery: Politics and Ideology in Antebellum South Carolina* (Chapel Hill: University of North Carolina Press, 2000), 208–15; Shearer Davis Bowman, *Masters and Lords: Mid-19th-Century U.S. Planters and Prussian Junkers* (New York: Oxford University Press, 1993), 157–58.

79. Charles C. Bolton, *Poor Whites of the Antebellum South: Tenants and Laborers in Central North Carolina and Northeast Mississippi* (Durham: Duke University Press, 1994), 56; Martin Crawford, *Ashe County's Civil War: Community and Society in the Appalachian South* (Charlottesville: University Press of Virginia, 2001), 64–65; Potter, *Impending Crisis*, 386–88; Freehling, *Road to Disunion*, vol. 2; John C. Inscoe, *Mountain Masters: Slavery and the Sectional Crisis in North Carolina* (1989; Knoxville: University of Tennessee Press, 1996), 145–49.

80. See esp. Freehling, *Road to Disunion*, 2:367–68; John Ashworth, *Slavery, Capitalism, and Politics in the Antebellum Republic*, vol. 2, *The Coming of the Civil War, 1850–1861* (Cambridge: Cambridge University Press, 2007), 136.

81. Roy Franklin Nichols, *The Disruption of American Democracy* (New York: Free Press, 1948), 370–71; Freehling, *Road to Disunion*, 2:406–8.

82. Anthony Gene Carey, *Politics, Slavery, and the Union in Antebellum Georgia* (Athens: University of Georgia Press, 1997), 237–38.

83. Dew, *Apostles of Disunion*, 46–47.

84. Emory M. Thomas, *The Confederate Nation, 1861–1865* (New York: Harper and Row, 1979), 78; Freehling, *Road to Disunion*, 2:503, 389.

CHAPTER 3

1. Julia M. H. Smith, *Europe after Rome: A New Cultural History, 500–1000* (Oxford: Oxford University Press, 2005), 101. Invaluable to any study of honor in the nineteenth-century United States is Samuel Haber, *The Quest for Authority and Honor in the American Professions, 1750–1900* (Chicago: University of Chicago Press, 1991), which focuses on the important interior river ports of Memphis and Cincinnati. My serious quest to understand honor historically began in a graduate school research seminar at the University of California at Berkeley directed by Professor Haber in which I wrote a paper, "Gentlemen and Gentry in Antebellum Virginia" (1976). Years later, I took another stab at understanding honor in "Honor and Martialism in the U.S. South and Prussian East Elbia in the Mid-Nineteenth Century," in *What Made the South Different?*, edited by Kees Gispen (Jackson: University Press of Mississippi, 1990), 19–40.

2. Robert M. Calhoun, *Evangelicals and Conservatives in the Early South, 1740–1861* (Columbia: University of South Carolina Press, 1988), 193–96; Erskine Clarke, *Dwelling Place: A Plantation Epic* (New Haven: Yale University Press, 2005), 397–99, 403–5, 485–86, 339.

3. James Bowman, *Honor: A History* (New York: Encounter, 2006), 15–92. Honor is "a creature of popular sentiment and opinion. It need not be connected to a clear moral impulse." In "actual honor cultures," people "regard as honorable what they honor"—that is, that which they respect and to which they assign elevated status. They view "as dishonorable what they despise, irrespective of what moral and political philosophers tell them they ought to honor or despise" (4, 35).

4. Clarke, *Dwelling Place*, 399; Robert Manson Myers, ed., *The Children of Pride: A True Story of Georgia and the Civil War* (New Haven: Yale University Press, 1972), 648.

5. Eric Walther, *The Fire-Eaters* (Baton Rouge: Louisiana State University Press, 1992), 176–77, 188.

6. John C. Rives, ed., *The Congressional Globe: Containing the Debates and Proceedings of the Second Session of the Thirty-sixth Congress* (Washington, D.C.: Congressional Globe Office, 1861), 71–76, 85–87.

7. Bertram Wyatt-Brown, *The Shaping of Southern Culture: Honor, Grace, and War, 1760s–1890s* (Chapel Hill: University of North Carolina Press, 2001), 178.

8. Roswell Hawks Lamson, *Lamson of the Gettysburg: The Civil War Letters of Lieutenant Roswell H. Lamson, U.S. Navy*, edited by James M. McPherson and Patricia R. McPherson (New York: Oxford University Press, 1997), 11.

9. Rives, *Congressional Globe*, 99–104.

10. Hans L. Trefousse, "Wade, Benjamin Franklin," in *American National Biography*, edited by John A. Garraty and Mark C. Carnes (New York: Oxford University Press, 1999), 22:431–32; James M. McPherson, *Battle Cry of Freedom: The Civil War Era* (New York: Oxford University Press, 1988), 227–28.

11. Walter Brian Cisco, *Wade Hampton: Confederate Warrior, Conservative Statesman* (Washington, D.C.: Brassey's, 2004), 47–48; Rod Andrew Jr., *Wade Hampton: Confed-

erate *Warrior to Southern Redeemer* (Chapel Hill: University of North Carolina Press, 2008), 32–35, 452–53. See also Drew Gilpin Faust, *James Henry Hammond and the Old South: A Design for Mastery* (Baton Rouge: Louisiana State University Press, 1982), 241–43: "The Hamptons and their kin . . . determined that Hammond must be destroyed." Faust sees "the unquestioning devotion" of these young girls as "a temptation that this desperately lonely and needy man could not resist." It subsequently became known that Hammond also had long-term affairs with a slave mother and her daughter.

12. After the Civil War, Morris, like Wade, received a federal appointment to a position with the Union Pacific Railroad, Morris as a commissioner, Wade as a government director (*Biographical Directory of United States Congress, 1774–Present*, http:/bioguide .congress.gov/biosearch/biosearch.asp [accessed 9 January 2010]).

13. Rives, *Congressional Globe*, appendix, 51–57.

14. Jonathan Worth, *The Correspondence of Jonathan Worth*, edited by J. G. de Roulhac Hamilton (Raleigh, N.C.: Edwards and Broughton, 1909), 141; Robert Jefferson Breckinridge, *The Civil War: Its Nature and End* (Cincinnati, 1861), in *Southern Unionist Pamphlets and the Civil War*, edited by Jon L. Wakelyn (Columbia: University of Missouri Press, 1999), 29–30.

15. Although Confederate cannon caused no casualties among Anderson's troops, Morris proved prescient about the patriotic anger and indignation that came out of the trans-Appalachian free states after the Confederate bombardment of Fort Sumter (McPherson, *Battle Cry of Freedom*, 274).

16. *Boston Globe* as quoted in Russell McClintock, *Lincoln and the Decision for War: The Northern Response to Secession* (Chapel Hill: University of North Carolina Press, 2008), 109.

17. David Detzer, *Allegiance: Fort Sumter, Charleston, and the Beginning of the Civil War* (New York: Harcourt, 2001), 184–86.

18. Nicole Etcheson, *The Emerging Midwest: Upland Southerners and the Political Culture of the Old Northwest, 1787–1861* (Bloomington: Indiana University Press, 1996).

19. Ibid.; Bertram Wyatt-Brown, *Honor and Violence in the Old South* (New York: Oxford University Press, 1986), 20. This volume is an abbreviated and somewhat revised version of Bertram Wyatt-Brown, *Southern Honor: Ethics and Behavior in the Old South* (New York: Oxford University Press, 1982). Other provocative studies that present analogous views of southern honor include Peter W. Bardaglio, *Reconstructing the Household: Families, Sex, and the Law in the Nineteenth-Century South* (Chapel Hill: University of North Carolina Press, 1995); Kenneth S. Greenberg, *Honor and Slavery* (Princeton: Princeton University Press, 1996); Ariela J. Gross, *Double Character: Slavery and Mastery in the Southern Courtroom* (Athens: University of Georgia Press, 2000); Christopher J. Olsen, *Political Culture and Secession in Mississippi: Masculinity, Honor, and the Antiparty Tradition* (New York: Oxford University Press, 2000); Peter S. Carmichael, *The Last Generation: Young Virginians in Peace, War, and Reunion* (Chapel Hill: University of North Carolina Press, 2005); Andrew, *Wade Hampton*, esp. xii–xiv, where the author introduces "three themes to explain the cultural influences and socialization of Hampton in the first half of his life. 'Paternalism,' 'honor,' and 'chivalry' are terms that historians have often used to define the ideals of men and women of Hampton's place and time."

20. Orville Vernon Burton, *The Age of Lincoln* (New York: Hill and Wang, 2007),

107–9. Burton's explanation for Thomas Lincoln's decision to leave Kentucky for Indiana seems seriously incomplete (112). For a more convincing account, see Lowell H. Harrison, *Lincoln of Kentucky* (Lexington: University Press of Kentucky, 2000), 22–24.

21. See Shearer Davis Bowman, "Honor and Martialism." On the fatal 1838 duel between Congressmen Jonathan Cilley of Maine and William Graves of Kentucky, see Steven M. Stowe, *Intimacy and Power in the Old South: Ritual in the Lives of the Planters* (Baltimore: Johns Hopkins University Press, 1987), 38–49.

22. David Herbert Donald, *Lincoln* (New York: Simon and Schuster, 1996), 91.

23. Ibid., 90–93; Harrison, *Lincoln of Kentucky*, 72–73; Catherine Clinton, *Mrs. Lincoln: A Life* (New York: HarperCollins, 2009), 56–57.

24. Amy Greenberg, *Manifest Manhood and the Antebellum American Empire* (Cambridge: Cambridge University Press, 2005), 139. See also Christopher Phillips, *Missouri's Confederate: Claiborne Fox Jackson and the Creation of Southern Identity in the Border West* (Columbia: University of Missouri Press, 2000), 97–98; Douglas Montagna, "'Choked Him til His Tongue Protruded': Violence, the Code of Honor, and Methodist Clergy in the Antebellum Ohio Valley," *Ohio Valley History* 7 (Winter 2007): esp. 27.

25. Robert W. Johannsen, *Stephen A. Douglas* (New York: Oxford University Press, 1973), 850.

26. Herschel Gower, *Charles Dahlgren of Natchez: The Civil War and Dynastic Decline* (Washington, D.C.: Brassey's, 2002), 41–42, 12–13: "The years at sea taught all three Dahlgren brothers the code expected of a nineteenth-century naval officer. 'Dueling was the ritualistic expression of honor, the code of the gentlemen,' as John Dahlgren's biographer observed."

27. Julia M. H. Smith, *Europe after Rome*, 108.

28. *McPherson, Battle Cry of Freedom*, 231; Abraham Lincoln, "Proclamation Calling Militia and Convening Congress, April 15, 1861," in Abraham Lincoln, *Speeches and Writings, 1859–1865*, edited by Don E. Fehrenbacher (New York: Library of America, 1989), 232.

29. David J. Silbey, *A War of Frontier and Empire: The Philippine-American War, 1899–1902* (New York: Hill and Wang, 2007), 90.

30. Debby Applegate, *The Most Famous Man in America: The Biography of Henry Ward Beecher* (New York: Three Leaves/Doubleday, 2006), 281.

31. *Dubuque Herald* as quoted in McPherson, *Battle Cry of Freedom*, 225; Louis Auchincloss, ed., *The Hone and Strong Diaries of Old Manhattan* (New York: Abbeville, 1989), 197–98.

32. Calhoun, *Evangelicals and Conservatives*, 145–46. Armstrong's name does not appear in Ernest Trice Thompson, *Presbyterians in the South*, vol. 1, *1607–1861* (Richmond, Va.: Knox, 1963).

33. Robert W. Johannsen, *Lincoln, the South, and Slavery: The Political Dimension* (Baton Rouge: Louisiana State University Press, 1991), 90 n. 26.

34. Harold Holzer, *Lincoln at Cooper Union: The Speech That Made Abraham Lincoln President* (New York: Simon and Schuster, 2004), 203, 246–47.

35. On slavery as dishonor and therefore "social death" throughout history, the classic argument comes from historical sociologist Orlando Patterson, *Slavery and Social Death: A Comparative Study* (Cambridge: Harvard University Press, 1982); on the Old South,

see esp. 94–97. For valuable insights into northern racial attitudes, see John Corrigan, *Business of the Heart: Religion and Emotion in the Nineteenth Century* (Berkeley: University of California Press, 2002), 241–48, which discusses white Bostonians' construction of African American emotionality as "outside the range of acceptable or even human emotionality." Consequently, like blacks, abolitionists "were made out to be both fanatics and emotionally deficient, unfeeling promoters of a grand scheme of social change." In 1855, Boston had 2,216 black residents (about 1.3 percent of the population); 60 percent had been born in Massachusetts.

36. James Oakes, *Slavery and Freedom: An Interpretation of the Old South* (New York: Knopf, 1990), 15; Gross, *Double Character*, 50.

37. Cobb's speech is available, with fine editorial commentary, in William W. Freehling and Craig M. Simpson, eds., *Secession Debated: Georgia's Showdown in 1860* (New York: Oxford University Press, 1992), 3–30; quotation on 11–12.

38. A powerful and highly readable narrative account is Stephen B. Oates, *The Fires of Jubilee: Nat Turner's Fierce Rebellion* (New York: Harper and Row, 1975); but see also Deborah Gray White, "Let My People Go: 1804–1860," in *To Make Our World Anew: A History of African Americans*, edited by Robin D. G. Kelley and Earl Lewis (New York: Oxford University Press, 2000), 197–98.

39. Philip J. Schwarz, *Twice Condemned: Slaves and the Criminal Law of Virginia, 1705–1865* (Baton Rouge: Louisiana State University Press, 1988), 239, ix, citing Patterson, *Slavery and Social Death*, 39, 339.

40. Olsen, *Political Culture and Secession*, 8–9. Olsen emphasizes the absence of a "real party tradition" and the presence of both "a regional ethic of honor" and a "manly imperative" in antebellum Mississippi and the Lower South.

41. Manisha Sinha, *The Counterrevolution of Slavery: Politics and Ideology in Antebellum South Carolina* (Chapel Hill: University of North Carolina Press, 2000), 248.

42. *Douglass' Monthly*, February 1863, as cited in Rogan Kersch, *Dreams of a More Perfect Union* (Ithaca: Cornell University Press, 2001), 188; Frederick Douglass, *My Bondage and My Freedom*, edited by William L. Andrews (1855; Urbana: University of Illinois Press, 1987), 152; William S. McFeely, *Frederick Douglass* (New York: Norton: 1991), 218. See also Patterson, *Slavery and Social Death*, 13.

43. Quoted in Holzer, *Lincoln at Cooper Union*, 244–45.

44. Although François Furstenberg does not explicitly address the meaning or issue of honor, I am indebted to insights provided by *In the Name of the Father: Washington's Legacy, Slavery, and the Making of a Nation* (New York: Penguin, 2006), which takes as its overarching thesis the idea that the "exigency of reconciling slavery within a republican nationalism had, in short, promoted an impoverished meaning of [political] consent [to constitutional authority] based on an idealized image of individual achievement [embodied in civic texts about George Washington]. The conviction that Americans had single-handedly emancipated themselves from political slavery [to Britain] allowed them to shackle others in the bonds of slavery" (220–21).

45. David W. Blight, introduction to Frederick Douglass, *Narrative of the Life of Frederick Douglass, an American Slave, Written by Himself, with Related Documents*, 2nd ed. (Boston: Bedford/St. Martin's, 2003), 20.

46. Douglass, *My Bondage and My Freedom*, 158; Douglass, *Narrative*, 76.

47. Douglas L. Wilson, *Honor's Voice: The Transformation of Abraham Lincoln* (New York: Knopf, 1998), 8, 278–79, 289–91; William Lee Miller, *Lincoln's Virtues: An Ethical Biography* (New York: Knopf, 2002), 77–79; Stephen Berry, *House of Abraham: Lincoln and the Todds, a Family Divided by War* (Boston: Houghton Mifflin, 2007), 32–37; Clinton, *Mrs. Lincoln*, 51. Wilson offers a convincing account of Lincoln's apparently "conscious emphasis on honorable, or at least unobjectionable, behavior," including his feeling of obligation to follow the gentleman's code of honor and his feeling "honor bound" to wed Mary Todd.

48. Constance Brittain Bouchard, *Strong of Body, Brave and Noble: Chivalry and Society in Medieval France* (Ithaca: Cornell University Press, 1998), 103–16. On courtliness, see also Julia M. H. Smith, *Europe after Rome*, 175–76.

49. Miri Rubin, *The Hollow Crown: A History of Britain in the Late Middle Ages* (New York: Penguin, 2005), 109–13, 300.

50. Carmichael, *Last Generation*, 10–15, discusses the connections between Victorian culture, the Christian gentleman, and the "modernizing" or "bourgeois" spirit. John Kasson, *Rudeness and Civilities: Manners in Nineteenth-Century Urban America* (New York: Hill and Wang, 1990), argues for the growing importance of polite, mannerly decorum among those becoming "middle class."

51. Julia M. H. Smith, *Europe after Rome*, 123; Haber, *Quest for Authority*, 102–3. "While evangelical Protestantism, political democracy, and market capitalism frequently discountenanced customary rankings in society, they did not challenge rankings as such" (Haber, *Quest for Authority*, 98).

52. Joanne B. Freeman, *Affairs of Honor: National Politics in the New Republic* (New Haven: Yale University Press, 2001), xvi; Wyatt-Brown, *Honor and Violence*, viii.

53. Max Weber, "National Character and the Junkers," in *From Max Weber: Essays in Sociology*, translated and edited by H. H. Gerth and C. Wright Mills (New York: Oxford University Press, 1946), 292; Julia M. H. Smith, *Europe after Rome*, 177; Amy Greenberg, *Manifest Manhood and the Antebellum American Empire*, esp. 140.

54. Applegate, *Most Famous Man*, 319–21. Beecher's message came back to haunt him after his sexual indiscretions came to light; he knew that his church's leading men, in the words of trustee Henry Bowen, were "troubled about the extremely suspicious relations of Mr. Beecher with certain ladies of the church. It was a matter of common talk, and excited the gravest apprehensions." On Beecher during the 1850s and 1860s and on the Tipton scandal, see also Milton Rugoff, *The Beechers: An American Family in the Nineteenth Century* (New York: Harper and Row, 1981), chapters 20, 25.

55. Edward L. Ayers, *Vengeance and Justice: Crime and Punishment in the 19th-Century American South* (New York: Oxford University Press, 1984), 28.

56. Clement Eaton, *Jefferson Davis* (New York: Free Press, 1977), 50.

57. Haber, *Quest for Authority*, 98; James Bowman, *Honor*, 120.

58. Mark Voss-Hubbard, *Beyond Party: Cultures of Antipartisanship in Northern Politics before the Civil War* (Baltimore: Johns Hopkins University Press, 2002), 7. Corrigan, *Business of the Heart*, 253, concludes that during evangelical revivals—in particular, Boston's emotional 1857–58 "Businessmen's Revival," which had clear parallels in New York and Chicago—"The difference between the masculinized public sphere and the feminized private sphere each leaked into the other, informing and altering it."

59. Elizabeth Scott Neblett, *A Rebel Wife in Texas: The Diary and Letters of Elizabeth Scott Neblett, 1852–1964*, edited and introduction by Erika L. Murr (Baton Rouge: Louisiana State University Press, 2001), 35. The editor notes that even after Scott married and bore five children, she "never reconciled the tensions between her personal ambitions and society's expectations of her as a woman" (12).

60. Anne C. Rose, *Voices of the Marketplace: American Thought and Culture, 1830–1860* (Lanham, Md.: Rowman and Littlefield, 1995), esp. 40–41, 73–76; Glenna Matthews, "'Little Women' Who Helped Make This Great War," in *Why the Civil War Came*, edited by Gabor S. Boritt (New York: Oxford University Press, 1996), 42–43; Elizabeth R. Varon, *We Mean to Be Counted: White People and Politics in Antebellum Virginia* (Chapel Hill: University of North Carolina Press, 1998).

61. Allan Nevins, *Ordeal of the Union: Selected Chapters*, edited by E. B. Long (New York: Scribner's, 1973), 207, 214.

62. Larry Ceplair, ed., *The Public Years of Sarah and Angelina Grimké: Selected Writings, 1835–1839* (New York: Columbia University Press, 1989), 103; Gerda Lerner, *The Grimké Sisters from South Carolina: Pioneers for Woman's Rights and Abolition* (1967; New York: Schocken, 1971), 10–11.

63. Basil Armstrong Thomassen, *North Carolina Yeoman: The Diary of Basil Armstrong Thomassen, 1853–1862*, edited by Paul D. Escott (Athens: University of Georgia Press, 1996), 29, 141; see also 315.

64. Stephanie McCurry, *Masters of Small Worlds: Yeoman Households, Gender Relations, and the Political Culture of the Antebellum South Carolina Low Country* (New York: Oxford University Press, 1995), 221–23; Louisa Susanna Cheves McCord, *Louisa S. McCord: Political and Social Essays*, edited by Richard C. Lounsbury (Charlottesville: University Press of Virginia, 1995), 1–11, 222–44.

65. McFeely, *Frederick Douglass*, 155–56; for the photograph, see Rose, *Voices of the Marketplace*, 16.

66. McCurry, *Masters of Small Worlds*, 304.

67. Elizabeth Fox-Genovese and Eugene D. Genovese, *The Mind of the Master Class: History and Faith in the Southern Slaveholders' Worldview* (Cambridge: Cambridge University Press, 2005), 118.

68. William J. Cooper Jr. and Thomas E. Terrill, *The American South: A History*, 3rd ed. (Boston: McGraw-Hill, 2002), 277.

69. Wyatt-Brown, *Honor and Violence*, ix.

70. John C. Calhoun, "Speech on the Reception of Abolition Petitions, February 6, 1837, Revised Report," in *Union and Liberty: The Political Philosophy of John C. Calhoun*, edited by Ross M. Lence (Indianapolis: Liberty Fund, 1992), 469, 474. "The defensive tone of much proslavery rhetoric was provoked by the rise of militant abolitionism in the North after 1830" (James M. McPherson, *This Mighty Scourge: Perspectives on the Civil War* [New York: Oxford University Press, 2007], 13).

71. *Philadelphia Inquirer*, 23 February 1861, in Howard Cecil Perkins, ed., *Northern Editorials on Secession* (1942; Gloucester, Mass.: Smith, 1964), 1:286.

72. Wyatt-Brown, *Honor and Violence*, ix.

73. Tilden as quoted in McClintock, *Lincoln and the Decision for War*, 30–33.

74. Tryphena Blanche Holder Fox, *A Northern Woman in the Plantation South: Letters*

of Tryphena Blanche Holder Fox, 1856–1876, edited by Wilma King (Columbia: University of South Carolina Press, 1993), 57, 86, 61, 114–116.

75. Joshua D. Rothman, *Notorious in the Neighborhood: Sex and Families across the Color Line in Virginia, 1787–1861* (Chapel Hill: University of North Carolina Press, 2003), 228–42. See also Norrece T. Jones Jr., "Rape in Black and White: Sexual Violence in the Testimony of Enslaved and Free Americans," in *Slavery and the American South,* edited by Winthrop D. Jordan (Jackson: University Press of Mississippi, 2003), 93–108, and the commentary by Jan Lewis, 108–16.

76. Bruce Thornton, *Greek Ways: How the Greeks Created Western Civilization* (New York: MJF, 2000), 27.

77. See esp. E. M. Halliday, *Understanding Thomas Jefferson* (New York: Harper-Collins, 2001), 100–101, which includes a very helpful reproduction of van der Werff's painting. Halliday makes use of a perceptive and underappreciated biography by Page Smith, *Jefferson: A Revealing Biography* (1976; republished as *Jefferson: Architect of America* [New York: iBooks, 2002]). This was the first biography to respond favorably to the psychological hypotheses presented two years earlier by Fawn Brodie in *Thomas Jefferson, an Intimate History* (New York: Norton, 1974) about how Jefferson turned to Sally Hemings for romantic solace after the end of his roller-coaster affair with Cosway. The attractive Hemings was the half-sister of Jefferson's deceased and beloved wife, and there is no way to determine what mixture of coercion and affection characterized their relationship, as is the case with many interracial liaisons in the Old South.

78. See David Brion Davis, *Inhuman Bondage: The Rise and Fall of Slavery in the New World* (New York: Oxford University Press, 2006), esp. 145, 155.

79. George M. Fredrickson, *The Black Image in the White Mind: The Debate on Afro-American Culture and Destiny, 1817–1914* (New York: Harper Torchbooks, 1971), xiii.

80. Ella Gertrude Clanton Thomas, *The Secret Eye: The Journal of Ella Gertrude Clanton Thomas, 1848–1889,* edited by Virginia Ingraham Burr, introduction by Nell Irvin Painter (Chapel Hill: University of North Carolina Press, 1990), 45–46, 50–52.

81. Ibid. Thomas's journal from mid-March 1859 to early July 1861 is not extant; however, on 13 July 1861, she paid homage to "the glory of the gallant little state of South Carolina" (183).

82. Painter, introduction to Thomas, *Secret Eye,* Edward E. Baptist, "'Cuffy,' 'Fancy Maids,' and 'One-Eyed Men': Rape, Commodification, and the Domestic Slave Trade in the United States," in *The Chattel Principle: Internal Slave Trades in the Americas,* edited by Walter Johnson (New Haven: Yale University Press, 2004), 182. Melton McLaurin, *Celia, a Slave* (Athens: University of Georgia Press, 1991), tells a harrowing tale from the 1850s of a widowed master in Missouri who repeatedly raped his young female slave, who in turn murdered him and disposed of his body in gruesome fashion.

83. See Richard E. Beringer, Herman Hattaway, Archer Jones, and William N. Still Jr., *Why the South Lost the Civil War* (Athens: University of Georgia Press, 1986), chapter 14, "God, Guilt, and the Confederacy in Collapse."

CHAPTER 4

1. Harold Holzer, *Lincoln at Cooper Union: The Speech That Made Abraham Lincoln President* (New York: Simon and Schuster, 2004), 4.

2. Jonathan M. Berkey, "Douglass, Frederick," in *The Oxford Companion to United States History*, edited by Paul S. Boyer (New York: Oxford University Press, 2001), 193. See also David W. Blight's first-rate introduction to Frederick Douglass, *Narrative of the Life of Frederick Douglass, an American Slave, Written by Himself, with Related Documents*, 2nd ed. (Boston: Bedford/St. Martin's, 2003).

3. For more on Douglas, see Robert W. Johannsen, "Douglas, Stephen Arnold," in *American National Biography*, edited by John A. Garraty and Mark C. Carnes (New York: Oxford University Press, 1991), 6:805–8; Robert W. Johannsen, *Stephen A. Douglas* (New York: Oxford University Press, 1973).

4. Johannsen, "Douglas."

5. See Hendrik V. Booraem, *The Formation of the Republican Party in New York: Politics and Conscience in the Antebellum North* (New York: New York University Press, 1983), 83–84.

6. Joel H. Silbey, *Martin Van Buren and the Emergence of American Popular Politics* (Lanham, Md.: Rowman and Littlefield, 2002), 12–15. After the War of 1812, Van Buren emerged as chief first of the Bucktail faction of the state's Jeffersonian Republican Party and later of the Albany Regency, which rewarded loyalty by appointments to public office or perhaps by public contracts to private contractors—i.e., patronage. At the state constitutional convention of 1821, Van Buren anticipated his coming political alliance with Jackson's egalitarian persona by supporting lower property qualifications for voting. Yet his "habitual caution" in the face of demands for radical change, plus his focus on building a strong and unified Jeffersonian Republican organization in the state, explain his opposition to populist demands that more state and local offices be popularly elected; he preferred to maintain the governor's power to appoint these officeholders.

7. As Martin traveled all over the state attending courts of common pleas and courts of chancery, according to biographer John Niven, Hannah's "lack of pretense, her unruffled disposition, and her thoughtfulness were just what her husband needed." Possibly "more than anything else, she made no demands upon him" (*Martin Van Buren: The Romantic Age of American Politics* [New York: Oxford University Press, 1983], 24–25).

8. James Henretta, "Martin Van Buren," in *The American Presidency*, edited by Alan Brinkley and Davis Dyer (New York: Houghton Mifflin, 2004), 104–5; Joel H. Silbey, *Martin Van Buren*, 157–60. According to Daniel Walker Howe, "Van Buren's relaxed style in the White House, emphasizing gracious living, did not make for effective legislative management" (*What Hath God Wrought: The Transformation of America, 1815–1848* [New York: Oxford University Press, 2007], 507).

9. Robert V. Remini, *Henry Clay, Statesman for the Union* (New York: Norton, 1991), 237–38, 260, 268–69, 286.

10. Jonathan H. Earle, *Jacksonian Antislavery and the Politics of Free Soil, 1824–1854* (Chapel Hill: University of North Carolina Press, 2004), 6.

11. Howe, *What Hath God Wrought*, 544. Workers in manufactures might vote Democrat or Whig, but "in the long run a majority of the industrial working-class ended up captured by the Democrats," especially after the mass migration of relatively inexpensive Irish laborers began in the 1840s. As president, Van Buren in fact orchestrated but a single "small achievement for labor" when "he mandated a ten-hour day for laborers on federal public works" by executive order in March 1840 (544, 549–50).

12. John F. Marszalek, *The Petticoat Affair: Manner, Mutiny, and Sex in Andrew Jackson's White House* (Baton Rouge: Louisiana State University Press, 1997), 21, vii, 239; William W. Freehling, *The Road to Disunion* (New York: Oxford University Press, 2007), 1:270; Howe, *What Hath God Wrought*, 336–39.

13. Nicholas Onuf and Peter Onuf, *Nations, Markets, and War: Modern History and the American Civil War* (Charlottesville: University of Virginia Press, 2006), 165.

14. John C. Calhoun, "Speech on the Reception of Abolition Petitions [February 6, 1837], Revised Report," in *Union and Liberty: The Political Philosophy of John C. Calhoun*, edited by Ross M. Lence (Indianapolis: Liberty Fund, 1992), 473. For a lengthy reiteration of this argument on the eve of the Civil War by a Democratic northern journalist sympathetic to the South (but who supported the Union during the war), see Thomas P. Kettell, *Southern Wealth and Northern Profits*, edited by Fletcher M. Green (1860; University: University of Alabama Press, 1965). Kettell noted Calhoun's support for the first protective tariff of 1816 and his opposition to the protective tariffs of 1828 and 1832, when South Carolina undertook "gallant resistance" to the federal government during the nullification controversy of 1832–33. "It was thus that Mr. Calhoun supported the government when it was too weak, and opposed it when it was too strong" (162–63).

15. For a clear and concise discussion of the crucial distinction between postmillennial and premillennial perspectives in Christianity, see Howe, *What Hath God Wrought*, 285–89.

16. Robert Cook, *Baptism of Fire: The Republican Party in Iowa, 1838–1878* (Ames: Iowa State University Press, 1994), 23–24; Larry Schweikert, *Banking in the American South from the Age of Jackson to Reconstruction* (Baton Rouge: Louisiana State University Press, 1987), 278.

17. Sean Wilentz, *The Rise of American Democracy, Jefferson to Lincoln* (New York: Norton, 2005), 455. Jackson rewarded his loyal political lieutenant with the vice presidential spot on the 1832 ticket, railroading him through the Democratic National Convention by imposing the two-thirds rule for party nominees that would survive until 1936. In 1835–36, Van Buren was presented as the alternative to a third term in office for Jackson, who wanted to respect the precedent set by Washington. Van Buren won the election of 1836 against a trio of regional opposition candidates who had hoped that together they might deny the Little Magician a majority in the Electoral College and thereby throw the election into the House of Representatives. Daniel Webster of Massachusetts and future president William Henry Harrison of Ohio were put forward by anti-Jackson National Republicans, who were in the process of becoming nationalistic Whigs. In the South, Hugh Lawson White of Tennessee, with Tyler as his running mate, represented former Jacksonians (including Calhoun, South Carolina's most eminent nullifier and proslavery spokesman) who viewed Jackson's aggressive use of executive power as a violation of their state's rights principles and thus indirectly a potential threat to the stability of slave society. Although Van Buren won the election of 1836 outright, Harrison and Tyler came together in 1840 to deny the New Yorker a second term. In 1836, Van Buren won the Electoral College 170–113, much closer than Jackson's 1832 margin of 219–32.

18. David Brion Davis, *Inhuman Bondage: The Rise and Fall of Slavery in the New World* (New York: Oxford University Press, 2006), 156.

19. Ibid., 160.

20. Edward P. Crapol, *John Tyler, the Accidental President* (Chapel Hill: University of North Carolina Press, 2006), 255; Leonard L. Richards, *"Gentlemen of Property and Standing": Anti-Abolition Mobs in Jacksonian America* (New York: Oxford University Press, 1970), 55–58.

21. Crapol, *John Tyler*, 47–48; William G. Shade, *Democratizing the Old Dominion: Virginia and the Second Party System, 1824–1861* (Charlottesville: University Press of Virginia, 1996), 23; Michael F. Holt, *The Fate of Their Country: Politicians, Slavery Extension, and the Coming of the Civil War* (New York: Hill and Wang, 2004), 6; Shearer Davis Bowman, *Masters and Lords: Mid-19th-Century U.S. Planters and Prussian Junkers* (New York: Oxford University Press, 1993), 143.

22. Crapol, *John Tyler*, 58–59, 235.

23. See Freehling, *Road to Disunion*, 1:313–36; Howe, *What Hath God Wrought*, 513.

24. Howe, *What Hath God Wrought*, 513; Bruce Levine, *Half Slave and Half Free: The Roots of the Civil War*, rev. ed. (New York: Hill and Wang/Farrar, Straus, and Giroux, 2005), 168.

25. In Georgia, Calhounites were defined by "their virulent antiparty spirit, their emphasis on southern unity, and their willingness to attack the national party system to promote sectional goals" (Anthony Gene Carey, *Politics, Slavery, and the Union in Antebellum Georgia* [Athens: University of Georgia Press, 1997], 66).

26. Joel H. Silbey, *Martin Van Buren*, 103; Joel H. Silbey, *Storm over Texas: The Annexation Controversy and the Road to the Civil War* (New York: Oxford University Press, 2005), 103, 21. A good study of Calhoun is John Niven, *John C. Calhoun and the Price of Union: A Biography* (Baton Rouge: Louisiana State University Press, 1988).

27. Jules Witcover, *Party of the People: A History of the Democrats* (New York: Random House, 2003), chapter 8.

28. Don E. Fehrenbacher and Ward M. McAfee, *The Slaveholding Republic: An Account of the United States Government's Relations to Slavery* (New York: Oxford University Press, 2001), 120, 126.

29. See Crapol, *John Tyler*, 3–6; Howe, *What Hath God Wrought*, 589–90.

30. Onuf and Onuf, *Nations, Markets, and War*, 291, 271.

31. Crapol, *John Tyler*; 61, 249.

32. On Polk, see esp. William Dusinberre, *Slavemaster President: The Double Career of James Polk* (New York: Oxford University Press, 2003), chapter 11, "Texas and the Mexican War."

33. Larry K. Menna, "Southern Whiggery and Economic Development: The Meaning of Slavery within a National Context," in *The Meaning of Slavery in the North*, edited by Martin Blatt and David Roediger (New York: Garland, 1998), 55, 67.

34. Gary J. Kornblith, "Rethinking the Coming of the Civil War: A Counterfactual Exercise," *Journal of American History* 90 (June 2003): 102. In addition, both the 1840 and 1844 election can be seen as the zenith of second party system, after which the economic issues that had separated the parties nationally began to lose their salience.

35. See Carey, *Politics, Slavery, and the Union*, esp. 58–76, 220, 233; quotation on 72. Also helpful is Brooks D. Simpson, "Cobb, Howell," in *American National Biography*, edited by Garraty and Carnes, 5:99–100.

36. See Crapol, *John Tyler*, 259–65. Still helpful is Robert Gray Gunderson, *Old*

Gentlemen's Convention: The Washington Peace Conference of 1861 (Madison: University of Wisconsin Press, 1961), quotation on 6.

37. Earle, *Jacksonian Antislavery*, esp. 12–13.

38. Ibid., 188; Doris Kearns Goodwin, *Team of Rivals: The Political Genius of Abraham Lincoln* (New York: Simon and Schuster, 2005), 135; Howe, *What Hath God Wrought*, 546. On northern Democrats who intended to make the Democracy antislavery during the 1850s and even hoped that President Franklin Pierce would help their cause, see Yonatan Eyal, *The Young America Movement and the Transformation of the Democratic Party, 1828–1861* (Cambridge: Cambridge University Press, 2007), esp. 189.

39. On Loco-Focoism, see Earle, *Jacksonian Antislavery*, 218 n. 8; Howe, *What Hath God Wrought*, 546.

40. Robert J. Scarry, *Millard Fillmore* (Jefferson, N.C.: McFarland, 2001), 311–12.

41. Joseph P. Reidy, *From Slavery to Agrarian Capitalism in the Cotton Plantation South: Central Georgia, 1800–1880* (Chapel Hill: University of North Carolina Press, 1992), 89.

42. Carey, *Politics, Slavery, and the Union*, 215.

43. Howell Cobb, *Letter . . . to the People of Georgia* (1860), in *Southern Pamphlets on Secession, November 1860–April 1861*, edited by Jon L. Wakelyn (Chapel Hill: University of North Carolina Press, 1996), 88–100; quotations on 89, 94, 98. During the Civil War, Cobb achieved the rank of major general. On the organization of the Confederacy, a recent and readable account is William C. Davis, *Look Away: A History of the Confederate States of America* (New York: Free Press, 2003), chapter 3.

44. Forrest McDonald, *States' Rights and the Union: Imperium in Imperio, 1776–1876* (Lawrence: University Press of Kansas, 2000), 184; Abraham Lincoln, *Speeches and Writings, 1859–1865*, edited by Don E. Fehrenbacher (New York: Library of America, 1989), 117.

45. Tracy Campbell, *Deliver the Vote: A History of Election Fraud, an American Political Tradition, 1742–2004* (New York: Carroll and Graf, 2005), 49.

46. Many recent historians have asked, as William E. Gienapp did, why the Democratic Party survived if it was responsible for the Kansas-Nebraska Act "while the more strongly antislavery Whig party disappeared" and why the Republican Party, "which sought to capitalize on antislavery and anti-Nebraska sentiment in the free states by opposing the expansion of slavery," was "so weak in its first years of existence." Gienapp summarizes what has come to be known as the ethnocultural explanation: "What checked any Whig comeback and led to the party's rapid demise was the emergence in the early 1850s of ethnocultural issues, particularly temperance and nativism, in northern politics," as evidenced in the short-lived success of the Know-Nothings, who "attacked the political power of Catholics and immigrants" ("The Crisis of American Democracy: The Political System and the Coming of the Civil War," in *Why the Civil War Came*, edited by Gabor S. Boritt [New York: Oxford University Press, 1996], 96–99). In response, it can be asked whether the anti-Nebraska state coalitions that organized the Republican Party in 1854–55 were really so weak in the free states, since the new party almost captured the presidency in 1856.

47. This willingness to denounce Buchanan and Lecompton even prompted some eastern Republicans to consider backing Douglas for reelection to the Senate in 1858.

48. Douglas as quoted in James M. McPherson, *Battle Cry of Freedom: The Civil War*

Era (New York: Oxford University Press, 1988), 176–77, which identifies this statement as anticipating the Freeport Doctrine enunciated by Douglas during the 1858 Lincoln-Douglas debates.

49. Ibid., 193–95.

50. Robert W. Johannsen, *Lincoln, the South, and Slavery: The Political Dimension* (Baton Rouge: Louisiana State University Press, 1991), 34, 29, 96–97.

51. Johannsen, *Stephen A. Douglas*, 788–90; William C. Harris, *North Carolina and the Coming of the Civil War* (Raleigh: North Carolina Division of Archives and History, 1989), 32–33.

52. Mark E. Neely Jr., *The Union Divided: Party Conflict in the Civil War North* (Cambridge: Harvard University Press, 2002), 12.

53. Johannsen, *Stephen A. Douglas*, 865–67. See also Neely, *Union Divided*, 14. The story of Douglas's meeting with Lincoln the night of 14 April and of the roles played by both Republican George Ashmun of Massachusetts and Adele Cutts Douglas in the background to that meeting is told well in David Detzer, *Dissonance: The Turbulent Days between Fort Sumter and Bull Run* (Orlando: Harcourt, 2006), 24–26.

54. Adam I. P. Smith, *No Party Now: Politics in the Civil War North* (New York: Oxford University Press, 2006), 3–9; George C. Rable, *The Confederate Republic: A Revolution against Politics* (Chapel Hill: University of North Carolina Press, 1994), 5.

55. See James C. Klotter, *The Breckinridges of Kentucky* (1986; Lexington: University Press of Kentucky, 2006).

56. See Lewis O. Saum, *The Popular Mood of Pre–Civil War America* (Westport, Conn.: Greenwood, 1980), 169, 275. All Luark quotations are from his diary, which he kept from 1846 to 1899 and which is housed in the Michael Fleenen Luark Papers, Special Collections Division, University of Washington Libraries, Seattle; a microfilm copy is available via interlibrary loan.

57. On Lane, see Robert W. Johannsen, *Frontier Politics on the Eve of the Civil War* (Seattle: University of Washington Press, 1955), 59–62.

58. Holman Hamilton, *Prologue to Conflict: The Crisis and Compromise of 1850* (New York: Norton, 1964), 115, 60. See also Daniel W. Crofts, "Bell, John," in *American National Biography*, edited by Garraty and Carnes, 2:509–11; Dusinberre, *Slavemaster President*, 161–65; Joseph H. Parks, *John Bell of Tennessee* (Baton Rouge: Louisiana State University Press, 1950), 244–51. A helpful discussion of unionism in Bell's Nashville and Middle Tennessee can be found in Stephen V. Ash, *Middle Tennessee Society Transformed, 1860–1870: War and Peace in the Upper South* (Baton Rouge: Louisiana State University Press, 1988), esp. 64–72.

59. Daniel Walker Howe, "Everett, Edward," in *American National Biography*, edited by Garraty and Carnes, 7:629–30; Richards, *"Gentlemen of Property and Standing,"* 53.

60. Richard H. Abbott, *Cotton and Capital: Boston Businessmen and Antislavery Reform, 1854–1868* (Amherst: University of Massachusetts Press, 1991), 66; Thomas H. O'Connor, *Civil War Boston: Home Front and Battlefield* (Boston: Northeastern University Press, 1997), 40–44.

61. Quoted in Ollinger Crenshaw, *The Slave States in the Presidential Election of 1860* (1945; Gloucester, Mass.: Smith, 1969), 261.

62. Martha Jane Brazy, *An American Planter: Stephen Duncan of Antebellum Natchez and New York* (Baton Rouge: Louisiana State University Press, 2006), 150–53.

63. William C. Harris, *North Carolina*, 34–39; William Banks Taylor, *King Cotton and Old Glory: Natchez in the Age of Sectional Controversy and Civil War* (Hattiesburg, Miss.: Fox, 1977); Christopher Morris, *Becoming Southern: The Evolution of a Way of Life, Warren County and Vicksburg, 1770–1860* (New York: Oxford University Press, 1995), 168–79; Katharine J. Adams and Lewis L. Gould, eds., *Inside the Natchez Trace Collection: New Sources for Southern History* (Baton Rouge: Louisiana State University Press, 1999), esp. the essays by William G. Shade, Morton Rothstein, and Bowman.

64. William Gannaway Brownlow, *Secessionists and Other Scoundrels: Selections from Parson Brownlow's Book*, edited and introduction by Steven B. Ash (Baton Rouge: Louisiana State University Press, 1999), 3–5, 26–30; Mary Emily Robertson Campbell, *The Attitude of Tennesseans toward the Union, 1847–1861* (New York: Vantage, 1961), 128, 147–49, 186–88, 193–94, 200; Joe A. Mobley, "Vance, Zebulon," in *American National Biography*, edited by Garraty and Carnes, 22:168–70; William Gannaway Brownlow, *Speech against the Great Rebellion* (1862), in *Southern Unionist Pamphlets and the Civil War*, edited by Jon L. Wakelyn (Columbia: University of Missouri Press, 1999), 105–19, but the editor is mistaken in the assertion that Brownlow "supported Lincoln for president in 1860" (105). On Vance; his ultra southern rival, Thomas Clingman; and western North Carolina in 1860–61, see John C. Inscoe and Gordon B. McKinney, *The Heart of Confederate Appalachia: Western North Carolina in the Civil War* (Chapel Hill: University of North Carolina Press, 2000), chapter 2, "Secession."

65. Brownlow, *Secessionists and Other Scoundrels*, 27; Michael Les Benedict, "Johnson, Andrew," in *Oxford Companion to United States History*, edited by Boyer, 406–7.

66. H. Draper Hunt, "Hamlin, Hannibal," in *American National Biography*, edited by Garraty and Carnes, 9:936–38.

67. Martin M. Rosenberg, *Iowa on the Eve of the Civil War: A Decade of Frontier Politics* (Norman: University of Oklahoma Press, 1972), 222–23.

68. Almost all historians today would argue that Lincoln's behavior and actions from December to April were hardly dictated by what Luark termed "ultra sectional and Abolition" ideas or men. Even so, politicians who considered themselves moderates also spoke words and took actions that helped moved the country toward disunion and military conflict.

69. William C. Harris, *North Carolina*, 33; Crenshaw, *Slave States*, 197.

70. Basil Armstrong Thomassen, *North Carolina Yeoman: The Diary of Basil Armstrong Thomassen, 1853–1862*, edited by Paul D. Escott (Athens: University of Georgia Press, 1996), xx, xlix, 291, 305, 307; William C. Harris, *North Carolina*, 39, 45, 54.

71. Luke E. Harlow, "Religion, Race, and Robert J. Breckinridge: The Ideology of an Antislavery Slaveholder, 1830–1860," *Ohio Valley History* 6 (Fall 2006): 1–24; Harold D. Tallant, *Evil Necessity: Slavery and Political Culture in Antebellum Kentucky* (Lexington: University Press of Kentucky, 2003), 155–58; James F. Hopkins, *A History of the Hemp Industry in Kentucky* (1951; Lexington: University Press of Kentucky, 1998), 29–30; Robert J. Breckinridge, *The Civil War: Its Nature and End* (1861), in *Southern Unionist Pamphlets*, edited by Wakelyn, 27–55.

72. Frank H. Heck, *Proud Kentuckian: John C. Breckinridge, 1821-1875* (Lexington: University Press of Kentucky, 1976), 12.

73. Ibid., 32.

74. Klotter, *Breckinridges*, 107-8; Heck, *Proud Kentuckian*, 45-46.

75. Heck, *Proud Kentuckian*, 25-26.

76. Ibid., 49.

77. "Emigration from the Slave to the Free States," *Chicago Press and Tribune*, 21 October 1858.

78. Freehling, *Road to Disunion*, 2:320.

79. Lowell H. Harrison and James C. Klotter, *A New History of Kentucky* (Lexington: University Press of Kentucky, 1997), 184-87; Heck, *Proud Kentuckian*, 89; Freehling, *Road to Disunion*, 2:283-84; Eric H. Walther, *William Lowndes Yancey and the Coming of the Civil War* (Chapel Hill: University of North Carolina Press, 2006), 251-52; Johannsen, *Stephen A. Douglas*, 790.

CHAPTER 5

1. William J. Cooper Jr., *Jefferson Davis, American* (New York: Knopf, 2000), 12, 15.

2. Ibid., 21-22; William J. Cooper Jr., ed., *Jefferson Davis: The Essential Writings* (New York: Modern Library, 2003), 5-8; Paul Escott, "Davis, Jefferson," in *American National Biography*, edited by John A. Garraty and Mark C. Carnes (New York: Oxford University Press, 1999), 6:201-4.

3. Escott, "Davis," 201-4; Cooper, *Jefferson Davis: The Essential Writings*, 37-39.

4. Escott, "Davis"; William C. Davis, *Jefferson Davis: The Man and the Hour* (New York: HarperCollins, 1991), 69.

5. Charles S. Sydnor, *Slavery in Mississippi* (1933; Baton Rouge: Louisiana State University Press, 1966), 243; Cooper, *Jefferson Davis: The Essential Writings*, 88.

6. Cooper, *Jefferson Davis, American*, 226, 223. According to another biographer, Jefferson Davis "would not allow his blacks to be whipped and insisted that their health be of paramount importance to his crops" (William C. Davis, *Jefferson Davis*, 219).

7. Shearer Davis Bowman, *Masters and Lords: Mid-19th-Century U.S. Planters and Prussian Junkers* (New York: Oxford University Press, 1993), 77, 276 n. 223.

8. This is the title of chapter 3 in Mitchell Snay, *Gospel of Disunion: Religion and Separatism in the Antebellum South* (1993; Chapel Hill: University of North Carolina Press, 1997).

9. Cooper, *Jefferson Davis, American*, 234.

10. Lynda Lasswell Crist, "Jefferson Davis and Abraham Lincoln: A Comparison," *Journal of Mississippi History* 70 (Spring 2008): 32.

11. Snay, *Gospel of Disunion*, 3, 8, 13, 39.

12. Albert J. Raboteau, *Slave Religion: The "Invisible Institution" in the Antebellum South* (New York: Oxford University Press, 1978), 313-18; Wilma A. Dunaway, *Slavery and the American Mountain South* (Cambridge: Cambridge University Press, 2003), 230-40; David W. Blight, introduction to Frederick Douglass, *Narrative of the Life of Frederick Douglass, an American Slave, Written by Himself*, 2nd ed. (Boston: Bedford/St. Martin's, 2003), 16.

13. Clement Eaton, *Jefferson Davis* (New York: Free Press, 1977), 24–26.

14. Joan E. Cashin, *First Lady of the Confederacy: Varina Davis's Civil War* (Cambridge: Belknap Press of Harvard University Press, 2006), 30, 55, 28, 79, 46; Eaton, *Jefferson Davis*, 24–26. See also Catherine Clinton, *Fanny Kemble's Civil Wars* (New York: Oxford University Press, 2000).

15. John Ashworth has suggested that "Southern Democrats viewed plantation slavery as the foundation of the southern social order, southern Whigs viewed it as an interest." Since Whigs north and south emphasized "the interdependence of the various interests in society," southern Whigs proved more willing to compromise on the issue than Democrats in the region and attached greater importance to the Union. Yet antislavery attitudes penetrated northern Whiggery far more than southern Whigs, in part because of the free-labor preferences that emerged first in New England. "The Whig party was an alliance between commercial and capitalist groups in the North and those in the South who perceived no necessary conflict between slavery and capitalism" (*Slavery, Capitalism, and Politics in the Antebellum Republic*, vol. 1, *Commerce and Compromise, 1820–1850* [Cambridge: Cambridge University Press, 1995], 484–91). More recently, Ashworth has argued with regard to the Civil War that "there is no obvious reason to single out the war experience or the war itself as crucial to the success or development of American capitalism" (*Slavery, Capitalism, and Politics in the Antebellum Republic*, vol. 2, *The Coming of the Civil War, 1850–1861* [Cambridge: Cambridge University Press, 2007], 644).

16. Cooper, *Jefferson Davis: The Essential Writings*, 21.

17. Ibid., 69.

18. Ibid., 64–71.

19. Davis's 12 July 1848 speech on the admission of Oregon to the Union as quoted in James L. Huston, *Calculating the Value of the Union: Slavery, Property Rights, and the Economic Origins of the Civil War* (Chapel Hill: University of North Carolina Press, 2003), 128; Leonard L. Richards, *The California Gold Rush and the Coming of the Civil War* (New York: Knopf, 2007), 64–65.

20. Christopher Clark, *Social Change in America, from the Revolution through the Civil War* (Chicago: Dee, 2006), 173; Richards, *California Gold Rush*, 36–37, 103, 132; Craig M. Simpson, *A Good Southerner: The Life of Henry Wise of Virginia* (Chapel Hill: University of North Carolina Press, 1985), 87, 104; Shearer Davis Bowman, "Conditional Unionism and Slavery in Virginia, 1860–1861," *Virginia Magazine of History and Biography* 96 (January 1988): 42–43.

21. Cooper, *Jefferson Davis, American*, 106, 109; Eaton, *Jefferson Davis*, 26; Richards, *California Gold Rush*, 73, 93, 172, 176, 211, 228, 234; Cashin, *First Lady of the Confederacy*, 102; Russell McClintock, *Lincoln and the Decision for War: The Northern Response to Secession* (Chapel Hill: University of North Carolina Press, 2008), 207; Catherine Clinton, *Mrs. Lincoln: A Life* (New York: HarperCollins, 2009), 124.

22. Roy F. Nichols, *Franklin Pierce: Young Hickory of the Granite Hills* (Philadelphia: University of Pennsylvania Press, 1958), 136.

23. William C. Davis, *Look Away! A History of the Confederate States of America* (New York: Free Press, 2003), 80; Escott, "Davis," 202–3; Crist, "Jefferson Davis and Abraham Lincoln," 37; Cooper, *Jefferson Davis, American*, 310; Cashin, *First Lady of the Confederacy*, 50.

24. Harold Holzer, *Lincoln at Cooper Union: The Speech That Made Abraham Lincoln President* (New York: Simon and Schuster, 2004), 45, 85.

25. William C. Davis, *Jefferson Davis*, 266–85.

26. Cooper, *Jefferson Davis: The Essential Writings*, 166–72; William C. Davis, *Jefferson Davis*, 273, 189; Cooper, *Jefferson Davis, American*, 236; Cashin, *First Lady of the Confederacy*, 61.

27. James E. Bagwell, *Rice Gold: James Hamilton Couper and Plantation Life on the Georgia Coast* (Macon, Ga.: Mercer University Press, 2000), 121, 163; Shearer Davis Bowman, review of James E. Bagwell, *Rice Gold*, in *Journal of American History* 87 (March 2001): 1477–78; Elizabeth Fox-Genovese and Eugene D. Genovese, *The Mind of the Master Class: History and Faith in the Southern Slaveholders' World View* (Cambridge: Cambridge University Press, 2005), 670–71.

28. William W. Freehling, *The Road to Disunion* (New York: Oxford University Press, 2007), 1:17–18; *Charlottesville Review*, 23 November 1860, in Dwight Lowell Dumond, ed., *Southern Editorials on Secession* (1931; Gloucester, Mass.: Smith, 1964), 261–62.

29. William G. Shade, *Democratizing the Old Dominion: Virginia and the Second Party System, 1824–1861* (Charlottesville: University Press of Virginia, 1996), 269–77.

30. David Goldfield, *Region, Race, and Cities: Interpreting the Rural South* (Baton Rouge: Louisiana State University Press, 1997), 66–86, 189–246. "The popular fascination with internal improvements—especially railroads—consumed the state during the 1850s" (William A. Link, *Roots of Secession: Slavery and Politics in Antebellum Virginia* [Chapel Hill: University of North Carolina Press, 2003], 35).

31. See esp. Mark Voss-Hubbard, "The Infrapolitics of Slavery?," *Reviews in American History* 32 (March 2004): 44.

32. See Elizabeth Brown Pryor, *Reading the Man: A Portrait of Robert E. Lee through His Private Letters* (New York: Viking, 2007), 260–75. Many large slaveholders in Virginia's Tidewater and Piedmont regions had long since shifted from tobacco to wheat. Since cultivating an acre of wheat required less labor than did an acre of tobacco or cotton, substantial slaveholders might rent the labor of their surplus slaves. In the northern Piedmont county of Cumberland, wheat and corn were the dominant crops. While corn fed livestock, slaves, and free people, wheat was "the biggest money crop," thanks in part to the Orange and Alexandria Railroad, which had reached the county in 1851 and connected it to the Potomac River port of Alexandria to the north as well as to Richmond to the south. Culpeper farmers belonged "among the southern leaders of progressive, diversified agriculture." Slave prices were high on the eve of the Civil War, leading many free residents to hire rather than purchase black labor. Ten percent of the slave population was hired out, and fewer than 70 percent of slaveholders owned all the slaves who worked for them. See Donald E. Sutherland, *Seasons of War: The Ordeal of a Confederate Community, 1861–1865* (Baton Rouge: Louisiana State University Press, 1995), v–vii, 5–12.

33. Richard Eppes Diary, 1859–1862, entries for 28, 30 November 1859, Virginia Historical Society, Richmond. See also Shearer Davis Bowman, "Conditional Unionism," 32 n. 2.

34. Shearer Davis Bowman, "Conditional Unionism," 43–52; George H. Reese, ed., *Proceedings of the Virginia State Convention of 1861, February 13–May 1* (Richmond: Virginia State Library, 1965), 2:241–44; Ralph A. Wooster, *Secession Conventions of the*

South (Princeton: Princeton University Press, 1962), 144–45. On Upper South planters who invested in Deep South lands for surplus slaves, see also Stanley Lebergott, *The Americans: An Economic Record* (New York: Norton, 1984), 207; Daniel W. Crofts, *Old Southampton: Politics and Society in a Virginia County, 1834–1869* (Charlottesville: University Press of Virginia, 1992), 25–33. For a planter in the Virginia Piedmont who rented out slaves for labor on the James River and Kanawha Canal and considered investing in a Deep South sugar plantation, see Elijah Fletcher, *Letters*, edited by Martha von Briesen (Charlottesville: University Press of Virginia, 1965), 207, 226.

35. Link, *Roots of Secession*, 86.

36. James M. McPherson, *Battle Cry of Freedom: The Civil War Era* (New York: Oxford University Press, 1988), 87.

37. Marie Tyler-McGraw, *At the Falls: Richmond, Virginia, and Its People* (Chapel Hill: University of North Carolina Press for the Valentine Museum, 1994), 134. See also Link, *Roots of Secession*, 64.

38. Gregg D. Kimball, *American City, Southern Place: A Cultural History of Antebellum Richmond* (Athens: University of Georgia Press, 2000), 34–35.

39. Francesco L. Napa, "Stewart, Alexander Turney," in *American National Biography*, edited by Garraty and Carnes, 20:740–42.

40. Edwin G. Burrows and Mike Wallace, *Gotham: A History of New York City to 1898* (New York: Oxford University Press, 1999), 639, 716; Thomas Kessner, *Capital City: New York City and the Men behind America's Rise to Economic Dominance* (New York: Simon and Schuster, 2003), 12–16.

41. Mary Winfield Scott, *Houses of Old Richmond* (New York: Bonanza, 1941), 235; Robert A. Granniss Diary, entry for 9 April 1860, Virginia Historical Society, Richmond.

42. Horace L. Kent to John Y. Mason, 22 April 1857, John Y. Mason Papers, Virginia Historical Society, Richmond; Kimball, *American City, Southern Place*, 34–35.

43. Pryor, *Reading the Man*, 282. In the 1880s, Lee's former neighbor, Constance Cary Harrison, recalled that at her family home in Fairfax, "there seemed to be no especial reason for us to share in the apprehension of an uprising by the blacks. But there was the fear . . . dark, boding, oppressive, and altogether hateful. . . . In the daytime it seemed impossible to associate suspicion with those familiar tawny or sable faces that surrounded us. . . . What subtle influence was at work that should transform them into tigers thirsting for our blood? The idea was preposterous. But when evening came again, and with it the hour when the coloured people . . . assembled themselves together for dance or prayer-meeting, the ghost that refused to be laid [to rest] was again at one's elbow."

44. Granniss Diary, October–December 1859.

45. W. Ashbury Christian, *Richmond, Her Past and Present* (Richmond: Jenkins, 1912), 158, 174–75; Kimball, *American City, Southern Place*, 86, 219–20; Elizabeth R. Varon, *Southern Lady, Yankee Spy: The True Story of Elizabeth Van Lew, a Union Agent in the Heart of the Confederacy* (New York: Oxford University Press, 2003), 35–38.

46. Granniss Diary, April 1860; Kimball, *American City, Southern Place*, 55–57; Christian, *Richmond*, 163; Mary H. Mitchell, *Hollywood Cemetery: The History of a Southern Shrine* (Richmond: Virginia State Library, 1985), 6–7. The example of Mount Auburn came earlier to New York than to Virginia. An 1832 visit to Mount Auburn inspired Henry F. Pierrepont to envision a similar city of the dead in Brooklyn, across Gowanus

Bay, on the wooded heights of Gowanus. His vision was also propelled by "the fortune he could make importing corpses from Manhattan." Green-Wood Cemetery was incorporated in 1838, and lots went on sale the following year. By the early 1850s, it had become "in effect, the preeminent park for both Brooklyn and Manhattan," receiving the dead as residents and the quick as visitors" (Burrows and Wallace, *Gotham*, 582, 639, 732).

47. Ernest B. Furgurson, *Ashes of Glory: Richmond at War* (New York: Knopf, 1996), 20.

48. Granniss Diary, October 1858; Kimball, *American City, Southern Place*, 76–77.

49. Link, *Roots of Secession*, 146, 201–2; Voss-Hubbard, "Infrapolitics of Slavery?," 43; Varon, *Southern Lady, Yankee Spy*, 36–37.

50. Edmund Ruffin, *The Diary of Edmund Ruffin*, edited by William Kauffman Scarborough (Baton Rouge: Louisiana State University Press, 1982), 1:482.

51. Varon, *Southern Lady, Yankee Spy*, 4, 36–41; Link, *Roots of Secession*, 145–46.

52. Granniss Diary, December 1860–April 1861.

53. Pryor, *Reading the Man*, 291–97; Edward M. Coffman, *The Old Army: A Portrait of the American Army in Peacetime* (New York: Oxford University Press, 1986), 92.

54. Granniss Diary, May–August 1861.

55. Varon, *Southern Lady, Yankee Spy*, 85–86, 213.

56. Scott, *Houses of Old Richmond*, 235–36.

57. Christopher Phillips, *Missouri's Confederate: Claiborne Fox Jackson and the Creation of Southern Identity in the Border West* (Columbia: University of Missouri Press, 2000), 35, 131, 159, 182, 194, 159, 258–59; R. Douglas Hurt, *Agriculture and Slavery in Missouri's Little Dixie* (Columbia: University of Missouri Press, 1992), 235. On rates of return from agriculture, see Richard G. Lowe and Randolph B. Campbell, *Planters and Plain Folk: Agriculture in Antebellum Texas* (Dallas: Southern Methodist University Press, 1987), esp. 169: "With the exception of small slaveholders (1–9 slaves), all groups [of slaveholding cotton farmers] enjoyed rates of return (i.e., profits as a percentage of investment) of approximately 6 percent or better in 1850 and 1860."

58. Christopher Clark, *Social Change*, 202–5. For a recent study of Baltimore, Louisville, and New Orleans, see Frank Towers, *The Urban South and the Coming of the Civil War* (Charlottesville: University of Virginia Press, 2004). See also John E. Clark Jr., *Railroads in the Civil War: The Impact of Management on Victory and Defeat* (Baton Rouge: Louisiana State University Press, 2001), esp. 2–4, 126, 229, 227, 69, 223. Clark concludes that "southern planters demonstrated sound managerial instincts and a bias toward risk taking in the business of growing cotton." Yet "the mismanagement of southern railroads" during the Civil War clearly illustrates how "the southern economy produced too few people with management expertise adequate for the trials the Confederacy faced." Clark's mentor at Princeton, James M. McPherson, has emphasized that "The Puritan work ethic was strongest among New Englanders in general, and among Congregationalists, Unitarians, Presbyterians, and Quakers in particular. It is no coincidence that New England was at the cutting edge of American modernization or that a disproportionate number of entrepreneurs and inventors were New England Yankees of Calvinist background" (*Ordeal by Fire: The Civil War and Reconstruction* [New York: Knopf, 1982], 14).

59. Larry Schweikert, *Banking in the American South from the Age of Jackson to Reconstruction* (Baton Rouge: Louisiana State University Press, 1987), 277–78, 282–84,

290–91. More recently, another scholar has confirmed much of Schweikert's analysis: "During the panics of 1847–48 and 1857–58 regional markets did not disintegrate as they had in 1837. . . . [T]he movement of funds both within and between regions slowed during the panic of 1857, but did not altogether cease as it had during the panics of 1837 and 1839" (Howard Bodenhorn, *A History of Banking in the Antebellum United States: Financial Markets and Economic Development in an Era of Nation-Building* [Cambridge: Cambridge University Press, 2000], 156).

60. Goldfield, *Region, Race, and Cities*, 74–75.

61. William G. Shade, "In re Those 'Prebourgeois' Planters," in *Inside the Natchez Trace Collection: New Sources for Southern History*, edited by Katharine J. Adams and Lewis L. Gould (Baton Rouge: Louisiana State University Press, 1999), 173. See also Morton Rothstein, "Acquisitive Pursuits in a Slaveholding Society: Business History in the Natchez Trace Collection," in *Inside the Natchez Trace Collection*, edited by Adams and Gould, 93–114.

62. James C. Cobb, *Industrialization and Southern Society, 1877–1984* (Chicago: Dorsey, 1984), 8–9; Christopher Morris, *Becoming Southern: The Evolution of a Way of Life: Warren County and Vicksburg, Mississippi, 1770–1860* (New York: Oxford University Press, 1995), 164–68; Richard T. Archer Family Papers, Boxes 2E646 and 2E647, Natchez Trace Collection, Center for American History, University of Texas, Austin; Shearer Davis Bowman, "Industrialization and Economic Development in the Nineteenth-Century U.S. South: Some Interregional and Intercontinental Comparative Perspectives," in *Global Perspectives on Industrial Transformation in the American South*, edited by Susanna Delfino and Michele Gillespie (Columbia: University of Missouri Press, 2005), 100; Shearer Davis Bowman, "Reflections of Sectional Conflict in the Natchez Trace Collection," in *Inside the Natchez Trace Collection*, edited by Adams and Gould, 117–21.

63. Fred Bateman and Thomas Weiss, *A Deplorable Scarcity: The Failure of Industrialization in the Slave Economy* (Chapel Hill: University of North Carolina Press, 1981), 152–55; William N. Parker, *Europe, America, and the Wider World: Essays on the Economic History of Western Capitalism*, vol. 1, *Europe and the World Economy* (Cambridge: Cambridge University Press, 1984), 144–46; Goldfield, *Region, Race, and Cities*, 199; Bodenhorn, *History of Banking*, 101.

64. Lebergott, *Americans*, 214; Curtis J. Evans, *The Conquest of Labor: Daniel Pratt and Southern Industrialization* (Baton Rouge: Louisiana State University Press, 2001), 205; Bess Beatty, *Alamance: The Holt Family and Industrialization in a North Carolina County, 1847–1900* (Baton Rouge: Louisiana State University Press, 1999), xiii–xv, 30–31, 61–62.

65. Ulrich Bonnell Phillips, *Life and Labor in the Old South* (New York: Grosset and Dunlap, 1929), 3.

66. Robert W. Fogel, *Without Consent or Contract: The Rise and Fall of American Slavery* (New York: Norton, 1989); Michael Tadman, *Speculators and Slaves: Masters, Traders, and Slaves in the Old South* (Madison: University of Wisconsin Press, 1989); Gavin Wright, *Slavery and American Economic Development* (Baton Rouge: Louisiana State University Press, 2006). This discussion draws on Shearer Davis Bowman, "Industrialization and Economic Development."

67. Gavin Wright, *Slavery and American Economic Development*, 74.

68. See Robert Margo, "The South as an Economic Problem: Fact or Fiction?" in *The South as an American Problem*, edited by Larry J. Griffin and Don H. Doyle (Athens: University of Georgia Press, 1995), 165. See also the discussion of profitability and efficiency in Mark Smith, *Debating Slavery: Economy and Society in the Antebellum South* (Cambridge: Cambridge University Press, 1998), 60–61.

69. Patrick O'Brien, *The Economic Effects of the American Civil War* (Atlantic Highlands, N.J.: Humanities, 1988), 15. According to Lebergott, "Overall slave prices almost quadrupled from the de jure end of the foreign slave trade in 1808 to the eve of the Civil War in 1860. Underlying that increase was the quadrupling by 1860 in Southern crop production per slave" (*Americans*, 213–14).

70. O'Brien, *Economic Effects*, 22; Lebergott, *Americans*, 208–9; Mark Smith, *Debating Slavery*, 85. Per capita income was generally higher in the Lower than in the Upper and Border Souths, and the western Cotton Belt, particularly the alluvial soils of the Mississippi River Valley, contained more fertile and productive land than did the eastern Cotton Belt. Per capita income in the seven states of the Lower South averaged $97 in 1860, led by Louisiana's $131. In the four states of the Upper South, the average was $91, led by $95 for Arkansas. For the Border South, per capita income in Kentucky came to $83, while the estimates for Missouri and Maryland are $90 (O'Brien, *Economic Effects*, 15). According to Donghu Yang, "The inequality of wealth distribution in the rural South at the eve of the Civil War was far higher than the inequality of the rural North; and southern wealth distribution lies somewhere between the position of the planter dominance thesis and the simple view that there was a prospering middle class" ("Recent Findings on the Distribution of Wealth, on Social Structure, and on Economic Mobility among Free Southerners during the Late Antebellum Era," in *Without Consent or Contract: The Rise and Fall of American Slavery: Evidence and Methods*, edited by Robert W. Fogel, Ralph A. Galantine, and Richard L. Manning [New York: Norton, 1992], 244).

71. Kenneth Pomeranz, *The Great Divergence: China, Europe, and the Making of the Modern World Economy* (Princeton: Princeton University Press, 2000), 214. Until the twentieth century, what Susan Archer Mann has termed "the unpredictability and capriciousness of nature"—that is, drought and flood, insects and disease—played a major role in Western agricultural history. Farms confronted more formidable natural obstacles than did factories to the "predictability and standardization" associated with industrial capitalism and its use of advanced technology operated by wage labor. Mann concludes "that the industrial revolutions of the late eighteenth and nineteenth centuries, while sufficient to industrialize industry, were not sufficient to industrialize many spheres of agriculture" (*Agrarian Capitalism in Theory and Practice* [Chapel Hill: University of North Carolina Press, 1990], 127, 139). With regard to the Old South, Clement Eaton points out that the cotton harvest could last from the second half of August until early January. Because cotton bolls ripened unevenly, fields might need to be picked over three or more times. "This unequal ripening was the most important reason for the failure until the 1930s to develop a successful mechanical picker" (*The Growth of Southern Civilization, 1790–1860* [New York: Harper Torchbooks, 1963], 28). According to Robert C. McMath Jr., "The [mechanical] cotton picker more nearly resembles the mechanical tomato harvester, developed in the 1960s, than does the machinery that revolutionized grain harvesting before the Civil

War" in the North. That is, the mechanical cotton picker involved a much higher degree of technological sophistication than did McCormick's reaper ("Variations on a Theme by Henry Grady, Technology, Modernization, and Social Change," in *The Future South: A Historical Perspective for the Twenty-first Century*, edited by Joe P. Dunn and Howard L. Preston [Urbana: University of Illinois Press, 1991], 89).

72. Lacy Ford, "Reconsidering the Internal Slave Trade: Paternalism, Markets, and the Character of the Old South," in *The Chattel Principle: Internal Slave Trades in the Americas*, edited by Walter Johnson (New Haven: Yale University Press, 2004), 152.

73. McPherson, *Battle Cry of Freedom*, 227–28; David L. Lightner, *Slavery and the Commerce Power: How the Struggle against the Interstate Slave Trade Led to the Civil War* (New Haven: Yale University Press, 2006).

74. Walter Johnson, *Soul by Soul: Life inside the Antebellum Slave Market* (Cambridge: Harvard University Press, 1999).

75. Nina Silber, *Daughters of the Union: Northern Women Fight the Civil War* (Cambridge: Harvard University Press, 2005), 6.

76. Steven Deyle, *Carry Me Back: The Domestic Slave Trade in American Life* (New York: Oxford University Press, 2005), 239, 206. It is important not to underestimate "the self-deception by which southern slave sellers rationalized their behavior and generated a social portrait of themselves as paternalistic masters loathe to break up slave families and eager to avoid participation in the unseemly traffic in human beings" (Ford, "Reconsidering the Internal Slave Trade," 142).

77. Johnson, *Soul by Soul*, 113–15; Edward E. Baptist, "'Cuffy,' 'Fancy Maids,' and 'One-Eyed Men': Rape, Commodification, and the Domestic Slave Trade in the United States," in *Chattel Principle*, edited by Johnson, 182–83; James A. Ramage, *Rebel Raider: The Life of General John Hunt Morgan* (Lexington: University Press of Kentucky, 1986), 14–18.

78. Brenda S. Stevenson, *Life in Black and White: Family and Community in the Slave South* (New York: Oxford University Press, 1996), 325, x.

79. For good historiographical discussions of the capitalism issue, see Mark Smith, *Debating Slavery*; Hugh Tulloch, *The Debate on the American Civil War Era* (Manchester: Manchester University Press, 1999).

80. Stanley L. Engerman in the forum "Antebellum North and South in Comparative Perspective: A Discussion," *American Historical Review* 85 (December 1980): 1159. "There was a sharp increase in cotton output from small, non-slave farms in the 1850s, with the extension of railroads within the South" (1157).

81. John Majewski, *A House Dividing: Economic Development in Pennsylvania and Virginia before the Civil War* (Cambridge: Cambridge University Press, 2000), 3, 9–11, 171–72.

82. Kenneth Morgan, *Slavery, Atlantic Trade, and the British Economy, 1660–1800* (Cambridge: Cambridge University Press, 2000), 89–90.

83. Morton Rothstein, "The Cotton Frontier of the Antebellum United States: A Methodological Battleground," *Agricultural History* 44 (April 1970): 151–52. See also Fogel, *Without Consent or Contract*, 108–9.

84. Fox-Genovese and Genovese, *Mind of the Master Class*, 112.

CHAPTER 6

1. Medill as quoted in Allan Nevins, *Ordeal of the Union: Selected Chapters*, edited by E. B. Long (New York: Scribner's, 1973), 212.

2. William C. Harris, *Lincoln's Rise to the Presidency* (Lawrence: University Press of Kansas, 2007), 48; Kenneth M. Stampp, *The Imperiled Union: Essays on the Background of the Civil War* (New York: Oxford University Press, 1980), 161; Robert W. Johannsen, *Lincoln, the South, and Slavery: The Political Dimension* (Baton Rouge: Louisiana State University Press, 1991), 107; Anne C. Rose, *Voices of the Marketplace: American Thought and Culture, 1830–1860* (Lanham, Md.: Rowman and Littlefield, 1995), 77; Merrill D. Peterson, *The Great Triumvirate: Webster, Clay, and Calhoun* (New York: Oxford University Press, 1987), 8, 380; Robert V. Remini, *Henry Clay: Statesman for the Union* (New York: Norton, 1991), 2–5. More recently, Jill Lepore has written that the phrase "self-made man" was coined during the presidency of Andrew Jackson ("Bound for Glory: Writing Campaign Lives," *New Yorker*, 20 October 2008, 82). David Detzer, *Dissonance: The Turbulent Days between Fort Sumter and Bull Run* (Orlando: Harcourt, 2006), 7, recognizes that many voters were drawn to Lincoln, like Jackson, as a man of the people or common man. This image ignored the reality that Jackson was "an extraordinarily wealthy planter" and "that Lincoln had pocketed wads of money as a shrewd and successful lawyer, acting on behalf of powerful business interests." This argument overlooks the fact that both Jackson and Lincoln had achieved their financial and political successes without the advantages of substantial family wealth and connections. Hence, they had in fact risen from the ranks of the common people (i.e., white males) and were widely viewed as having proven their mettle in the process of their ascents.

3. See Bruce Levine, *Half Slave and Half Free: The Roots of the Civil War*, rev. ed. (New York: Hill and Wang/Farrar, Straus, and Giroux, 2005), 41, 136.

4. Christopher Clark, *Social Change in America, from the Revolution through the Civil War* (Chicago: Dee, 2006), 20; Edward G. Burrows and Mike Wallace, *Gotham: A History of New York City to 1898* (New York: Oxford University Press, 1999), 726–27: in colonial times "the middling sorts had stood far closer to the poor plebeians than to aristocratic elites," in contrast to the new middle class circa 1850, which was "becoming closer to the upper echelons."

5. Eric Foner, *Free Soil, Free Labor, Free Men: The Ideology of the Republican Party before the Civil War* (London: Oxford University Press, 1970), 11, 261–62.

6. Abraham Lincoln, *Speeches and Writings, 1859–1865*, edited by Don E. Fehrenbacher (New York: Library of America, 1989), 144.

7. Christopher Clark, *Social Change*, 231–33.

8. *Indianapolis Indiana Daily State Sentinel*, 22 February 1860, as quoted in Nicole Etcheson, *The Emerging Midwest: Upland Southerners and the Political Culture of the Old Northwest, 1787–1861* (Bloomington: Indiana University Press, 1996), 130.

9. George Fitzhugh, "Southern Thought," in *The Ideology of Slavery: Proslavery Thought in the Antebellum South, 1830–1860*, edited by Drew Gilpin Faust (Baton Rouge: Louisiana State University Press, 1981), 272–88.

10. George Fitzhugh, "Slavery Justified" (Fredericksburg, 1850), published as an appendix to *Sociology for the South; or, The Failure of Free Society* (1854; New York:

Franklin, 1964), 255; George Fitzhugh, "The Message, the Constitution, and the Times," *DeBow's Review*, February 1861, 163–64.

11. [George Frederick Holmes], "Slavery and Freedom," *Southern Quarterly Review*, April 1856, 81–82. The *Southern Quarterly Review* was published in Columbia, South Carolina, at that time. Neal C. Gillespie, *The Collapse of Orthodoxy: The Intellectual Ordeal of George Frederick Holmes* (Charlottesville: University Press of Virginia, 1972), 254–55, identifies Holmes as the author of this and a similar article, "Failure of Free Societies," *Southern Literary Messenger*, March 1855, 136–37.

12. *Domestic Slavery Considered as a Scriptural Institution: In a Correspondence between the Rev. Richard Fuller of Beaufort, S.C., and the Rev. Francis Wayland, of Providence, R.I., Revised and Corrected by the Authors*, 5th ed. (New York: Colby, 1847), 25–34, 90–91, 99, 105; Mark S. Schantz, *Piety in Providence: Class Dimensions of Religious Experience in Antebellum Rhode Island* (Ithaca: Cornell University Press, 2000), 153–61, 238–39. For a helpful discussion of the Fuller-Wayland exchange, see E. Brooks Holifield, *Theology in America: Christian Thought from the Age of the Puritans to the Civil War* (New Haven: Yale University Press, 2003), chapter 25, "The Dilemma of Slavery."

13. Burrows and Wallace, *Gotham*, 725; Sven Beckert, *The Monied Metropolis: New York City and the Consolidation of the American Bourgeoisie, 1850–1896* (Cambridge: Cambridge University Press, 2001), 90, 73.

14. Rose, *Voices of the Marketplace*, 80. Anthony Gronowicz, *Race and Class Politics in New York City before the Civil War* (Boston: Northeastern University Press, 1998), 167, offers a very different interpretation: "At the historical moment for national implementation of a new liberal capitalist order [based on free rather than slave labor as of 1865] to serve the large private industrial corporation, Lincoln took political advantage of the little man's desire to expand his own economic horizons. . . . The political hostility that Northern workingmen harbored against Northern monopoly capitalists was deflected to the Southern slaveholders." However, the number of actual "Northern monopoly capitalists" appears to have been rather small in 1860–61.

15. Paul G. Faler, *Mechanics and Manufacturers in the Early Industrial Revolution: Lynn, Massachusetts, 1780–1860* (Albany: State University of New York Press, 1981), 222.

16. Ibid., 166–67; James M. McPherson, *Battle Cry of Freedom: The Civil War Era* (New York: Oxford University Press, 1988), 12–13.

17. Lincoln, *Speeches and Writings, 1859–1865*, 144–45.

18. Fitzhugh, "Southern Thought," 281.

19. This account relies heavily on Faler, *Mechanics and Manufacturers*, 167–68, 186–88, 222–33. See also Bruce Laurie, *Artisans into Workers: Labor in Nineteenth-Century America* (New York: Noonday/Farrar, Straus and Giroux, 1989), 110–11; Levine, *Half Slave and Half Free*, 220–23. "Ethnic hostilities, rife in a town that had returned a resounding nativist vote, were submerged by the rising class feeling," explains Laurie. "Though still a minority, the Irish overlooked the sins of workmates and marched in parades and processions that maintained morale throughout the cold winter."

20. Charles B. Dew, *Ironmaker to the Confederacy: Joseph R. Anderson and the Tredegar Iron Works* (1966; Richmond: Library of Virginia, 1999), 23–34: "By the time Ander-

son and Company paid freight charges on the Northern iron, however, their raw materials costs had risen well above those of their competitors to the north."

21. Dew cites the *New York Commercial Advertiser* in 1847 to this effect (ibid., 25).

22. George B. Forgie, *Patricide in the House Divided: A Psychological Interpretation of Lincoln and His Age* (New York: Norton, 1979), chapter 2, "Lincoln at the Lyceum: The Problem of Ambition in the Post-Heroic Age"; Don E. Fehrenbacher, *Prelude to Greatness: Lincoln in the 1850s* (Stanford: Stanford University Press, 161); Johannsen, *Lincoln, the South, and Slavery,* 7.

23. Abraham Lincoln, *The Political Thought of Abraham Lincoln,* edited by Richard N. Current (Indianapolis: Bobbs-Merrill, 1967), 134.

24. Susan-Mary Grant, *The War for a Nation: The American Civil War* (New York: Routledge/Taylor and Francis, 2006), 15.

25. See James Oakes, *The Ruling Race: A History of American Slaveholders* (New York: Knopf, 1983), 44–49. Of course, the upward mobility of April Ellison and Free Frank McWhorter was hardly typical of even mulatto slaves in the Old South. McWhorter was born to a West African native, Juda, probably impregnated by her Scots-Irish master, George McWhorter. After buying freedom for himself and his wife in Kentucky, Frank McWhorter eventually moved in 1829 from Kentucky to Illinois, where he established the short-lived biracial town of New Philadelphia. He ultimately purchased freedom for himself and fifteen relatives at a total cost of some fourteen thousand dollars (equivalent to about one hundred thousand dollars in 1980). Ellison was born to a slave mother impregnated by either her owner, William Ellison, or his father. After being apprenticed to a manufacturer and repairer of cotton gins in South Carolina, April Ellison purchased freedom for himself, his wife, and their daughter between 1816 and 1820. By 1840, he "owned a home, a gin shop, thirty slaves, and more than 330 prime Sumter District acres." In 1860 he was master of Wisdom Hall plantation, including 900 acres and fifty-nine slaves. He seems to have retained a racial distance from his black chattel by not owning any mulattoes like himself. See Juliet E. K. Walker, *Free Frank: A Black Pioneer on the Antebellum Frontier* (Lexington: University Press of Kentucky, 1983); Michael P. Johnson and James L. Roark, *Black Masters: A Free Family of Color in the Old South* (New York: Norton, 1984), 79–80.

26. Stephen Berry, *House of Abraham: Lincoln and the Todds, a Family Divided by War* (Boston: Houghton Mifflin, 2007), 26; Lowell Harrison, *Lincoln of Kentucky* (Lexington: University Press of Kentucky, 2000), 22–24.

27. George M. Fredrickson, *Big Enough to Be Inconsistent: Abraham Lincoln Confronts Slavery and Race* (Cambridge: Harvard University Press, 2008), 47.

28. James F. Simon, *Lincoln and Chief Justice Taney: Slavery, Secession, and the President's War Powers* (New York: Simon and Schuster, 2006), 48; Michael Burlingame, *The Inner World of Abraham Lincoln* (Urbana: University of Illinois Press, 1994), xvi-xviii.

29. Quoted in Harold Holzer, *Lincoln at Cooper Union: The Speech That Made Abraham Lincoln President* (New York: Simon and Schuster, 2004), 181.

30. Fredrickson, *Big Enough,* 35–36; see also 82.

31. David Herbert Donald, *Lincoln* (New York: Simon and Schuster, 1995), 93; Catherine Clinton, *Mrs. Lincoln: A Life* (New York: HarperCollins, 2009), 98.

32. William C. Harris, *Lincoln's Rise*, 30, citing Burlingame, *Inner World*, esp. xvi.

33. Lynda Lasswell Crist, "Jefferson Davis and Abraham Lincoln: A Comparison," *Journal of Mississippi History* 70 (Spring 2008): 38; Burlingame, *Inner World*, xvi.

34. Harrison, *Lincoln of Kentucky*, 216–20.

35. William C. Harris, *Lincoln's Rise*, 22; Simon, *Lincoln and Chief Justice Taney*, 17, 53, 58–62, 65, 68–72, 75.

36. Simon, *Lincoln and Chief Justice Taney*, 68. See also Michael F. Holt, *The Rise and Fall of the American Whig Party: Jacksonian Politics and the Onset of the Civil War* (New York: Oxford University Press, 1999), 195.

37. Lincoln as quoted in Holzer, *Lincoln at Cooper Union*, 209; see also William C. Harris, *Lincoln's Rise*, 58.

38. David M. Potter, *The Impending Crisis, 1848–1861*, completed and edited by Don E. Fehrenbacher (New York: Harper and Row, 1976), 113; Simon, *Lincoln and Chief Justice Taney*, 80.

39. Nevins, *Ordeal of the Union*, 160.

40. Stampp, *Imperiled Union*, 138; George H. Mayer, *The Republican Party, 1854–1966*, 2nd ed. (New York: Oxford University Press, 1967), 36.

41. Harrison, *Lincoln of Kentucky*, 87; William C. Harris, *Lincoln's Rise*, 68, 92–93.

42. Kenneth M. Stampp, ed., *The Causes of the Civil War*, 3rd rev. ed. (New York: Touchstone/Simon and Schuster, 1991), 139–40.

43. Ibid., 138–39.

44. Phillip Shaw Paludan, *The Presidency of Abraham Lincoln* (Lawrence: University Press of Kansas, 1994), 13: "Dred Scott marked the first time that due process clause had been used by the Supreme Court as a substantive doctrine upholding slavery. Taney's innovations lacked the secure authority of precedent. . . . [T]he idea that only the Supreme Court could declare the meaning of the Constitution had not yet been established."

45. Robert W. Johannsen, *Frontier Politics on the Eve of the Civil War* (Seattle: University of Washington Press, 1955), 78–80.

46. Stampp, *Imperiled Union*, 144–52.

47. Donald, *Lincoln*, 246.

48. James Oakes, *The Radical and the Republican: Frederick Douglass, Abraham Lincoln, and the Triumph of Antislavery Politics* (New York: Norton, 2007), 127–30.

49. William C. Harris, *Lincoln's Rise*, 97–98, 131–32.

50. Frederick Douglass declared at midcentury that the Negro could and must escape slavery's legacy of degradation through "the power of his native intelligence and his own right arm" (Margaret Washington, introduction to Olive Gilbert, *Narrative of Sojourner Truth* [1850; New York: Vintage, 1993], x).

51. Donald, *Lincoln*, 155.

52. Jeremy Atack and Peter Passell, *A New Economic View of American History*, 2nd ed. (New York: Norton, 1994), 435–36.

53. D. W. Meinig, *The Shaping of America: A Geographical Perspective on 500 Years of History*, vol. 2, *Continental America, 1800–1867* (New Haven: Yale University Press, 1993), 318–21.

54. Christopher Clark, *Social Change*, 226.

55. Gavin Wright, *Slavery and American Economic Development*, 61, 58.

56. Christopher Clark, *Social Change*, 138.

57. Atack and Passell, *New Economic View*, 433; Daniel Walker Howe, *What Hath God Wrought: The Transformation of America, 1815–1848* (New York: Oxford University Press, 2007), 562–69.

58. Part of this process involved the ongoing concentration of specie reserves and banking capital in northeastern cities.

59. Peter A. Coclanis, "The Paths before Us/U.S.," in *The South, the Nation, and the World: Perspectives on Southern Economic Development*, edited by David L. Carlton and Peter A. Coclanis (Charlottesville: University of Virginia Press, 2003), 19; Jeff Horn, *The Industrial Revolution: Milestones in Business History* (Westport, Conn.: Greenwood, 2007), 106–7.

60. George Rogers Taylor, *The Transportation Revolution, 1815–1860* (1951; New York: Harper Torchbooks, 1968), 86; Donald L. Miller, *City of the Century: The Epic of Chicago and the Making of America* (New York: Simon and Schuster, 1996), 103–11.

61. This involved standardized grading of wheat by quality and a system of receipts for grain stored in elevators that in effect provided a new form of currency.

62. Donald L. Miller, *City of the Century*, 99.

63. Ibid., 99; Meinig, *Shaping of America*, 283.

64. John F. Stover, *American Railroads*, 2nd ed. (Chicago: University of Chicago Press, 1997), 82; Atack and Passell, *New Economic View*, 436–39; Robert Cook, *Baptism of Fire: The Republican Party in Iowa, 1838–1878* (Ames: Iowa State University Press, 1994), 106, 97–100. Cook points out that during the depression following the financial panic of 1857, hard-pressed out-of-state banks called in so many loans that only thirty-five miles of track were constructed in Iowa during all of 1858.

65. Donald L. Miller, *City of the Century*, 114, 99; Meinig, *Shaping of America*, 283.

66. "Emigration from the Slave to the Free States," *Chicago Press and Tribune*, 21 October 1858.

67. Henry B. Waller Papers, 1809–1943, Box 6, Huntington Library, San Marino, California. This excellent collection has apparently not been examined carefully by historians of either Kentucky or Illinois.

68. Between 1839 and November 1860, Waller owned a modest farm, Auvergne, just outside the Ohio River port of Maysville and close to the Lexington Turnpike. His Mason County tax records show that he owned six slaves in 1856 and eleven in 1859. Henry and Bell had six sons and four daughters between 1838 and 1858.

69. *Speech of Henry Waller, Esq. on the Dred Scott Decision and Other National Issues Involved in the Senatorial Canvass in Illinois* (Chicago, 1858).

70. Waller Papers, Boxes 10 and 11.

71. Henry Waller Letterpress Book, 1878–92, 12 March 1879, Filson Historical Society Library, Louisville, Kentucky.

72. George Rogers Taylor, *Transportation Revolution*, 85; Atack and Passell, *New Economic View*, 427; Beckert, *Monied Metropolis*, 20, 84–88.

73. Holzer, *Lincoln at Cooper Union*, 230–31; Debby Applegate, *The Most Famous Man in America: The Biography of Henry Ward Beecher* (New York: Three Leaves/Doubleday, 2006), 221.

74. Beckert, *Monied Metropolis*, 23, 29. Beckert points out that more merchants were becoming investors in domestic factories that manufactured the particular products they shipped west, although "manufacturing lacked either the financial security or the dignified reputation that came along with the more gentlemanly trade." Consequently, "for some merchants-cum-manufacturers, southern trade became less important, internal improvements mattered substantially more than before, and even the traditional bête noire of traders, tariffs, might be countenanced." During the Civil War, military contracts, the underwriting of federal debt, and even the protective tariff implemented in 1861 proved a boon to New York's business and financial community.

75. Burrows and Wallace, *Gotham*, 655, xvii.

76. Roy Franklin Nichols, *The Disruption of American Democracy* (New York: Free Press, 1948), 342; Burrows and Wallace, *Gotham*, 655. See also Gronowicz, *Race and Class Politics*; Beckert, *Monied Metropolis*, 79.

77. Edward L. Lach, "Cooper, Peter," in *American National Biography*, edited by John A. Garraty and Mark C. Carnes (New York: Oxford University Press, 1999), 5:454–55; Beckert, *Monied Metropolis*, 53–54, 63; Burrows and Wallace, *Gotham*, 713, 662; Howe, *What Hath God Wrought*, 563, 567.

78. During the 1850s, Manhattan became the nation's information center as well as its economic hub. The new Associated Press and American Telegraph Company located in the city, and the transatlantic cable connected it to England in 1858. New technology was crucial. The speedy rotary presses pioneered by the city's Richard Hoe in the 1840s, combined with new papermaking machines producing cheap newsprint from wood pulp (as opposed to relatively scarce cotton and linen rags), had enabled 2 of the city's 174 newspapers, James Gordon Bennett's *Herald* and Greeley's *Tribune*, to become the nation's most profitable dailies. The less prominent *New York Times* appeared in 1851. Lorman A. Ratner and Dwight L. Teeter Jr., *Fanatics and Fire-Eaters: Newspapers and the Coming of the Civil War* (Urbana: University of Illinois Press, 2003), 12; Burrows and Wallace, *Gotham*, 674–77.

79. Benjamin Thomas, *Abraham Lincoln, a Biography* (New York: Knopf, 1952), 202; Hendrik V. Booraem, *The Formation of the Republican Party in New York: Politics and Conscience in the Antebellum North* (New York: New York University Press, 1983), 106–7; Burrows and Wallace, *Gotham*, 674–79, 777; Beckert, *Monied Metropolis*, 92; Holzer, *Lincoln at Cooper Union*, 25, 69–71.

80. Lincoln, *Political Thought*, 139; Holzer, *Lincoln at Cooper Union*, 73, 115, 233.

81. See Paludan, *Presidency of Abraham Lincoln*, 17.

82. Ibid., 77, 103, 202; Milton Rugoff, *The Beechers: An American Family in the Nineteenth Century* (New York: Harper and Row, 1981), 388–89; Applegate, *Most Famous Man*, 5, 15, 201–2, 230.

83. William C. Harris, *Lincoln's Rise*, 183–84; Holzer, *Lincoln at Cooper Union*, 64, 158–62.

84. Holzer, *Lincoln at Cooper Union*, 33.

85. Ibid., 101–2; Robert W. Johannsen, *Stephen A. Douglas* (New York: Oxford University Press, 1973), 709–10.

86. Lincoln's "Address at Cooper Institute, New York City," in Lincoln, *Speeches and Writings, 1859–1865*, 111–30, and in Lincoln, *Political Thought*, 139–62.

87. Frederick Douglass, *My Bondage and My Freedom*, edited by William L. Andrews (1855; Urbana: University of Illinois Press, 1987), 55.

88. Hunter quoted in Holzer, *Lincoln at Cooper Union*, 84.

89. William C. Harris, *Lincoln's Rise*, 280; Lincoln to Stephens, 20 December 1860, in Lincoln, *Speeches and Writings, 1859–1865*, 194.

90. On the report issued in June 1860 by the Republican-dominated Covode Committee, which detailed "corruption ranging from Kansas to the navy yards in the East," see Paludan, *Presidency of Abraham Lincoln*, 22–23; Mark W. Summers, *The Plundering Generation: Corruption and the Crisis of the Union* (New York: Oxford University Press, 1987), 239–60.

91. Records from the Republican conventions of both 1856 and 1860 are reprinted in Horace Greeley and John P. Cleveland, *A Political Textbook for 1860* (1860; New York: Negro Universities Press/Greenwood, 1969), 22–23, 26–29.

92. William C. Harris, *Lincoln's Rise*, 224, 241.

93. *New Orleans Daily Crescent*, 28 November 1860, in Dwight Lowell Dumond, ed., *Southern Editorials on Secession* (1931; Gloucester, Mass.: Smith, 1964), 272–74.

94. Russell McClintock, *Lincoln and the Decision for War: The Northern Response to Secession* (Chapel Hill: University of North Carolina Press, 2008), 45, 165; Paludan, *Presidency of Abraham Lincoln*, 45.

95. *St. Louis Daily Missouri Republican*, 21 November 1860, in Dumond, *Southern Editorials*, 258–61. The newspaper reported that during the prior week in Lincoln's home state, a slave was "rescued from the proper officers of the law" and taken to Canada while the owner was "insulted and abused by the mob."

96. William C. Harris, *Lincoln's Rise*, 241–43; Richard J. Carwardine, *Lincoln* (Harlow, Eng.: Pearson/Longman, 2003), 140.

97. Lincoln to John A. Gilmer, 15 December 1860, Lincoln to Henry J. Raymond, 18 December 1860, both in Lincoln, *Speeches and Writings, 1859–1865*, 190–94.

98. Carwardine, *Lincoln*, 137.

99. In the Border South (including the future state of West Virginia), Lincoln won just over 26,300 votes. Almost two-thirds of these votes came from Missouri, which Douglas carried, and most of them were cast by voters among St. Louis's substantial population of both immigrants from Germany and migrants from the free states.

100. Applegate, *Most Famous Man*, 326.

101. McClintock, *Lincoln and the Decision for War*, 49, 54.

102. Bessie Louise Pierce, *A History of Chicago*, vol. 2, *From Town to City, 1848–1871* (New York: Knopf, 1940), 509.

103. *Chicago Press and Tribune*, 7 January 1861.

104. Ibid.

105. Ibid.

106. Ibid.

107. Ibid.

CHAPTER 7

1. Keziah Goodwyn Hopkins Brevard, *A Plantation Mistress on the Eve of the Civil War: The Diary of Keziah Goodwyn Hopkins Brevard, 1860–61*, edited by John Ham-

mond Moore (Columbia: University of South Carolina Press, 1993), 92–93. See also Drew Gilpin Faust, *Mothers of Invention: Women of the Slaveholding South in the American Civil War* (Chapel Hill: University of North Carolina Press, 1996), esp. 7; Kirsten E. Wood, *Masterful Women: Slaveholding Widows from the American Revolution through the Civil War* (Chapel Hill: University of North Carolina Press, 2004).

2. Historians such as Kate Adams and Morton Rothstein have examined newly available sources and reexamined others with fresh eyes and have discovered a wide range of written records "documenting the entrepreneurial drive and talents of women" (Morton Rothstein, "Acquisitive Pursuits in a Slaveholding Society," in *Inside the Natchez Trace Collection: New Sources for Southern History*, edited by Katharine J. Adams and Lewis L. Gould [Baton Rouge: Louisiana State University Press, 1999], 102).

3. Brevard seems to have been exceptional. According to a historian who has studied planter women moving from the settled Southeast to the southwestern frontier, "most women's kinship networks deteriorated, just as they had feared." This deterioration contributed to these women becoming "even more dependent on men than they had been at home" (Joan E. Cashin, *A Family Venture: Men and Women on the Southern Frontier* [New York: Oxford University Press, 1991], 120).

4. Brevard, *Plantation Mistress*, 10–14.

5. Frederick Douglass, *My Bondage and My Freedom*, edited by William L. Andrews (1855; Urbana: University of Illinois Press, 1987), 61. For example, Alabama planter Augustus Benners recorded in his diary on 24 April 1861, "Give Burke a thrashing for impudence" (*Disunion, War, Defeat, and Recovery in Alabama: The Journal of Augustus Benners, 1850–1885*, edited by Glenn Linden and Virginia Linden [Macon, Ga.: Mercer University Press, 2007], 64).

6. Brevard, *Plantation Mistress*, 2–40, 85. Jessie Benton Frémont, the wife of the 1856 Republican presidential candidate and later Union general, wrote similarly in early 1861, "The fear of what may be in store for us all if this cloud of civil war takes shape, makes me restless & I am unfortunate in not being able to live more away from myself just now." At about the same time, Frémont cited one of the last letters written by Hortense, stepdaughter of Napoleon I and mother of Napoleon III: "Believe firmly there is another life. Mine here has been such as to render this hope a necessary belief without which I could not endure it" (*The Letters of Jessie Benton Frémont*, edited by Pamela Herr and Mary Lee Spence [Urbana: University of Illinois Press, 1993], 233–34).

7. Brevard, *Plantation Mistress*, 43–49.

8. Ibid., 51–64.

9. Ibid., 69–75, 85; Paul Conkin, *The Uneasy Center: Reformed Christianity in Antebellum America* (Chapel Hill: University of North Carolina Press, 1995), 264–65; C. C. Goen, *Broken Churches, Broken Nation: Denominational Schisms and the Coming of the American Civil War* (Macon, Ga.: Mercer University Press, 1985), 74–75. On the importance of Thornwell and this sermon, see Mark M. Smith, ed., *The Old South* (Malden, Mass.: Blackwell, 2001), 123–26. Another South Carolina clergyman, Lutheran John Bachman (a native New Yorker who delivered the opening prayer to the state's secession convention), also "advocated a patriarchal and paternalistic form of slavery aimed at civilizing and Christianizing the slaves." He "seemed genuinely outraged by abolitionist claims that slavery was a sin and anti-Christian" (Peter McCandless, "The Political Evo-

lution of John Bachman: From New York Yankee to South Carolina Secessionist," *South Carolina Historical Magazine* 108 [January 2007]: 9, 15).

10. Brevard, *Plantation Mistress*, 95–105.

11. Ibid., 108–12.

12. Margaret Washington, introduction to Olive Gilbert, *Narrative of Sojourner Truth* (1850; New York: Vintage, 1993), ix.

13. Nell Irvin Painter, *Sojourner Truth: A Life, a Symbol* (New York: Norton, 1996), 113.

14. "Black participation in the struggle against England, Quaker antislavery activity, and formation of the New York Manumission Society in 1785 were the impetus for eventual emancipation" (Washington, introduction, xx).

15. See Joanne Pope Melish, *Disowning Slavery: Gradual Emancipation and Race in New England, 1780–1860* (Ithaca: Cornell University Press, 1998).

16. Nell Irvin Painter, introduction to Olive Gilbert, *Narrative of the Life of Sojourner Truth* (New York: Penguin, 1998), xii–xiii.

17. Painter, *Sojourner Truth*, 15–17.

18. Ibid., 18.

19. Ibid., 17, 22.

20. Ibid., 27–8.

21. Ibid., 32–35.

22. Conkin, *Uneasy Center*, 86.

23. Washington, introduction, xxvi.

24. See Robert H. Abzug, *Passionate Liberator: Theodore Dwight Weld and the Dilemma of Reform* (New York: Oxford University Press, 1980), 129–30. "The abolitionists envisioned their campaign as one to save the churches from potential divine retribution for failing in their duty to rebuke sin" (John R. McKivigan, "The Northern Churches and the Moral Problem of Slavery," in *The Meaning of Slavery in the North*, edited by Martin Blatt and David Roediger [New York: Garland, 1998], 78).

25. Anne C. Rose, *Voices of the Marketplace: American Thought and Culture, 1840–1860* (Lanham, Md.: Rowman and Littlefield, 1995), 166; Shearer Davis Bowman, *Masters and Lords: Mid-19th-Century U.S. Planters and Prussian Junkers* (New York: Oxford University Press, 1993), 214–15; George M. Fredrickson, *The Black Image in the White Mind: The Debate on Afro-American Character and Destiny, 1817–1914* (New York: Harper Torchbooks, 1971), esp. 119–21, 157–58.

26. Painter, *Sojourner Truth*, 47, 54. On the Prophet Matthias, see also Paul E. Johnson and Sean Wilentz, *The Kingdom of Matthias: A Story of Sex and Salvation in 19th-Century America* (New York: Oxford University Press, 1994).

27. Washington, introduction, xv.

28. Painter, introduction, xv.

29. Painter, *Sojourner Truth*, 98, 181. However, Washington emphasizes that Truth's four children whose names have survived—Diana, Elizabeth, Peter, and Sophia—"were named for parents and siblings, thus creating a collective identity and recreating her family" (introduction, xxiv).

30. Painter, *Sojourner Truth*, 109–10.

31. "Exploiting James Madison's notes on the Constitutional Convention, which first

appeared in 1840, Garrisonians gleefully debunked the framers' reputation as opponents of slavery. They charged the southern delegates had demanded protection for slavery and that northerners had cravenly abandoned their principles and acquiesced in provisions that protected, even promoted slavery," such as the three-fifths compromise (Donald C. Nieman, *Promises to Keep: African-Americans and the Constitutional Order, 1776 to the Present* [New York: Oxford University Press, 1991], 34).

32. See esp. Milton C. Sernett, *Harriet Tubman: Myth, Memory, and History* (Durham: Duke University Press, 2007), 158–60.

33. Frances Dana Gage, account of Sojourner Truth Speech, *Anti-Slavery Standard*, 2 May 1863, http://www.sojournertruth.org/Library/Speeches/AintIAWoman.htm (accessed 9 January 2010).

34. Painter, *Sojourner Truth*, 164–82.

35. Ibid., 179–82, 200–207; Jennifer Fleischner, *Mrs. Lincoln and Mrs. Keckly: The Remarkable Story of the Friendship between a First Lady and a Former Slave* (New York: Broadway, 2003), 264–65, 277–78; Kate Clifford Larson, *Bound for the Promised Land: Harriet Tubman, Portrait of an American Hero* (New York: Ballantine, 2004), 168–69.

36. Gilbert, *Narrative of the Life of Sojourner Truth*, 120–21.

37. Painter, *Sojourner Truth*, 206–7.

38. James Oakes, *The Radical and the Republican: Frederick Douglass, Abraham Lincoln, and the Triumph of Antislavery Politics* (New York; Norton, 2007), 213.

39. Ibid., 210–17; William S. McFeely, *Frederick Douglass* (New York: Norton, 1991), 232–35; Fleischner, *Mrs. Lincoln and Mrs. Keckly*, 278.

40. George M. Fredrickson, *Big Enough to Be Inconsistent: Abraham Lincoln Confronts Slavery and Race* (Cambridge: Harvard University Press, 2008), 118.

CHAPTER 8

1. Jean H. Baker, *James Buchanan* (New York: Times Books/Holt, 2004), 9; William E. Gienapp, "Buchanan, James," in *American National Biography*, edited by John A. Garraty and Mark C. Carnes (New York: Oxford University Press, 1999), 3:835–39; David Detzer, *Allegiance: Fort Sumter, Charleston, and the Beginning of the Civil War* (New York: Harcourt, 2001), 67.

2. Kenneth M. Stampp, *America in 1857: A Nation on the Brink* (New York: Oxford University Press, 1990), viii, 48; Leonard L. Richards, *The California Gold Rush and the Coming of the Civil War* (New York: Knopf, 2007), 208–10.

3. Martin M. Rosenberg, *Iowa on the Eve of the Civil War: A Decade of Frontier Politics* (Norman: University of Oklahoma Press, 1972), 224; Jean H. Baker, *James Buchanan*, 117; David M. Potter, *The Impending Crisis, 1848-1861*, completed and edited by Don E. Fehrenbacher (New York: Harper and Row, 1976), 391.

4. James Buchanan, *The Works of James Buchanan*, edited by John Bassett Moore (New York: Antiquarian, 1960), 11:7–43.

5. In significant ways, "presidential power was more limited before the Civil War" than it subsequently became (William E. Gienapp, "The Crisis of American Democracy: The Political System and the Coming of the Civil War," in *Why the Civil War Came*, edited by Gabor S. Boritt [New York: Oxford University Press, 1996], 113).

6. Some antisecessionists in the Upper South raised the possibility of a "Border State

convention" that might negotiate Union-saving compromises. See esp. Daniel W. Crofts, *Reluctant Confederates: Upper South Unionists in the Secession Crisis* (Chapel Hill: University of North Carolina Press, 1989).

7. Potter, *Impending Crisis*, 519.

8. Buchanan, *Works of James Buchanan*, 11:55.

9. Roy Franklin Nichols, *The Disruption of American Democracy* (New York: Free Press, 1948), 404–5.

10. Toombs cited in William Y. Thompson, *Robert Toombs of Georgia* (Baton Rouge: Louisiana State University Press, 1966), 152.

11. J. G. Randall and David Herbert Donald, *Civil War and Reconstruction*, 2nd ed. (Lexington, Mass.: Heath, 1969), 154–55. As Detzer explains, Anderson "was under very clear orders, repeated several times, to avoid anything that might initiate a conflict. If he ordered his own guns to fire, a national civil war would certainly ensue" (*Allegiance*, 160). South Carolina guns on Morris Island "were doing no damage" to the *Star of the West*. That spring this same ship, then docked in Galveston, became part of the Confederate fleet after being seized by some ninety Texans on 17 April (314).

12. Wigfall in John C. Rives, ed., *The Congressional Globe: Containing the Debates and Proceedings of the Second Session of the Thirty-sixth Congress* (Washington, D.C.: Congressional Globe Office, 1861), 1373; Robert W. Johannsen, *Stephen A. Douglas* (New York: Oxford University Press, 1973), 863–64; Keziah Goodwyn Hopkins Brevard, *A Plantation Mistress on the Eve of the Civil War: The Diary of Keziah Goodwyn Hopkins Brevard, 1860–61*, edited by John Hammond Moore (Columbia: University of South Carolina Press, 1993), 70.

13. Russell McClintock, *Lincoln and the Decision for War: The Northern Response to Secession* (Chapel Hill: University of North Carolina Press, 2008), 132; Detzer, *Allegiance*, 171–72, 217–18.

14. Gienapp, "Buchanan"; Jean H. Baker, *James Buchanan*, 140–43. See also the summary of Allan Nevins's judgment that Buchanan was "helpless" and Congress "blundering and legalistic" during the crucial six weeks after Lincoln's election (*Ordeal of the Union: Selected Chapters*, edited and introduction by E. B. Long [New York: Scribner's, 1971], 137); Hans L. Trefousse, *Thaddeus Stevens: Nineteenth-Century Egalitarian* (Chapel Hill: University of North Carolina Press, 1997), 103, 106.

15. McClintock, *Lincoln and the Decision for War*, 68. As political scientist Herman Belz makes clear, "The Constitution, in express terms, neither conferred or prohibited the right of a state to secede from the Union, nor authorized or denied the right of the federal government to coerce a state to remain in the Union should it seek to withdraw" ("Lincoln's Construction of the Executive Power in the Secession Crisis," *Journal of the Abraham Lincoln Association* 27 [Winter 2006]: 21–22).

16. Rives, *Congressional Globe*, 1373.

17. Ernest William Winkler, ed., *Journal of the Secession Convention of Texas, 1861* (Austin: Texas Library and Historical Commission, 1912), 61–65; Rives, *Congressional Globe*, 1373. Rice had served a term in the House before his election to the Senate in 1856 (*Biographical Directory of United States Congress, 1774–Present*, http://bioguide.congress .gov/biosearch/biosearch.asp [accessed 9 January 2010]).

18. Potter, *Impending Crisis*, 530. Nevins, *Ordeal of the Union*, 212, also employs the term "chieftains."

19. Thomas E. Stephens, "Crittenden, John Jordan," in *American National Biography*, edited by Garraty and Carnes, 5:140–42. Crittenden, a Frankfort attorney, served as U.S. attorney general in addition to several terms in the Senate. In 1856 he had "half-heartedly supported" the nativist Know-Nothing Party (Potter, *Impending Crisis*, 530–31). On the House Committee of Thirty-three, see also Randall and Donald, *Civil War and Reconstruction*, 148–49.

20. James M. McPherson, *Battle Cry of Freedom: The Civil War Era* (New York: Oxford University Press, 1988), 255.

21. Potter, *Impending Crisis*, 530–33, 553; *Newark Daily Advertiser*, 22 January 1861, in Howard Cecil Perkins, ed., *Northern Editorials on Secession* (1942; Gloucester, Mass.: Smith, 1964), 1:252–54.

22. Dwight Lowell Dumond, ed., *Southern Editorials on Secession* (1931; Gloucester, Mass.: Smith, 1964), 203.

23. William J. Cooper Jr., *Jefferson Davis, American* (New York: Knopf, 2000), 317–20; Potter, *Impending Crisis*, 532. Eli N. Evans, *Judah P. Benjamin: The Jewish Confederate* (New York: Free Press, 1988), briefly discusses Benjamin's state's rights principles and his switch in the 1850s from Whig to Democrat (87–88). Evans also presents a far less flattering portrait of Davis than the more complete one provided by Cooper. A very judicious evaluation of the Crittenden Compromise's failure in the Committee of Thirteen is presented in William Y. Thompson, *Robert Toombs*, 152. Although Toombs "believed Seward to be intractably opposed to the Crittenden proposals," in reality "the New Yorker was only conforming—reluctantly—with Lincoln's stated position" (John M. Taylor, *William Henry Seward, Lincoln's Right Hand* [Washington: Brassey's, 1991], 129–30). According to McClintock, among Republicans "the firmness of the hard-line majority—and as we have seen and will see again, of the president-elect in particular—continued to dictate the party's response" (*Lincoln and the Decision for War*, 151).

24. Nichols, *Disruption*, 400.

25. McClintock, *Lincoln and the Decision for War*, 162–63.

26. Potter, *Impending Crisis*, 530; William C. Harris, *Lincoln's Rise to the Presidency* (Lawrence: University Press of Kansas, 2007), 287, 232.

27. McClintock, *Lincoln and the Decision for War*, 94–95.

28. McPherson, *Battle Cry of Freedom*, 256.

29. Cited in Nevins, *Ordeal of the Union*, 191.

30. *Raleigh North Carolina Standard*, 1 December 1860, in Dumond, *Southern Editorials*, 284–86.

31. Harold Holzer, *Lincoln, President-Elect: Abraham Lincoln and the Great Secession Winter 1860–1861* (New York: Simon and Schuster, 2008), 377–419.

32. See McClintock, *Lincoln and the Decision for War*, 194–99; Detzer, *Allegiance*, 212. The report of Lincoln's words to Rives came later from Kentuckian Charles S. Morehead, and his is "the only one extant" from someone present.

33. "Silent on secession though the Constitution was, its preamble proclaimed among its purposes the creation of 'a more perfect Union.' But the Articles of Confederation had

already pronounced the Union perpetual. What sensible man could think a confederation dissoluble at the whim of any of its constituent parts an improvement?" (Mark Wahlgren Summers, "'Freedom and Law Must Die ere They Sever': The North and the Coming of the Civil War," in *Why the Civil War Came*, edited by Boritt, 181).

34. See William C. Wright, *The Secession Movement in the Middle Atlantic States* (Rutherford, N.J.: Fairleigh Dickinson University Press, 1973), 176–80; Edwin G. Burrows and Mike Wallace, *Gotham: A History of New York City to 1898* (New York: Oxford University Press, 1999), 867–68; William W. Freehling, *The Road to Disunion* (New York: Oxford University Press, 2007), 2:348.

35. Lincoln as quoted in Harold Holzer, *Lincoln at Cooper Union: The Speech That Made Abraham Lincoln President* (New York: Simon and Schuster, 2004), 241.

36. Detzer, *Allegiance*, 285; Summers, "'Freedom and Law Must Die ere They Sever,'" 186; Anthony Gronowicz, *Race and Class Politics in New York City before the Civil War* (Boston: Northeastern University Press, 1998), 159.

37. Perkins, *Northern Editorials*, 1:265, 251.

38. *Omaha and Council Bluffs (Iowa) Daily Telegraph*, 24 February 1861, at the Huntington Library, San Marino, California.

39. McClintock, *Lincoln and the Decision for War*, 142, 145.

40. Nelson D. Lankford, *Cry Havoc!: The Crooked Road to Civil War, 1861* (New York: Viking, 2007), 82.

41. Owen Lovejoy, *His Brother's Blood: Speeches and Writings, 1838-64*, edited by William F. Moore and Jane Ann Moore (Urbana: University of Illinois Press, 2004), xxix, 142, 145–56; McClintock, *Lincoln and the Decision for War*, 197; Eric H. Walther, *The Shattering of the Union: America in the 1850s* (Wilmington, Del.: Scholarly Resources, 2004), 176.

42. Abraham Lincoln, *The Political Thought of Abraham Lincoln*, edited by Richard N. Current (Indianapolis: Bobbs-Merrill, 1967), 168–79; Potter, *Impending Crisis*, 565. On Seward's advice, see Nevins, *Ordeal of the Union*, 171.

43. Detzer, *Allegiance*, 214–17. Scott, age seventy-four, very tall (at six feet, four inches), and a War of 1812 veteran, "had held the rank of general for nearly half a century, and that of commanding general for two decades, and he was the only lieutenant general the United States Congress had ever created, even by brevet." Nonetheless, he had become very corpulent and was infamous for "the pomposity of his prose and plumery." After stern Unionist Joseph Holt replaced the sleazy John Floyd in December, "General Scott outlined a plan to introduce more soldiers into Washington gradually, to avoid the inflammatory impression that he was amassing troops to march against the insurgent states" (William Marvel, *Mr. Lincoln Goes to War* [Boston: Houghton Mifflin, 2006], 4).

44. Both Douglas and Seward seemed to hope that orchestrating a peaceful preservation of the Union would enable them to emerge as a leader in "a revitalized national party system" that would in turn work to control sectional tensions (McPherson, *Battle Cry of Freedom*, 238–39). "Aside from revenue collection, what [Lincoln] proposed was essentially passive. He would not sacrifice the Union in order to maintain peace, neither did he intend to provoke a needless civil war" (McClintock, *Lincoln and the Decision for War*, 187).

45. McClintock, *Lincoln and the Decision for War*, 227–28; Detzer, *Allegiance*, 221–

29. According to Detzer, "Some of the most talented, mentally nimble leaders in American history were acting in ways somewhere between slapdash and daft" (239–40). This judgment seems to apply to a good many episodes in U.S. history. For Nevins's classic summary of Lincoln's "three errors" during the crucial run-up to Fort Sumter, see *Ordeal of the Union*, 207.

46. Allan Nevins, *The War for the Union*, vol. 1, *The Improvised War, 1861–1862* (New York: Scribner's, 1955), 55, quoted by Daniel W. Crofts in his introduction to David M. Potter, *Lincoln and His Party in the Secession Crisis* (1942; Baton Rouge: Louisiana State University Press, 1995), xxiv. Crofts's introductory remarks constitute the best essay-length historiography of the secession crisis.

47. McClintock, *Lincoln and the Decision for War*, 246, 252.

48. Detzer, *Allegiance*, 225, 243–47; Nevins, *Ordeal of the Union*, 178; William Y. Thompson, *Robert Toombs*, 168.

49. See esp. McClintock, *Lincoln and the Decision for War*, 11; Kenneth M. Stampp, "Lincoln and the Secession Crisis," in *Imperiled Union: Essays on the Background of the Civil War* (New York: Oxford University Press, 1980), 163–88.

50. William Y. Thompson, *Robert Toombs*, 168; Detzer, *Allegiance*, 254.

51. Detzer, *Allegiance*, 256–57, 275, 304, 308–9.

52. Detzer, *Allegiance*, 36. According to Maury Klein, *Days of Defiance: Sumter, Secession, and the Coming of the Civil War* (New York: Knopf, 1997), 419, this private, whose name is spelled Galloway, "suffered fatal wounds and died three days later." Detzer, *Allegiance*, 309, reports that Gallway died later that night in the hospital.

53. Klein, *Days of Defiance*, 416–18; Detzer, *Allegiance*, 294–306.

54. Lankford, *Cry Havoc!*, 36–37, 68–69, 83–85.

55. For a helpful overview of Lincoln's constitutional outlook in general, see Daniel Farber, *Lincoln's Constitution* (Chicago: University of Chicago Press, 2003).

56. Donald L. Robinson, *"To the Best of My Ability": The Presidency and the Constitution* (New York: Norton, 1987), 128–29.

57. Ibid., 129–30; Charles A. Stevenson, *Congress at War: The Politics of Conflict since 1789* (Washington, D.C.: National Defense University Press and Potomac Books, 2007), 17, 30. According to Stevenson, prior Congresses had provided earlier presidents with such explicit authorizations of force in the quasi-war of 1798 with France, in 1802 against Tripoli, and against Algeria in 1815 (15–22, 30).

58. Andrew S. Coopersmith, *Fighting Words: An Illustrated History of Newspaper Accounts of the Civil War* (New York: Free Press, 2004), xvii.

59. Charles Hoffmann and Tess Hoffmann, *North by South: The Two Lives of Richard James Arnold* (Athens: University of Georgia Press, 1988), 7–8, 220, 232. Allen married James Arnold's twin sister, Eliza Harriet Arnold, and before the war often acted as agent for and trustee of his brother-in-law's properties in the North when Arnold lived on his estates in Georgia.

60. Bayly Ellen Marks and Mark Norton Schatz, eds., *Between North and South: A Maryland Journalist Views the Civil War* (Rutherford, N.J.: Fairleigh Dickinson Press, 1976), 26–27; William W. Freehling, *The South versus the South: How Anti-Confederate Southerners Shaped the Course of the Civil War* (New York: Oxford University Press, 2001), 62.

61. Kenneth M. Stampp, *And the War Came: The North and the Secession Crisis, 1860–1861* (1950; Baton Rouge: Louisiana State Press, 1970), 231–39.

62. The grand sachem of Tammany Hall, Isaac Vanderbeck Fowler, saw John Brown's raid as "riot, treason and murder" (Gronowicz, *Race and Class Politics*, 156).

63. E. N. Tailer Diaries, 1860–61, New-York Historical Society, New York.

64. *The Most Fearful Ordeal: Original Coverage of the Civil War by Writers and Reporters of the New York Times*, edited by James M. McPherson (New York: St. Martin's 2004), 75. The North had significant numbers of antiwar Democrats and outspoken Copperheads, most famously Ohio's Clement L. Vallandigham. See esp. Jennifer L. Weber, *Copperheads: The Rise and Fall of Lincoln's Opponents in the North* (New York: Oxford University Press, 2006).

65. Cited in Coopersmith, *Fighting Words*, 5, 301.

66. Leon F. Litwack, *Been in the Storm So Long: The Aftermath of Slavery* (New York: Vintage, 1980).

Guide to Further Reading

INTRODUCTION

The best historical surveys of the antebellum era are provided in two volumes of the Oxford History of the United States: Daniel Walker Howe, *What Hath God Wrought: The Transformation of America, 1815–1848* (New York: Oxford University Press, 2007); and James M. McPherson, *Battle Cry of Freedom: The Civil War Era* (New York: Oxford University Press, 1988). However, it is helpful to read Howe's volume alongside Charles G. Sellers, *The Market Revolution: Jacksonian America, 1815–1846* (New York: Oxford University Press, 1991), and John Ashworth, *Slavery, Capitalism, and Politics in the Antebellum Republic*, vol. 1, *Commerce and Compromise, 1820–1850* (Cambridge: Cambridge University Press, 1995). Likewise, it is best to read McPherson's chapters on late antebellum sectionalism and the secession crisis (chapters 1–10) in conjunction with Roy Franklin Nichols, *The Disruption of American Democracy* (New York: Free Press, 1948); J. G. Randall and David Herbert Donald, *Civil War and Reconstruction*, 2nd ed. (Lexington, Mass.: Heath, 1969), chapters 1–9; Peter J. Parish, *The American Civil War* (New York: Holmes and Meier, 1975), chapters 1–4; David M. Potter, *The Impending Crisis, 1846–1861*, completed and edited by Don E. Fehrenbacher (New York: Harper and Row, 1976); Kenneth M. Stampp, *The Imperiled Union: Essays on the Background of the Civil War* (New York: Oxford University Press, 1980); Bruce Levine, *Half Slave and Half Free: The Roots of the Civil War*, rev. ed. (New York: Hill and Wang/Farrar, Straus, and Giroux, 2005); and John Ashworth, *Slavery, Capitalism, and Politics in the Antebellum Republic*, vol. 2, *The Coming of the Civil War, 1850–1861* (Cambridge: Cambridge University Press, 2007).

Every historian of the Civil War era should do substantial reading in the eight gracefully written, deeply researched, and often wise volumes by Allan Nevins known collectively as *The Ordeal of the Union* (New York: Scribner's, 1947–71), the final two volumes published in the year of his death. Every student of the secession crisis must read, at a minimum, chapter 15, "Lincoln Takes the Helm," in *The Emergence of Lincoln*, vol. 2, *Prologue to Civil War, 1859–1861* (1950). This chapter is also included in Allan Nevins, *Ordeal of the Union: Selected Chapters*, edited and introduction by E. B. Long (New York: Scribner's, 1971), which provided me with my initial introduction to Nevins's work.

For insights into how postbellum Americans tried to make sense of the Civil War years, the essential books are Eric Foner, *Reconstruction: America's Unfinished Revolution, 1862–1877* (New York: Harper and Row, 1988); David W. Blight, *Race and Reunion: The Civil War in American Memory* (Cambridge: Belknap Press of Harvard University Press, 2001); Heather Cox Richardson, *West from Appomattox: The Reconstruction of America after the Civil War* (New Haven: Yale University Press, 2007); and Douglas A. Blackmon, *Slavery by Another Name: The Reenslavement of Black Americans from the Civil War to World War II* (New York: Anchor, 2008–9).

McPherson's *Battle Cry of Freedom* closes with a "Bibliographical Note" (pp. 865–75), which provides the best guide to essential monographic literature on the background to the Civil War and the secession crisis available at the time. The interested reader is strongly encouraged to review McPherson's titles, since most of them do not appear here. Nor does this guide presume to encompass every relevant monograph published since the mid-1980s. It focuses on books—monographs, edited sources, and occasional essay collections—that have been especially helpful to me in the composition of this volume. Additional titles, published both before and since McPherson wrote, would no doubt be listed here but for the author's deficiencies in time, energy, and perspicacity.

Extremely valuable edited works include the twenty-four volumes of the *American National Biography*, edited by John A. Garraty and Mark C. Carnes (New York: Oxford University Press, 1999), which contain a wealth of invaluable biographical sketches by a variety of distinguished scholars. A much briefer but often useful reference work is Paul S. Boyer, ed., *The Oxford Companion to United States History* (New York: Oxford University Press, 2001). A very old but remarkable collection of primary sources is Frank Moore, ed., *The Rebellion Record: A Diary of American Events, with Documents, Narratives, Illustrative Events, Poetry, Etc.*, vol. 1 (New York: Putnam, 1864). Historians of the secession crisis in particular are heavily indebted to two editions of excerpts from newspapers of the time originally prepared under the auspices of the American Historical Association: Dwight Lowell Dumond, ed., *Southern Editorials on Secession* (1931; Gloucester, Mass.: Smith, 1964); and Howard Cecil Perkins, ed., *Northern Editorials on Secession*, 2 vols. (1942; Gloucester, Mass.: Smith, 1964). Two scholars have compiled valuable pamphlet collections: Frank Freidel, ed., *Union Pamphlets of the Civil War Era, 1861–1865*, 2 vols. (Cambridge: Belknap Press of Harvard University Press, 1967); and Jon L. Wakelyn, ed., *Southern Pamphlets on Secession, November 1860–April 1861* (Chapel Hill: University of North Carolina Press, 1996). Two marvelous collections of essays are Gabor S. Boritt, ed., *Why the Civil War Came* (New York: Oxford University Press, 1996); and Martin H. Blatt and David Roediger, eds., *The Meaning of Slavery in the North* (New York: Garland, 1998). The best one-volume collection of documents is Kenneth M. Stampp, ed., *The Causes of the Civil War*, 3rd rev. ed. (New York: Touchstone/Simon and Schuster, 1991).

What follows is a topical bibliography, with each section organized alphabetically by author's last name. Titles that appear in McPherson's 1988 "Bibliographical Note" are included if they proved important to my approach and inquiries.

SYNTHESIS

Abzug, Robert H., and Stephen E. Maizlish, eds. *New Perspectives on Race and Slavery in America: Essays in Honor of Kenneth M. Stampp*. Lexington: University Press of Kentucky, 1986.

Clark, Christopher. *Social Change in America, from the Revolution through the Civil War*. Chicago: Dee, 2006.

Coopersmith, Andrew S. *Fighting Words: An Illustrated History of Newspaper Accounts of the Civil War*. New York: Free Press, 2004.

Detzer, David. *Allegiance: Fort Sumter, Charleston, and the Beginnings of the Civil War*. New York: Harcourt, 2001.

Einhorn, Robin L. *American Taxation, American Slavery*. Chicago: University of
Chicago Press, 2006.

Fehrenbacher, Don E. *The Slaveholding Republic: An Account of the United States
Government's Relations to Slavery*. Completed and edited by Ward M. McAfee.
New York: Oxford University Press, 2001.

Foner, Eric. *Politics and Ideology in the Age of the Civil War*. New York: Oxford
University Press, 1980.

Goodman, Paul. *Of One Blood: Abolitionism and the Origins of Racial Equality*.
Berkeley: University of California Press, 1998.

Grant, Susan-Mary. *The War for a Nation: The American Civil War*. New York:
Routledge/Taylor and Francis, 2006.

Guelzo, Allen C. *The Crisis of the Republic: A History of the Civil War and
Reconstruction*. New York: St. Martin's, 1995.

Holt, Michael F. *The Fate of Their Country: Politicians, Slavery Extension, and the
Coming of the Civil War*. New York: Hill and Wang, 2004.

———. *The Rise and Fall of the American Whig Party: Jacksonian Politics and the
Onset of the Civil War*. New York: Oxford University Press, 1999.

Hummel, Jeffrey Rogers. *Emancipating Slaves, Enslaving Free Men: A History of the
American Civil War*. Chicago: Open Court, 1996.

Huston, James L. *Calculating the Value of the Union: Slavery, Property Rights, and the
Economic Origins of the Civil War*. Chapel Hill: University of North Carolina Press,
2003.

Knupfer, Peter. *The Union as It Is: Constitutional Unionism and Sectional Compromise*.
Chapel Hill: University of North Carolina Press, 1991.

Lankford, Nelson D. *Cry Havoc!: The Crooked Road to Civil War, 1861*. New York:
Viking, 2007.

Lightner, David L. *Slavery and the Commerce Power: How the Struggle against the
Interstate Slave Trade Led to the Civil War*. New Haven: Yale University Press, 2006.

Maizlish, Stephen E., and John J. Kushma, eds. *Essays on Antebellum American
Politics*. College Station: Texas A & M University Press, 1982.

McDonald, Forrest. *States' Rights and the Union: Imperium in Imperio, 1776–1876*.
Lawrence: University Press of Kansas, 2000.

McPherson, James M. *This Mighty Scourge: Perspectives on the Civil War*. New York:
Oxford University Press, 2007.

Meinig, D. W. *The Shaping of America: A Geographical Perspective on 500 Years of
History*. Vol. 2, *Continental America, 1800–1867*. New Haven: Yale University Press,
1993.

Mitchell, Reid. *The American Civil War, 1861–1865*. Harlow, Eng.: Longman/Pearson,
2001.

Morrison, Michael A. *Slavery and the American West: The Eclipse of Manifest Destiny
and the Coming of the Civil War*. Chapel Hill: University of North Carolina Press,
1997.

Onuf, Nicholas, and Peter Onuf. *Nations, Markets, and War: Modern History and the
American Civil War*. Charlottesville: University of Virginia Press, 2006.

Ransom, Roger L. *Conflict and Compromise: The Political Economy of Slavery,*

Emancipation, and the American Civil War. Cambridge: Cambridge University Press, 1989.

Richards, Leonard L. The California Gold Rush and the Coming of the Civil War. New York: Knopf, 2007.

———. The Slave Power: The Free North and Southern Domination, 1780–1860. New York: Oxford University Press, 2000.

Rose, Anne C. Voices of the Marketplace: American Thought and Culture, 1830–1860. Lanham, Md.: Rowman and Littlefield, 1995.

Sewell, Richard H. A House Divided: Sectionalism and Civil War, 1848–1865. Baltimore: Johns Hopkins University Press, 1988.

Silbey, Joel. Storm over Texas: The Annexation Controversy and the Road to the Civil War. New York: Oxford University Press, 2005.

Summers, Mark W. The Plundering Generation: Corruption and the Crisis of the Union. New York: Oxford University Press, 1987.

Vorenberg, Michael. Final Freedom: The Civil War, the Abolition of Slavery, and the Thirteenth Amendment. Cambridge: Cambridge University Press, 2001.

Wilentz, Sean. The Rise of American Democracy, Jefferson to Lincoln. New York: Norton, 2005.

POLITICS PRIOR TO 1859

Earle, Jonathan H. Jacksonian Antislavery and the Politics of Free Soil, 1824–1854. Chapel Hill: University of North Carolina Press, 2004.

Formisano, Ronald P. For the People: American Populist Movements from the Revolution to the 1850s. Chapel Hill: University of North Carolina Press, 2008.

Hamilton, Holman. Prologue to Conflict: The Crisis and Compromise of 1850. New York: Norton, 1964.

Horsman, Reginald. Race and Manifest Destiny: The Origins of American Racial Anglo-Saxonism. Cambridge: Harvard University Press, 1981.

Marszalek, John F. The Petticoat Affair: Manner, Mutiny, and Sex in Andrew Jackson's White House. Baton Rouge: Louisiana State University Press, 1997.

Richards, Leonard L. "Gentlemen of Property and Standing": Anti-Abolition Mobs in Jacksonian America. New York: Oxford University Press, 1970.

Watson, Harry. Liberty and Power: The Politics of Jacksonian America. Rev. ed. New York: Hill and Wang, 2006.

INTERNATIONAL AND INTERSECTIONAL STUDIES

Ayers, Edward. In the Presence of Mine Enemies: The Civil War in the Heart of America, 1859–1863. New York: Norton. 2003.

Beran, Michael Knox. Forge of Empires, 1861–1871: Three Revolutionary Statesmen and the World They Made [President Abraham Lincoln, Tsar Alexander II, and Chancellor Otto von Bismarck]. New York: Free Press, 2007.

Bowman, Shearer Davis. Masters and Lords: Mid-19th-Century U.S. Planters and Prussian Junkers. New York: Oxford University Press, 1993.

Cunliffe, Marcus. Chattel Slavery and Wage Slavery: The Anglo-American Context, 1830–1860. Athens: University of Georgia Press, 1979.

Dal Lago, Enrico. *Agrarian Elites: American Slaveholders and Southern Italian Landowners, 1815–1861*. Baton Rouge: Louisiana State University Press, 2005.

Davis, David Brion. *Inhuman Bondage: The Rise and Fall of Slavery in the New World*. New York: Oxford University Press, 2006.

Degler, Carl N. *Neither Black nor White: Slavery and Race Relations in Brazil and the United States*. New York: Macmillan, 1971.

Dunlavy, Colleen. *Politics and Industrialization: Early Railroads in the United States*. Princeton: Princeton University Press, 1994.

Fredrickson, George M. *The Black Image in the White Mind: The Debates over African-American Culture and Destiny, 1815–1914*. New York: Harper and Row, 1973.

———. *White Supremacy: A Comparative Study in American and South African History*. New York: Oxford University Press, 1981.

Hindus, Michael Stephen. *Prison and Plantation: Crime, Justice, and Authority in Massachusetts and South Carolina, 1767–1878*. Chapel Hill: University of North Carolina Press, 1980.

Kolchin, Peter. *A Sphinx on the American Land: The Nineteenth-Century South, a Comparative Perspective*. Baton Rouge: Louisiana State University Press, 2003.

———. *Unfree Labor: American Slavery and Russian Serfdom*. Cambridge: Belknap Press of Harvard University Press, 1987.

Majewski, John. *A House Dividing: Economic Development in Pennsylvania and Virginia before the Civil War*. Cambridge: Cambridge University Press, 2000.

McPherson, James M. *What They Fought For, 1861–1865*. New York: Anchor, 1994.

Pease, Jane H., and William H. Pease. *Ladies, Women, and Wenches: Choice and Constraint in Antebellum Charleston and Boston*. Chapel Hill: University of North Carolina Press, 1990.

Pease, William H., and Jane H. Pease. *The Web of Progress: Private Values and Public Styles in Boston and Charleston, 1828–1845*. New York: Oxford University Press, 1986.

Quist, John W. *Restless Visionaries: The Social Roots of Antebellum Reform in Alabama and Michigan*. Baton Rouge: Louisiana State University Press, 1998.

Taylor, William R. *Cavalier and Yankee: The Old South and American National Character*. Cambridge: Harvard University Press, 1979.

Van den Berghe, Pierre L. *Race and Racism: A Comparative Perspective*. 2nd ed. New York: Wiley, 1978.

"HONOR"

Ayers, Edward L. *Vengeance and Justice: Crime and Punishment in the 19th-Century American South*. New York: Oxford University Press, 1984.

Bouchard, Constance Brittain. *Strong of Body, Brave and Noble: Chivalry and Society in Medieval France*. Ithaca: Cornell University Press, 1998.

Bowman, James. *Honor: A History*. New York: Encounter, 2006.

Freeman, Joanne B. *Affairs of Honor: National Politics in the New Republic*. New Haven: Yale University Press, 2001.

Greenberg, Kenneth M. *Honor and Slavery*. Princeton: Princeton University Press, 1996.

Gross, Ariela J. *Double Character: Slavery and Mastery in the Antebellum Southern Courtroom*. Athens: University of Georgia Press, 2000.

Haber, Samuel. *The Quest for Authority and Honor in the American Professions, 1750–1900*. Chicago: University of Chicago Press, 1991.

Oakes, James. *Slavery and Freedom: An Interpretation of the Old South*. New York: Knopf, 1990.

Patterson, Orlando. *Slavery and Social Death: A Comparative Study*. Cambridge: Harvard University Press, 1982.

Rubin, Miri. *The Hollow Crown: A History of Britain in the Late Middle Ages*. New York: Penguin, 2005.

Smith, Julia M. H. *Europe after Rome: A New Cultural History, 500–1000*. Oxford: Oxford University Press, 2005.

Stewart, Frank Henderson. *Honor*. Chicago: University of Chicago Press, 1994.

Wilson, Douglas L. *Honor's Voice: The Transformation of Abraham Lincoln*. New York: Knopf, 1998.

Wyatt-Brown, Bertram. *Honor and Violence in the Old South*. New York: Oxford University Press, 1986.

———. *The Shaping of Southern Culture: Honor, Grace, and War, 1760s–1890s*. Chapel Hill: University of North Carolina Press, 2001.

RELIGIOUS ISSUES

Abzug, Robert H. *Cosmos Crumbling: American Reform and the Religious Imagination*. New York: Oxford University Press, 1994.

Applegate, Debby. *The Most Famous Man in America: The Biography of Henry Ward Beecher*. New York: Three Leaves/Doubleday, 2006.

Beringer, Richard E., Herman Hattaway, Archer Jones, and William N. Still Jr. *Why the South Lost the Civil War*. Athens: University of Georgia Press, 1986.

Calhoun, Robert M. *Evangelicals and Conservatives in the Early South, 1740–1861*. Columbia: University of South Carolina Press, 1988.

Conkin, Paul. *The Uneasy Center: Reformed Christianity in Antebellum America*. Chapel Hill: University of North Carolina Press, 1995.

Corrigan, John. *Business of the Heart: Religion and Emotion in the Nineteenth Century*. Berkeley: University of California Press, 2002.

Fuller, A. James. *Chaplain to the Confederacy: Basil Manly and Life in the Old South*. Baton Rouge: Louisiana State University Press, 2000.

Goen, C. C. *Broken Churches, Broken Nation: Denominational Schisms and the Coming of the American Civil War*. Macon, Ga.: Mercer University Press, 1985.

Heyrman, Christine Leigh. *Southern Cross: The Beginnings of the Bible Belt*. New York: Knopf, 1997.

Holifield, E. Brooks. *Theology in America: Christian Thought from the Age of the Puritans to the Civil War*. New Haven: Yale University Press, 2003.

Johnson, Paul E., and Sean Wilentz. *The Kingdom of Matthias: A Story of Sex and Salvation in 19th-Century America*. New York: Oxford University Press, 1994.

Mathews, Donald G. *Religion in the Old South*. Chicago: University of Chicago Press, 1977.

Miller, Robert J. *Both Prayed to the Same God: Religion and Faith in the American Civil War*. Lanham, Md.: Lexington, 2007.

Moorhead, James H. *American Apocalypse: Yankee Protestants and the Civil War, 1860–1869*. New Haven: Yale University Press, 1978.

Noll, Mark A. *The Civil War as a Theological Crisis*. Chapel Hill: University of North Carolina Press, 2006.

Raboteau, Albert J. *Slave Religion: The "Invisible Institution" in the Antebellum South*. New York: Oxford University Press, 1978–80.

Robins, Glenn. *The Bishop of the Old South: The Ministry and Civil War Legacy of Leonidas Polk*. Mercer, Ga.: Mercer University Press, 2006.

Schantz, Mark S. *Piety in Providence: Class Dimensions of Religious Experience in Antebellum Rhode Island*. Ithaca: Cornell University Press, 2000.

Sernett, Milton C., ed. *African American Religious History: A Documentary Witness*. 2nd ed. Durham: Duke University Press, 1999.

Smith, H. Shelton. *In His Image, but . . . : Racism in Southern Religion, 1780–1910*. Durham: Duke University Press, 1972.

Smith, Morton, and R. Joseph Hoffmann, eds. *What the Bible Really Says*. New York: Harper San Francisco/HarperCollins, 1989.

Snay, Mitchell. *Gospel of Disunion: Religion and Separatism in the Antebellum South*. 1993; Chapel Hill: University of North Carolina Press, 1997.

Stout, Harry S. *Upon the Altar of the Nation: A Moral History of the American Civil War*. New York: Viking, 2006.

Wills, Gary. *Head and Heart: A History of Christianity in America*. New York: Penguin, 2007.

CULTURAL, ECONOMIC, INTELLECTUAL, AND SOCIAL HISTORY

Adams, Katharine J., and Lewis L. Gould, eds. *Inside the Natchez Trace Collection: New Sources for Southern History*. Baton Rouge: Louisiana State University Press, 1999.

Atack, Jeremy, and Peter Passell. *A New Economic View of American History*. 2nd ed. New York: Norton, 1994.

Bateman, Fred, and Thomas Weiss. *A Deplorable Scarcity: The Failure of Industrialization in the Slave Economy*. Chapel Hill: University of North Carolina Press, 1981.

Bender, Thomas, ed. *The Antislavery Debate: Capitalism and Abolitionism as a Problem of Historical Interpretation*. Berkeley: University of California Press, 1992.

Bodenhorn, Howard. *A History of Banking in Antebellum America: Financial Markets and Economic Development in an Era of Nation-Building*. Cambridge: Cambridge University Press, 2000.

Carlton, David L., and Peter Coclanis, eds. *The South, the Nation, and the World: Perspectives on Southern Economic Development*. Charlottesville: University of Virginia Press, 2003.

Clark, John E., Jr. *Railroads in the Civil War: The Impact of Management on Victory and Defeat*. Baton Rouge: Louisiana State University Press, 2001.

Delfino, Susanna, and Michele Gillespie, eds. *Global Perspectives on Industrial*

Transformation in the American South. Columbia: University of Missouri Press, 2005.

Faust, Drew Gilpin. *The Creation of Confederate Nationalism: Ideology and Identity in the Civil War South.* Baton Rouge: Louisiana State University Press, 1988.

Goldfield, David. *Region, Race, and Cities: Interpreting the Rural South.* Baton Rouge: Louisiana State University Press, 1997.

Grant, Susan-Mary. *North over South: Northern Nationalism and American Identity in the Antebellum Era.* Lawrence: University Press of Kansas, 2000.

Laurie, Bruce. *Artisans into Workers: Labor in Nineteenth-Century America.* New York: Noonday/Farrar, Straus, and Giroux, 1989.

O'Brien, Patrick. *The Economic Effects of the American Civil War.* Atlantic Highlands, N.J.: Humanities, 1988.

Parker, William N. *Europe, America, and the Wider World: Essays on the Economic History of Western Capitals.* Vol. 1, *Europe and the World Economy.* Cambridge: Cambridge University Press, 1984.

Ryan, Mary P. *Civic Wars: Democracy and Public Life in the American City during the Nineteenth Century.* Berkeley: University of California Press, 1997.

Saum, Lewis O. *The Popular Mood of Pre–Civil War America.* Westport, Conn.: Greenwood, 1980.

Schweikert, Larry. *Banking in the American South from the Age of Jackson to Reconstruction.* Baton Rouge: Louisiana State University Press, 1987.

Stover, John F. *American Railroads.* 2nd ed. Chicago: University of Chicago Press, 1997.

Stowe, Steven M. *Intimacy and Power in the Old South: Ritual in the Lives of the Planters.* Baltimore: Johns Hopkins University Press, 1987.

GENDER ISSUES

Cashin, Joan E. *A Family Venture: Men and Women on the Southern Frontier.* New York: Oxford University Press, 1991.

Faust, Drew Gilpin. *Mothers of Invention: Women of the Slaveholding South in the American Civil War.* Chapel Hill: University of North Carolina Press, 1996.

Fox-Genovese, Elizabeth. *Within the Plantation Household: Black and White Women of the Old South.* Chapel Hill: University of North Carolina Press, 1988.

Greenberg, Amy. *Manifest Manhood and the Antebellum American Empire.* Cambridge: Cambridge University Press, 2005.

Horowitz, Helen Lefkowitz. *Rereading Sex: Battles over Sexual Knowledge and Suppression in Nineteenth-Century America.* New York: Knopf, 2004.

Rable, George C. *Civil Wars: Women and the Crisis of Southern Nationalism.* Urbana: University of Illinois Press, 1989.

Silber, Nina. *Daughters of the Union: Northern Women Fight the Civil War.* Cambridge: Harvard University Press, 2005.

Varon, Elizabeth. *We Mean to Be Counted: White People and Politics in Antebellum Virginia.* Chapel Hill: University of North Carolina Press, 1998.

Boles, John B. *The South through Time: A History of an American Region*. Englewood Cliffs, N.J.: Prentice Hall, 1995.

Cooper, William J., Jr., and Thomas E. Terrill. *The American South: A History*. 3rd ed. Boston: McGraw-Hill, 2002.

Crofts, Daniel W. *Reluctant Confederates: Upper South Unionists in the Secession Crisis*. Chapel Hill: University of North Carolina Press, 1988.

Davis, William C. *Look Away: A History of the Confederate States of America*. New York: Free Press, 2003.

Fox-Genovese, Elizabeth, and Eugene D. Genovese. *The Mind of the Master Class: History and Faith in the Southern Slaveholders' Worldview*. New York: Cambridge University Press, 2005.

Freehling, William W. *The Road to Disunion*. 2 vols. New York: Oxford University Press, 1990, 2007.

———. *The South versus the South: How Anti-Confederate Southerners Shaped the Course of the Civil War*. New York: Oxford University Press, 2001.

Jordan, Winthrop D., ed. *Slavery and the American South*. Jackson: University Press of Mississippi, 2003.

Rable, George C. *The Confederate Republic: A Revolution against Politics*. Chapel Hill: University of North Carolina Press, 1994.

Rubin, Anne Sarah. *A Shattered Nation: The Rise and Fall of the Confederacy, 1861–1868*. Chapel Hill: University of North Carolina Press, 2005.

Scarborough, William Kauffman. *Masters of the Big House: Elite Slaveholders of the Mid–Nineteenth Century South*. Baton Rouge: Louisiana State University Press, 2003.

Shore, Laurence. *Southern Capitalists: The Ideological Leadership of an Elite, 1832–1885*. Chapel Hill: University of North Carolina Press, 1986.

Towers, Frank. *The Urban South and the Coming of the Civil War*. Charlottesville: University of Virginia Press, 2004.

Walther, Eric H. *The Fire-Eaters*. Baton Rouge: Louisiana State University Press, 1992.

Crofts, Daniel. Introduction to David M. Potter, *Lincoln and His Party in the Secession Crisis*. 1942. Baton Rouge: Louisiana State University Press, 1995.

Etcheson, Nicole. *The Emerging Midwest: Upland Southerners and the Political Culture of the Old Northwest, 1787–1861*. Bloomington: Indiana University Press, 1996.

Eyal, Yonatan. *The Young America Movement and the Transformation of the Democratic Party, 1828–1861*. Cambridge: Cambridge University Press, 2007.

Foner, Eric. *Free Soil, Free Labor, Free Men: The Ideology of the Republican Party before the Civil War*. London: Oxford University Press, 1970.

Hess, Earl J. *Liberty, Virtue, and Progress: Northerners and Their War for the Union*. 2nd ed. New York: Fordham University Press, 1997.

McClintock, Russell. *Lincoln and the Decision for War: The Northern Response to Secession*. Chapel Hill: University of North Carolina Press, 2008.

Neely, Mark, Jr. *The Union Divided: Party Conflict in the Civil War North.* Cambridge: Harvard University Press, 2002.

Oakes, James. *The Radical and the Republican: Frederick Douglass, Abraham Lincoln, and the Triumph of Antislavery Politics.* New York: Norton, 2007.

Smith, Adam I. P. *No Party Now: Politics in the Civil War North.* New York: Oxford University Press, 2006.

Stampp, Kenneth M. *And the War Came: The North and the Secession Crisis, 1860–1861.* 1950. Baton Rouge: Louisiana State University Press, 1970.

Voss-Hubbard, Mark. *Beyond Party: Cultures of Partisanship in Northern Politics before the Civil War.* Baltimore: Johns Hopkins University Press, 2002.

Weber, Jennifer L. *Copperheads: The Rise and Fall of Lincoln's Opponents in the North.* New York: Oxford University Press, 2006.

LINCOLN AND HIS FAMILY

Berry, Stephen. *House of Abraham: Lincoln and the Todds, a Family Divided by War.* Boston: Houghton Mifflin, 2007.

Burlingame, Michael. *The Inner World of Abraham Lincoln.* Urbana: University of Illinois Press, 1994.

Carwardine, Richard J. *Lincoln.* Harlow, Eng.: Longman/Pearson, 2003.

Clinton, Catherine. *Mrs. Lincoln: A Life.* New York: HarperCollins, 2009.

Current, Richard N., ed. *The Political Thought of Abraham Lincoln.* Indianapolis: Bobbs-Merrill, 1967.

Donald, David Herbert. *Lincoln.* New York: Simon and Schuster, 1995.

Fredrickson, George M. *Big Enough to Be Inconsistent: Abraham Lincoln Confronts Slavery and Race.* Cambridge: Harvard University Press, 2008.

Forgie, George B. *Patricide in the House Divided: A Psychological Interpretation of Lincoln and His Age.* New York: Norton, 1979.

Goodwin, Doris Kearns. *Team of Rivals: The Political Genius of Abraham Lincoln.* New York: Simon and Schuster, 2005.

Harris, William C. *Lincoln's Rise to the Presidency.* Lawrence: University Press of Kansas, 2007.

Harrison, Lowell. *Lincoln of Kentucky.* Lexington: University Press of Kentucky, 2000.

Holzer, Harold. *Lincoln at Cooper Union: The Speech That Made Abraham Lincoln President.* New York: Simon and Schuster, 2004.

———. *Lincoln, President-Elect: Abraham Lincoln and the Great Secession Winter 1860–1861.* New York: Simon and Schuster, 2008.

Johannsen, Robert W. *Lincoln, the South, and Slavery: The Political Dimension.* Baton Rouge: Louisiana State University Press, 1991.

Lincoln, Abraham. *This Fiery Trial: The Speeches and Writings of Abraham Lincoln.* Edited by William E. Gienapp. New York: Oxford University Press, 2002.

———. *Speeches and Writings, 1832–1858: Speeches, Letters, and Miscellaneous Writings, the Lincoln-Douglas Debates.* New York: Library of America, 1989.

———. *Speeches and Writings, 1859–1865: Speeches, Letters, and Miscellaneous*

Writings, Presidential Messages and Proclamations. New York: Library of America, 1989.

Miller, William Lee. *Lincoln's Virtues: An Ethical Biography*. New York: Knopf, 2002.

Paludan, Phillip Shaw. *The Presidency of Abraham Lincoln*. Lawrence: University Press of Kansas, 1994.

Simon, James F. *Lincoln and Chief Justice Taney: Slavery, Secession, and the President's War Powers*. New York: Simon and Schuster, 2006.

JEFFERSON DAVIS AND HIS FAMILY

Cashin, Joan E. *First Lady of the Confederacy: Varina Davis's Civil War*. Cambridge: Belknap Press of Harvard University Press, 2006.

Cooper, William J., Jr. *Jefferson Davis, American*. New York: Knopf, 2000.

Davis, Jefferson. *The Messages and Papers of Jefferson Davis and the Confederacy: Including Diplomatic Correspondence, 1861–1865*. Edited and compiled by James D. Richardson. 2 vols. Philadelphia: Chelsea House, 2001.

Davis, William C., ed. *Jefferson Davis: The Essential Writings*. New York: Modern Library, 2003.

———. *Jefferson Davis, the Man and His Hour: A Biography*. New York: HarperCollins, 1991.

Eaton, Clement. *Jefferson Davis*. New York: Free Press, 1977.

THOMAS JEFFERSON AND HIS LEGACY

Ellis, Joseph J. *American Sphinx: The Character of Thomas Jefferson*. New York: Knopf, 1997.

Gordon-Reed, Annette. *The Hemingses of Monticello: An American Family*. New York: Norton, 2008.

———. *Thomas Jefferson and Sally Hemings: An American Controversy*. Charlottesville: University Press of Virginia, 1997.

Halliday, E. M. *Understanding Thomas Jefferson*. New York: HarperCollins, 2001.

Maier, Pauline. *American Scripture: Making the Declaration of Independence*. New York: Knopf, 1997.

McLaughlin, Jack. *Jefferson and Monticello: The Biography of a Builder*. New York: Holt, 1988.

Miller, John Chester. *The Wolf by the Ears: Thomas Jefferson and Slavery*. New York: Free Press, 1977.

Peterson, Merrill D. *The Jeffersonian Image in the American Mind*. New York: Oxford University Press, 1960.

Sheldon, Garrett Ward. *The Political Philosophy of Thomas Jefferson*. Baltimore: Johns Hopkins University Press, 1991.

Simon, James F. *What Kind of Nation: Thomas Jefferson, John Marshall, and the Epic Struggle to Create a United States*. New York: Simon and Schuster, 2002.

Sloan, Herbert E. *Principle and Interest: Thomas Jefferson and the Problem of Debt*. New York: Oxford University Press, 1995.

Smith, Page. *Jefferson: Architect of America*. New York: iBooks, 2002. Originally published as *Jefferson: A Revealing Biography*. New York: American Heritage, 1976.

SLAVERY AS AN INSTITUTION

Berlin, Ira. *Generations of Captivity: A History of African-American Slaves*. Cambridge: Belknap Press of Harvard University Press, 2003.

Deyle, Steven. *Carry Me Back: The Domestic Slave Trade in American Life*. New York: Oxford University Press, 2005.

Dunaway, Wilma A. *Slavery in the American Mountain South*. Cambridge: Cambridge University Press, 2003.

Fogel, Robert William. *Without Consent or Contract: The Rise and Fall of American Slavery*. New York: Norton, 1989.

Franklin, John Hope, and Alfred A. Moss Jr. *From Slavery to Freedom: A History of African Americans*. 8th ed. New York: Knopf, 2000.

Horton, James Oliver, and Lois E. Horton. *Slavery and the Making of America*. New York: Oxford University Press, 2005.

Johnson, Walter. *Soul by Soul: Life inside the Antebellum Slave Market*. Cambridge: Harvard University Press, 1999.

Kelley, Robin D. G., and Earl Lewis, eds. *To Make Our World Anew: A History of African Americans*. New York: Oxford University Press, 2000.

Kolchin, Peter. *American Slavery, 1619–1877*. Rev. ed. New York: Hill and Wang, 2003.

Litwack, Leon F. *Been in the Storm So Long: The Aftermath of Slavery*. New York: Vintage, 1980.

Morris, Thomas D. *Southern Slavery and the Law, 1619–1860*. Chapel Hill: University of North Carolina Press, 1996.

Schwarz, Philip J. *Twice Condemned: Slaves and the Criminal Law of Virginia, 1705–1865*. Baton Rouge: Louisiana State University Press, 1988.

Smith, Mark. *Debating Slavery: Economy and Society in the Antebellum South*. Cambridge: Cambridge University Press, 1998.

Tadman, Michael. *Speculators and Slaves: Masters, Traders, and Slaves in the Old South*. Madison: University of Wisconsin Press, 1989.

Wright, Gavin. *Slavery and American Economic Development*. Baton Rouge: Louisiana State University Press, 2006.

PRIMARY SOURCES ON THE OLD SOUTH (PUBLISHED SINCE 1986)

Benners, Augustus. *Disunion, War, Defeat, and Recovery in Alabama: The Journal of Augustus Benners, 1850–1885*. Edited by Glenn Linden and Virginia Linden. Macon, Ga.: Mercer University Press, 2007.

Brevard, Keziah Goodwyn Hopkins. *A Plantation Mistress on the Eve of the Civil War: The Diary of Keziah Goodwyn Hopkins Brevard, 1860–61*. Edited by John Hammond Moore. Columbia: University of South Carolina Press, 1993.

Brownlow, William Gannaway. *Secessionists and Other Scoundrels: Selections from Parson Brownlow's Book*. Edited and introduction by Steven B. Ash. Baton Rouge: Louisiana State University Press, 1999.

Calhoun, John C. *Union and Liberty: The Political Philosophy of John C. Calhoun.* Edited by Ross M. Lence. Indianapolis: Liberty Fund, 1992.

Freehling, William W., and Craig M. Simpson, eds. *Secession Debated: Georgia's Showdown in 1860.* New York: Oxford University Press, 1992.

McCord, Louisa Susanna Cheves. *Louisa S. McCord: Political and Social Essays.* Edited by Richard C. Lounsbury. Charlottesville: University Press of Virginia, 1995.

Neblett, Elizabeth Scott. *A Rebel Wife in Texas: The Diary and Letters of Elizabeth Scott Neblett, 1852–1964.* Edited and introduction by Erika L. Murr. Baton Rouge: Louisiana State University Press, 2001.

Russell, William Howard. *My Diary North and South.* Edited by Eugene H. Berwanger. New York: Knopf, 1988.

Smith, Mark M., ed. *The Old South.* Malden, Mass.: Blackwell, 2001.

Thomas, Ella Gertrude Clanton. *The Secret Eye: The Journal of Ella Gertrude Clanton Thomas, 1848–1889.* Edited by Virginia Ingraham Burr. Introduction by Nell Irvin Painter. Chapel Hill: University of North Carolina Press, 1990.

Thomassen, Basil Armstrong. *North Carolina Yeoman: The Diary of Basil Armstrong Thomassen, 1853–1862.* Edited by Paul D. Escott. Athens: University of Georgia Press, 1996.

Wakelyn, Jon L., ed. *Southern Unionist Pamphlets and the Civil War.* Columbia: University of Missouri Press, 1999.

PRIMARY SOURCES FROM ANTEBELLUM FREE STATES
(PUBLISHED SINCE 1986)

Auchincloss, Louis, ed. *The Hone and Strong Diaries of Old Manhattan.* New York: Abbeville, 1989.

Bryant, William Cullen. *Power for Sanity: Selected Editorials of William Cullen Bryant, 1829–1861.* Compiled and annotated by William Cullen Bryant II. New York: Fordham University Press, 1994.

Ceplair, Larry, ed. *The Public Years of Sarah and Angelina Grimké: Selected Writings, 1835–1839.* New York: Columbia University Press, 1989.

Donald, Robert Bruce, ed. *Manhood and Patriotic Awakening in the American Civil War: The John E. Mattoon Letters, 1859–1866.* Lanham, Md.: Hamilton, 2008.

Folmar, John Kent, ed. *This State of Wonders: The Letters of an Iowa Frontier Family, 1858–1861.* Iowa City: University of Iowa Press, 1986.

Lamson, Roswell Hawks. *Lamson of the Gettysburg: The Civil War Letters of Lieutenant Roswell H. Lamson, U.S. Navy.* Edited by James M. McPherson and Patricia R. McPherson. New York: Oxford University Press, 1997.

Lovejoy, Owen. *His Brother's Blood: Speeches and Writings, 1838–64.* Edited by William F. Moore and Jane Ann Moore. Urbana: University of Illinois Press, 2004.

Lytle, William Haines. *For Honor, Glory, and Union: The Mexican and Civil War Letters of Brig. Gen. William Haines Lytle.* Edited by Ruth C. Carter. Lexington: University Press of Kentucky, 1999.

Meigs, John Rodgers. *A Civil War Soldier of Christ and Country: The Selected Correspondence of John Rodgers Meigs, 1859–64.* Edited by Mary A. Giunta. Urbana: University of Illinois Press, 2006.

The Most Fearful Ordeal: Original Coverage of the Civil War by Writers and Reporters of the New York Times. Introduction and notes by James M. McPherson. New York: St. Martin's, 2004.

SLAVE STATES AND SOUTHERN COMMUNITIES

Ash, Stephen V. *Middle Tennessee Society Transformed, 1860–1870: War and Peace in the Upper South.* Baton Rouge: Louisiana State University Press, 1988.

Baum, Dale. *The Shattering of Texas Unionism: Politics in the Lone Star State during the Civil War Era.* Baton Rouge: Louisiana State University Press, 1998.

Bolton, Charles C. *Poor Whites of the Antebellum South: Tenants and Laborers in Central North Carolina and Northeast Mississippi.* Durham: Duke University Press, 1994.

Bond, Bradley G. *Political Culture in the Nineteenth-Century South: Mississippi, 1830–1860.* Baton Rouge: Louisiana State University Press, 1995.

Campbell, Randolph B. *An Empire for Slavery: The Peculiar Institution in Texas.* Baton Rouge: Louisiana State University Press, 1989.

Carey, Anthony Gene. *Politics, Slavery, and the Union in Antebellum Georgia.* Athens: University of Georgia Press, 1997.

Carmichael, Peter S. *The Last Generation: Young Virginians in Peace, War, and Reunion.* Chapel Hill: University of North Carolina Press, 2005.

Clarke, Erskine. *Dwelling Place: A Plantation Epic.* New Haven: Yale University Press, 2005.

Cobb, James C. *The Most Southern Place on Earth: The Mississippi Delta and the Roots of Regional Identity.* New York: Oxford University Press, 1992.

Crofts, Daniel W. *Old Southampton: Politics and Society in a Virginia County, 1834–1869.* Charlottesville: University Press of Virginia, 1992.

Harris, William C. *North Carolina and the Coming of the Civil War.* Raleigh: North Carolina Division of Archives and History, 1989.

Harrison, Lowell H., and James C. Klotter. *A New History of Kentucky.* Lexington: University Press of Kentucky, 1997.

Hurt, R. Douglas. *Agriculture and Slavery in Missouri's Little Dixie.* Columbia: University of Missouri Press, 1992.

Jordan, Winthrop D. *Tumult and Silence at Second Creek: An Inquiry into a Civil War Slave Conspiracy.* Baton Rouge: Louisiana State University Press, 1993.

Kimball, Gregg D. *American City, Southern Place: A Cultural History of Antebellum Richmond.* Athens: University of Georgia Press, 2000.

Lowe, Richard G., and Randolph B. Campbell. *Planters and Plain Folk: Agriculture in Antebellum Texas.* Dallas: Southern Methodist University Press, 1987.

McCurry, Stephanie. *Masters of Small Worlds: Yeoman Households, Gender Relations, and the Political Culture of the Antebellum South Carolina Low Country.* New York: Oxford University Press, 1995.

Morris, Christopher. *Becoming Southern: The Evolution of a Way of Life, Warren County and Vicksburg, 1770–1860.* New York: Oxford University Press, 1995.

Olsen, Christopher J. *Political Culture and Secession in Mississippi: Masculinity,*

Honor, and the Antiparty Tradition, 1830–1860. New York: Oxford University Press, 2000.

Reidy, Joseph P. From Slavery to Agrarian Capitalism in the Cotton Plantation South: Central Georgia, 1800–1880. Chapel Hill: University of North Carolina Press, 1992.

Reynolds, Donald E. Texas Terrors: The Slave Insurrection Panic of 1860 and the Secession of the Lower South. Baton Rouge: Louisiana State University Press, 2007.

Rothman, Joshua D. Notorious in the Neighborhood: Sex and Families across the Color Line in Virginia, 1787–1861. Chapel Hill: University of North Carolina Press, 2003.

Shade, William G. Democratizing the Old Dominion: Virginia and the Second Party System, 1824–1861. Charlottesville: University Press of Virginia, 1996.

Sinha, Manisha. The Counterrevolution of Slavery: Politics and Ideology in Antebellum South Carolina. Chapel Hill: University of North Carolina Press, 2000.

Stevenson, Brenda S. Life in Black and White: Family and Community in the Slave South. New York: Oxford University Press, 1996.

Sutherland, Donald E. Seasons of War: The Ordeal of a Confederate Community, 1861–1865. Baton Rouge: Louisiana State University Press, 1995.

Takagi, Midori. Rearing Wolves to Our Own Destruction: Slavery in Richmond, Virginia, 1782–1865. Charlottesville: University Press of Virginia, 1999.

Tallant, Harold D. Evil Necessity: Slavery and Political Culture in Antebellum Kentucky. Lexington: University Press of Kentucky, 2003.

Woods, James L. Rebellion and Realignment: Arkansas's Road to Secession. Fayetteville: University of Arkansas Press, 1987.

FREE STATES AND NORTHERN COMMUNITIES

Abbott, Richard H. Cotton and Capital: Boston Businessmen and Antislavery Reform, 1854–1868. Amherst: University of Massachusetts Press, 1991.

Beckert, Sven. The Monied Metropolis: New York City and the Consolidation of the American Bourgeoisie, 1850–1896. Cambridge: Cambridge University Press, 2001.

Booraem, Hendrik V. The Formation of the Republican Party in New York: Politics and Conscience in the Antebellum North. New York: New York University Press, 1983.

Burrows, Edward G., and Mike Wallace. Gotham: A History of New York City to 1898. New York: Oxford University Press, 1999.

Cook, Robert. Baptism of Fire: The Republican Party in Iowa, 1838–1878. Ames: Iowa State University Press, 1994.

Current, Richard N. The History of Wisconsin. Vol. 2, The Civil War Era, 1848–1873. Madison: State Historical Society of Wisconsin, 1976.

Faler, Paul G. Mechanics and Manufacturers in the Early Industrial Revolution: Lynn, Massachusetts, 1780–1860. Albany: State University of New York Press, 1981.

Gronowicz, Anthony. Race and Class Politics in New York City before the Civil War. Boston: Northeastern University Press, 1998.

Kessner, Thomas. Capital City: New York City and the Men behind America's Rise to Economic Dominance. New York: Simon and Schuster, 2003.

McKay, Ernest A. The Civil War and New York City. Syracuse: Syracuse University Press, 1990.

Miller, Donald L. *City of the Century: The Epic of Chicago and the Making of America.*
New York: Simon and Schuster, 1996.

O'Connor, Thomas H. *Civil War Boston: Home Front and Battlefield.* Boston:
Northeastern University Press, 1997.

Pierce, Bessie Louise. *A History of Chicago.* Vol. 2, *From Town to City, 1848–1871.*
New York: Knopf, 1940.

INDIVIDUAL SLAVES AND FORMER SLAVES

Clinton, Catherine. *Harriet Tubman: The Road to Freedom.* Boston: Little, Brown,
2004.

Douglass, Frederick. *My Bondage and My Freedom.* Edited by William L. Andrews.
1855. Urbana: University of Illinois Press, 1987.

———. *Narrative of the Life of Frederick Douglass, an American Slave, Written by
Himself, with Related Documents.* Edited and introduction by David W. Blight.
2nd ed. Boston: Bedford/St. Martin's, 2003.

Fleischner, Jennifer. *Mrs. Lincoln and Mrs. Keckly: The Remarkable Story of the
Friendship between a First Lady and a Former Slave.* New York: Broadway, 2003.

Gilbert, Olive. *Narrative of Sojourner Truth.* Edited and introduction by Margaret
Washington. 1850; New York: Vintage, 1993.

———. *Narrative of the Life of Sojourner Truth.* Edited and introduction by Nell Irvin
Painter. New York: Penguin, 1998.

Larson, Kate Clifford. *Bound for the Promised Land: Harriet Tubman, Portrait of an
American Hero.* New York: Ballantine, 2004.

McFeely, William S. *Frederick Douglass.* New York: Norton, 1991.

McLaurin, Melton A. *Celia, a Slave.* Athens: University of Georgia Press, 1991.

Painter, Nell Irvin. *Sojourner Truth: A Life, a Symbol.* New York: Norton, 1996.

Sernett, Milton C. *Harriet Tubman: Myth, Memory, and History.* Durham: Duke
University Press, 2007.

WHITE SOUTHERNERS

Ambrose, Douglas. *Henry Hughes and Proslavery Thought in the Old South.* Baton
Rouge: Louisiana State University Press, 1996.

Andrew, Rod, Jr. *Wade Hampton: Confederate Warrior to Southern Redeemer.* Chapel
Hill: University of North Carolina Press, 2008.

Bagwell, James E. *Rice Gold: James Hamilton Couper and Plantation Life on the
Georgia Coast.* Macon, Ga.: Mercer University Press, 2000.

Beatty, Bess. *Alamance: The Holt Family and Industrialization in a North Carolina
County, 1847–1900.* Baton Rouge: Louisiana State University Press, 1999.

Brazy, Martha Jane. *An American Planter: Stephen Duncan of Antebellum Natchez and
New York.* Baton Rouge: Louisiana State University Press, 2006.

Cisco, Walter Brian. *Wade Hampton: Confederate Warrior, Conservative Statesman.*
Washington, D.C.: Brassey's, 2004.

Crapol, Edward P. *John Tyler, the Accidental President.* Chapel Hill: University of North
Carolina Press, 2006.

Dew, Charles B. *Ironmaker to the Confederacy: Joseph R. Anderson and the Tredegar Iron Works*. 1966. Richmond: Library of Virginia, 1999.

Duisenberre, William. *Slavemaster President: The Double Career of James Polk*. New York: Oxford University Press, 2003.

Evans, Curtis J. *The Conquest of Labor: Daniel Pratt and Southern Industrialization*. Baton Rouge: Louisiana State University Press, 2001.

Faust, Drew Gilpin. *James Henry Hammond and the Old South: A Design for Mastery*. Baton Rouge: Louisiana State University Press, 1982.

Gower, Herschel. *Charles Dahlgren of Natchez: The Civil War and Dynastic Decline*. Washington, D.C.: Brassey's, 2002.

Heck, Frank H. *Proud Kentuckian: John C. Breckinridge, 1821–1875*. Lexington: University Press of Kentucky, 1976.

Niven, John. *John C. Calhoun and the Price of Union: A Biography*. Baton Rouge: Louisiana State University Press, 1987.

Parrish, T. Michael. *Richard Taylor: Soldier Prince of Dixie*. Chapel Hill: University of North Carolina Press, 1992.

Phillips, Christopher. *Missouri's Confederate: Claiborne Fox Jackson and the Creation of Southern Identity in the Border West*. Columbia: University of Missouri Press, 2000.

Pryor, Elizabeth Brown. *Reading the Man: A Portrait of Robert E. Lee through His Private Letters*. New York: Viking, 2007.

Ramage, James A. *Rebel Raider: The Life of General John Hunt Morgan*. Lexington: University Press of Kentucky, 1986.

Remini, Robert V. *Henry Clay: Statesman for the Union*. New York: Norton, 1991.

Rosengarten. Theodore. *Tombee: Portrait of a Cotton Planter, with the Journal of Thomas B. Chaplin, 1822–1890*. New York: Morrow, 1986.

Varon, Elizabeth R. *Southern Lady, Yankee Spy: The True Story of Elizabeth Van Lew, a Union Agent in the Heart of the Confederacy*. New York: Oxford University Press, 2003.

Walther, Eric H. *William Lowndes Yancey and the Coming of the Civil War*. Chapel Hill: University of North Carolina Press, 2006.

WHITE NORTHERNERS

Applegate, Debby. *The Most Famous Man in America: The Biography of Henry Ward Beecher*. New York: Three Leaves/Doubleday, 2006.

Baker, Jean. *James Buchanan*. New York: Times Books/Holt, 2004.

Donald, David H. *Charles Sumner and the Coming of the Civil War*. New York: Knopf, 1960.

Johannsen, Robert W. *Stephen A. Douglas*. New York: Oxford University Press, 1973.

Niven, John. *Martin Van Buren: The Romantic Age of American Politics*. New York: Oxford University Press, 1983.

Peterson, Merrill D. *John Brown: The Legend Revisited*. Charlottesville: University of Virginia Press, 2002.

Remini, Robert. *Daniel Webster: The Man and His Time*. New York: Norton, 1997.

Reynolds, David S. *John Brown, Abolitionist: The Man Who Killed Slavery, Sparked the Civil War, and Seeded Civil Rights*. New York: Knopf, 2005.

Rugoff, Milton. *The Beechers: An American Family in the Nineteenth Century*. New York: Harper and Row, 1981.

Silbey, Joel H. *Martin Van Buren and the Emergence of American Popular Politics*. Lanham, Md.: Rowman and Littlefield, 2002.

Taylor, John M. *William Henry Seward: Lincoln's Right Hand*. Washington, D.C.: Brassey's, 1991.

Trefousse, Hans L. *Thaddeus Stevens: Nineteenth-Century Egalitarian*. Chapel Hill: University of North Carolina Press, 1997.

Acknowledgments

Many years ago in Austin, Texas, Gary Gallagher and Mike Parrish invited me to do the volume on the 1860–61 secession crisis for the Littlefield Sesquicentennial History of the Civil War. They seemed to expect that I, like my graduate school mentor Ken Stampp, could do creditable historical research and analysis both north and south of the Mason-Dixon Line and Ohio River. They may have also hoped that my earlier work as a transatlantic comparative historian, published as *Masters and Lords: Mid-19th-Century U.S. Planters and Prussian Junkers* (1993), indicated that I could treat accurately and fairly both southern secessionists and northern Unionists on the eve of the Civil War. Readers and reviewers, of course, will decide for themselves whether I have succeeded. I regret that Ken Stampp did not live to see the final product; my appreciation for his scholarship and guidance only grew as we aged.

Mike Parrish and Bill Link provided scorching yet hopeful commentary on an earlier version of the book, and Mike frequently made helpful recommendations and even gifts of particular articles and monographs. Like all scholars, I could not have completed this project without the invaluable aid of many librarians and archivists. Particularly helpful over the past decade were staff members at Berea College, the Chicago Historical Society, the Huntington Library, the New York Public Library, the New-York Historical Society, the Newberry Library, the University of Kentucky Library, the University of Texas at Austin Library, and the Virginia Historical Society.

During the many years in which I researched, composed, and revised this book, a number of friends and colleagues provided support and encouragement at opportune moments: Tighe and Hugh Antrim, Kathy DeBoer, Bill Freehling, Chesley and Lee Garrett, David Hamilton, Helen and Steve Kelly, Bruce Levine, Howard Miller, Bob Moeller, Jim Oakes, Mark Pittman, Jim Sidbury, and Mark Summers. Because I have asked none of them to read and comment on any chapter of this book, they are all absolved of any responsibility for knowing exactly what to expect, much less agreeing with it.

Lee Willey Bowman, Kate Bowman, and Willis Bowman never seriously doubted that someday the book would be finished and even published. After all, nearly two decades passed before my initial vision of a monographic study juxtaposing planters and Junkers became a reality.

Although editor in chief David Perry of UNC Press may have had occasional doubts that this volume would ever make it into print, he was and is too much the consummate professional to let those doubts surface. Zach Read helped shepherd the manuscript along when it was submitted to the Press.

My siblings and their spouses probably wondered whether a book on the secession crisis was worth the expenditure of so much time and energy, but they still expressed hopeful interest in the final product. Because John and Ginny Bowman, Jane and John Fain, Susan and David Reynolds, John and Andrea Willey, and Willis and Vance Willey have helped teach me that siblings and in-laws can become friends as well as relatives, the book is dedicated to them.

Publisher's note: The University of North Carolina Press gratefully acknowledges the assistance of George C. Herring in reviewing the copyedited manuscript and page proof for this book upon the untimely death of the author.

Index

Abolitionists: antislavery literature and, 124–25; John Brown and, 2, 180, 253; Fugitive Slave Act of 1850 and, 22, 24, 103, 191, 255; from Great Britain, 124–25, 202, 256; Lincoln and, 5, 137, 210, 216, 217, 255, 257–60, 275; petitions to Congress, 45, 105, 127–28; proslavery and, 105, 154, 308 (n. 70); radical, 34, 63, 94, 95, 103, 146, 216, 255–56; religion and, 2, 21–22, 24, 235, 252–53, 332 (n. 24); Republican Party and, 2–3, 72, 191, 275, 277; rise of, 2, 27, 250, 308 (n. 70); southern feeling about, 63, 68, 103, 125–26, 127, 166–67, 246, 247, 305–6 (n. 35); U.S. Constitution and, 216, 255, 332–33 (n. 31); white southerners as, 71–72, 102–3, 110; women, 22, 35, 102, 103, 110, 249, 254, 255. *See also* Beecher, Henry Ward; Douglass, Frederick; Garrison, William Lloyd; Truth, Sojourner

Abzug, Robert H., 21

Adams, James Hopkins, 244

Adams, John, 51

Adams, John Quincy, 53, 123, 134; as president, 119–20, 121

Affleck, Thomas, 163

African Americans, 20, 57, 277, 284; American dream and, 206, 326 (n. 25); John Brown and, 301 (n. 61); escaping slavery, 59, 62, 107, 300–301 (n. 55), 301 (n. 58); interracial marriages, 217; in New York City, 230, 252, 253–54; proposed colonization of freed slaves, 23, 64, 66, 109, 126–27, 154, 171, 183, 208, 214, 216, 237, 253; proposed suffrage for freed slaves, 230, 260; in Richmond, Va., 176; slavery and honor

and, 94–95, 217–18, 305–6 (n. 35), 306 (n. 44), 327 (n. 50); Union Army black troops, 36, 94–95. *See also* Douglass, Frederick; Emancipation; Racism; Slavery; Truth, Sojourner

Age of Reason, The (Paine), 208

Agriculture: in border states, 185–86, 320 (n. 57); hemp, 122, 154, 185, 189, 192; indigo, 70; in Midwest, 224, 230; northern vs. southern, 192–94, 196; rice, 70, 189; southern, 189–91, 318 (n. 32); tobacco, 70, 187, 189, 318 (n. 32); wheat, 224, 230, 318 (n. 32), 328 (n. 61). *See also* Cotton

Alabama, 38, 215; secession, 73, 75, 152

Albany Atlas and Argus, 273

Albany Regency, 118–19, 123, 233, 310 (n. 6)

Alien and Sedition Acts of 1798, 51

Allen, William, 166

Allen, Zechariah, 284, 337 (n. 59)

Alternative, The (Holcombe), 253

Amalgamation (white-black sexual relations), 3, 64, 106–11, 154, 165–66, 206, 217, 248, 309 (nn. 77, 82), 326 (n. 25)

American Antislavery Society, 124–25, 253, 255

American Colonization Society, 21

American dream, 195, 197, 206, 231, 326 (n. 25)

American nationalism, 10–14, 17–19, 25–26

American Party. *See* Know-Nothings

American Revolution, 13–14, 17, 48, 64, 113, 160, 206

American System, 122, 123, 182, 208, 218. *See also* Clay, Henry; Whig Party

Anderson, Eba Clinch, 86

Boston, 94, 122, 135, 145, 146–47, 181, 222, 257, 274, 301 (n. 60), 305–6 (n. 35)

Boston Courier, 86

Botts, John Minor, 174, 182, 183

Bowen, Henry Chandler, 234

Bowman, James, 78, 97, 98, 100

Brady, Mathew, 273

Branch, Thomas, 43

Brazy, Martha Jane, 147

Breckinridge, John (grandfather), 153

Breckinridge, John C., 225–26; early life, 155; as lawyer, 155, 156–57; as one of two 1860 Democratic candidates, 4, 106, 112, 114–15, 142, 145, 153, 157–58; secession crisis and, 158–59, 268; slavery and, 155–56, 157; state's rights and, 114, 116; 1860 support for, 113, 133, 142–43, 144, 148, 149, 152, 153, 169, 182, 241, 289 (n. 7); as vice president, 113, 143, 157, 262, 268, 289 (n. 7)

Breckinridge, Joseph Cabell, 153

Breckinridge, Polly Cabell, 153

Breckinridge, Robert Jefferson, 85, 153–54

Bremer, Frederika, 171–72

Brevard, Joseph, 244

Brevard, Keziah Goodwyn Hopkins, 10, 27–28, 244–49, 265, 331 (n. 3)

Brevard, Theodore, 244

Brooks, Preston, 2, 22, 56, 80, 81, 91, 299 (n. 37)

Brown, Elizabeth Pryor, 184

Brown, John, 3, 63, 67, 72, 108, 141, 152, 246, 277, 338 (n. 62); abolitionists and, 2, 180, 253; African American reaction to raid of, 301 (n. 61); hanging of, 2, 126, 146, 180, 275; Lincoln and, 5, 179, 236, 238, 275; Richmond reaction to raid of, 176, 179, 180

Brown, Joseph E., 265

Brown, Peronneau, 44

Browning, Elizabeth Barrett, 101–2

Browning, Orville H., 278

Brownlow, William Gannaway, 148–51, 315 (n. 64)

Brownlow's Knoxville Whig, 149

Brownson, Orestes, 199

Brown University, 61, 199, 284

Bruce, James Cole, 176

Bruce, Rebecca, 192

Bruce, Sanders, 192

Bryant, William Cullen, 233

Buchanan, James, 137, 198; John Brown and, 126; corruption and, 238, 330 (n. 90); Cuba and, 56, 114, 141, 167; Douglas and, 114, 140, 141, 313 (n. 47); 1856 election, 4, 113–14, 157, 172, 213, 261; 1860 elections and, 145; homestead bill and, 141, 262; as lame-duck president, 6, 36, 80, 86, 262–66; secession crisis and, 6, 7, 262–66, 272, 279, 334 (n. 14); slavery and, 4, 56, 91, 92, 114, 128, 170, 261–63, 266, 297–98 (n. 28); Supreme Court and, 56; Unionism of, 6, 124, 264–65, 266

Bullitt, William C., 155

Bullock and Breckinridge, 155

Burch, Mary Cyrene, 155

Burlingame, Michael, 207, 209

Burr, Aaron, 89, 118

Burrows, Edwin G., 230

Burton, Orville Vernon, 88

Butler, Andrew P., 53, 299 (n. 37)

Calhoun, John C., 161, 168, 194, 268, 270, 311 (n. 17); as Jackson's vice president, 121; nullification crisis and, 58, 70, 122–23, 311 (n. 14); sectional separation and, 6, 39, 58, 132, 312 (n. 25); slavery and, 6, 45, 105, 127–28, 129, 131, 133, 138, 156, 167, 215, 263, 269; Texas annexation and, 129

California, 57, 134, 138, 146, 167–69

Campbell, David, 35

Campbell, William B., 35

Canton Iron Works, 231

Capitalism, 192–94, 198, 199–200, 317 (n. 15), 325 (n. 14)

Carey, Anthony Gene, 75, 133

Cashin, Joan, 165

Cass, Lewis, 155, 264

Catholic Church, 1, 56, 92, 140, 161, 163, 199, 212, 313 (n. 46)

Charles Scribner publishers, 77

Charleston, S.C., 69–70, 73–74, 79, 102; 1860 Democratic Party convention, 114, 158; Fort Sumter and, 7, 59, 152, 280, 281, 282, 283, 284

Charleston and Savannah Railroad, 73

Charleston Mercury, 272

Chase, Salmon P., 11, 82, 136, 210, 211, 212, 232, 238

Chesnut, James, Jr., 59, 75

Chesnut, Mary Boykin Miller, 59, 74, 110

Chicago, 195, 238; businessmen and, 227, 228–29; 1860 elections and, 241; industrial development of, 224, 225–27; Kentucky and, 157, 189, 196, 226–27, 228–29, 241–42; as railroad center, 139, 193, 221–22, 223–24, 226–27, 229–30; secession and, 241–43

Chicago Press and Tribune, 157, 226, 235, 241

Chicago Tribune, 195

Christian, Letitia, 129

Christy, George, 235

Civil War, 49, 73, 144, 317 (n. 15); American nationalism and, 11–14, 18–19; expectation of, 9, 37, 151–52, 183, 263–64, 267, 280–82; failure to avoid, 9, 30–31, 34, 160; Mexican War as cause of, 132; slavery as root cause of, 18, 50; slavery brought to an end by, 28, 34–35, 36, 37, 62, 287; slaves during, 62, 300–301 (n. 55), 301 (n. 56); Sojourner Truth during, 256–57

Clark, Christopher, 186, 221

Clark, Erskine, 77

Clarke, William Penn, 225

Clay, Clement Claiborne, 40

Clay, Henry, 131, 149, 226; 1844 election defeat, 132, 210; 1824 elections and, 119; as Great Compromiser, 5, 30–31, 156, 182, 211, 242, 268; Kentucky and, 55, 113, 145, 154, 156, 157; Lincoln and,

182, 196, 208, 209, 210, 211, 218, 243; protectionism and, 122, 123; as "self-made man," 195; slavery and, 55, 154, 298–99 (n. 35)

Clemens, Sherman, 277

Clemson, Thomas Green, 194

Clinton, Catherine, 96

Clinton, DeWitt, 118

Cobb, Howell, 113, 264; Compromise of 1850 and, 31, 74, 137, 138; Confederacy and, 31, 112, 137, 313 (n. 43); early life, 132–33

Cobb, James, 38

Cobb, Thomas R. R., 93–94, 133

Cocke, John Hartwell, 176

Cocke, Philip St. George, 176

Coclanis, Peter A., 222

College of William and Mary, 44, 129, 187

Colman, Lucy, 257, 258–59

Columbia Theological Seminary, 77

Compromise of 1850, 1, 24, 155, 185, 214; Henry Clay and, 30–31, 146, 211, 268; Cobb, Howell, and, 31, 74, 137, 138; Crittenden Compromise and, 268, 271; Davis and, 167, 169; Douglas and, 31, 138, 211; favoring Slave Power, 136, 210; Fugitive Slave Act of 1850 and, 53

Confederacy: American nationalism and, 10–14, 17–18, 19; border slave states joining, 7–8, 16; constitution of, 6, 11, 14, 35, 36–37, 47, 144; cotton and, 48–49; Davis chosen as president, 5, 40, 76, 112, 137, 160; Davis inauguration as president, 46, 47, 67; disunion and, 13, 14, 18, 19–20, 25, 48; establishment of, 5, 6, 27–28, 31, 41, 66, 76, 112, 134, 137, 248, 271–72, 274; international slave trade and, 11, 294 (n. 3); Morrill Tariff and, 285; Richmond as capital, 7, 36, 175, 203; slavery and, 18, 30, 36, 48, 50, 287; southerners against, 150–51; state's rights and, 14, 18, 19–20, 36, 48, 49–51, 297 (n. 25); Stephens as vice president, 47, 48; U.S. Constitution

and, 13–14, 15, 16, 18, 19–20, 33, 50–51.
See also Fort Sumter
Congregationalist Church, 23–24, 99,
   234
Conkin, Paul, 247, 252
Constitutional Union Party, 4, 91, 106,
   113, 145, 146, 147, 148, 182
Cook, Jane, 160, 161
Cook, Robert, 64
Cooper, Edward, 232
Cooper, Peter, 231–32, 233, 234, 270
Cooper, William J., Jr., 69, 161, 163, 269
Cooper Union for the Advancement of
   Science and Art, 234, 235
Corning, Erastus, 235
Corwin, Thomas, 191, 268
Cosway, Maria, 109, 309 (n. 77)
Cotton, 38, 48–49, 185, 186, 320
   (nn. 57–58); Cotton Whigs of Massa-
   chusetts and, 146, 147; increase in value
   of, 190–91, 220, 322 (n. 70); New York
   City and, 229–31; secession and, 69–70,
   154; slavery and, 189–91, 322 (n. 69),
   322–23 (n. 71); transportation of, 219–
   20, 323 (n. 80)
*Cotton Plantation Record and Account
   Book* (Affleck), 163
Couper, James Hamilton, 171, 172
Covey, Edward, 94
Craven, Avery, 31
Crawford, William H., 119
Crist, Lynda Casswell, 170, 209
Crittenden, John J., 5, 39, 40, 145, 242,
   243, 268, 269, 270–71, 335 (n. 19)
Crittenden Compromise, 241, 268; Davis
   and, 6, 39, 40, 268, 269–70, 294–95
   (n. 6); failure of, 5, 6, 39, 40, 184, 270,
   271, 272, 273, 279, 335 (n. 23); Mis-
   souri Compromise of 1820 and, 5, 39,
   242, 243, 269, 270, 271
Cuba, 56, 114, 141, 167, 170
Current, Richard N., 58, 233
Cushing, Caleb, 56, 198
Custis, George Washington Parke, 175
Cutting, Francis B., 156

Dahlgren, Charles, 89, 305 (n. 26)
Dahlgren, John Adolphus, 89–90, 305
   (n. 26)
Daily Atlas and Bee (Boston), 274
Daily Minnesotan, 275
Daniel, John Moncure, 176
Davis, David Brion, 124, 125
Davis, Garrett, 154
Davis, Jefferson, 143, 159, 168, 209, 273;
   accepting presidency of the Confederacy, 5, 40–41, 46, 47, 67, 76, 112, 137,
   160, 295 (n. 9); bid for Mississippi
   governorship, 169; as cooperationist,
   38–39, 69, 171; Crittenden Compromise
   and, 6, 39, 40, 268, 269–70, 294–95
   (n. 6); Declaration of Independence
   and, 20, 28–29; early life, 160–64; Fort
   Sumter and, 281–82; honor and, 96,
   99–100; military service of, 162, 166;
   as plantation owner, 162–63, 188, 194;
   religion and, 99, 163–64, 245; secession and, 100, 160, 170–71, 269–70;
   as secretary of war under Pierce, 169,
   170, 187; as senator, 6, 38, 141, 160, 162,
   166, 169, 170–71; as slaveholder, 38,
   162–64, 165–66, 171, 245, 316 (n. 6);
   slavery and, 20, 47, 48, 49, 50, 127, 141,
   161, 162, 166–67, 171, 214–15, 263, 297
   (n. 23); temperament of, 170; U.S. Constitution and, 11, 20, 28–29, 39–40, 47,
   50, 162, 166, 167
Davis, Joseph, 161, 162, 163, 165, 166, 171
Davis, Samuel Emory, 160, 161
Davis, Varina, 164, 165, 166, 168, 171, 209,
   257
Davis, William C., 170
DeBow, James D. B., 71
DeBow's Review, 69, 71, 103, 198
Declaration of Independence, 13, 25, 32,
   98; right of rebellion and, 18, 29, 66, 67,
   142; secession and, 13, 14, 67, 142, 267;
   slavery and, 18, 20, 28–29, 199, 205–6,
   234, 252
Delaware, 8, 173
Democratic Party: antislavery and, 136,

139, 313 (n. 38); antiwar Democrats during Civil War, 287, 338 (n. 64); 1860 Convention, 114, 158, 211; corruption and, 238, 330 (n. 90); 1840 elections and, 128, 132–33; 1844 elections and, 132, 135; 1848 elections and, 135, 136; 1852 elections and, 4, 113; 1856 elections and, 2, 4, 56, 113–14, 157, 172, 213, 261; 1860 elections and, 114–16, 230; Jacksonian Democrats, 27, 32, 117, 118, 120, 122, 123, 124, 166, 177, 311 (n. 17); Kansas-Nebraska Act of 1854 and, 83, 114, 138, 139, 140, 156, 211, 213, 225, 313 (n. 46); Loco-Focoism and, 136; in New York City, 285–86, 287, 338 (n. 62); railroads and, 221, 225; secession crisis and, 32, 84–85; Slave Power and, 1, 16, 17, 22, 54, 82, 141; slavery and, 22–23, 32, 38, 56, 72, 127–28, 166, 188, 317 (n. 15); 1860 split in, 3–4, 33, 75, 113, 114; working classes and, 120, 136, 310 (n. 11). *See also* Breckinridge, John C.; Douglas, Stephen A.

Detzer, David, 86

Dew, Thomas Roderick, 44–45

Deyle, Steven, 60, 192

District of Columbia Emancipation Act, 257. *See also* Washington, D.C.

"Dividing Line between Federal and Local Authority, The" (Douglas), 236

Divine Providence, 87, 200, 228, 292 (n. 41); American nationalism and, 25–26, 34; Civil War and, 34, 287; Confederacy and, 11, 47; Lincoln and, 28, 207; secession crisis and, 27–28, 78, 183, 264, 291–92 (n. 38)

Donald, David Herbert, 32, 218, 265

Douglas, Adele Cutts, 117, 142

Douglas, Stephen A., 155, 157; Compromise of 1850 and, 31, 138, 211; early life, 116–17; in Illinois, 117, 123–24, 143, 225, 270; Jacksonian Democrats and, 117, 118, 123, 196; Kansas-Nebraska Act of 1854 and, 114, 140, 156, 170, 211, 225; as one of two 1860 Democratic can-

didates, 4, 106, 112, 114–16; secession and, 143–44, 241, 267, 268, 280, 314 (n. 53), 336 (n. 44); 1858 senate race, 140–41, 208, 270; as senator, 41, 89, 116, 137–41, 222, 225, 313–14 (n. 48); slavery and, 36, 116, 139–40, 213, 228, 236, 299 (n. 37), 313 (n. 47); state's rights and, 114, 116, 138–39, 156, 227–28; support for, 47–48, 85, 113, 141–43, 144, 145, 149, 151–52, 169, 241, 330 (n. 99); Unionism of, 113, 142–43, 265

Douglass, Frederick, 62, 66, 237, 246, 257; as abolitionist, 10, 34, 103, 216; honor and, 94–95, 96, 327 (n. 50); Lincoln and, 116, 259–60; promoting black troops for U.S. Army, 94–95; Sojourner Truth and, 254–56

Douglass, Sarah Fisk, 117

Douglass, Stephen Arnold, 116, 117

Dred Scott decision, 6, 14, 47, 228; Lincoln and, 92, 141, 213, 214, 215, 238, 276, 278; northern reaction to, 2, 22, 23; President Buchanan and, 261–63; recognition of slavery and, 58, 92, 157, 263, 269, 327 (n. 44)

Duels: Davis and, 99–100, 168; Lincoln and, 88–89, 95; northerners and, 82, 305 (n. 21); southerners and, 78, 80, 81, 84, 87, 105, 156, 305 (n. 26). *See also* Honor

Dumont, John, 251, 255

Dumont, Sally, 251

Dunaway, Wilma, 164

Duncan, Stephen, 147–48

Earle, Jonathan, 120, 135

Eaton, John Henry, 121

Eaton, Margaret "Peggy," 121

Edward III (king of England), 97

Edwards, Matilda, 96

Edwards, Ninian, 96

1860 Association, 70, 71, 72, 73, 75

Elections, presidential: of 1824, 119; of 1828, 121; of 1832, 311 (n. 17); of 1836, 124, 311 (n. 17); of 1840, 119, 128–29,

132, 133, 209, 261, 311 (n. 17), 312
(n. 34); of 1844, 100, 131, 132, 133, 135,
169, 210, 261, 312 (n. 34); of 1848, 56,
113, 135, 136, 155, 162, 211; of 1852, 4,
113, 169, 211; of 1856 (*see* Democratic
Party: 1856 elections; Republican
Party: 1856 elections); of 1864, 144. *See
also* Lincoln, Abraham—election of, as
president
"Elegy Written in a Country Churchyard"
(poem, Gray), 195
Elements of Moral Science, The (Wayland), 199
Elements of Political Economy, The (Way-
land), 199
Elliot, Jeffrey M., 190
Emancipation, 2, 23–25, 37, 63–64, 109,
147, 154, 171, 183, 208, 214, 253, 266;
gradual and compensated, 5, 23, 126,
210, 216; in northern states, 17, 23,
51–52, 250, 332 (n. 14)
Emancipation Proclamation, 9, 36, 93,
95, 116, 257–58, 266
Emory College, 58
Engels, Friedrich, 200
Engerman, Stanley, 193
Episcopal Church, 102, 119, 129–30, 163,
192, 245, 246
*Epistle to the Clergy of the Southern
States, An* (S. Grimké), 102
Eppes, Richard, 42–44, 45, 168, 176
Erie Canal, 117, 181, 219, 222, 230
Erwin, Edward Jones, 72
Escott, Paul, 161, 170
Etcheson, Nicole, 57, 87, 88
Everett, Edward, 145, 146, 148, 150

Faler, Paul, 201, 202, 203
Federalist Party, 117, 118, 119, 130
Fehrenbacher, Don E., 52, 53, 129, 205
Fessenden, William, 89
Fillmore, Millard, 56, 137, 140, 145, 146,
225, 238, 298 (n. 30)
Finney, Charles G., 199
Fitzhugh, George, 198–99, 203

Fleischner, Jennifer, 259
Florida, 73, 131–32, 265–66; secession,
75, 152, 266
Floyd, John, 264
Fogel, Robert, 70, 189
Foner, Eric, 197
Ford, Lacy, 191
Forgie, George B., 205
Fort Moultrie, 71, 86, 265, 266
Fort Pickens, 169, 265–66, 283
Fort Pulaski, 265
Fort Sumter, 11, 31, 35, 91, 144, 150, 153,
159, 212; Confederate attack on, 7, 16,
17, 42, 59, 90, 113, 248, 249, 266, 274,
281, 282, 284, 304 (n. 15); Confederate thinking on, 16, 31–32, 169, 281–82;
crisis at, 279–83; Lincoln and, 7, 16, 17,
32, 273, 279–81; move from Fort Moultrie to, 71, 86, 266; northern reaction
to attack on, 7, 8–9, 17, 31, 32, 67, 173,
279, 281, 284–87, 304 (n. 15); President Buchanan and, 265–66, 279, 334
(n. 11); South Carolina and, 7, 42, 59,
85–86, 265, 266, 334 (n. 11); southern
reaction to surrender of, 43, 59, 183,
285; *Star of the West* incident and, 265,
334 (n. 11)
Fox, David Raymond, 107
Fox, Gustavus, 280, 283
Fox, Tryphena Blanche Holder, 106–7
Fox-Genovese, Elizabeth, 104, 172
Fredrickson, George M., 45, 110, 207
Freedmen and Soldiers Relief Associa-
tion, 258
Freedmen's Bureau, 258
Freedmen's Inquiry Commission, 258
Freehling, William W., 62, 69, 70, 76, 121,
158, 173, 285
Freeland, William, 95
Freeman, Joanne B., 98
Free-Soilers, 53, 54, 63, 68, 82, 113, 134,
139, 212
Free-Soil Party, 135–36, 210
Frémont, John C., 56, 57, 169, 331 (n. 6)
French Revolution, 130

and, 197, 200, 202–3, 205–6, 217, 231, 232, 233, 325 (n. 14); geographic containment of slavery and, 5, 92, 116, 172, 205, 210, 211, 214–15, 216–17, 239–40, 250, 269, 270, 271, 335 (n. 23); honor and, 88–89, 90, 92–93, 95–96, 307 (n. 47); "House Divided" speech, 41, 214; in Illinois, 88–89, 124, 195, 196, 207–10, 218; inauguration, 2, 6, 31, 67, 74, 76, 83, 113, 173, 183, 195, 248, 262, 272–73, 278–79, 281; Kansas-Nebraska Act of 1854 and, 92, 205, 212–14; as lawyer, 208, 211, 218, 223, 224, 280; Lincoln-Douglas debates and, 92, 208, 213, 216, 236, 313–14 (n. 48); marriage, 96, 209, 307 (n. 47); Mexican War and, 134, 210; mistakes in secession crisis, 240, 272–73, 280, 336–37 (n. 45); moderate stance on slavery by, 57, 116, 191, 208, 216–17, 233–34, 235, 236–38, 252, 315 (n. 68); national political life, 261; as 1860 presidential candidate, 93, 112–13, 114–15, 137, 149, 151, 195–96, 197, 211, 214, 216, 232–40; racial sensibilities, 217, 258–60; railroads and, 218, 223, 224; religion and, 92, 207; secession crisis and, 6–7, 65–66, 88, 212, 266–67, 270–74, 275–76, 279–80, 335 (nn. 23, 32), 336 (n. 44); as "self-made man," 195, 206, 324 (n. 2); 1858 senate race, 140–41, 208, 213, 255, 270; slavery and, 5–6, 15, 17, 23, 30, 35, 36, 41, 62–63, 266; Sojourner Truth and, 257, 258–59; state's rights and, 18, 278; temperament of, 170, 195, 208, 209; Thirteenth Amendment and, 35, 36; Unionism of, 36, 37, 143, 159, 273; U.S. Constitution and, 11, 18, 20, 28–29, 138–39, 213, 236, 238, 283–84, 292 (n. 42); U.S. Navy blockade and, 283–84; Whig Party and, 113, 124, 134, 156, 172, 195, 196, 208, 209, 210, 211, 212, 213, 243
—election of, as president: as affront to southern honor, 76, 106, 172, 182;

California and, 169; Chicago and, 241; Davis and, 38, 49, 50, 69, 171; Electoral College votes and, 4–5, 29–30, 132, 144, 148, 158, 289 (n. 5); first seven seceding slave states and, 14, 23, 29, 67–68, 113, 133; free vs. slave states, 30, 132, 142, 238, 289 (n. 7), 330 (n. 99); New York City and state and, 230; President Buchanan and, 262; secession crisis development after, 2, 4, 6–9, 23, 27, 69, 74, 79, 151–53, 173, 228, 286, 293 (n. 62), 334 (n. 14); slaveholders and, 33, 35, 69–71, 106, 137, 148, 168; slave states and, 5, 50, 71, 116, 152, 158, 171; southern anxiety about, 2, 41, 43, 45, 62–63, 68, 94, 129, 191, 218, 247, 253, 270–71, 276–78; state elections predicting, 4, 78, 239; unsuccessful candidates and, 4, 106, 112–13, 114–16, 141–42, 144–45, 148, 149–50, 151, 152, 157–58, 295–96 (n. 11); U.S. Constitution and, 16–17, 83, 132, 273–74; in Virginia, 182–83

Lincoln, Abraham (grandfather), 206
Lincoln, Mary Todd. *See* Todd, Mary
Lincoln, Mordecai, 206
Lincoln, Nancy Hanks, 206, 207
Lincoln, Robert, 235
Lincoln, Thomas, 206, 207, 304–5 (n. 20)
Lincoln and the Decision for War (McClintock), 18
Loco-Focoism, 136
Lodge, Henry Cabot, 90
Logan, David, 215
Logan, Stephen T., 215
Longstreet, Augustus Baldwin, 58
Louisiana, 85, 107, 161, 162, 176; secession, 76, 152
Louisiana Purchase, 1, 117, 126, 138, 140, 205
Louisville Journal, 239
Lovejoy, Owen, 275–76, 277
Luark, Michael Fleenen, 10, 144–45, 151–52, 153, 315 (n. 68)

Morgan, Edwin, 241

Morgan, John Hunt, 192

Morgan, Lewis, 192

Morrill Tariff, 285

Morris, Isaac Newton, 84–87, 90, 304
(nn. 12, 15)

Mount Auburn Cemetery (Cambridge,
Mass.), 181, 319–20 (n. 46)

Napoleonic Wars (1793–1815), 130

Narrative of the Life of Sojourner Truth
(Truth), 255

Nast, Thomas, 279

Natchez, Miss., 38, 65, 147–48, 161, 162,
165, 187, 188

National Antislavery Standard, 257

Nebraska, 114, 138, 140, 205, 212. *See also*
Kansas-Nebraska Act of 1854

"Negro-Mania" (McCord), 103

Nevins, Allan, 9, 33, 102, 212, 280

Newark Daily Advertiser, 269

New England Immigrant Aid Society,
215

New Jersey, 196, 231, 250, 269, 275

New Mexico, 138, 271

New Orleans, 107, 198, 207, 219, 222, 285

New Orleans Bee, 63

New Orleans Daily Crescent, 62, 239

New Orleans Daily Delta, 269

New York (state), 117, 135, 219; Albany
Regency of, 118–19, 123, 233, 310 (n. 6);
1860 elections and, 230; Loco-Focoism
and, 136; secession crisis and, 274;
slavery and, 173, 196, 249–50; Van
Buren and, 118–19, 120–21, 123, 310
(n. 6)

New York City, 60; African Americans
and, 230, 252, 253–54; business between North and South and, 177, 181;
commercial development of, 219, 229–
32, 274, 329 (n. 74); Democratic Party
and, 285–86, 287, 338 (n. 62); emporium pioneering in, 177–78; laboring
vs. middle classes in, 196–97, 200, 231;
as media center, 232–33, 329 (n. 78);

Morrill Tariff and, 285, 286; Republican Party and, 211–12, 216, 231, 232–38,
270, 274; secession crisis and, 66, 173,
272, 274, 286–87

New York Daily Tribune, 66

New York Evening Post, 233

New York Herald, 47

New York Independent, 102

New York Times, 60, 233, 287

New York Tribune, 216, 232, 233, 272

New York World, 287

Nichols, Roy Franklin, 31, 32, 73, 230

Noll, Mark, 25

"Non-Slaveholders of the South, The"
(DeBow), 71

No Party Now but All for Our Country
(Lieber), 144

Northampton Association for Education
and Industry, 254, 255

North Carolina, 71–72, 188; 1860 election and, 142, 152–53; non-slaveholding
yeomen of, 102–3, 152, 153; process
leading to secession, 65–66, 153, 174;
secession, 7–8, 66, 150, 173; Unionism
of, 85, 272

North Carolina Standard, 142–43, 272

Northrup, Solomon, 59

Northwest Ordinance of 1787, 23, 205,
213, 277

Notes on the State of Virginia (Jefferson),
109–10

Nugent, William L., 39

Nullification Controversy, 123, 130, 311
(n. 14)

Oakes, James, 30, 93, 217, 259

O'Brien, Michael, 44

Ohio, 82, 85

Olmsted, Frederick Law, 60–61

Onuf, Nicholas, 122

Onuf, Peter, 122

Order of the Garter, 97

Oregon Country, 134, 167

Oregon Territory, 145, 211, 215

Orr, James L., 75

Schantz, Mark, 199

Schweikert, Larry, 187

Scott, Lizzie, 101, 308 (n. 59)

Scott, Robert E., 183

Scott, Sir Walter, 97

Scott, Winfield, 211, 266, 280, 336 (n. 43)

Scripps, Jon Locke, 195

Secession: beginnings of crisis, 1, 2, 4, 27, 32, 36, 38–39; border slave states and, 8, 85, 154, 173, 174, 285; business between North and South and, 63, 301 (n. 62); businessmen and, 177, 180, 182, 186–87, 274–75, 285–86, 320 (n. 58); Civil War expected as result of, 263–64, 267, 280; cooperationists and, 38–39, 69, 75, 294 (n. 3), 295–96 (n. 11); disunion and, 11, 13, 16–17, 61, 67, 68, 149–50, 160; Divine Providence and, 27–28, 78, 183, 264, 291–92 (n. 38); failure to avoid Civil War during crisis of, 9, 30–31, 34, 160; first seven slave states to opt for, 6, 8, 10, 14–15, 17, 67–68, 76, 85, 113, 133, 152, 173, 280; histories of, 9–10; honor and, 79–87, 90, 91, 94, 272; international slave trade and, 75, 80, 84, 154–55, 294 (n. 3); northern vs. southern views of, 29–30, 31–32, 33, 66–67; politics and, 32–33, 293 (nn. 51–52); President Buchanan and, 6, 7, 262–66, 272, 279, 334 (n. 14); as preventing revolution in South, 39–40, 49, 294 (n. 5); Protestant church thinking and, 31, 164, 246, 331 (n. 6); referenda and, 67, 68; Republican Party and, 5, 17, 18, 90, 91, 241, 242, 271; slaveholders and, 35, 39–40, 42–44, 49, 68, 70–71, 73, 248–49, 265, 294 (nn. 2–3), 295 (n. 7); southerners against, 38–39, 42–45, 47, 61, 65–66, 137, 147–50, 152, 172, 180, 315 (n. 64); southern fire-eaters and, 67–68, 80, 84, 114, 158, 179, 182, 187–88, 215, 265, 267, 272, 294 (n. 3); southern Unionists and, 67, 68, 69, 74, 85, 113, 149–50, 157–59, 177, 182, 238, 271–72, 279,

280; state's rights and, 36, 50, 51, 58, 64, 80, 180, 297 (n. 25); subregions of South and, 172–74; Upper South slave states and, 7–8, 16, 85, 173, 174, 272, 280, 281, 296 (n. 12), 333–34 (n. 6). See also Crittenden Compromise; Lincoln, Abraham; Slavery; U.S. Constitution; U.S. Senate Committee of Thirteen; individual states

Second Bank of the United States, 26–27, 117–18, 121, 122, 123, 131, 209. See also Bank of the United States

Second Great Awakening, 21, 123, 148, 277

Second party system, 32, 112, 312 (n. 34)

"Secret Six," 253

Seward, William Henry, 39, 49, 151, 191, 277, 297 (n. 21); antislavery and, 35, 41, 154, 211, 214, 216; John Brown and, 179; Fort Sumter and, 212, 273, 280, 283; secession crisis and, 169, 212, 268, 271, 272, 278–79, 335 (n. 23), 336 (n. 44); as unsuccessful candidate for nomination, 211–12, 214, 216, 232–33, 238, 268

Sewing machines, 165, 201

Shade, William, 173, 187

Sharkey, William, 147

Shattered Nation, A (Rubin), 17

Shaw, Albert, 279

Shaw, John, 161

Sheperdstown Register, 59

Sherman, John, 72

Shields, James, 88, 89, 95

Shoe manufacturing, 200–203, 204, 325 (n. 19)

Silbey, Joel, 119, 128

Simon, James, 209

Simpson, Craig, 168

Slave Power, 287, 298 (n. 33); Compromise of 1850 and, 136, 210; as conspiracy, 3, 54, 56–57, 213–14; control of federal government by, 30, 232, 274, 278; Crittenden Compromise and, 269, 270, 271; Democratic Party and, 1, 16,

17, 22, 54, 82, 141; fear of nationalized slavery by northerners and, 54, 56, 92, 213, 238, 277; Fugitive Slave Act of 1850 and, 54, 62–63; geographic expansion of slavery and, 133, 134, 239; northern antagonism toward, 4, 5, 19, 22, 25, 27, 54, 136, 140, 241, 253, 262, 275; northern honor and, 91, 92, 128; proslavery and, 22–23, 198–99

Slavery: abolition of foreign slave trade and, 11, 23, 191, 205, 277, 294 (n. 3), 322 (n. 69); in border states, 185–86; capitalism and, 192–94, 198; climate and, 173, 189; Confederacy and, 18, 30, 36, 48, 50, 287; cotton and, 189–91, 322 (n. 69), 322–23 (n. 71); failure to compromise over, 30–31, 33, 39, 292 (n. 47); geographic containment of, 1, 5, 14–15, 33, 83, 92, 134, 167, 205, 210, 211, 228; geographic expansion of, 1, 5, 6, 20–21, 27, 48, 117, 126, 133, 299 (n. 37); industry use of, 187, 189, 192, 203–4, 205; international slave trade and, 11, 75, 80, 84, 154–55, 294 (n. 3); interstate slave trade and, 127, 155, 162, 181–82, 191–92, 250, 293 (n. 62), 323 (n. 76); marriage and families in, 192; mining in California and, 167, 168–69; non-slaveholding yeomen and, 71, 102–4, 152, 153; in the North, 23, 196, 249–50; paternalism and, 60, 61, 62, 93, 237, 300 (n. 48), 323 (n. 76); philosophy and, 44–45, 55, 198–99, 298–99 (n. 35); plantations and, 27, 35, 77–78, 84, 107, 110–11, 126, 246, 331 (n. 5); primary sources for, 10; proposed gag rule over in Congress, 127–28, 151; religion of slaves and, 163–65; slave hiring and transferring and, 175–76, 318 (n. 32), 318–19 (n. 34); slaveholders and, 38, 53, 54, 55, 60, 61, 77–78, 79, 99–100, 171–72, 187–89, 229; slave populations in southern states and, 38, 69, 70, 81, 186; slave rebellions and, 94, 110, 125, 164, 237; slaves hiding true feelings and, 59,

237; southerners against, 71–72, 110, 152, 199; southern fear of slave revolt and, 2, 68, 94, 110, 125, 147, 179, 180, 215, 237, 247, 264, 319 (n. 43); white-black sexual relations, 77–78, 79, 106–11, 154, 165–66, 206, 248, 251, 303–4 (n. 11), 309 (nn. 77, 82), 326 (n. 25); woman's rights and, 104, 110–11, 254, 255, 256; women slaves, 91, 108, 109, 111, 192, 246–47. *See also* Abolitionists; African Americans; Civil War; Declaration of Independence; Fugitive Slave Act of 1850; Honor; Lincoln, Abraham; Protestant church thinking; Secession; Slave Power; U.S. Constitution

Slemmer, Adam, 266

Smallwood, Arvin D., 190

Smith, Adam, 26

Smith, Adam I. P., 144

Smith, Gerritt, 57

Smith, Mary Clay, 153

Snay, Mitchell, 164

Sociology for the South (Fitzhugh), 198

South Alone Should Govern the South, The (Townsend), 70

South Carolina, 2, 22, 45, 56, 102; federal tariffs of 1828 and 1832 and, 63, 69, 70, 123, 311 (n. 14); Fort Sumter and, 7, 42, 59, 85–86, 265, 266, 285, 334 (n. 11); Fugitive Slave Act of 1850 and, 53; honor and, 84, 272; non-slaveholding yeomen and, 103–4; plantations in, 69–70, 244–46; process leading to secession, 64–65, 69–75, 263; secession, 6, 27, 38, 66, 69, 79–81, 151, 158, 180, 183, 266, 270, 302 (n. 71); slavery, extent of in, 38, 69, 70, 81

Southern Guardian, 58

Southern Literary Messenger, 253

"Southern Thought" (Fitzhugh), 198

Speed, Joshua, 96, 208

Sprague and Howell, 165

Springfield State Register, 277

Stampp, Kenneth M., 37, 262, 285

Stanton, Edwin, 264–65

annexation and, 132, 133; Unionism of, 6, 113, 130; as vice president, 124, 127

Vance, Zebulon B., 148, 150

Vanderbilt, Cornelius, 265

Van Lew, Elizabeth, 184

Van Wagenen, Isaac, 251

Van Wagenen, Maria, 251

Varon, Elizabeth, 12–13, 182, 184

Vicksburg, Miss., 38, 39, 40, 100, 107, 147, 169, 187

Vicksburg Whig, 147

Virginia, 35, 64, 198; business between North and South from, 63, 176–77, 181, 301 (n. 62); diversity of, 174–75, 318 (n. 32); 1860 election and, 182–83; Fugitive Slave Act of 1850 and, 59, 183; industry in, 188, 193, 203–4, 325–26 (n. 20); plantations in, 129, 167, 168, 174, 175–76; process leading to secession, 41–43, 134, 174, 176, 182–84, 273; railroads in, 174–75, 177, 178–79, 181, 187, 193; secession, 7–8, 44, 67, 113, 173, 177, 185, 302 (n. 71); 1831 slave rebellion, 94, 125, 164; slavery in, 107–8, 126, 175–76, 187, 192, 203–4, 318 (n. 32), 319 (n. 43); split in, after secession, 173–74, 185; suffrage for white males, 44, 104; Unionism in, 42–43. *See also* Richmond

"Virginia dynasty" (1801–25), 130

Virginia Historical and Philosophical Society, 44

Vorenberg, Michael, 35

Wade, Benjamin Franklin, 82–84, 87, 304 (n. 12)

Wagenen, Isabella. *See* Truth, Sojourner

Walker, David, 253

Walker, Leroy Pope, 274, 282

Wallace, Mike, 230

Waller, Catherine "Kitty" Breckinridge, 226

Waller, Henry, 10, 196, 226–29, 241–43, 328 (n. 68)

Waller, James Breckinridge, 226, 227

Waller, Kate, 229

Waller, Sarah Bell Langhorne, 227, 228–29, 328 (n. 68)

Waller, William S., 189, 226

Waller, Caulfield, and Bradley, 227

Walther, Eric, 158

Ward, John Elliott, 78

War of 1812, 51, 122, 129, 130, 165, 206–7, 336 (n. 43)

Washington, D.C., 175; proposed abolition of slavery in, 125, 126, 155, 191, 210, 257; slave trading in, 127, 162

Washington, George, 13–14, 42, 117–18

Washington, Margaret, 249, 252

Washington Peace Conference, 6, 134, 158

Wayland, Francis, 199–200

Webster, Daniel, 298 (n. 30), 311 (n. 17); protectionism and, 122, 123; slavery and, 53, 128, 131

Weed, Thurlow, 128, 211, 233

Weekly Tribune (New York), 233

Weems, Parson, 207

Weiss, Thomas, 188

Weld, Theodore Dwight, 124, 253

Welles, Gideon, 283

Wentworth, John, 225

Werff, Adriaen van der, 109

West Point, 27, 161–62, 226

West Virginia, 8, 173, 174, 185, 330 (n. 99)

Wheat, 224, 230, 318 (n. 32), 328 (n. 61)

Whig Party, 35, 53, 151, 188, 293 (n. 52); abolitionists and, 63; antislavery and, 82, 154; beginnings of, 123; Cotton Whigs and, 146, 147; disintegration of, 140, 172, 196, 211, 212, 214, 313 (n. 46); 1840 elections and, 119, 128–29, 132–33, 209, 311 (n. 17); 1848 elections and, 211; 1860 elections and, 4, 47, 149; "internal improvements" (railroads etc.) and, 120, 177, 218, 221; Know-Nothings and, 56, 145; Lincoln and, 113, 124, 134, 156, 172, 195, 196, 208, 209, 210, 211, 212, 213, 243; protectionism and, 122, 123; racism and, 215; second party system and, 32, 112; slavery and, 72, 127, 128, 131, 166, 212, 228, 317 (n. 15);

Unionism of, 226, 227, 243. *See also*
American System
White, John R., 185
Wigfall, Louis Trezevant, 80–81, 82, 83,
87, 265, 267, 281, 282
Wilentz, Sean, 124
Wilmot, David, 135, 210
Wilmot Proviso of 1846, 135, 138, 210
Winchester, Josiah, 147
Wisconsin Supreme Court, 57–58
Wise, Henry, 126, 167–68, 174, 179, 180
Witcover, Jules, 128
Woman's rights, 22, 291 (n. 35); African
Americans and, 249, 255, 256; ante-
bellum era and, 101, 102–3, 256, 308
(n. 59); slavery and, 104, 110–11, 254,
255, 256
Women: abolitionists, 125, 126; educa-
tion in the South for, 244; honor and,
99, 100–102, 106, 110, 121, 168, 244, 307
(n. 58); plantations and, 106–7, 165,
244–46, 331 (nn. 2–3); striking shoe-

makers and, 203. *See also* Brevard,
Keziah Goodwyn Hopkins; Slavery;
Truth, Sojourner
Wood, Fernando, 274
World Temperance Association, 233
World War I, 100
Worth, Daniel, 71–72
Worth, Jonathan, 65–66, 71, 85
Wright, Gavin, 189, 221
Wyatt-Brown, Bertram, 81, 87, 98, 105,
106

Yale University, 73, 74, 189
Yancey, William Lowndes, 76, 158, 215
Yates, Richard, 241
Yeatman, Jean Erwin, 146
Young, William Gourdin, 282
Young Men's Central Republican Union,
232–33

Zion African Church, 252